Abandoned Asylums

Matt Van der Velde

Foreword by Carla Yanni

JONGLEZ PUBLISHING

Matt Van der Velde

Matt Van der Velde, a photographer based in Ottawa, Canada, specialises in architecture, fine art, and event photography. Educated in Sociology at Brock University, Van der Velde is best known for his work touring internationally with Playboy's 50th Anniversary Playmate and DJ, Colleen Shannon. His interest in the evolution of mental health treatment arose from his experience as an infantry soldier in the Canadian Forces and his personal struggles with depression and PTSD.

Van der Velde has always had a passion for documenting places hidden from society. He understands the historic and architectural value in America's abandoned state hospital and psychiatric facilities. Partner that with an insatiable interest in history and you have the inspiration behind "Abandoned Asylums", which seeks to provide a visual record and last will and testament of these incredible institutions before they disappear forever.

Carla Yanni

Carla Yanni is the author of *The Architecture of Madness: Insane Asylums in the United States,* originally published by the University of Minnesota Press in 2007 and now in its third printing; it was selected as a 2007 "Book of Critical Interest" by the journal *Critical Inquiry*. She is currently writing a book on the architecture and social history of college dormitories. Yanni is a professor of architectural history at Rutgers, The State University of New Jersey. She holds a doctorate in Art History from the University of Pennsylvania and a B.A. from Wesleyan University in Connecticut.

Contents

Foreword

Carla Yanni

Matt Van der Velde has produced an arresting collection of photographs that capture abandoned places with no future and pasts redolent of despair. These photographs document a long history that includes the rise and fall of state hospitals as therapeutic places, their civic importance in the 19th century, the inhumane crowding that followed, the increasing role of drug-based therapy, and the dumping of mentally ill people into the streets during the last quarter of the 20th century. His photos serve as a testament to these places before they deteriorate further or disappear altogether.

The history of 19th-century and early 20th-century psychiatric hospitals

Based on the current reputation of Victorian insane asylums – variously called loony bins, funny farms, nuthouses, and booby hatches – these are not institutions that make later generations swell with pride. Indeed, today they are grim reminders of an often inhumane system. However, it was once believed that an improved environment could cure insanity and, during those times, these much-maligned institutions and the buildings that housed them exemplified civic munificence; in their attempts to communicate a message of generosity, they occupied buildings ranging in style from Greek temples to medieval castles. Their founders felt a sense of Christian kindness toward those less fortunate.

For most of the 19th century, doctors believed that between seventy and ninety percent of insanity cases were curable, but only if patients were treated in specially designed buildings. In the US and Canada, the dominant model was the linear or Kirkbride plan. Establishing a cure was Dr. Thomas S. Kirkbride's career-long preoccupation. Kirkbride, a Philadelphia Quaker, believed good architecture was essential for the comfort, security and recovery of lunatics. The linear plan was really not all that linear – asylum plans did not dictate a long straight building, but rather one in which the wards were set back *en échelon*, like a row of birds in flight. Kirkbride and his contemporaries promoted a method known as the moral treatment or moral management, wherein psychiatrists inculcated their subjects with self-control and positive thoughts. Diverting activities such as walking in the grounds, boat trips, acting in skits, and sleigh rides were part of the cure and part of the internal culture of the asylum.

Under moral management, the daily life of patients was controlled and simple; early to bed and early to rise was an asylum rule. They awoke around 5am, ate breakfast on the ward at 6am, and awaited the superintendent's rounds at 8am. In the morning, whenever the weather allowed, they spent a few hours outside with attendants. After lunch, middle class patients (such as lawyers and businessmen) read and played games, while working class patients worked on the farm or in the print shop. They ate dinner in the early evening, and retired to bed at 9:30pm. Medicines and hydrotherapy were issued in the morning after breakfast or at night after dinner. Patients spent daytime hours in the dayrooms or the ward hallways, but never in their bedrooms. For much of the 19th century, medical treatments (mostly opiate derivatives) took place on the ward or in the bathing rooms. Hydrotherapy (subduing patients with cold water

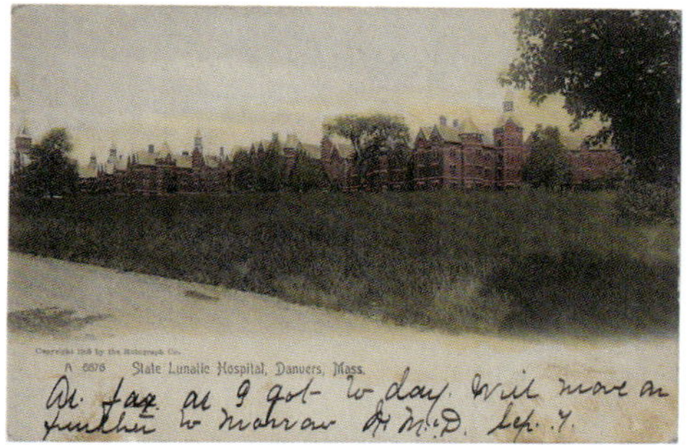

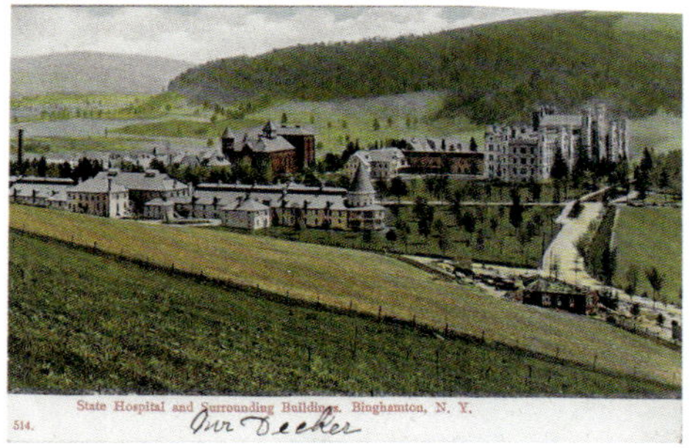

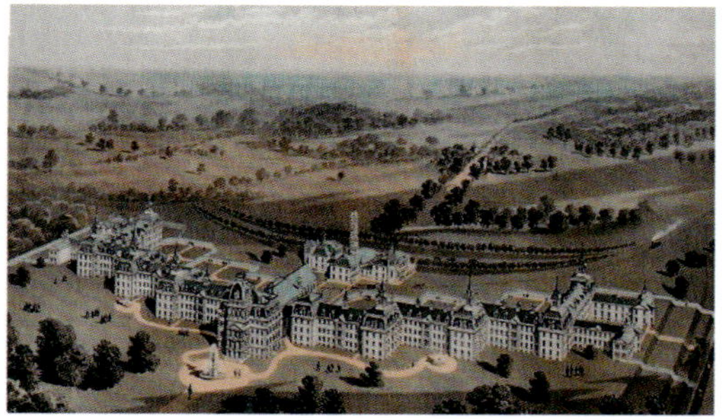

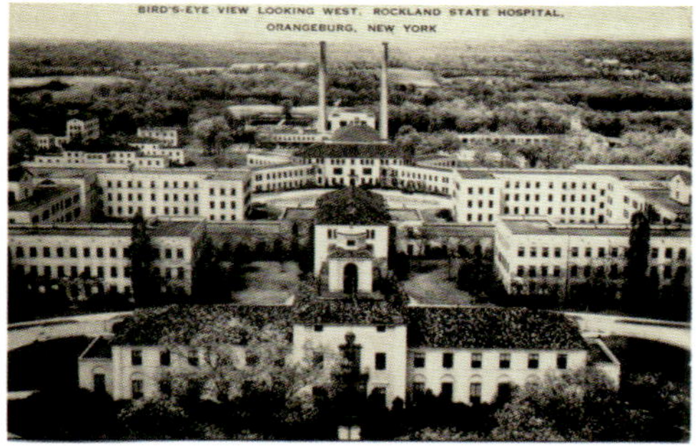

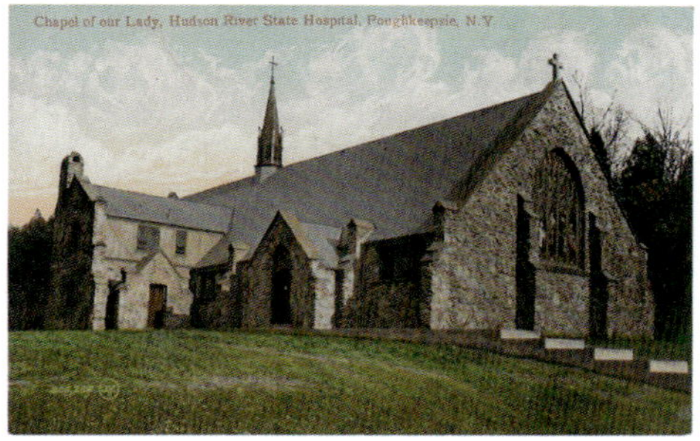

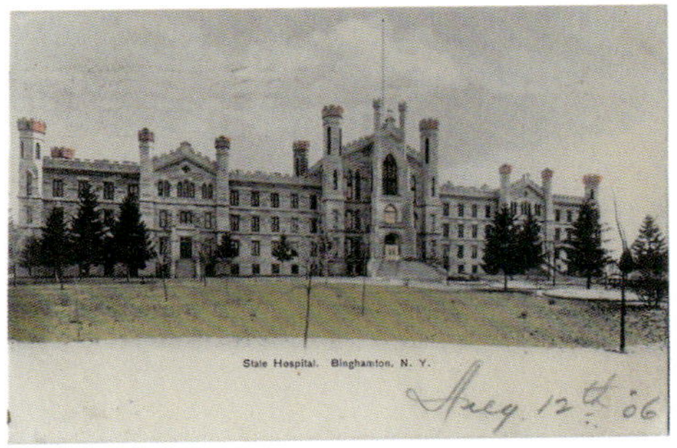

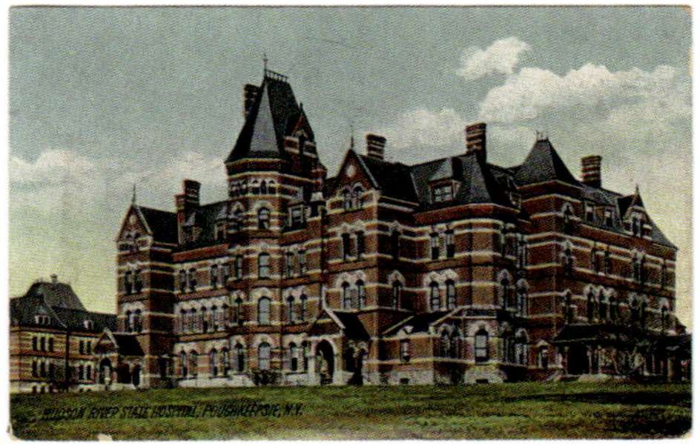

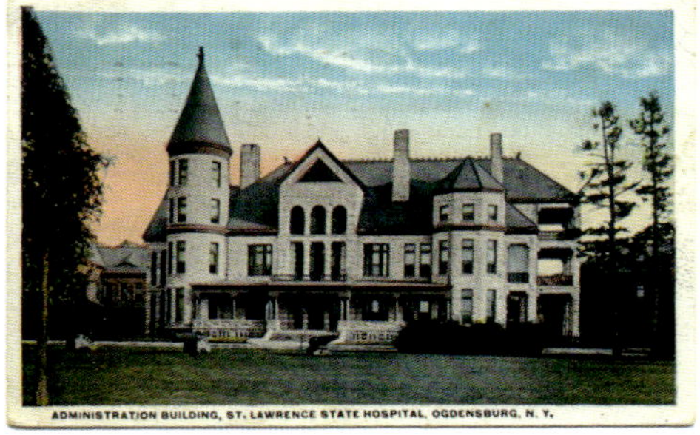

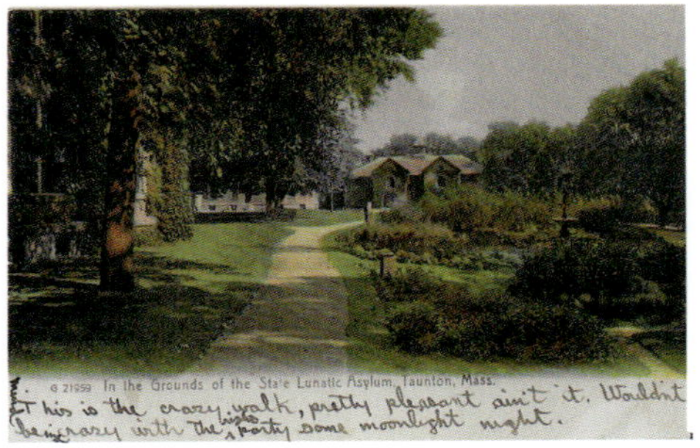

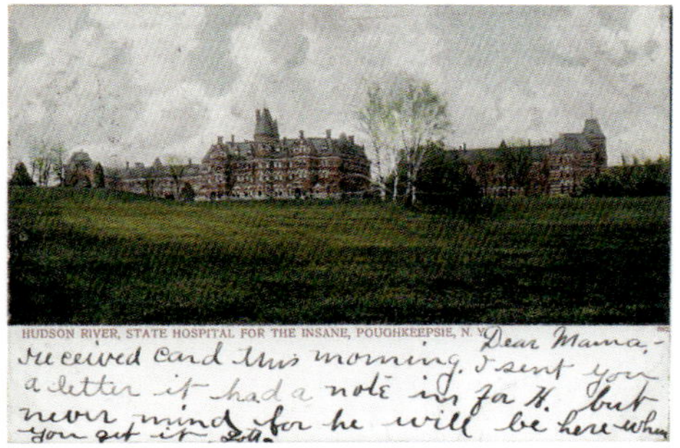

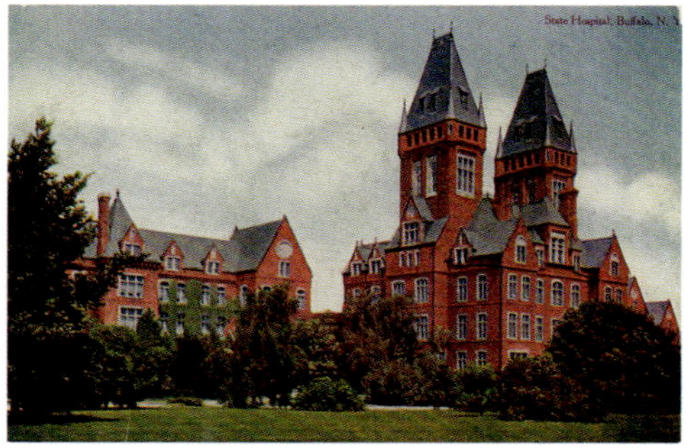

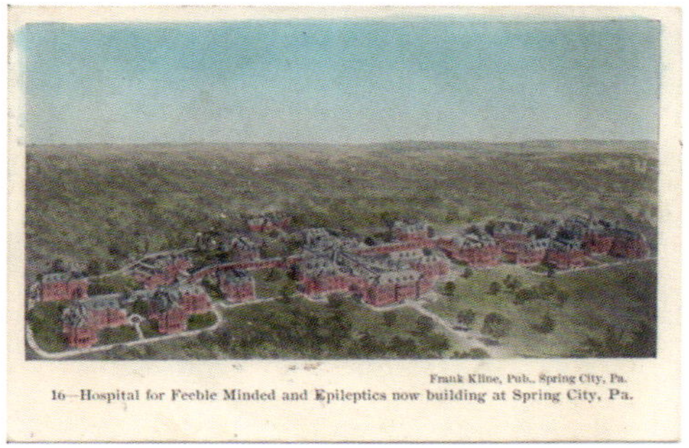

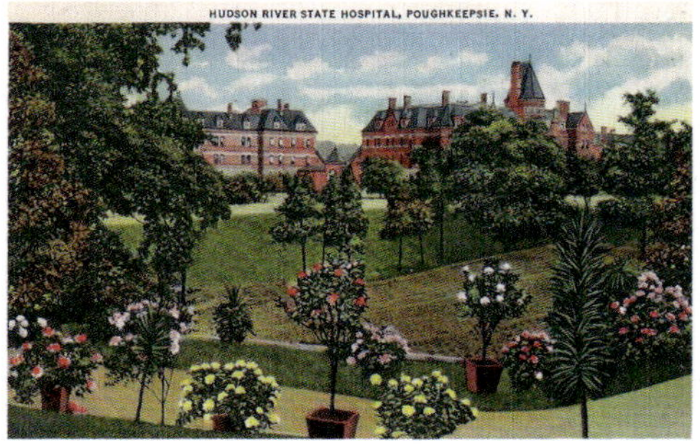

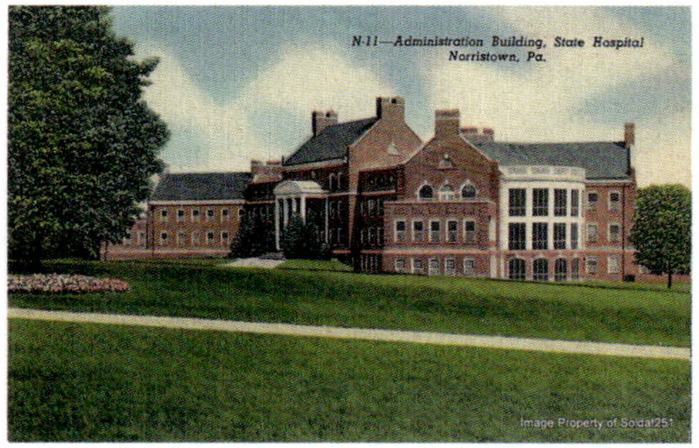

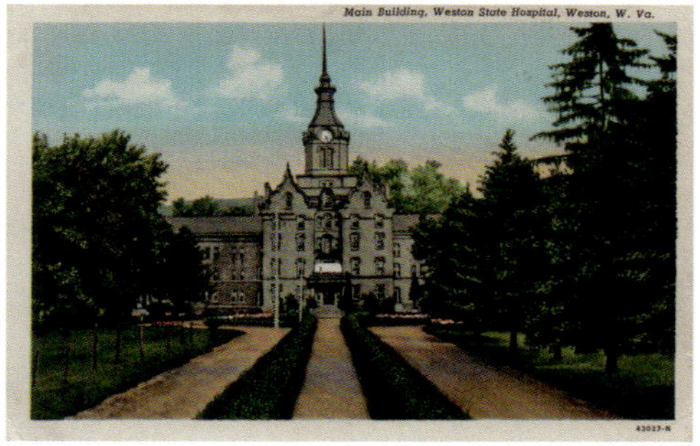

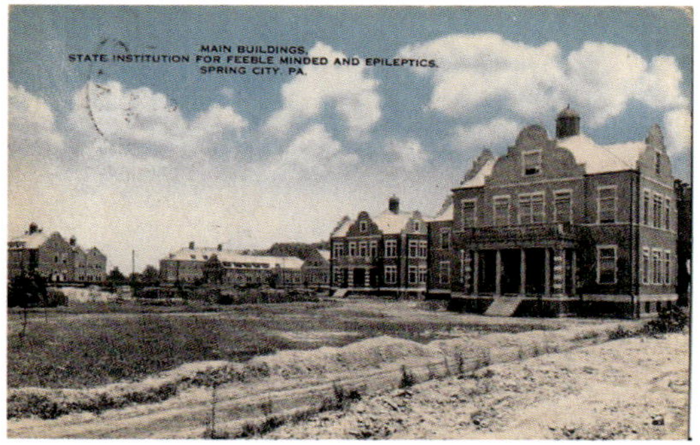

Historical postcards provided by the Piccola Collection

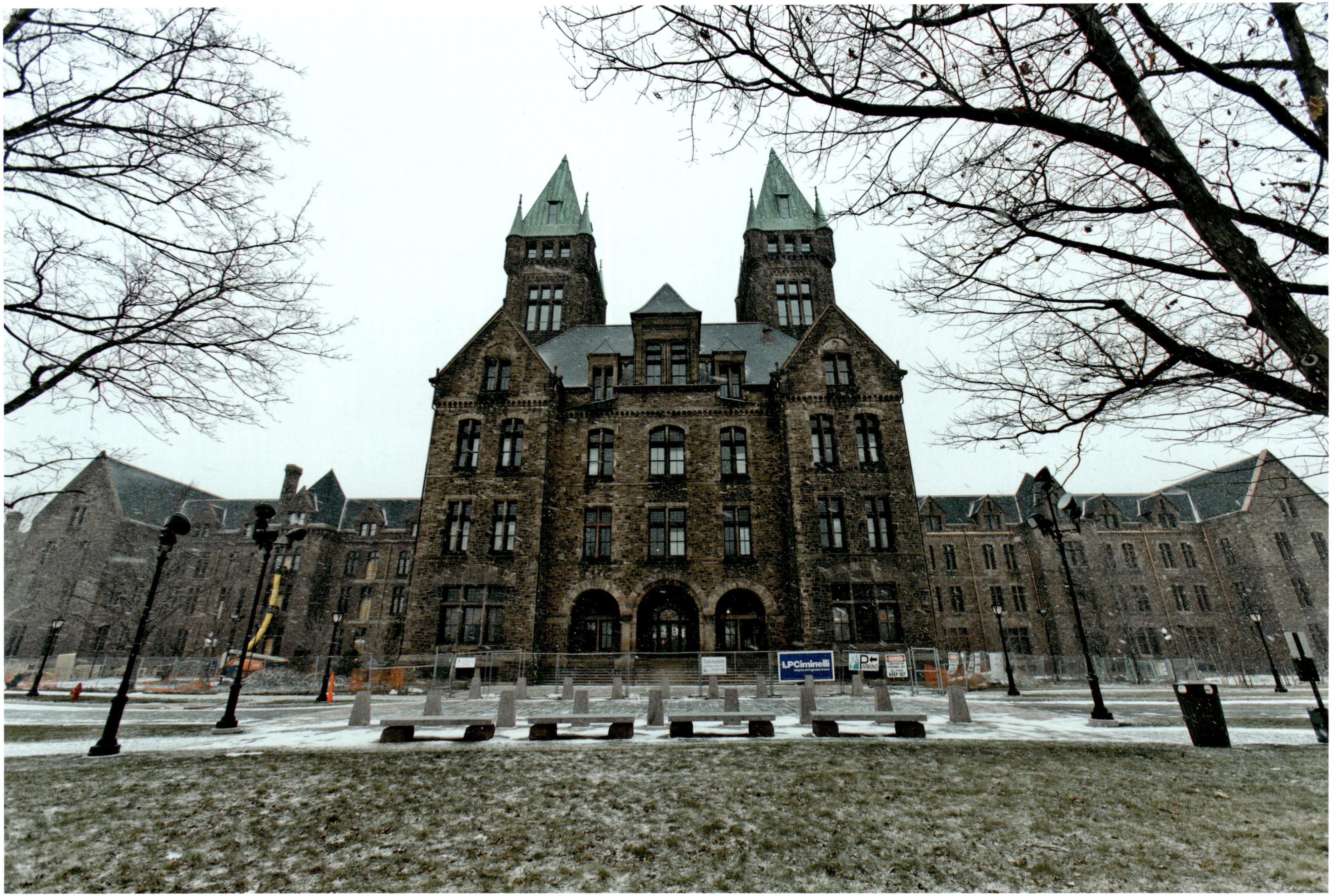

Buffalo State Asylum for the Insane adminsitration building

showers and baths) was commonly used. Van der Velde's photograph of a row of six covered bathtubs reminds the viewer of rows of patient beds, rows of tables in the cafeteria, and, ultimately, rows of identical headstones.

Kirkbride offered much advice on heating, flue design, and sewage removal, as well as firmly recommending the use of stone or brick to prevent fires. He promoted the characteristics seen at Trenton: the bilaterally symmetrical plan, consisting of a central building with flanking pavilions arranged in the echelon fashion. Pavilions were to be no more than three storeys high and short enough to allow a breeze to carry fresh air through the wards. These wards would be used to categorise patients by severity of disease, with the noisiest patients farthest from the centre.

A 19th-century Kirkbride-plan asylum followed a specific layout. Visitors would enter the main building at ground level to immediately face a spacious iron stairway leading up to the second storey, which housed business offices and reception rooms. The third storey was home to the chapel; this placement became standard. The centre main contained two dining rooms for the use of recovering or well-behaved patients. The outer refractory wards were for the noisiest or most violent patients; the outermost wards were comprised of single-loaded corridors, making surveillance easier, as the attendant never had to turn his or her back on a patient. Double-loaded corridors were standard for all the wards except the refractory ones, but if money had been no object, 19th-century doctors would have used single-loaded corridors throughout their hospitals. Hallways with rooms on one side only used space extravagantly; therefore most mental hospitals used double-loaded corridors. The view down this or any double-loaded corridor has come to symbolise *all* institutions. For example, architects in the 1960s, seeking reform in collegiate dormitories, avoided double-loaded corridors, as the corridors themselves were thought to reduce the inhabitants to inmates. But, because patients were not allowed in their bedrooms during the day, the ward hallway was the actual centre of a patient's daily life.

Each new state-funded asylum was a feather in the cap of Dorothea Dix, a charity reformer who considered the asylum in Trenton, New Jersey to be her earliest success. She later called it her "first child". Though legislators had discussed the possibility of a state mental hospital for seven years (from about 1838 to 1845), it was Dix's petition that catalysed the process. Formerly a schoolteacher, Dix travelled across the United States reporting on the desperate situation of almshouses and prisons. A Unitarian, she believed that within each person dwelled the possibility of continued spiritual development. She effectively coerced legislators in several states to fund asylums for the mentally ill. Generally, her appeals to state legislatures were filled with emotional descriptions of the conditions of dehumanised, pauper lunatics shivering in the cold of foul-smelling, dangerous almshouses. She did not speak herself, because women were not allowed to address state legislatures, but she prepared emotional statements that were read aloud by sympathetic politicians. Her entreaties on behalf of "those who ...are incapable of pleading their own cause" convinced many lawmakers. According to Dix, the situation for poor, mentally ill people was dire. Without institutions specifically for the insane, impoverished lunatics ended up in almshouses. County officials placed insane people in poorhouses when they were disruptive to the community, were dangerous to themselves, or carried some additional illness bringing them to the brink of death. Dix promoted the society-wide economic benefits of building therapeutic hospitals. But even if, as was widely believed, the insane could be cured, it was still cheaper for them to reside for a lifetime in an almshouse. However, counties and states looked uncaring when poorhouses burned to the ground, as happened in New Jersey just a week before Dix's petition was presented to the state legislature. No one died in the fire, but it served to illustrate that old buildings were unsafe and could not be adapted to this new purpose; since moral treatment required a changed setting anyway, a new building was the only way to house the nascent reform institution.

Nineteenth-century lunatic asylums were self-contained communities, almost like microcosmic cities. They had their own transportation systems, farms, kitchens, laundries, and print shops. Occupational therapy was an important part of the moral treatment; some patients were probably forced to work against their will, but other patients may have benefitted from gratifying work like growing flowers or making baskets. Court rulings of the 1970s ended patient labour abruptly. Although the change in the law was intended to protect patients from exploitation, it left them with yawning gaps of time. The loss of free labour marked the end of the asylum as a self-sustaining community.

During the last decades of the 19th century, outpatient care developed on several fronts, offering a reasonable, quick, inexpensive option for treating the mentally ill. In 1885, Massachusetts attempted to place docile patients with foster families. Reformers opened dispensaries, like the one attached to the Pennsylvania Hospital in 1885 and the Boston Dispensary in 1897. These clinics treated patients outside the traditional asylum, in the hope that if their diseases were caught early, the afflicted could be spared institutionalisation altogether. Aftercare programmes marked another innovation; these were programmes for those recently released from state hospitals. Similar types of care facilities exist in large numbers today and are related to halfway houses. Another type of institution, the psychopathic hospital, began around 1912. Its mission was to assess patients' illnesses for a few days, giving doctors a chance to observe acute cases before referring the most deranged patients to the state hospital, while sending others home. The extension of psychiatry 'beyond the walls' of the asylum was a bold step forward for the mentally ill – it allowed people to receive treatment without leaving their homes.

This would seem at first glance to be a welcome turn of events. But an insidious result ensued; the psychiatric profession gradually turned its attention away from the poorest, sickest patients, those who had no families, and those who were forced by circumstances to live in institutions. The budding field of psychiatry in the 1840s, as measured by the pronouncements of asylum doctors and the poignant petitions of Dix, once zealously attended to friendless and hopeless lunatics: by 1900, those lunatics were slipping from view. And today, the severely mentally ill are almost invisible. In the United States, the insurance industry refuses to pay for long-term stays in psychiatric hospitals, making it nearly impossible to find residential care for the mentally ill. Few ambitious graduates of a prestigious medical school seek employment at a state mental hospital; few young psychiatrists choose to work with institutionalised, impoverished schizophrenics or bipolar patients. As the profession has shifted its attention to non-institutionalised, milder cases, architecture has declined in importance to the field of psychiatry.

Today, mental illness is generally considered to be treatable, but it cannot be prevented or cured. Many patients recover, but their path is not an easy one. There is no vaccine for mental illness, such as that which has led to the eradication of smallpox. Nor is there a drug that purges mental illness from the body, in the way that a course of penicillin can conquer a staphylococcus infection. And no cure has reduced insanity to a minor problem, the way Vitamin C has made scurvy a mere medical nuisance. For many, mental illness remains shrouded in mystery, and that mystery creates further stigma for its sufferers. Those recovering from severe psychiatric illness must cope with this social stigma in addition to finding work, securing housing, and developing meaningful relationships. The difficulties faced by people in the 19th century did not disappear at the start of the 21st century, but architecture plays a far less significant role in the practice of psychiatry than it once did. As Melling and Forsythe explain in *Insanity, Institutions and Society*, since about 1980, most developed countries have abandoned the mass institutionalisation of the mentally ill.

It is true that long-term stays, those stretching from years into decades, are far less common now than in the past. Do we still need psychiatric hospitals? Do drugs make psychiatric hospitals obsolete? The questions are not easy to answer. Some psychiatrists envision that if drugs are properly prescribed and taken, all psychiatric patients could be integrated into society. Others say that even with drugs, there will always be mentally ill people who require confinement because they are dangerous to themselves and others. A middle ground might be that short-term care is the one form of confinement necessary, and that such short-term hospitalisation is required only for monitoring patients and establishing pharmaceutical regimens. Large hospitals where patients dwell for lifetimes are not a cherished or central part of the practice of psychiatric medicine, but they still exist.

Medical hospitals and lunatic asylums have had opposite historical trajectories. Today we need regular medical hospitals more than ever; for all their faults, they offer lifesaving technologies and treatments. That being said, we need psychiatric hospitals less and less. By 1920, the medical hospital was a highly valued aspect of any advanced city. Physicians, like those at the prestigious Johns Hopkins, associated themselves with universities, claiming higher status in society than ever before, and reinforcing their ranks with large, carefully organised, hygienic, technologically advanced hospitals. In this way, the status of the asylum and the medical hospital were at odds; as the medical hospital increased in eminence, the asylum declined. By comparison, state mental hospitals had lost status, drifting away from science, appearing to physicians as mere warehouses for humans. Doctors successfully aligned themselves with science (and all its socially constructed status), but asylum superintendents were still managing construction projects, repairing leaky roofs, fixing broken furnaces, and counting bales of hay. No new knowledge would ever come from a lunatic asylum.

Asylum doctors' focus on architecture was one of the signs of its failure. That alienists were once nearly obsessed with architecture was obvious in the 1850s, but such architectural dedication had dissipated by 1900. Around the turn of the 20th century, some critics accused traditional institutional doctors of claiming that the severely mentally ill needed to be institutionalised in order to keep their state hospitals up and running. These critics, again coming from the field of neurology, asserted that while public institutions were needed for the poor, any lunatic who had

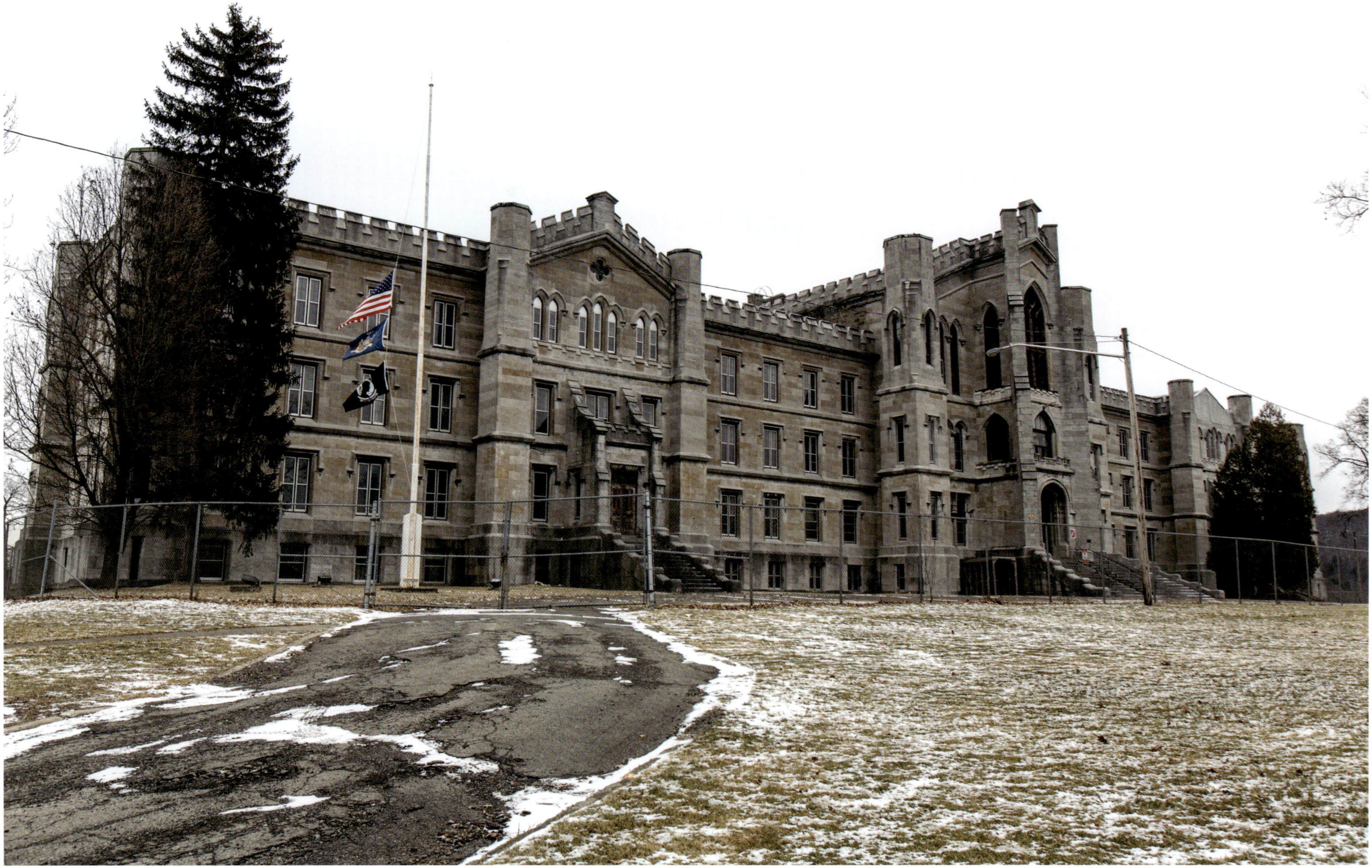

Binghamton State Hospital- the World's first asylum for inebriates

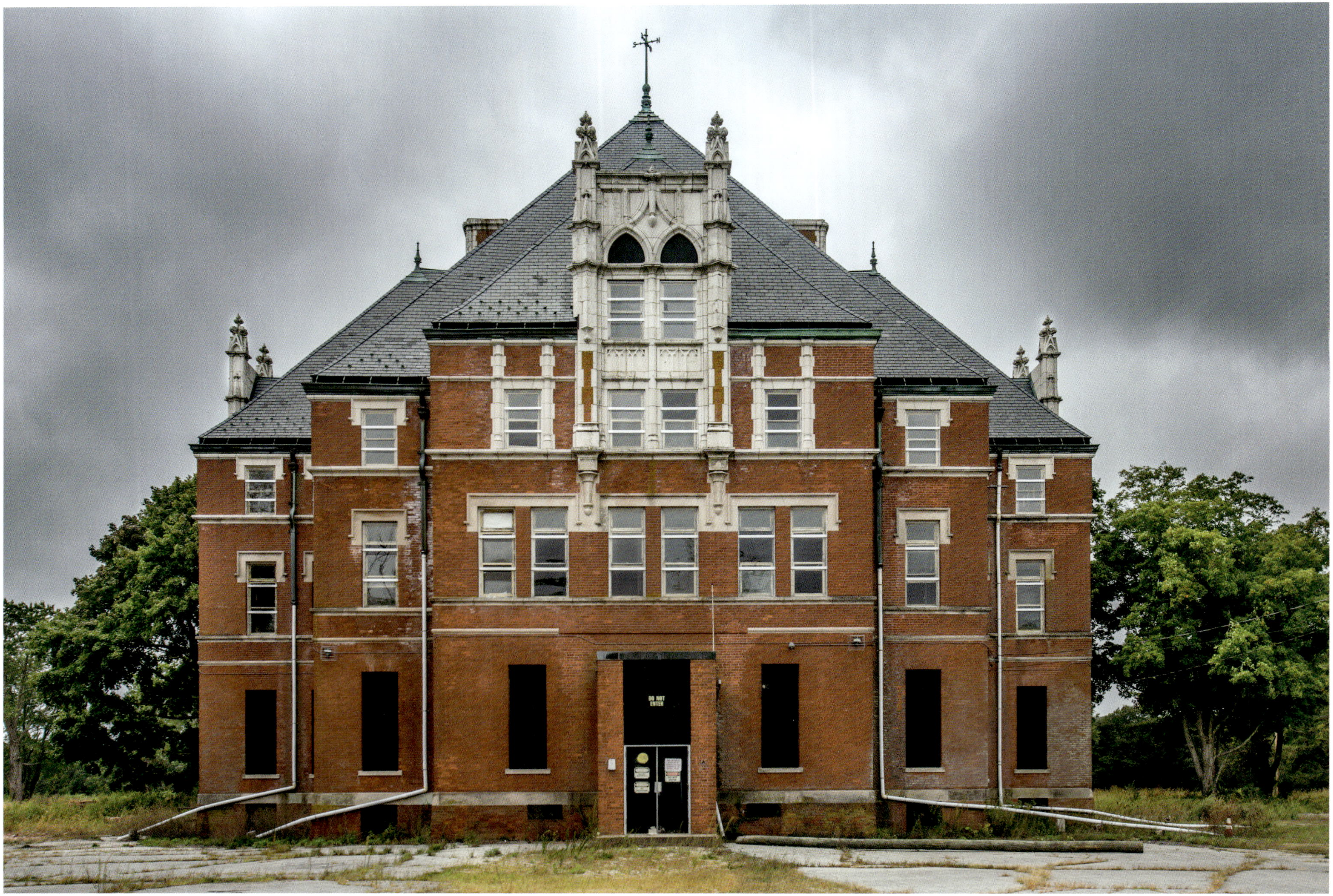

Norwich State Hospital for the Insane Administration building"

a family would be better off at home. In 1900, creating a therapeutic environment was not the key goal of asylum doctors. Indeed, it had become somewhat embarrassing that the allegedly therapeutic environments of the preceding sixty years were crowded with the lingering unwell. The profession needed to disassociate itself from the once grand claims of the asylum-as-cure Some doctors held dearly to the claim that if the patients had been admitted sooner, the asylum could have saved them; by the turn of the 20th century, this special pleading was difficult to accept. State mental hospitals embodied the times before psychiatry was serious medicine. Asylum doctors had managed the prosaic life of institutions, and this approach represented the past; the future of psychiatry would be to conduct research on diseases, rather than to manage institutions. The institutions themselves began to be neglected by both the doctors and the state because they carried negative associations. They were filled with incurable people who reminded both doctors and the public of past failures.

By the turn of the 20th century, the public distrusted all asylums, whether they looked like cottages or castles. The overcrowded asylums were decrepit; they had become custodial not curative. This building type – Asylums – as well as asylum medicine and the profession to which it was intimately connected, were at the end of their legitimacy as early as 1900. One might think that, given this sad state of affairs, the buildings would by now have just disappeared. In fact, many were torn down in pieces or as a whole. But for much of the 20th century, U.S. states actually needed these large buildings; where else would the underfunded mental health departments house thousands of people, people who could not care for themselves, had no one to speak for them, and had nowhere to go? So even as the respectability of asylum medicine declined, the buildings lingered.

The Photographs

Matt Van der Velde is an outstanding photographer who knows the conflicted and troubled history of this subject well. There are many evocative photos in this collection and Van der Velde's work will surely spark the interest of people who know little about the history of asylums, the treatment of the mentally ill in the 19th century, or the preservation of old buildings. Although I have some qualms about the genre, these compelling photographs of historic places are a potential path for historians to reach non-academics.

To offer readers a frame for understanding Van der Velde's haunting images, it helps to refer at least as far back as the 18th century. Piranesi's elegant etchings showed nature overtaking culture. Gandy made drawings for Soane that showed Soane's not-yet-built Bank of England in ruins. The decrepit state of the bank in these drawings only served to make the actual bank seem more important, as it drew a direct parallel between modern-day Great Britain and ancient Rome. In the late 18th century, wealthy British aristocrats constructed new ruins from scratch for their picturesque landscape gardens. In other words, the love affair with ruins is not restricted to the present post-industrial context – it extends far back in western culture.

Nick Yablon's book *Untimely Ruins: An Archeology of American Urban Modernity* (U of Chicago Press, 2009) evocatively describes two contemporary types of representation of urban ruins. First, there are the countless comic books, science fiction films, and video games set in post-apocalyptic space. Second, there are coffee table books (much like this one) of cities like Detroit in a crumbled state that seems to indicate the abandonment of inner cities. Who needs a coffee table book of a miserably sad subject? Yablon carefully traces the aggressive capitalism of America that occasionally led to unpredicted ruins made out of new materials. This was a break from the stone ruins of Greece and Rome that seemed to be part of a gradual process; a Roman ruin could serve as a reminder of the slow march of progress, or its opposite – the slow march of degeneracy. American ruins sprang up overnight, disturbing perceptions of time.

Cultural critic Sara Witty has convincingly placed the terror and beauty of the asylum in the art history category known as the Sublime; as she writes, there is something too alluring about tragedy, especially when that tragedy evokes the loss of one's mind. Nearly everyone knows someone who has survived mental illness or succumbed to it, and yet its nearness does not make it any less frightening. Witty objects to the use of patients' former possessions as stand-ins for the patients themselves. Much of this genre of photography includes aestheticising the contents of buildings: the typewriters, the pianos, the drum from the marching band, wheelchairs from every decade of the 20th century, peeling paint, mouldy carpet, mysterious medical instruments, measuring devices, rusty basketball hoops, and the gurneys that rolled away of their own volition. Witty sees photographs of ruined asylums as "…a means to quell contagion anxiety in a world without asylums." (Witty, *Asylum Myth and Material: A History of the St. Peter Regional Treatment Center, 1866 to the Present,* Ph.D. dissertation, Wisconsin, 2015). She argues that the ruined state of the asylum assures the outsider that mental illness can be contained, that it is not a threat, that it can be put away. Her research calls attention to the way that outsiders fetishise the asylum as a place of 'otherness', raising their own privileged status in the process.

Van der Velde's images remind us that large hospitals were once the *standard* form of care. The heaviness of the architectural materials (stone, brick, and iron), the quality of the finishes (inset panels in doors, Minton tiles, ornamental grill work on heating ducts) and the spaciousness of the hallways and chapels demonstrate the state investment in these buildings. These are not structures that crumbled because they were poorly built. In fact, it is just the opposite. The grandness and size of the original structure is essential to the effect of the ruin; a decrepit asylum recalls the scale of ancient Rome or Mexico. The devastation is more acute because the structure in its primary state was one of such high aspirations. The demolition of a building like Greystone in New Jersey was an absurd loss, a waste of architectural material and decorative arts that can never be replaced. More importantly, the intangible aspects of culture disappeared along with its demolition. Van der Velde's photograph of the spiral staircase in the Western State Hospital in Virginia reveals the craftsmanship that went into every detail of these buildings, evident in the scrollwork beneath the treads, which can be seen even in areas that almost nobody ever saw.

A standard facet of ruin representation is that the human-made object is overwhelmed and subdued by nature. Nature can be seen as out of bounds, in cases where operating rooms are choked with plants and library books are drenched in water. On the other hand, ruins suggest nature is merely returning to her rightful place, taking over where a vacuum was left. The intrusion of nature into these carefully wrought architectural spaces suggests the limitations of the built world, that all buildings are obsolescent. Peeling paint does not only mean neglect, it means the passage of time – it means that even a coat of paint was too much effort for the state to put into an edifice that once housed thousands of society's most infirm.

Victorian asylums present enormous challenges, both cultural and pragmatic, to historic preservation. On the pragmatic side, these are masonry buildings with hundreds of small rooms demarcated by load-bearing walls. They stubbornly resist new uses, whereas loft-like spaces in old factories are much more flexible. And culturally, of course, they carry a stigma that makes them difficult to repurpose. H. H. Richardson's Buffalo State Hospital was partly demolished many decades ago, but the remaining pavilions and the central administration block together form a National Historic Landmark. The building's survival is assured. In February 2006, then-Governor of New York George Pataki pledged state funds to stabilise the building and plan for its future. The process is now well advanced. The main building's unique character will be translated into its new role as an urban resort and conference centre.

The website for the Richardson Olmsted Complex politely but firmly rejects the language of ghosts and the appeal of the paranormal: "The Richardson Center Corporation focuses on the past, present, and future of the historic buildings and grounds. We are honoring the intent of the Complex as a place of hope and healing for people with mental illness. Horror- or paranormal-themed activities may be perceived as portraying those with mental illness in a negative light. The future of the site as a hospitality venue will draw visitors from all walks of life and we want to be inclusive to all future patrons."

The Richardson Olmsted Complex is wisely positioning itself as a compassionate site, where no ghosts of mental patients haunt the halls for the capitalistic gain of modern-day theme park owners. This cannot be said of the Trans-Allegheny Lunatic Asylum, whose website entices visitors to its ghost tours with the following : "Thousands have been committed to the asylum over the years, and hundreds unfortunately died here. Decide for yourself if they're still occupying the historic wards and treatment rooms." There are overnight Ghost Hunts and shorter Paranormal Tours. A few wards and part of the main administrative block have been renovated nicely – with the proceeds of the paranormal tours. Trans-Allegheny is still standing and Greystone is not. One doesn't like to trade in souls, but nothing about the history of psychiatric hospitals is easy or straightforward.

While doing research for my book, *The Architecture of Madness*, I visited a psychiatric ward for extremely difficult, chronic cases. Standing in the hallway was a woman wearing a shirt and underwear, but no pants. She was screaming at the doctor: "I am dying of cancer and I don't want a baloney sandwich for lunch. I want a hot lunch. I am dying here in this place." And I thought, no one should have to die in such object conditions. I thought about how her entire world had become reduced to a few rooms and how her death would take place within those few walls. How do we write history that acknowledges her struggle without objectifying her? In this volume, there is a photograph of the autopsy room in *her* hospital. I wonder if that is where her physical body met its end. No doubt others will have similar encounters with these images, for everyone who picks up this book probably has a reason to do so – a memory might be pried loose of its moorings.

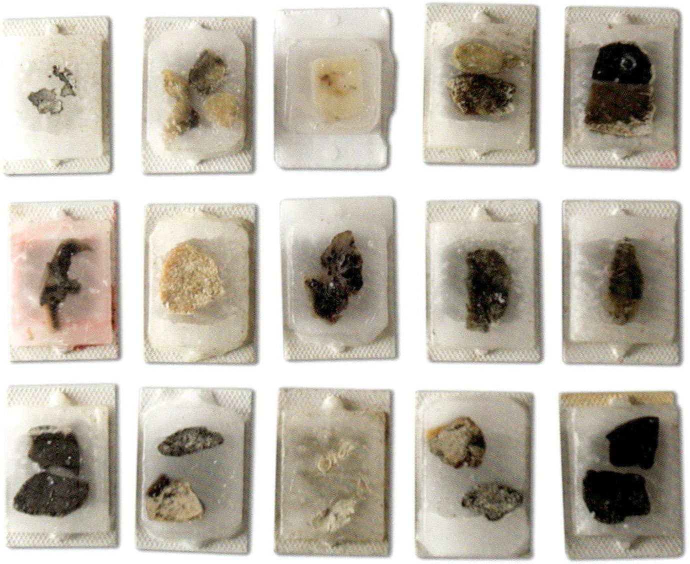

Patient brain, organ and tissue samples encased in wax for medical study

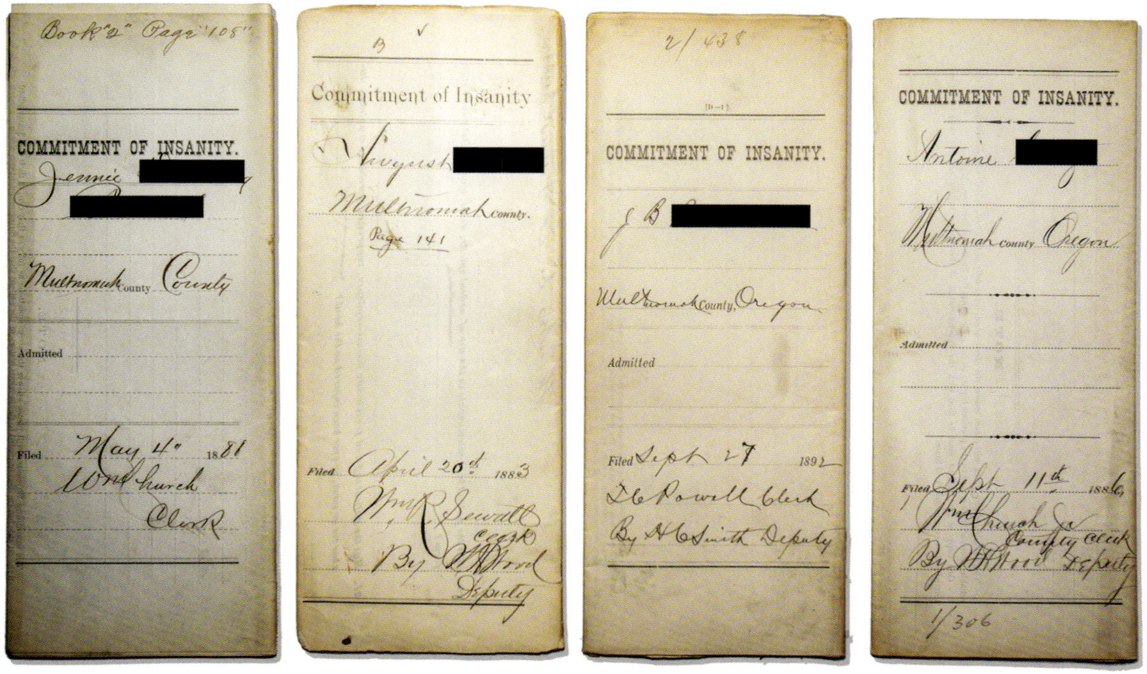

"Commitment of Insanity" files circa late 1800s

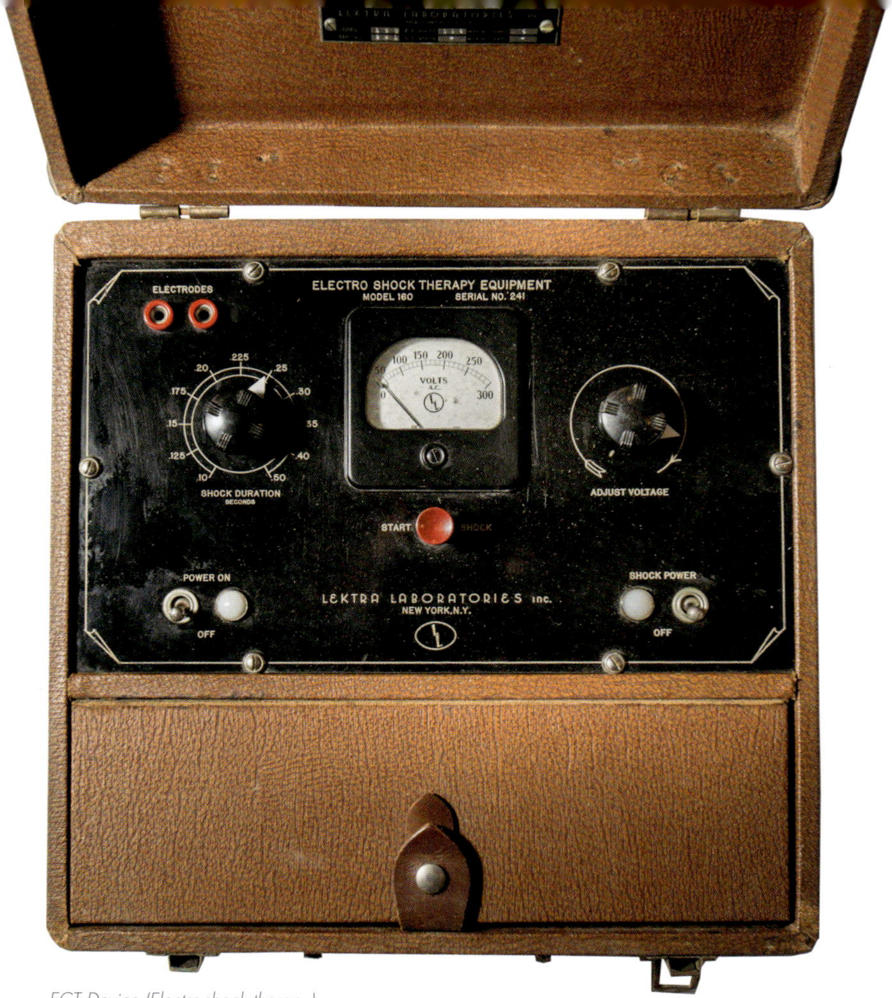

ECT Device (Electro-shock therapy)

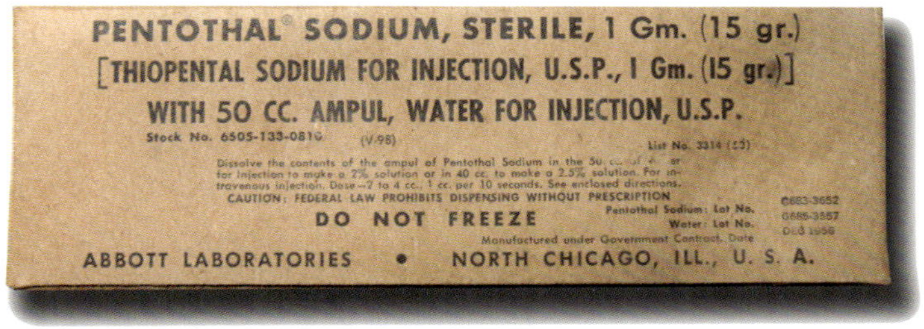

Pentothal Sodium (aka "Truth Serum" – utilised in psychiatry to desensitise patients suffering from phobias and to facilitate the recall of painful repressed memories)

Historical items provided by the Piccola Collection

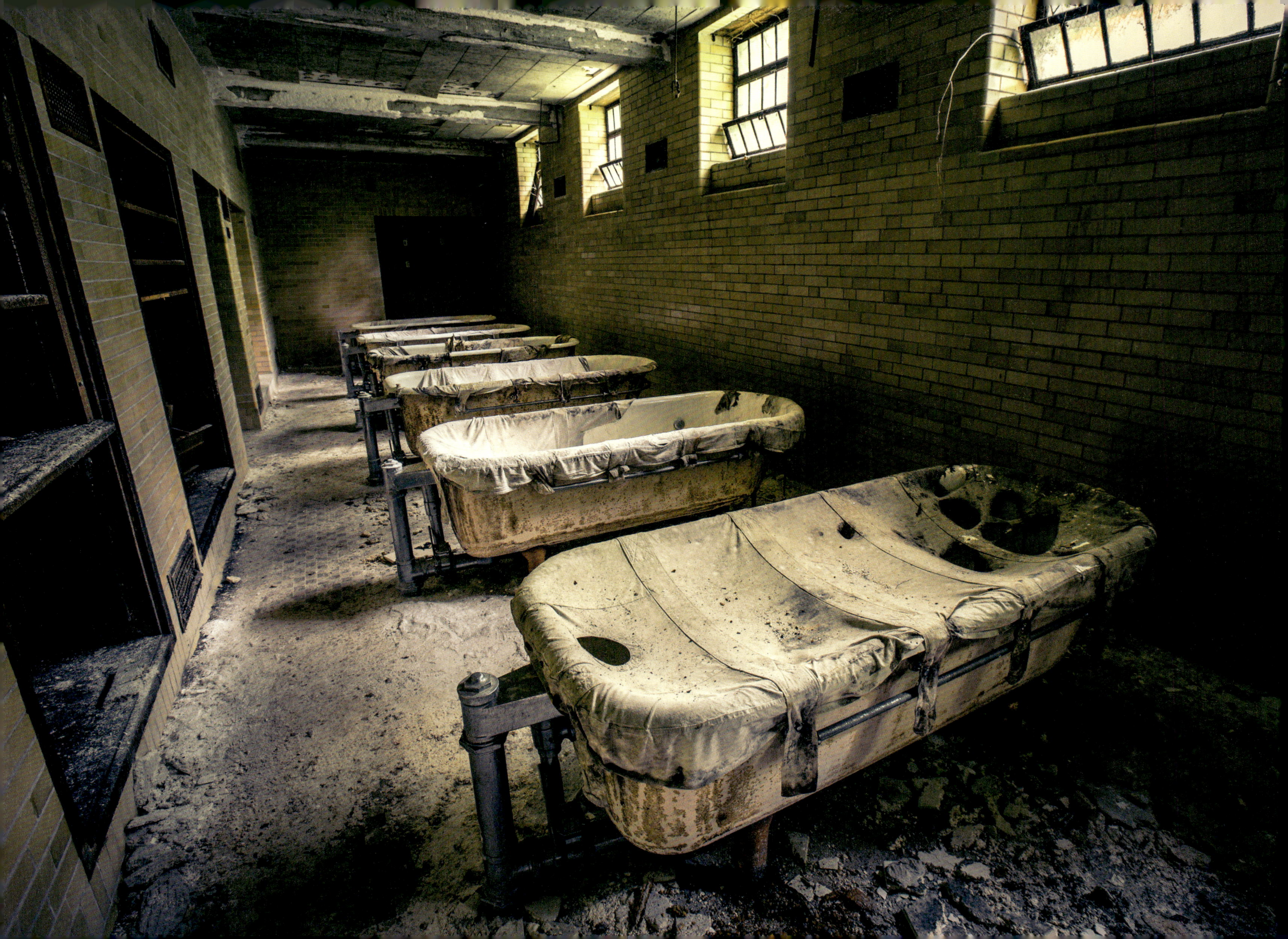

Comparisons between this book and Chris Payne's *Asylum* are inevitable; indeed, Van der Velde builds on but does not compete with Payne. The two books complement one another, especially because Van der Velde's pictures are more recent. Payne had the distinct advantage of the elegiac voice of the beloved Oliver Sacks. Dr. Sacks, the noted author and neurologist, had worked in a psychiatric hospital early in his career. Sacks wrote that even in the worst hospitals there were "pockets of human decency" (Payne, *Asylum*, 3). Sacks described Payne's photographs as offering "a mute and heartbreaking testimony both to the pain of those with severe mental illness and to the once-heroic structures we built to try to assuage that pain" (Payne, *Asylum*, 5). Van der Velde continues that important work here.

Generally, the photographs are stark and unpopulated. The absence of humans from architectural photographs has a long history, but in this case the absence may have emerged from a practical barrier – officials at most psychiatric hospitals request that photographers register their cameras and refrain from taking photos of people. Even though the humans at an abandoned hospital are likely to be repairmen or groundskeepers, the institutions understandably want to protect the identity of anyone who might wander into the frame. He captures the monumentality of these buildings without using people for scale. Nonetheless, we feel like we are trespassing on the spaces that patients called home.

Imaginative treatment of scale marks many of the images in *Abandoned Asylums*. Van der Velde's photographs capture a sense of architectural grandeur. But flipping through the images, one shifts from the colossal to the cramped, from the mammoth to the miniature. In addition to soaring rooftops and endless corridors, there are smaller measures of asylum life: a sneaker dangling from a suitcase, a cartoon bear in a folksy fresco, and a close-up of the number on a grave marker.

'Ruin Porn': Or is it?

Lastly, I feel the need to address the troubling term 'ruin porn'. The creeping use of the word 'porn' is my first complaint. Neither ruin porn nor food porn is really pornography. Photos of empty buildings and alluring food do not carry the same gendered, exploitative valence as posed images of objectified women. An éclair or a door is not fundamentally changed by having its likeness captured, but a woman might be. Same-sex pornography carries within it a power differential wherein the control is in the hands of the image-maker rather than the subject. I am arguing here that Van der Velde's photos ask the viewer to sympathise with the invisible individuals who moved through these spaces. There is only so much historical information that can be transmitted by a photo of a ruin, but since most people have an utter lack of historical knowledge about these places, these visual wake-up calls do more good than harm.

One caveat: on the many websites that show ruined buildings, often posted by people who call themselves urban explorers, the artists make vague claims about not trespassing. The photographers are then undone by their own popularity. The comment sections will be sprinkled with barely literate questions about 'getting past the cops'. My fear is that books like this one will encourage more so-called urban explorers who will be attracted to asylums for their creepy, forbidden quality, which apparently equates to counter-culture entertainment. I don't think people who break into historical asylums for fun should be encouraged. An abandoned asylum is not the same as a disused factory or an empty subway tunnel. Sneaking around a mental hospital diminishes the experience of the patients who suffered there. Curiosity about the patients doesn't erase stigma; it perpetuates stigma. It's not OK to lie in someone else's coffin; it's not OK to wear someone else's straitjacket. Furthermore, by scaling walls, cutting open fences, busting padlocks, and generally intruding, urban explorers put their own lives at risk and, by extension, they endanger the lives of rescue workers. This is not acceptable to me, as a historian (or as a taxpayer).

But what Van der Velde achieves here is something quite different; it is a balance between exposure and compassion. I would argue that these photographs are not 'ruin porn'. They are a kind of memorial for people who had a very limited voice in the body politic and almost no social clout. No single asylum campus exists today that offers a complete picture of the state mental hospital. But this composite portrait goes a long way towards capturing the ineffable spirit of these complex institutions.

Trenton State Hospital and the Infamous Dr. Cotton

Trenton State Hospital (formerly New Jersey State Lunatic Asylum) was founded in 1848 by Dorothea Dix; it served as the first psychiatric institution to be designed under the principle of the Kirkbride Plan. Not only was it revolutionary in terms of architectural design, but it also supplemented medical treatment with 'morale treatment', which aimed for a serene environment free of physical restraints. Treatments of the time included depletion (blood-letting), medicine, hydrotherapy, exercise and regulation of diet.

Throughout this era, psychiatrists operated under two popular beliefs: either generally accepting that major mental disorders were rooted in faulty heredity - rendering individuals biologically defective; or the Freudian approach, centred on the idea that mental illness was a result of childhood trauma and the collision of unconscious forces.

Between 1867 and 1907, Trenton's superintendent John Wesley Ward oversaw four decades of mundanity; the hospital's early ambitions were suppressed by surging chronic cases and an unrelenting growth in patient population, as asylums became human warehouses for anyone even remotely 'ill'. Superintendent Ward saw patients as "tainted creatures", preferring to spend as little time in their presence as possible, all the while operating Trenton under a low profile without attracting controversy or public attention.

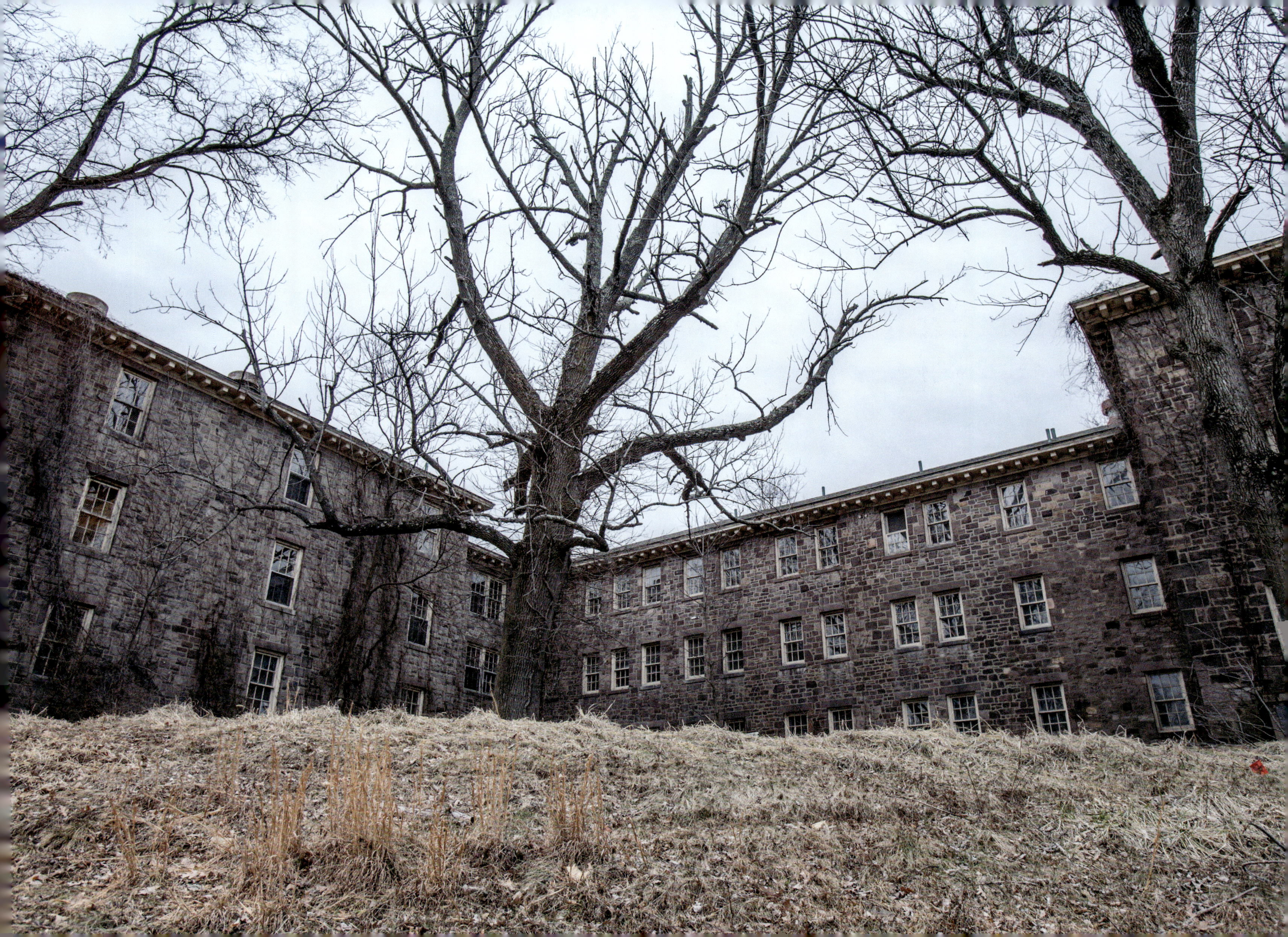

Laboratory

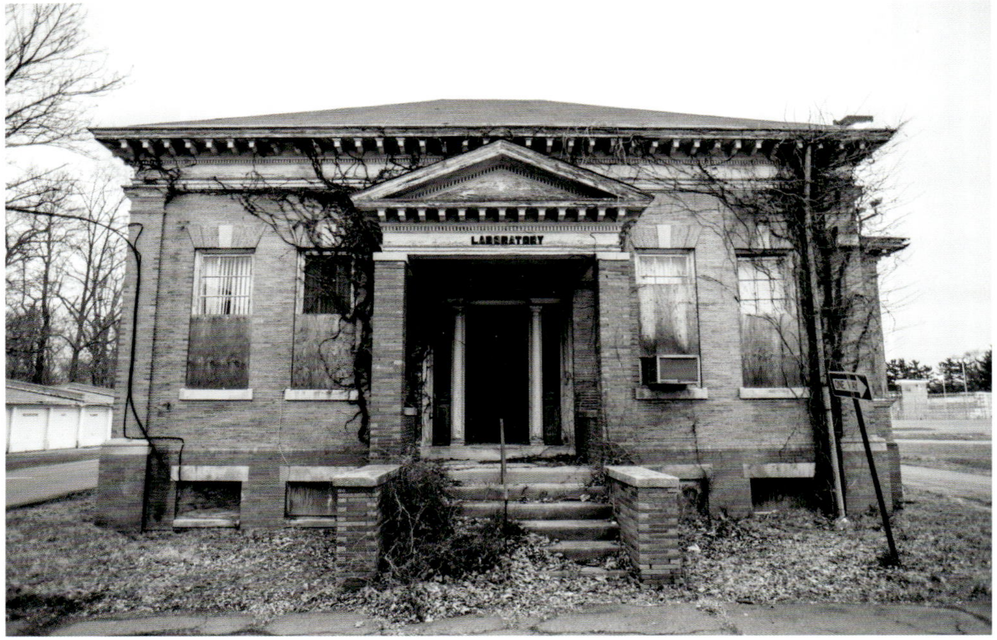

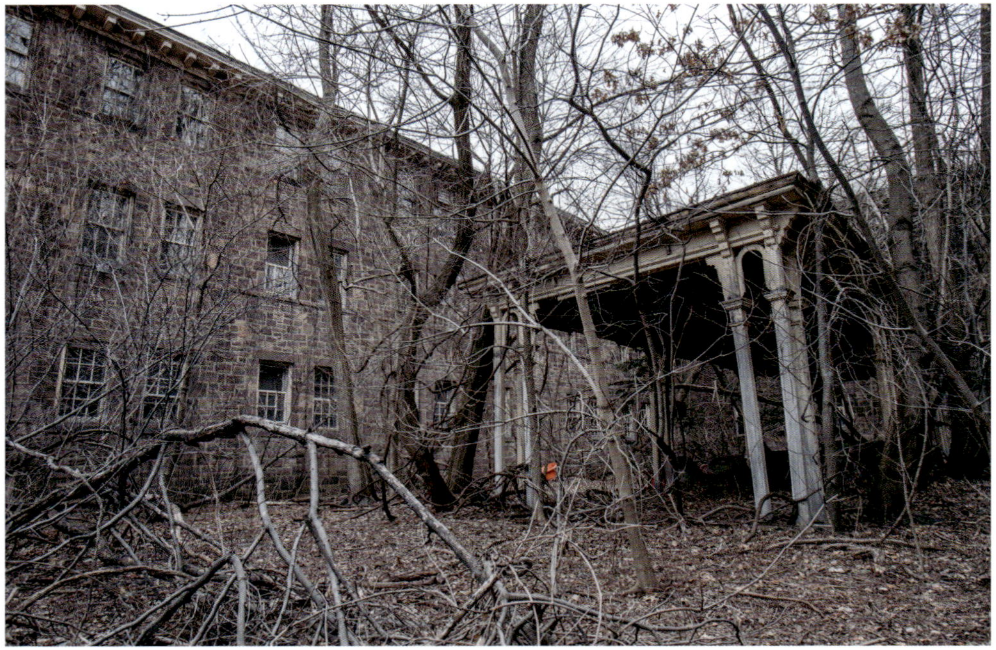

Patient courtyard

The superintendent was able to manage the status quo for 40 years, until 1907, when a massive outbreak of typhoid fever infected the hospital - patients and nursing staff fell ill at an alarming rate, as uncontrollable nausea, vomiting, and dysentery plagued the asylum. The hospital's administration paid no attention to the cause, choosing to continue operations as usual. The situation quickly worsened as those afflicted developed prolonged fevers, chills, agonising muscular pains and seizures, which led to intestinal hemorrhaging and sometimes death. Superintendent Ward's indifference to patients and lack of action in attempting to quell the outbreak decimating hospital staff, combined with reports of patient abuse and neglect, maladministration and corruption, forced an enquiry that ultimately led to his departure.

With the appointment of Dr. Henry Cotton as new medical director in 1907, the hospital saw a dramatic change in direction. His immense desire to discover the root of mental illness forced a new era in the methodology of treatment. Relative to his predecessor, Dr. Cotton took an active interest in the patients. Sadly, that did not equate to improvements in patient care or treatment.

Cotton's startling theories dismissed previous psychiatric understandings and methods as nothing but quackery and pseudo-science. He blamed germs for mental illness and operated under the principles of 'focal sepsis theory' - whereby infections were the root cause of disorders such as schizophrenia, psychosis and depression. As a result, Cotton used surgery as treatment to rid the body of focal infections, removing upwards of 11,000 teeth, limbs, and organs from his patients.

Asylum Fire Department"

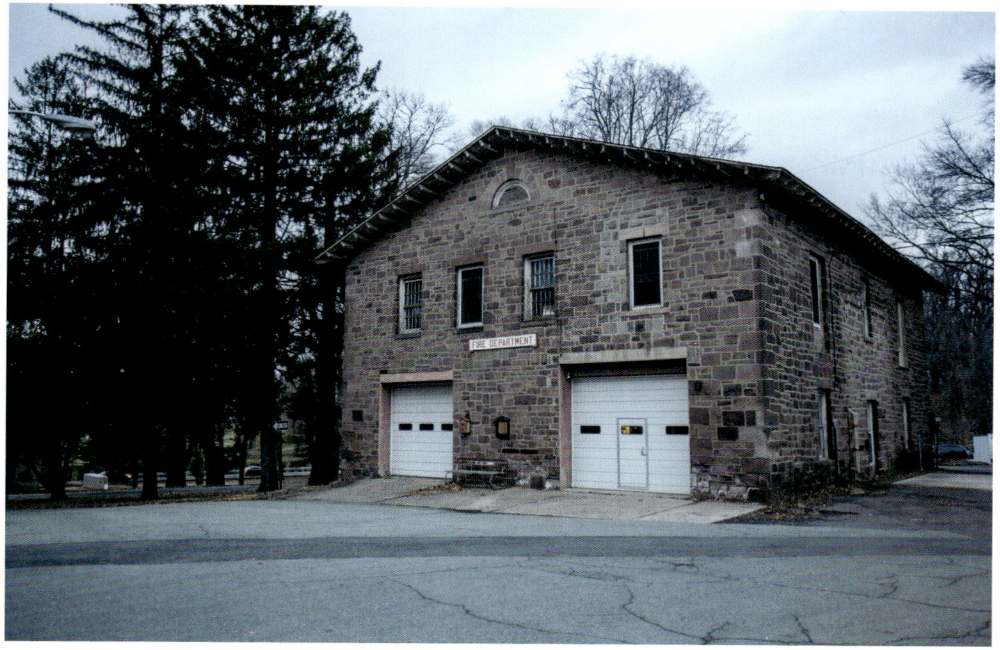

But how did such a foolish theory for the cause of madness come to be accepted in the first place? The truth is, it did not look so absurd at the time. The germ theory of disease (which stated that some diseases are caused by micro-organisms inside the human body) was relatively new, as was the discovery that syphilis was a root cause of the paralysis from which approximately 20% of the asylum population suffered. Even today, it is understood that hidden infections often result in acute confusion in the elderly, including hallucinations and delusions. While our current understanding of mental illness - both causes and treatment - has advanced far beyond 'focal sepsis theory', it was an entirely reasonable conclusion to draw at that time.

Surprisingly (and perhaps dangerously), Cotton was a master of self-promotion, who proclaimed his rate of success was 85% - thus he was lauded by his peers and other leading psychiatrists of the day. However, the adverse effects of his procedures were once again kept quiet and it was said that 30% of his patients died as a result of their treatments (hospital records indicate this rate was closer to 45%).

Dr. Cotton believed so thoroughly that his treatments were effective that he even removed some of his own teeth in 1926 after suffering something of a psychotic episode brought on by the political pressures he faced. Before dying of a heart attack in 1933, Cotton also extracted teeth from his wife and sons, who also suffered from mental illness. Tragically, the treatments were no cure for his sons, both of whom committed suicide. In hindsight, this would be seen as an era of inhumane and unethical treatment.

When analysing the evolution of mental health treatments and the institutions that harboured them, it's certainly easy to label Dr. Cotton as guilty of unethical conduct and medical malpractice. He directly caused the chronic suffering of countless maimed and traumatised patients, as well as an unacceptable number of patient deaths. Ironically, his tale is that of a psycho-pathological psychiatrist - one that history would rather soon forget. The truth, however, is that Cotton was neither an exception nor a lone crusader at war with germs and infection. Many of the world's leading scientists and psychiatrists shared these same beliefs and similar procedures continued worldwide decades after Dr. Cotton's death.

St Elizabeths and the "father of lobotomy"

Formerly known as the "Government Hospital for the Insane", St Elizabeths (note the lack of apostrophe) was built in 1855 using the Kirkbride Plan and was unique in both purpose and nomenclature. Unlike most asylums of the era – which served the general public, were run by the state and were referred to as "State Hospitals for the Insane" – St Elizabeths was a federal institution whose primary objective was to care for those in the military. Founded by Dorothea Dix, a key figure in mental health reform, the hospital aimed to provide the "most humane care and enlightened curative treatment of the insane of the Army, Navy, and the District of Columbia".

At the time that the asylum was built, the District of Columbia – much like elsewhere in the United States – was adopting a new approach to mental health. There was a pressing need to build institutions for the "insane" so that they could be moved from their inadequate accommodations at local jails, almshouses and general hospitals throughout the area.

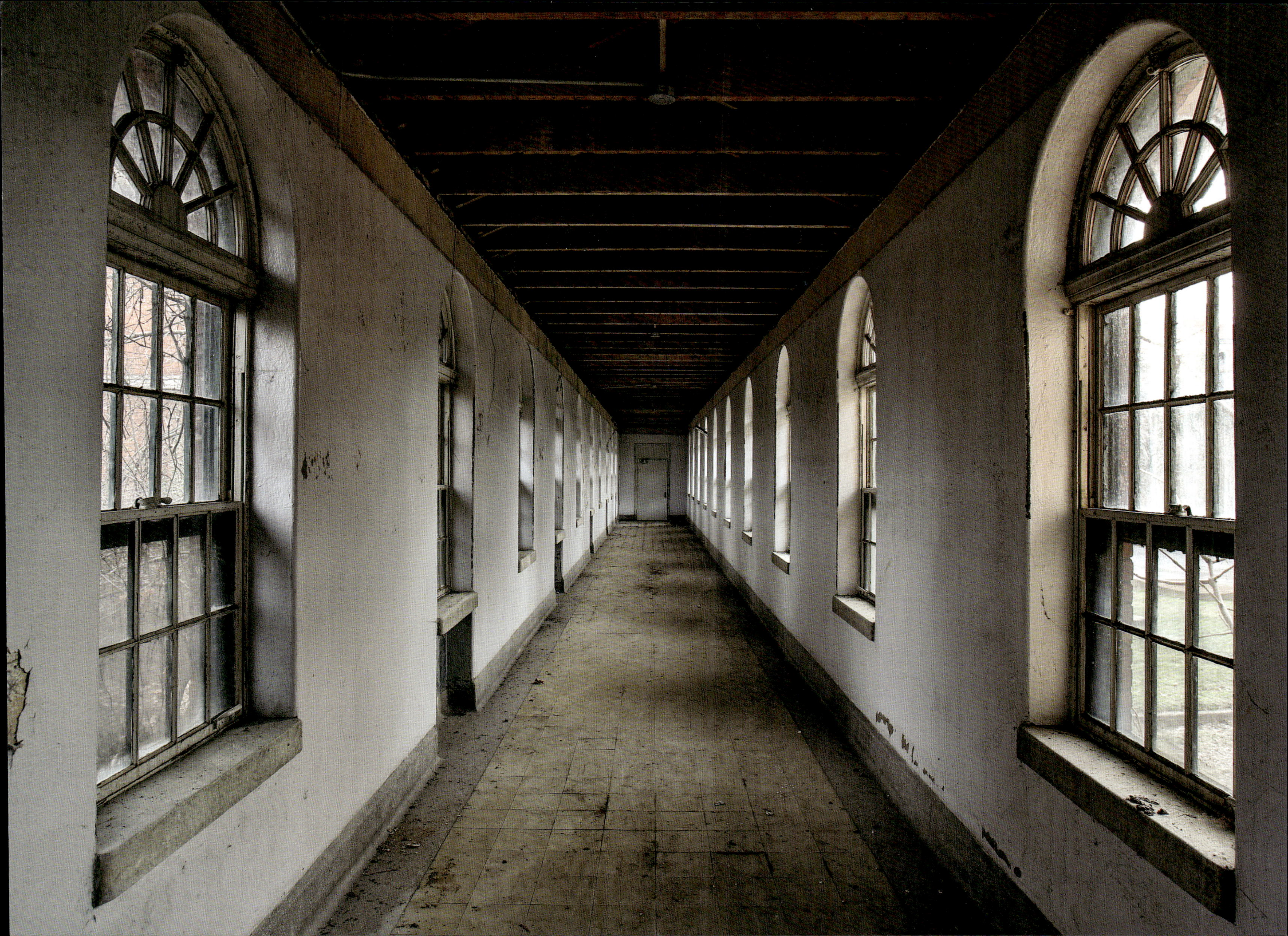

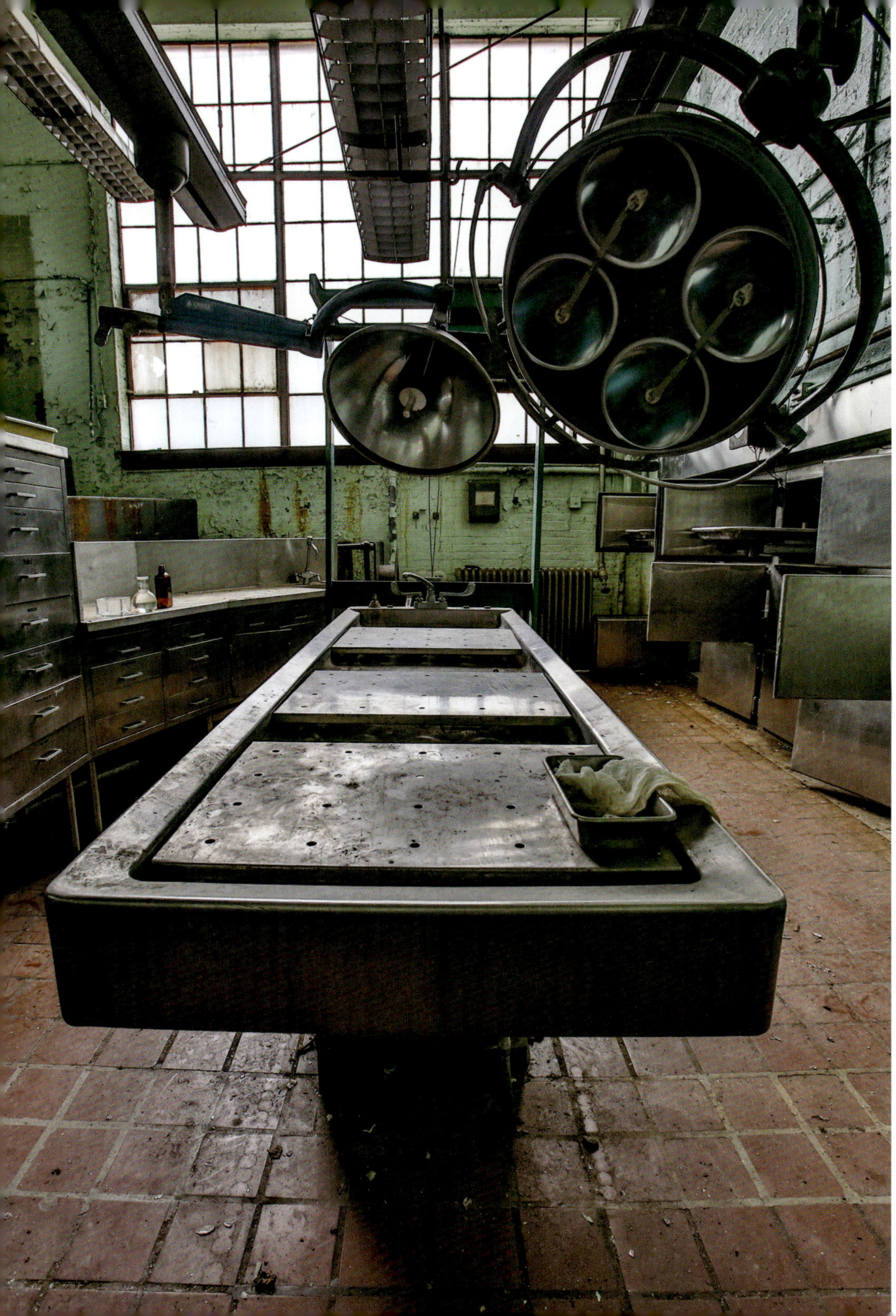

One of St Elizabeths' very first patients was none other than the infamous Richard Lawrence: in 1835 he aimed two misfiring pistols at President Andrew Jackson, thus becoming the first man to attempt to assassinate a US president. At the time, Lawrence was an unemployed house painter and he blamed the president for his struggles. He later told doctors that, with the president dead, "money would be more plenty" and that he "... could not rise until the president fell". Immediately after the failed attempt, he also told his interrogators that he was a deposed English king – specifically, Richard III (who, in reality, died in 1485). In 1838, while incarcerated at the DC jail, Lawrence was officially diagnosed as a "lunatic". It wasn't until 1855, with the opening of St Elizabeths, that he was able to receive more appropriate accommodations and treatment for his illness.

For many years, the hospital achieved its aim of being a leader in the field of mental health. In its heyday, it treated 8,000 patients and employed 4,000 staff. The first five of the institution's superintendents were all elected president of the American Psychiatric Association, and the Government Hospital for the Insane (St Elizabeths) was seen as the premier example of an institution offering moral treatment.

In 1903 Dr William Alanson White was appointed hospital superintendent by President Roosevelt – unofficially, he became known as the "chief psychiatrist of the United States". The hospital saw a change of direction with the introduction of psychotherapy and psychology, a desire for research and the application of internal medicine, occupational therapy and pathology. With these reforms came a change of name: the Government Hospital for the Insane became known as St Elizabeths.

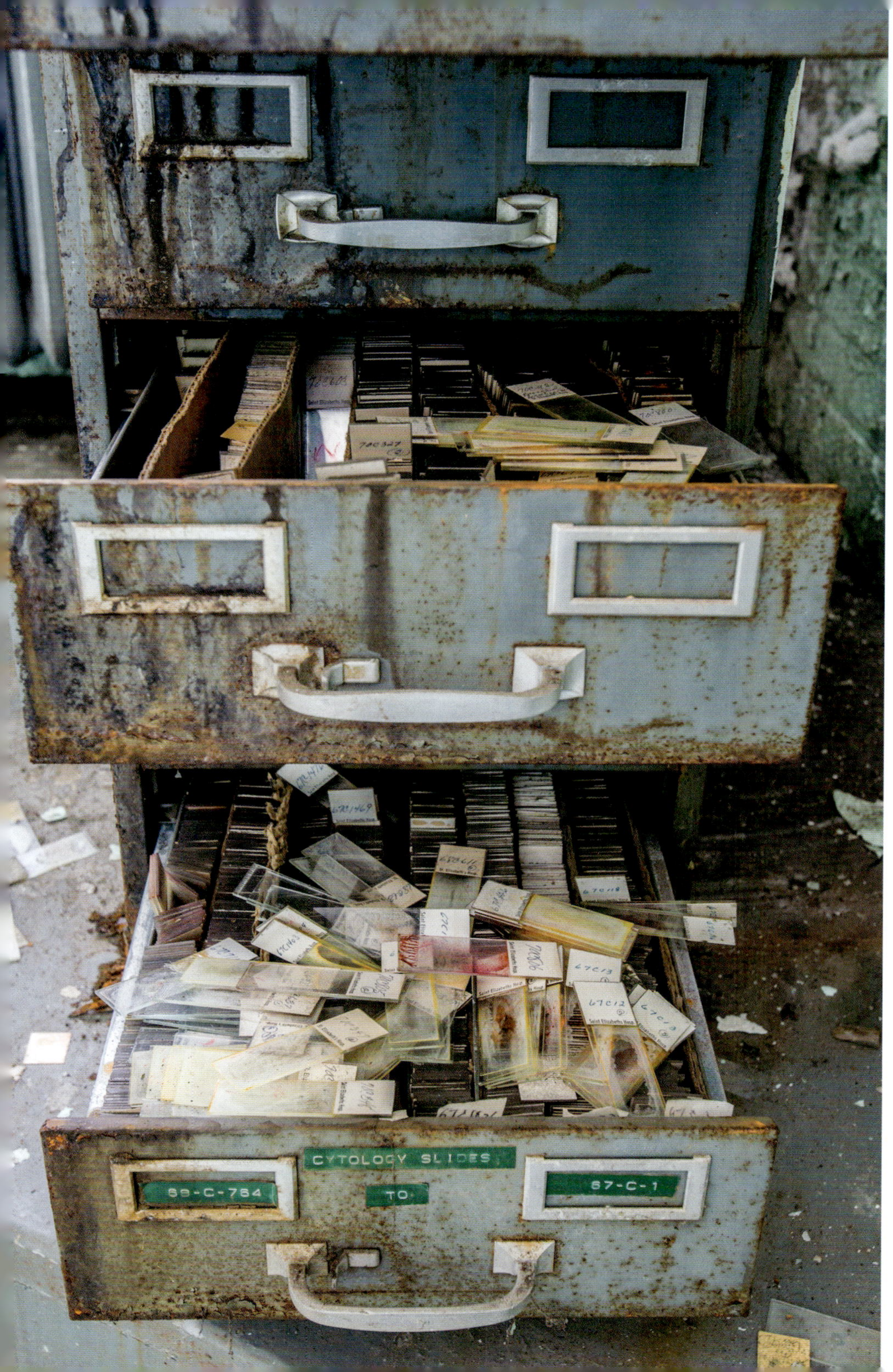

Patient blood and bodily fluid microscope slides

The desire to set a precedent in mental health care continued into 1919, when US Secretary of the Interior Franklin K. Lane suggested in a letter that St Elizabeths should use dogs as emotional therapy. He wrote: "A poor insane chap naturally reaches out for companionship and finds himself barred by the various limitations of his unfortunate associates, but he could develop a great friendship with a dog ... with his limited mind but unequalled capacity for affection." Dr White followed up on Lane's suggestion and experimented with pet therapy in order to encourage human-animal interaction. The hospital provided other progressive therapeutic activities, including "walks, rides, calisthenics, moving pictures, picnics, etc", which served to "attract the patient's interest, wake him so to speak, from his morbid phantasies and be the beginning of the re-socialization of his instincts".

In 1924 St Elizabeths appointed Dr Walter J. Freeman II – later to become known as the "father of lobotomy". Dr Freeman was the grandson of a nationally distinguished surgeon, William Keen – the first to successfully remove a brain tumor from a living person. Much like Keen, Freeman believed that he was destined for greatness. He had inherited Keen's showman-like qualities, which attempted to transform medical procedure into performance – an act to be observed by large and admiring audiences. As the scion of a medically prominent family, Freeman was appointed Director of Laboratories at St Elizabeths. He capitalized on his position to take the hospital in a more experimental direction, to the disapproval of his peers.

Like most neurologists, Freeman believed that mental illness was caused by physical defects in the human brain. He also believed that mental illness required direct action, not sympathy. This idea was in direct conflict with the moral therapies and humane treatments that St Elizabeths had stood for until then. Under Freeman, thousands of autopsies were performed at the Blackburn Laboratory at St Elizabeths. The aim was to discover correlations between psychosis, body type and endocrine functions (the glands that produce hormones).

The search for the root of mental health issues even brought Benito Mussolini to St Elizabeths ... well, his brain, at least. After Mussolini was executed in April 1945, an autopsy was performed and two samples of his brain tissue were sent to the United States. One went to the Army Institute of Pathology and the other to St Elizabeths. Dr Winfred Overholser, who was superintendent of St Elizabeths at the time, studied the sample for evidence that Mussolini had suffered from "paresis" (inflammation of the brain, causing dementia and paralysis) brought on by syphilis, but the tests came back negative. The army returned its sample to Mussolini's family in 1966 ... the whereabouts of the St Elizabeths sample is still unknown.

By this time, scientists were aware that the brain was composed of distinct regions that were responsible for physical, behavioral and emotional actions, but the source of mental illness was still elusive and unknown. Through his autopsies, Freeman would remove the brains of deceased patients, and then measure and photograph them meticulously. He hoped to discover the physical lesion from which mental illness originated, thus guiding scientists towards a solution. His experiment failed, however: he found no physical differences between samples from patients with serious mental illnesses and healthy individuals.

Frustrated in his attempts, but driven by ambition, Freeman decided to explore further into the realms of experimental psychiatry. He drew inspiration from a Portuguese neurologist, Egas Moniz, who in 1935 had performed a radical procedure dubbed the "leukotomy", where a small piece of a patient's brain is removed through a hole drilled in the skull. Moniz had no real explanation as to why this might work, but operated on the crude premise that, during the First World War, soldiers whose frontal lobe had been damaged were noticeably calmer and less prone to anxiety and depression. He concluded that one could simply damage a specific area of the brain, and while not being fatal to the patient, this would alter behavior.

This kind of procedure was abhorrent to most medical practitioners. To Freeman, however, it was an inspiration. Unfortunately for him, his surgical license had previously been revoked due to a death on the operating table. Because of this, he recruited a young and willing Dr James Watts to conduct the procedure. But yet another obstacle stood in their way. The superintendent of St Elizabeths (Dr William A. White) and the director of the New York State Psychiatric Institute both vehemently objected to the procedure, which, in their words, produced "zombies" and was "not an operation, but a mutilation". The practice was prohibited outright at St Elizabeths.

Unlike Moniz's "leukotomy", Freeman pushed his procedure even further, drilling several holes in the skull and inserting a spatula-shaped tool that was moved back and forth so as to sever the roots of the frontal lobe from the thalamus. The thalamus, a structure lying deep in the brain, transmits signals over nerve pathways to the frontal lobe and was purported by Freeman to be the "seat of human emotion". He dubbed his refined procedure the "lobotomy". And so, on September 14, 1936, Watts – under the explicit direction of Freeman, who dictated his every movement – conducted the very first lobotomy on US soil in Freeman's private Washington office. Four hours after the procedure, patient Alice Hammatt – who had wrestled with insomnia, anxiety and depression – awoke. She was alert and was noted as having a placid expression, with no signs of anxiety. The procedure was proclaimed a success, and Freeman wasted no time continuing to apply it.

In 1937, with the death of St Elizabeths' superintendent Dr William A. White and the appointment of Dr Winfred Overholser, the institution once again saw a dramatic change of policy. Although strictly regulated, Freeman would now be allowed to perform lobotomies on the campus as a last resort, should other treatments and more humane procedures be deemed ineffective.

As Freeman's procedure gained momentum, he would deny (and, in some cases, hide) any unsuccessful outcomes to avoid criticism from the medical profession. His observations and conclusions were usually only made within two days of the procedure – while the patient was still recovering and before the true results were apparent. While his track record proved that lobotomy could eliminate certain side effects, the reality was that others would take their place. Or the original condition would eventually return, so that the patient had to undergo multiple lobotomies. In some cases, the procedure was outright botched.

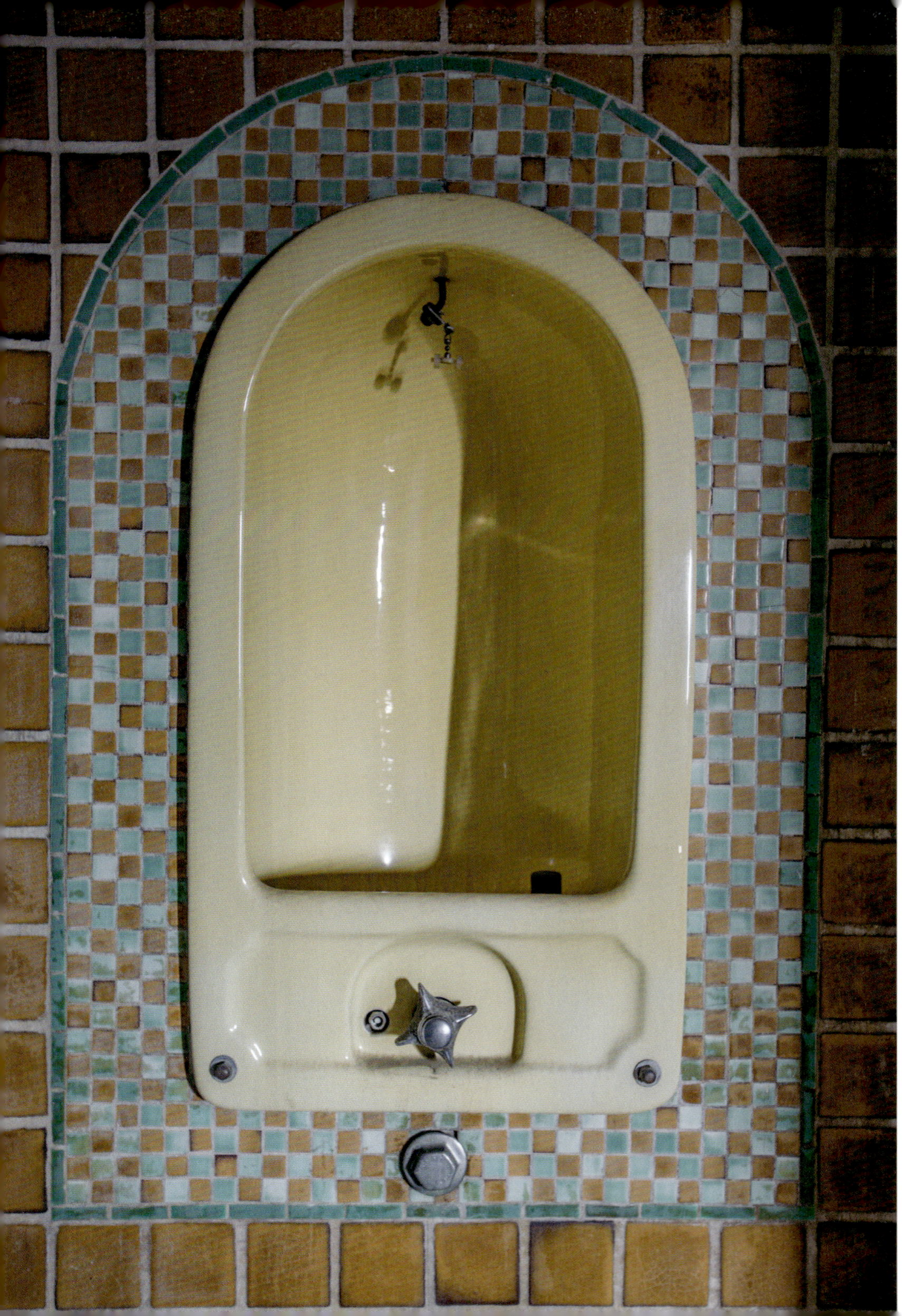

Many of Freeman's patients were so severely damaged that they needed to learn the most basic tasks all over again – how to eat, how to use the bathroom, how to walk. Some never fully recovered. Freeman's most famous patient, the "forgotten Kennedy" (Rosemary Kennedy), was left dependent and wheelchair-bound and was incarcerated in an institution for the rest of her life. A Washington police officer hemorrhaged after his lobotomy and was left in a persistent vegetative state. Sometimes the spatula-shaped tool used for the surgery broke off inside the skull. Another patient died on the operating table when Freeman stopped mid-surgery for a photography session – the tools slipped as he carelessly fumbled around with a camera in one hand and the implements in the other. Freeman realized that the procedure would need refining. Due to the overwhelmingly negative results, he started to conduct the operation on conscious patients, asking them questions, getting them to count down, or having them recite certain passages while he cut away at the brain.

By 1946, Freeman had had several years' experience of performing lobotomies. The procedure enjoyed limited popularity, however, because most state hospitals and mental institutions were not equipped to perform it. It was also expensive, requiring a neurologist, an anaesthesiologist and an operating room – at the time, most institutions had none of these. Because of this, Freeman decided to simplify his procedure radically to make it more accessible and efficient, so that it could be conducted outside the operating room – in an office, for instance. It was this change of procedure that ended the partnership between Freeman and Watts. Watts believed that entering the brain was a serious procedure that should only be conducted by a surgeon in an operating room.

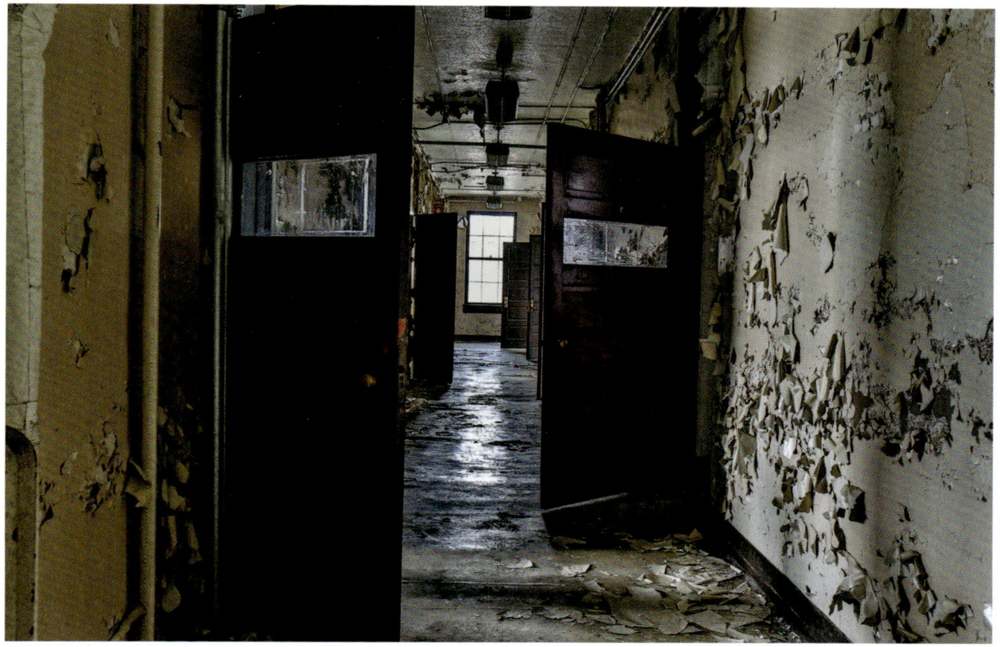

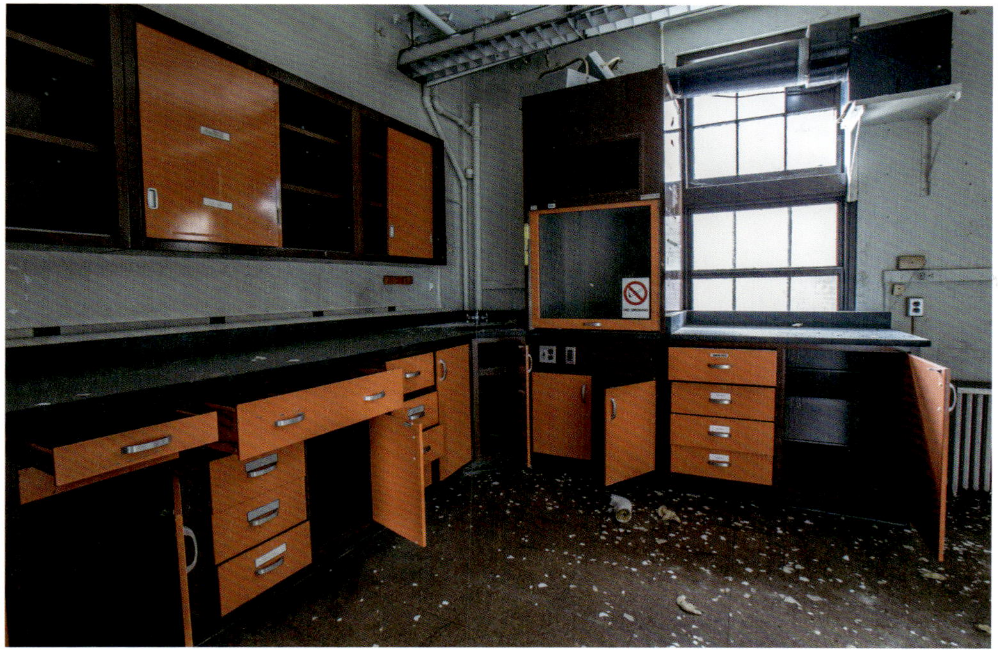

In his new procedure, instead of drilling into the skull, Freeman used an electric-shock machine to make the patient unconscious. He then entered the brain through the orbital cavity at the rear of the eye socket via a thin part of the skull, using an ice pick and a few taps with a hammer. The whole procedure lasted a few short minutes.

Eager to spread this radical new procedure, Freeman began travelling to many state hospitals throughout the US, including the Trans-Allegheny Lunatic Asylum (subsequently, Weston State Hospital) in West Virginia. He taught people with no surgical experience how to conduct the operation in a "production-line" fashion. On some days, Freeman would conduct as many as twenty-five transorbital lobotomies. To over-worked asylum doctors and administrators, the new procedure seemed a godsend – it could even be used on an out-patient basis. This quick, cheap, easy operation was conducted some 50,000 times between the late 1940s and the 1950s. For almost a decade, lobotomies were rampant in state hospitals. It was not until 1954 that the era of psychosurgery came to an end with the introduction of Chlorpromazine (Thorazine), known as the "chemical lobotomy".

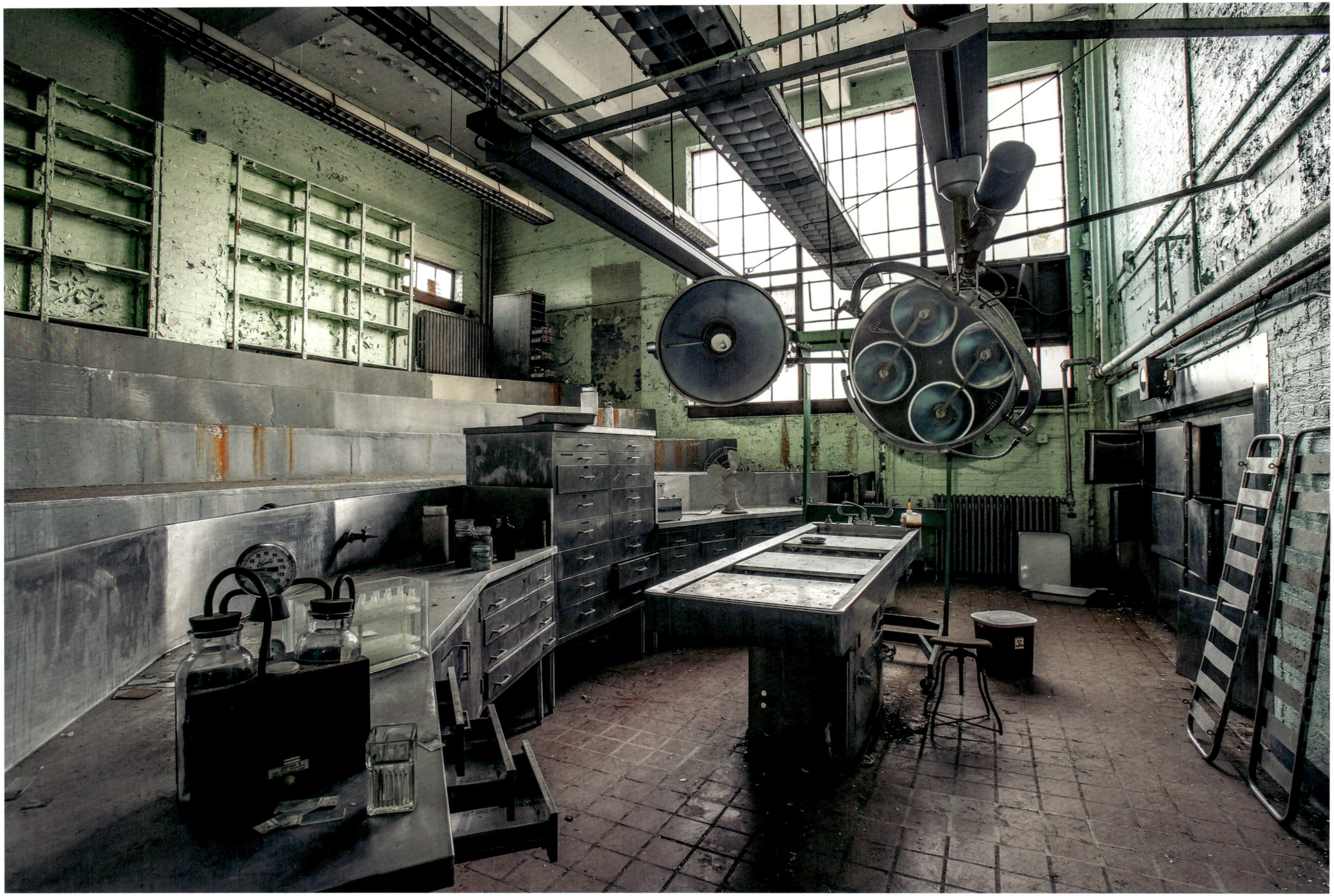

Walter Freeman's Blackburn Laboratory autopsy theatre

While some people consider Dr Walter Freeman a revolutionary, others see him as an infamous medical practitioner. The ethics involved in his work are no doubt controversial. However, his research and the time he spent at St Elizabeths have proved invaluable in our current understanding of the human body. His was a time when the desire for knowledge far outweighed the technology available for non-invasive surgical procedures. Institutions latched on to any procedure that might help with the problem of over-population and the overall decline of the institutions.

Today, there are major schemes to repurpose and stabilize the abandoned structures standing on the vacant parts of the St Elizabeths East Campus. Since 2010, only the part of the East Campus operated by the District of Columbia Department of Mental Health provides hospital facilities. (John Hinckley, Jr, who in 1981 attempted to assassinate Ronald Reagan, has been incarcerated at St Elizabeths ever since.) The remainder of the East Campus is slated for redevelopment by the District of Columbia, which owns the site. The West Campus is owned by the Federal government and is also being redeveloped.

Phase 1 at the East Campus is already under way: the aim is to create a vibrant, mixed-use development, with community amenities, that will also function as a marketplace for ideas, innovation and commercial activities. There are plans for an entertainment center; a sports arena serving as the new home of the NBA's Washington Wizards; a large residential neighborhood; and possibly a university campus. This will serve as the catalyst for economic development and growth, while also embracing the architecture and history of what was once a monument to civic pride.

Construction is also ongoing at the West Campus site (home to the original Kirkbride building). The Department of Homeland Security will set up their new national headquarters inside the halls of this historic institution. The US Coast Guard has also taken a large section of the property for their new headquarters. One of America's great institutions will be brought to life again and given a bright future – another Kirkbride scheme saved for the nation.

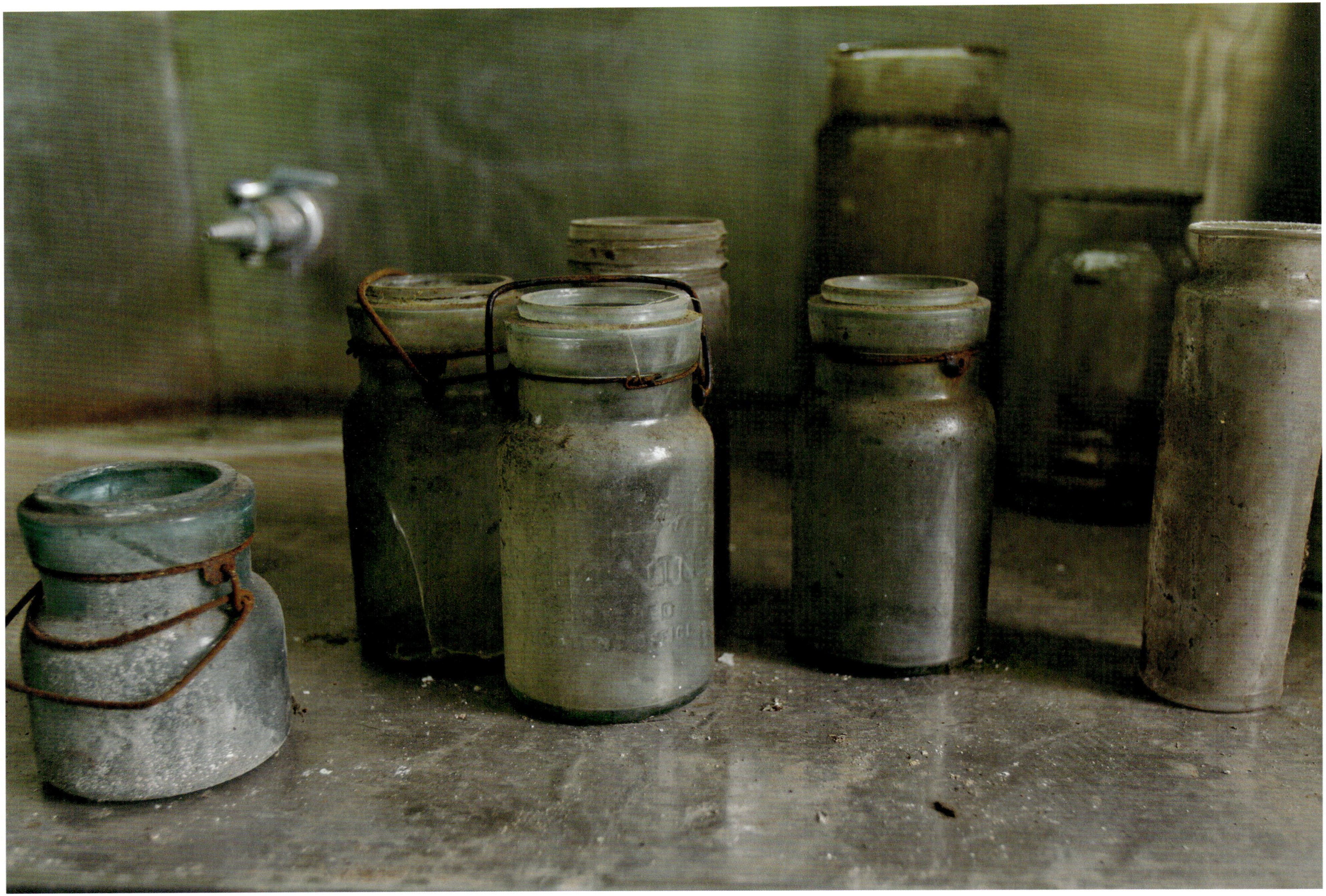

Autopsy specimen Jars

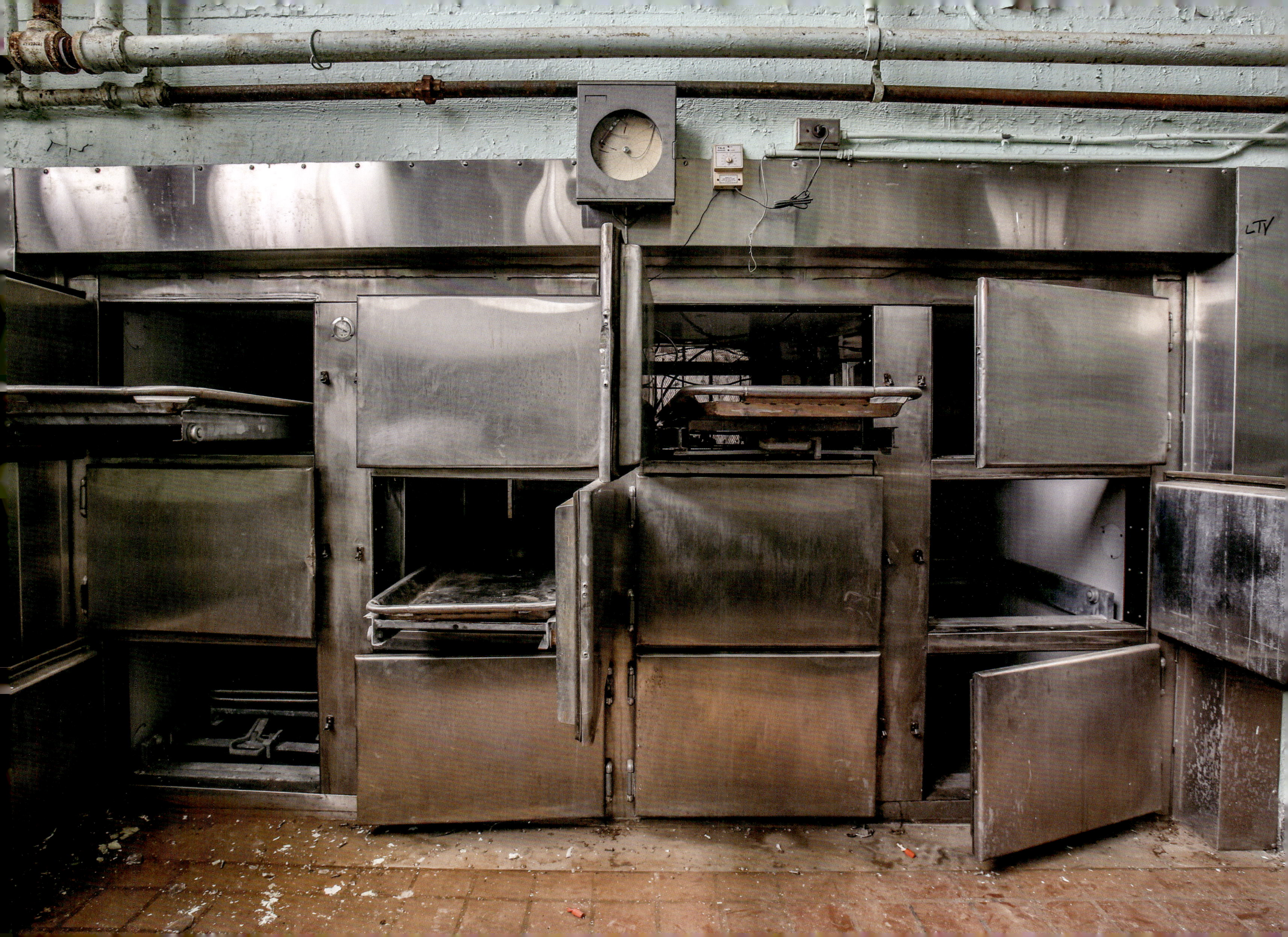
LTV

Saint Lawrence State Hospital and NYC's First Supermodel

In the early 1900s, before sophisticated cameras and runway fashion shows, the human form was most represented and appreciated through sculpture. During this time, Audrey Munson (due to her perfectly proportioned face and body) was to sculpture what Marilyn Monroe would later become to Hollywood - a true icon. Munson's depiction in monuments has survived generations. Her legacy can still be seen today, but her story is ultimately both tragic and piteous.

Diane Rozas (co-author of *American Venus: The Extraordinary Life of Audrey Munson, Model and Muse*) noted that Munson was "the first supermodel - and the first model to have a standing in society". She was a muse who took advantage of her ability to inspire artists. Because of this, it wasn't long before Munson was in high demand and the early notion of celebrity began. Her likeness can be found in dozens of NYC's most prominent sculptures. If you've ever visited the USS Maine Monument at Columbus Circle, or the entrance to Central Park, you've passed under her gaze. She was also the inspiration behind the *Civic Fame* sculpture atop the iconic Manhattan Municipal Building, and the *Spirit of Commerce* angel at the northern base of the Manhattan Bridge. Her beauty transcended the art world; Munson would cross over to work in silent films. She is credited as being the first actress to appear nude in a non-pornographic film.

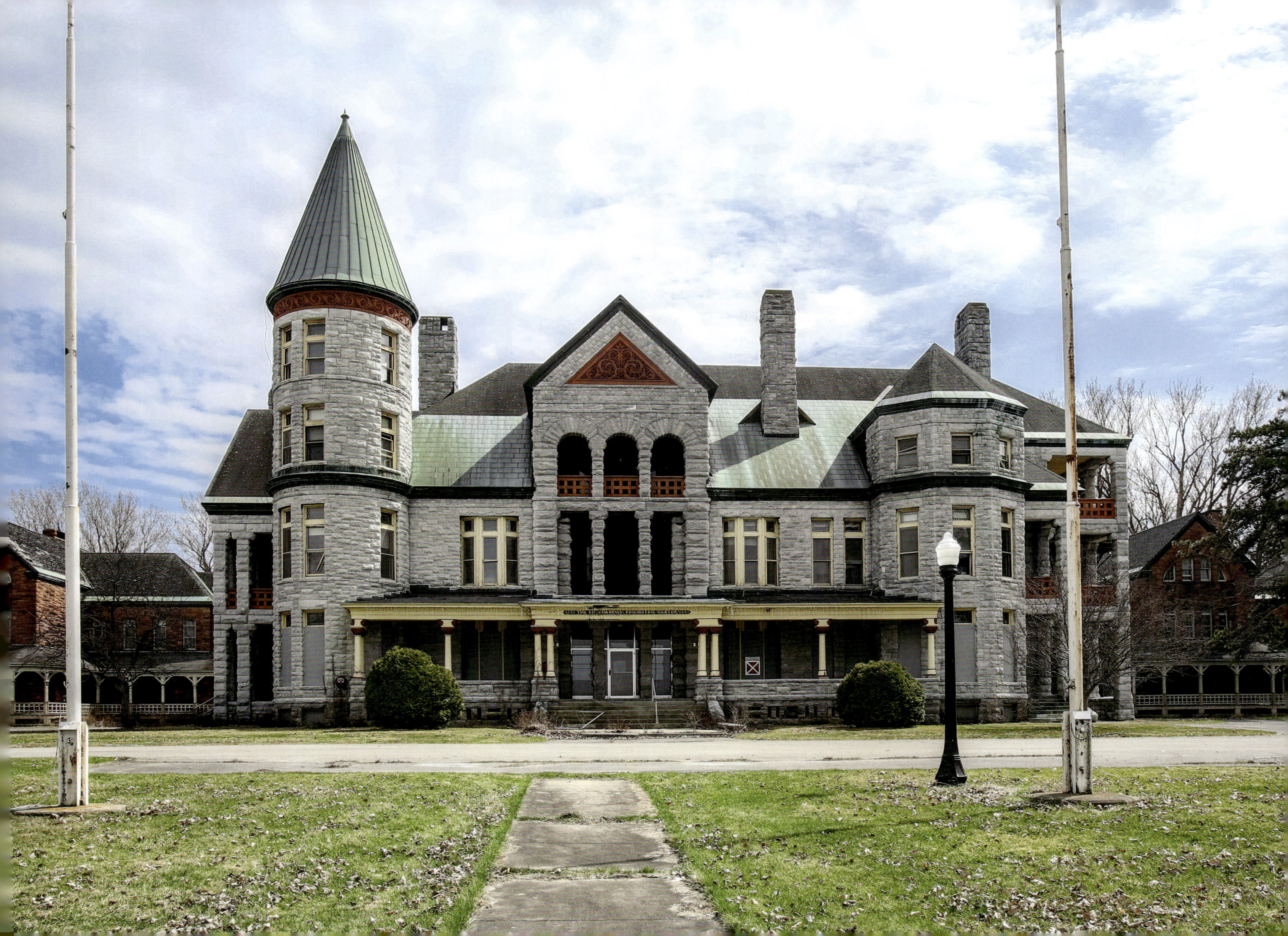

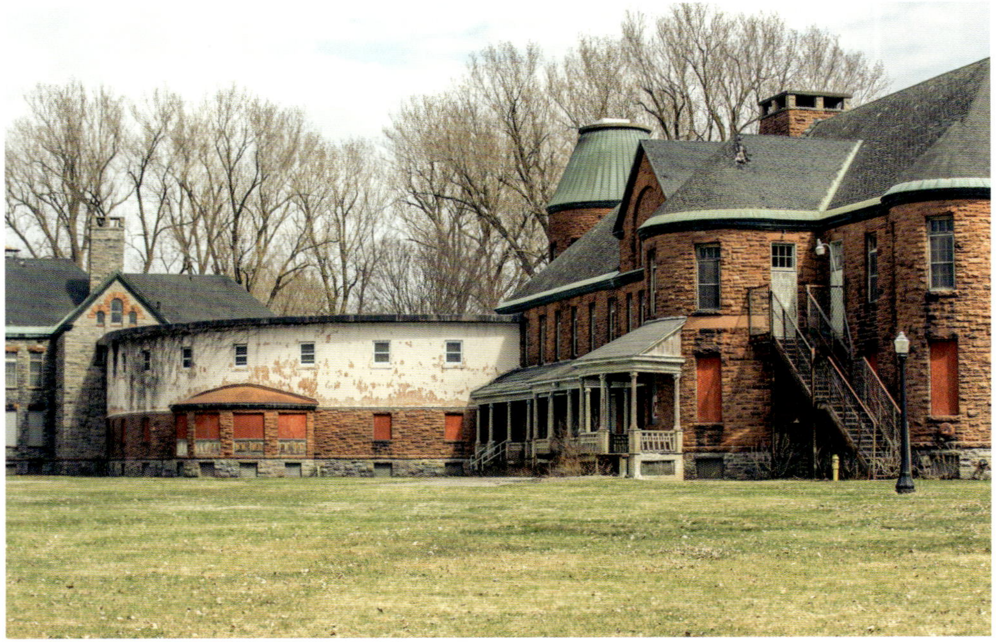

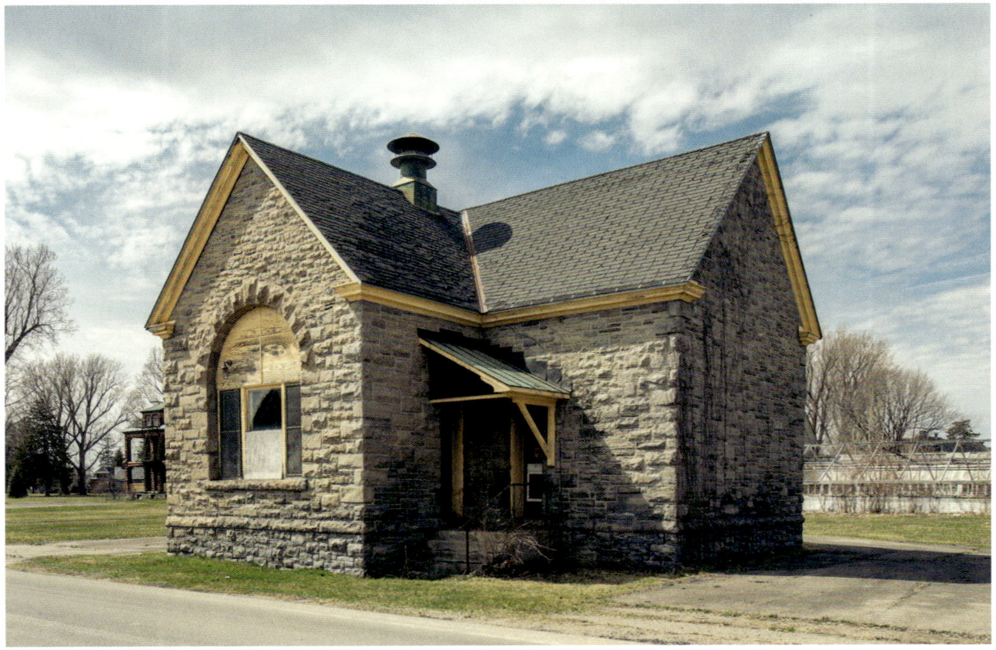

Morgue Building

In 1919, however, as quickly as her fame began it would come crumbling apart. Munson's life would be changed forever by a scandal involving her landlord, Dr. Walter Keene Wilkins, who, through an obsession for Audrey, had murdered his wife so he could start a new life with Munson. Although Munson had no knowledge or involvement in the plot, the negative publicity surrounding the situation destroyed her career. Her fall from grace proved too much to bear; Audrey was afflicted with depression and delusional behaviour. In 1922 she unsuccessfully attempted to commit suicide by swallowing a solution of Mercury Chloride.

Upon her recovery she was committed as a chronic case to Saint Lawrence State Hospital, where she would spend the remaining 64 years of her life until her death in 1996 at the age of 104. The question surrounding the legacy of beautiful women in art is hauntingly echoed through Audrey's words in a 1921 newspaper column: "What becomes of the artists' models?" - "I am wondering if many of my readers have not stood before a masterpiece of lovely sculpture ... and asked themselves the question, 'Where is she now, this model who was so beautiful?'". Next time you visit New York City, be sure to 'look up' and appreciate the tragic beauty that was Audrey Munson.

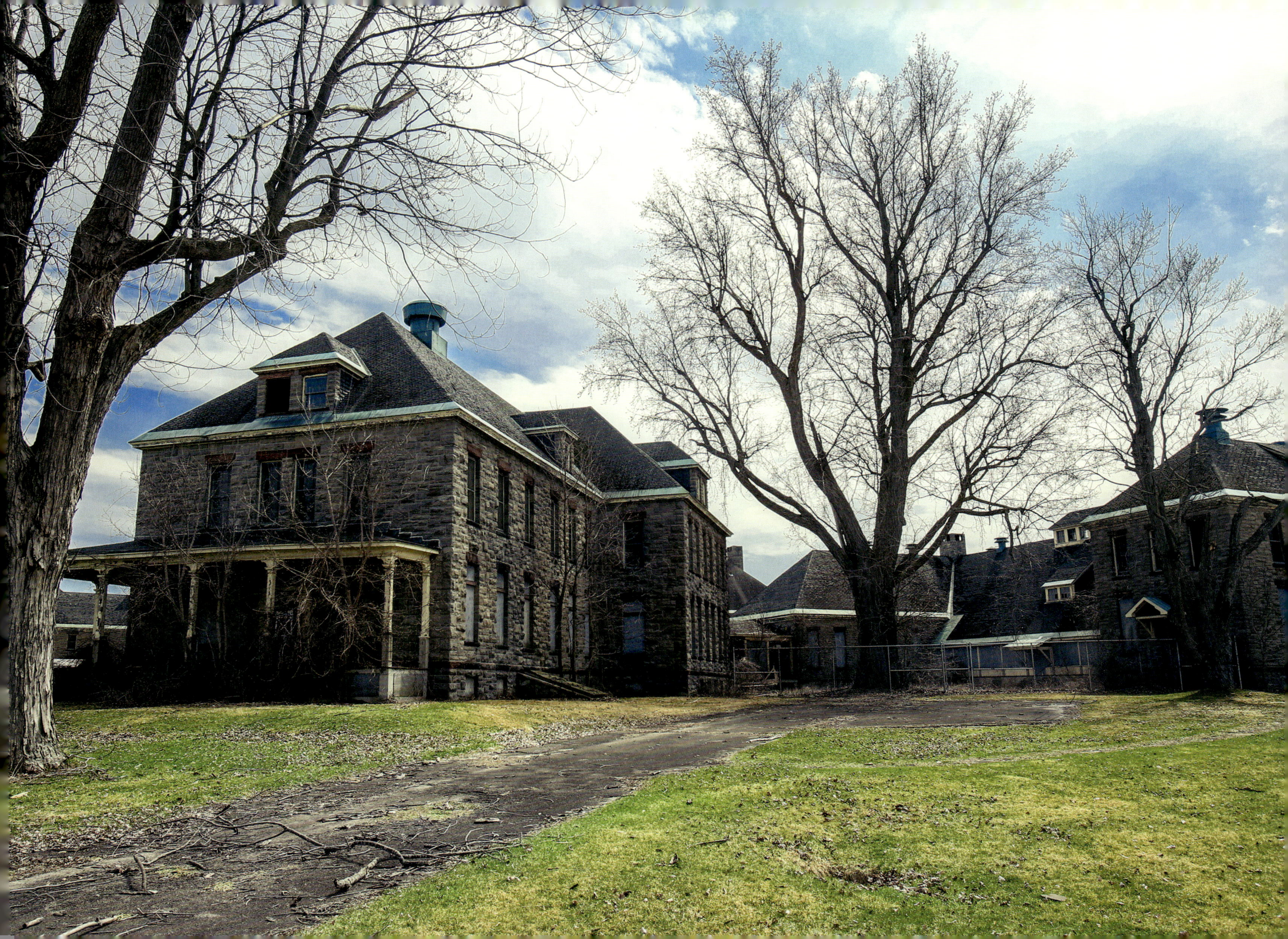

Trans-Allegheny Lunatic Asylum

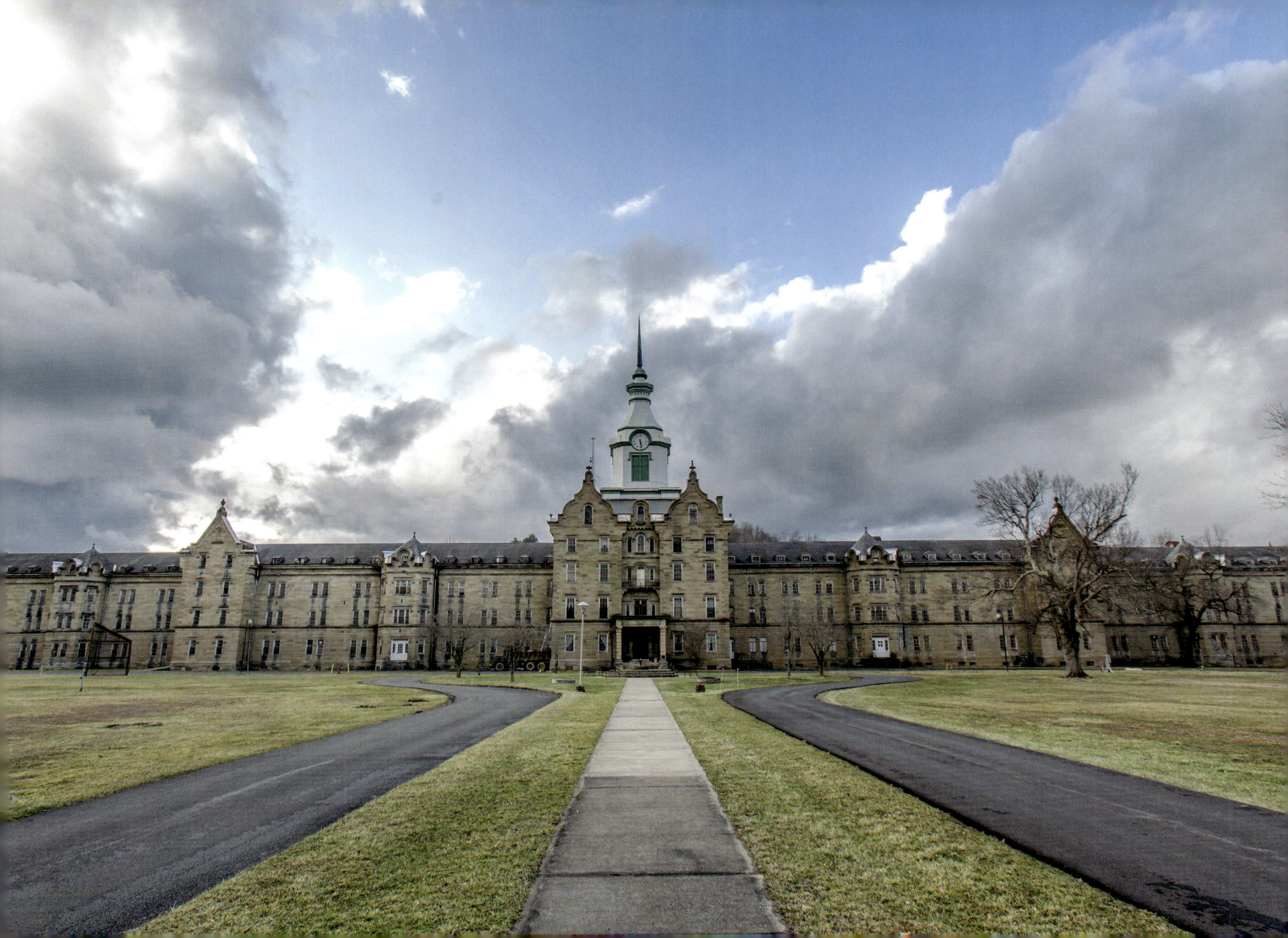

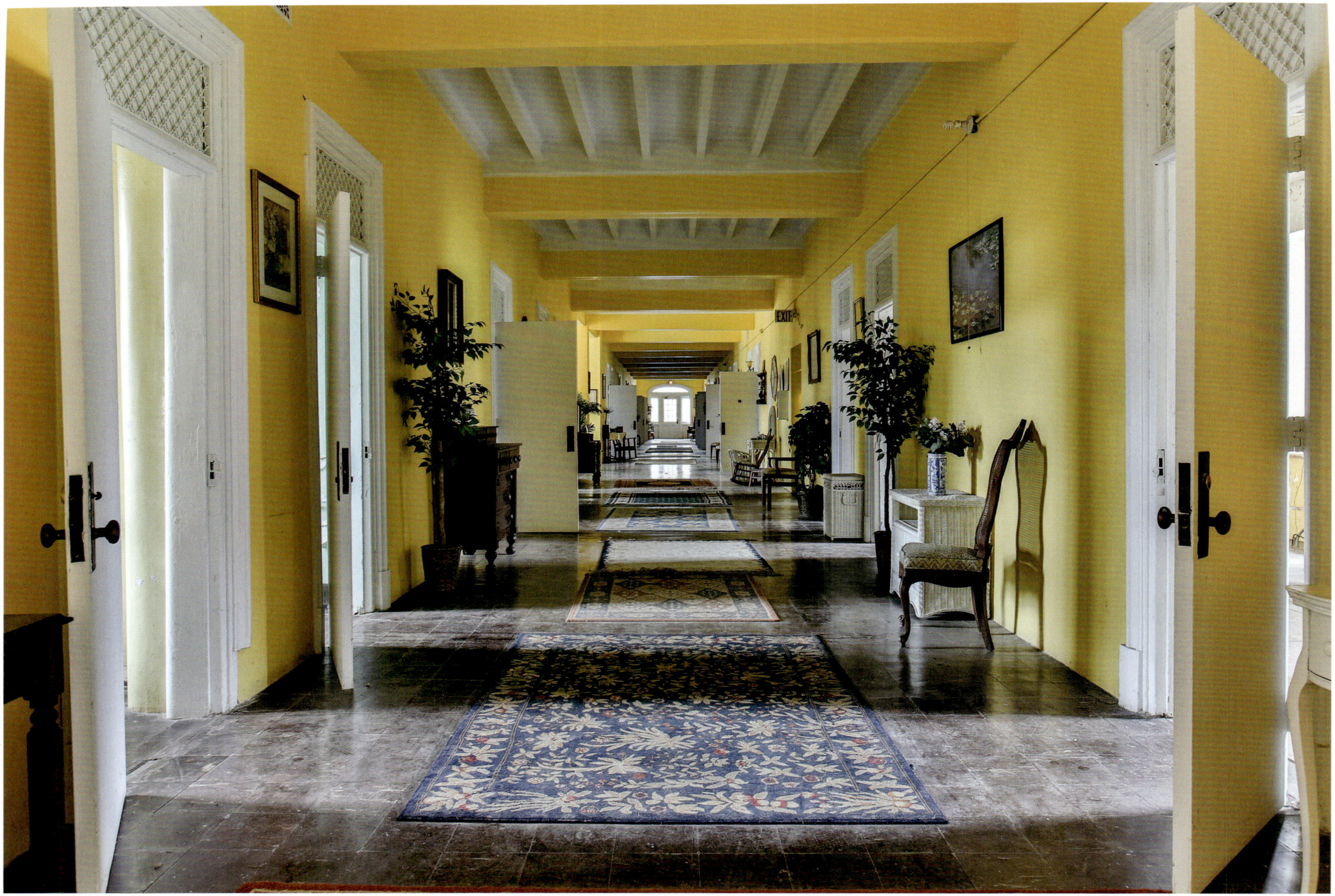

Fully restored 1864 patient Kirkbride plan ward

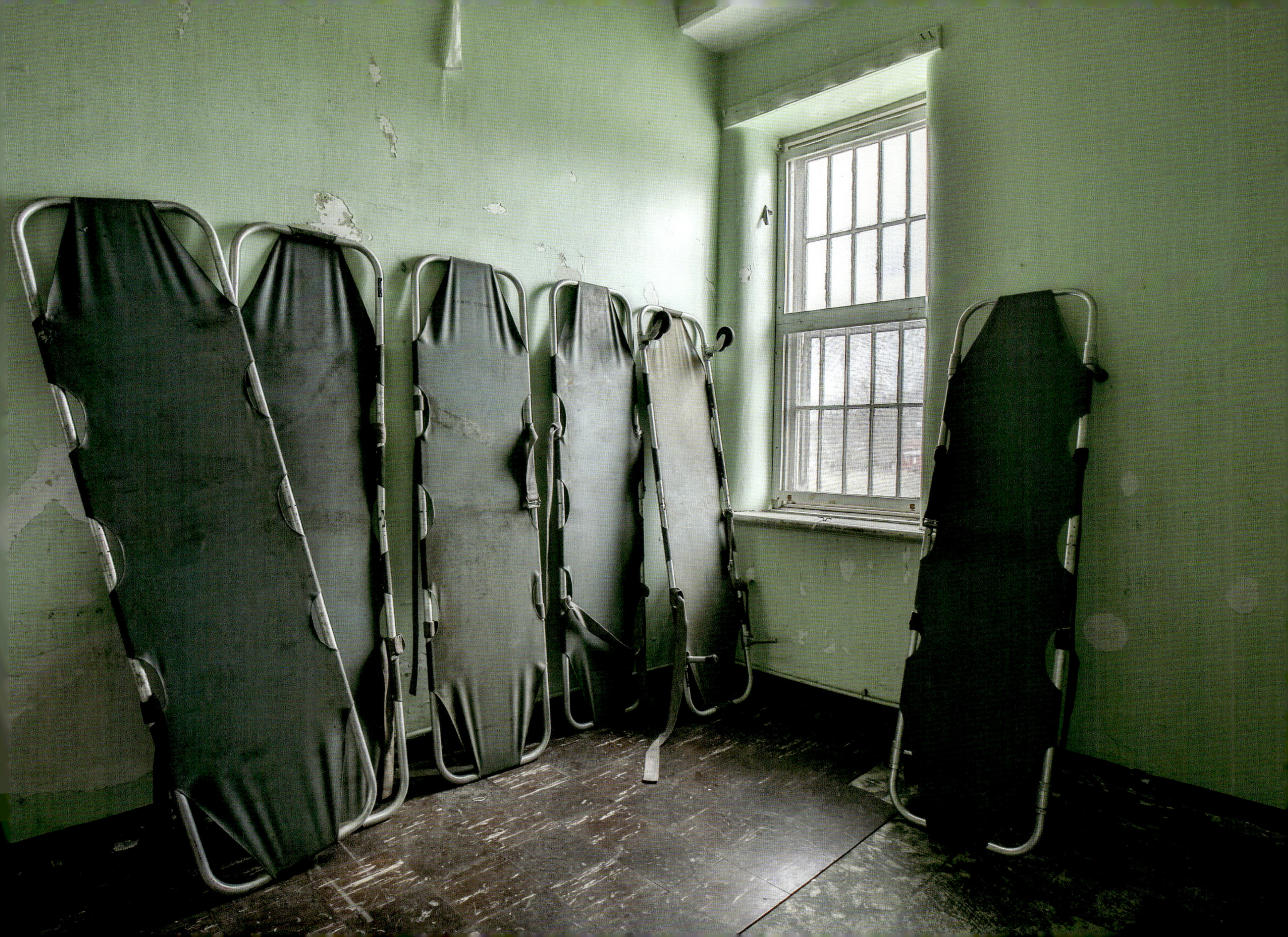

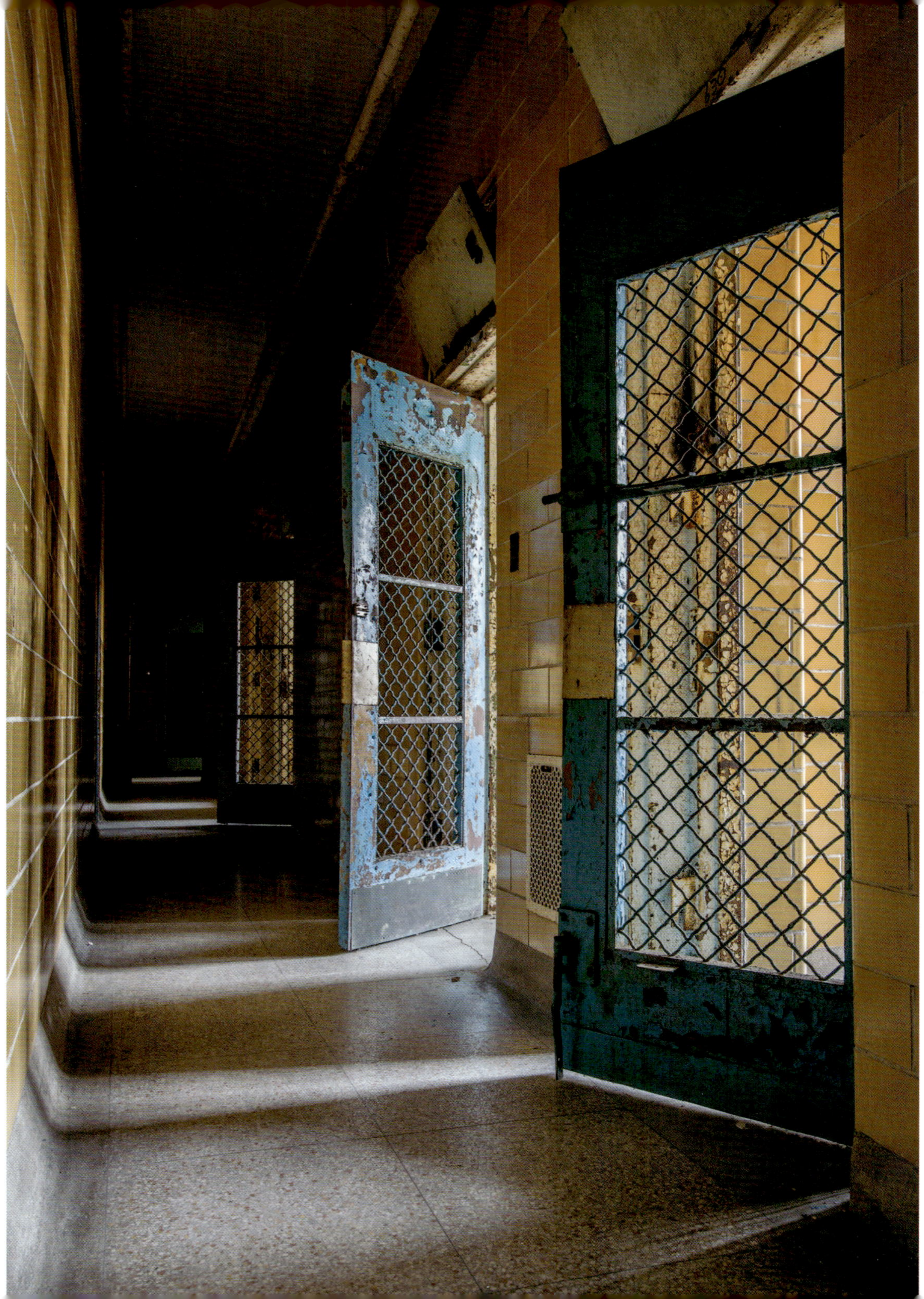

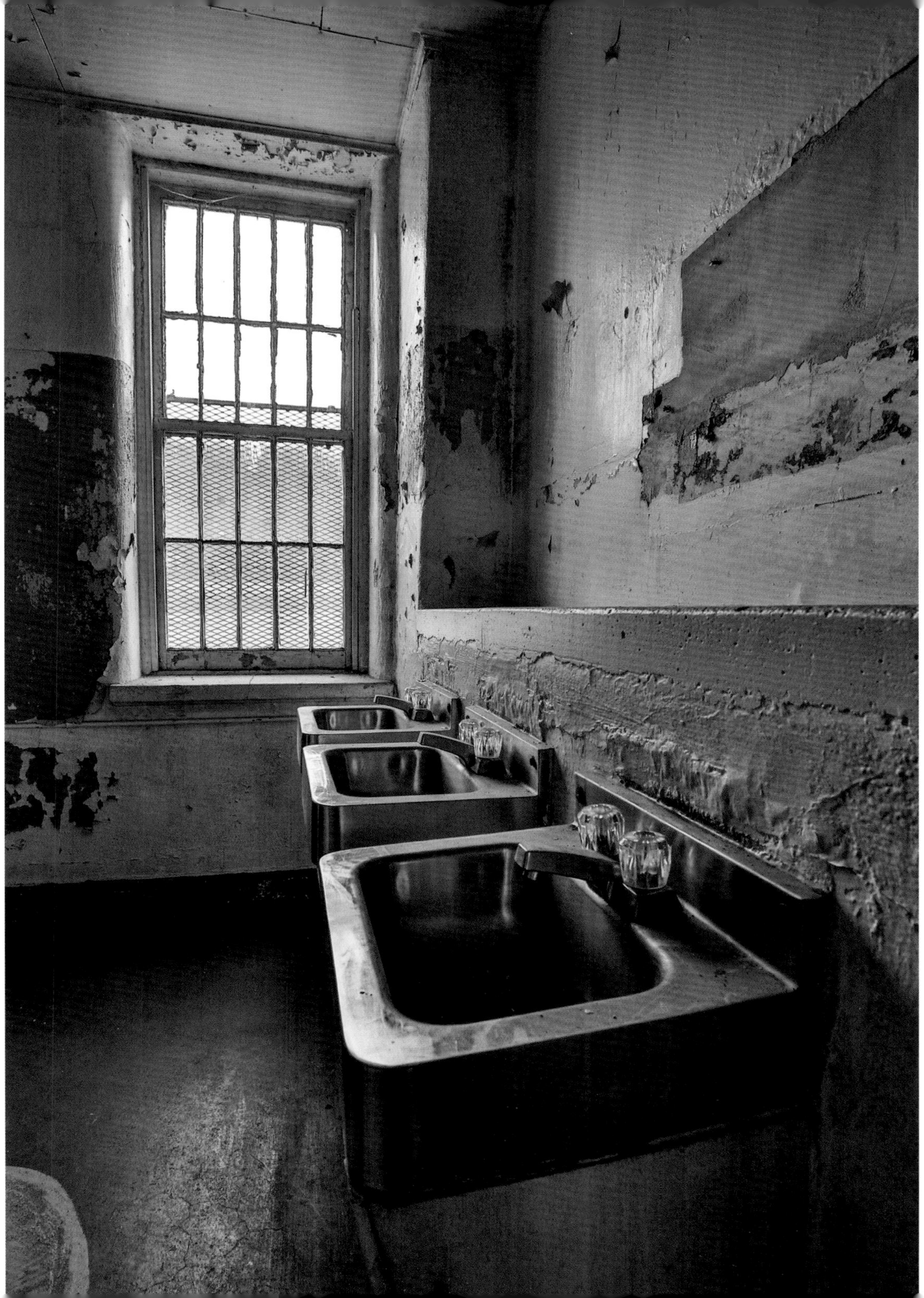

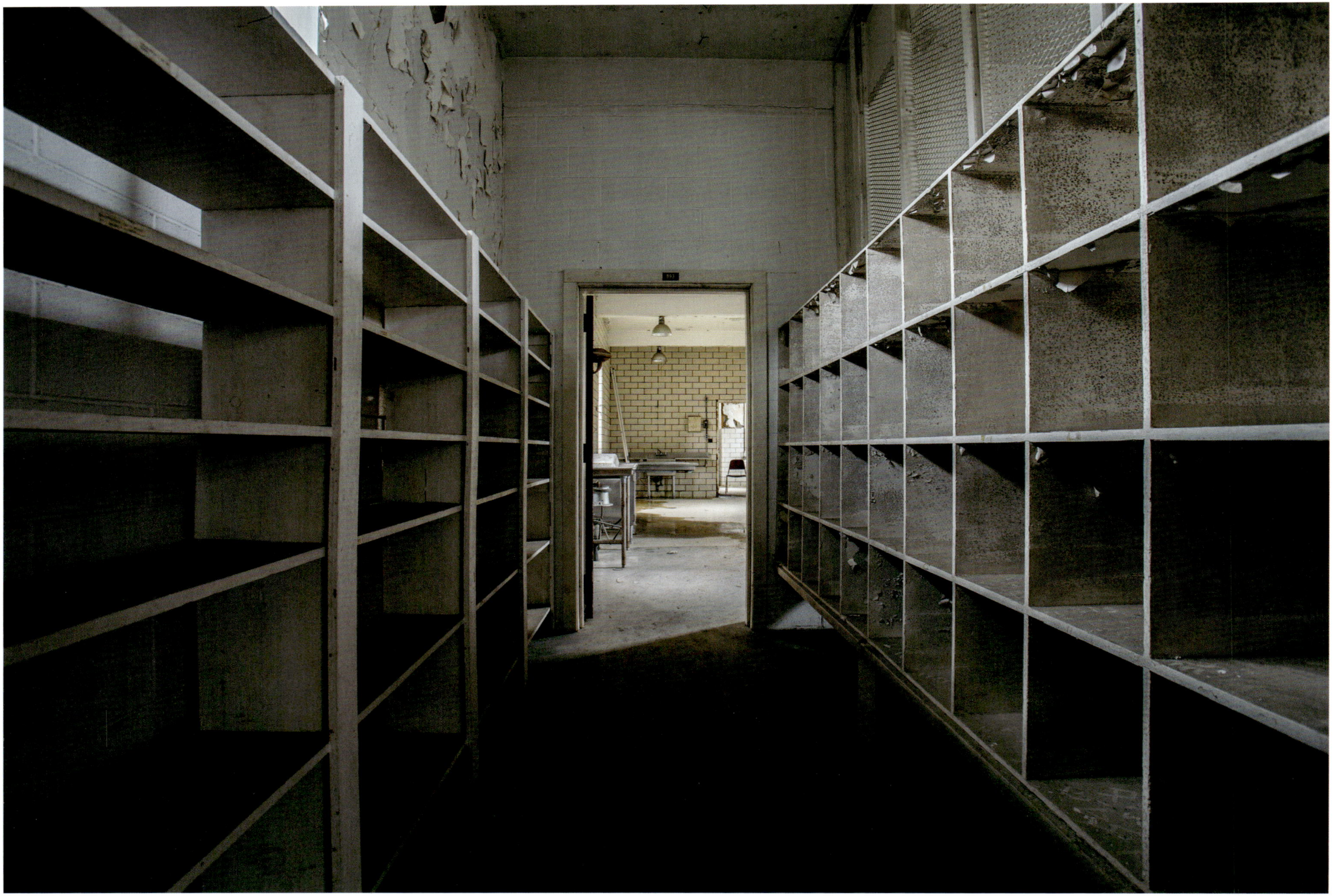

Kitchen food storage area

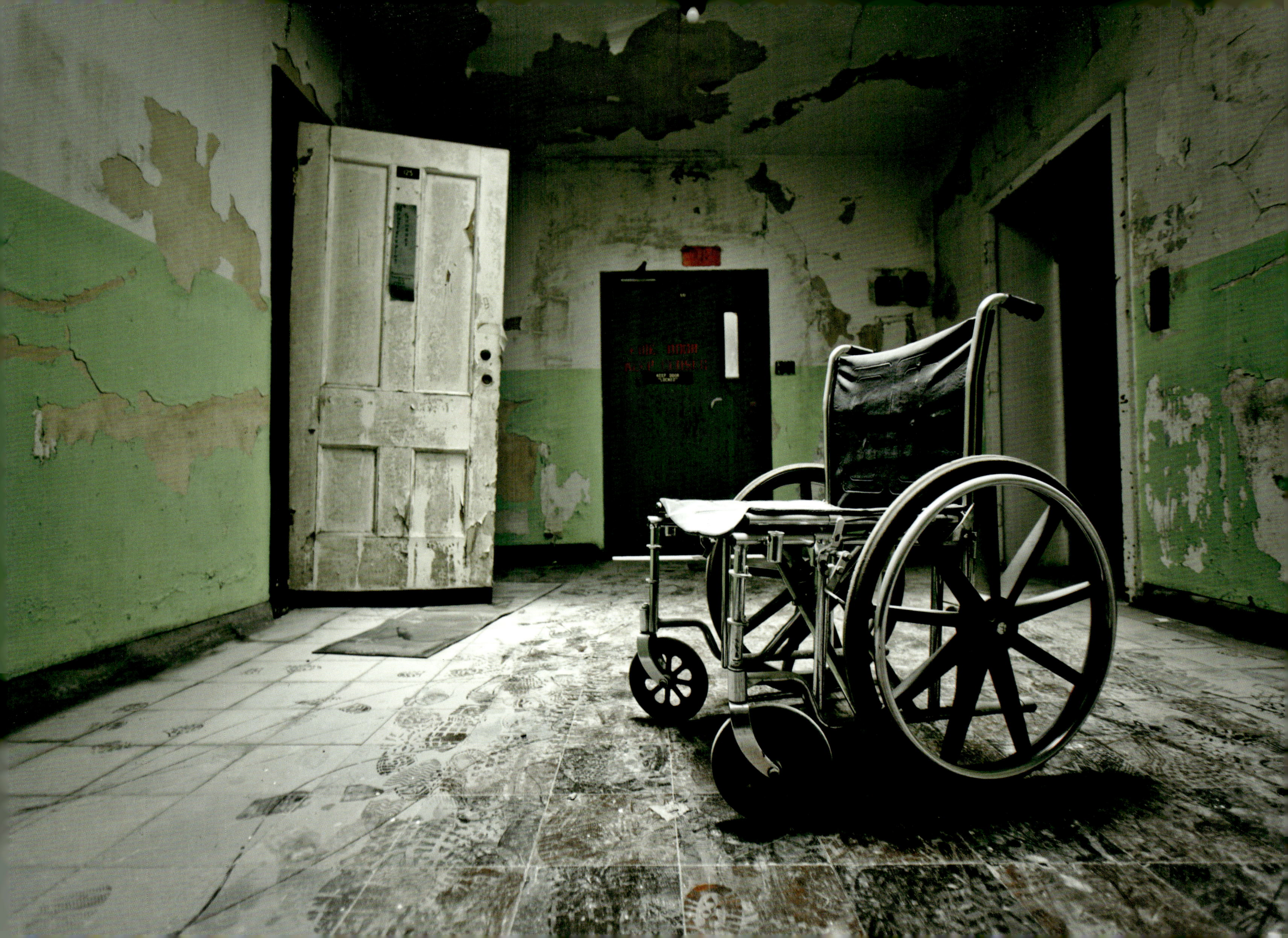

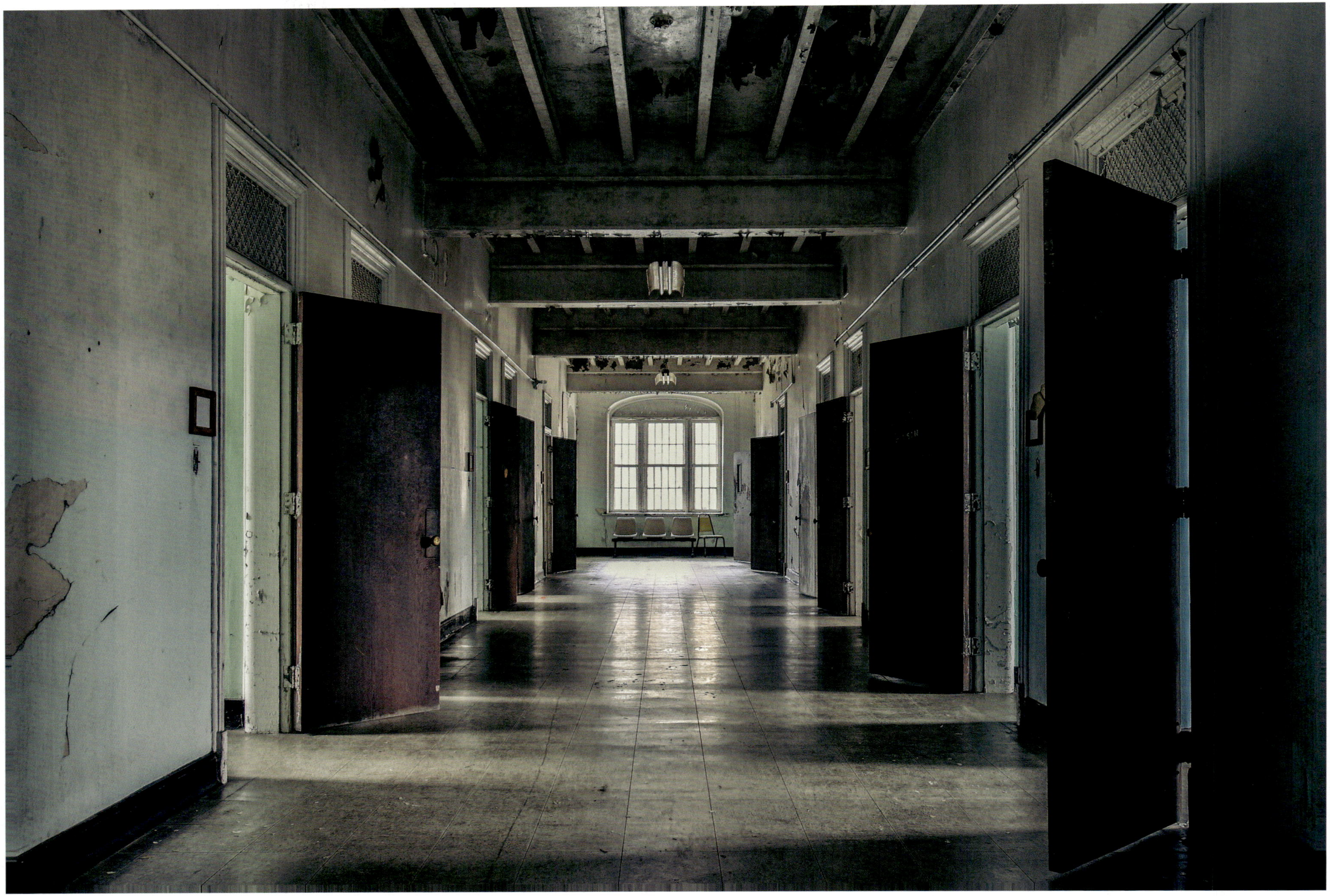

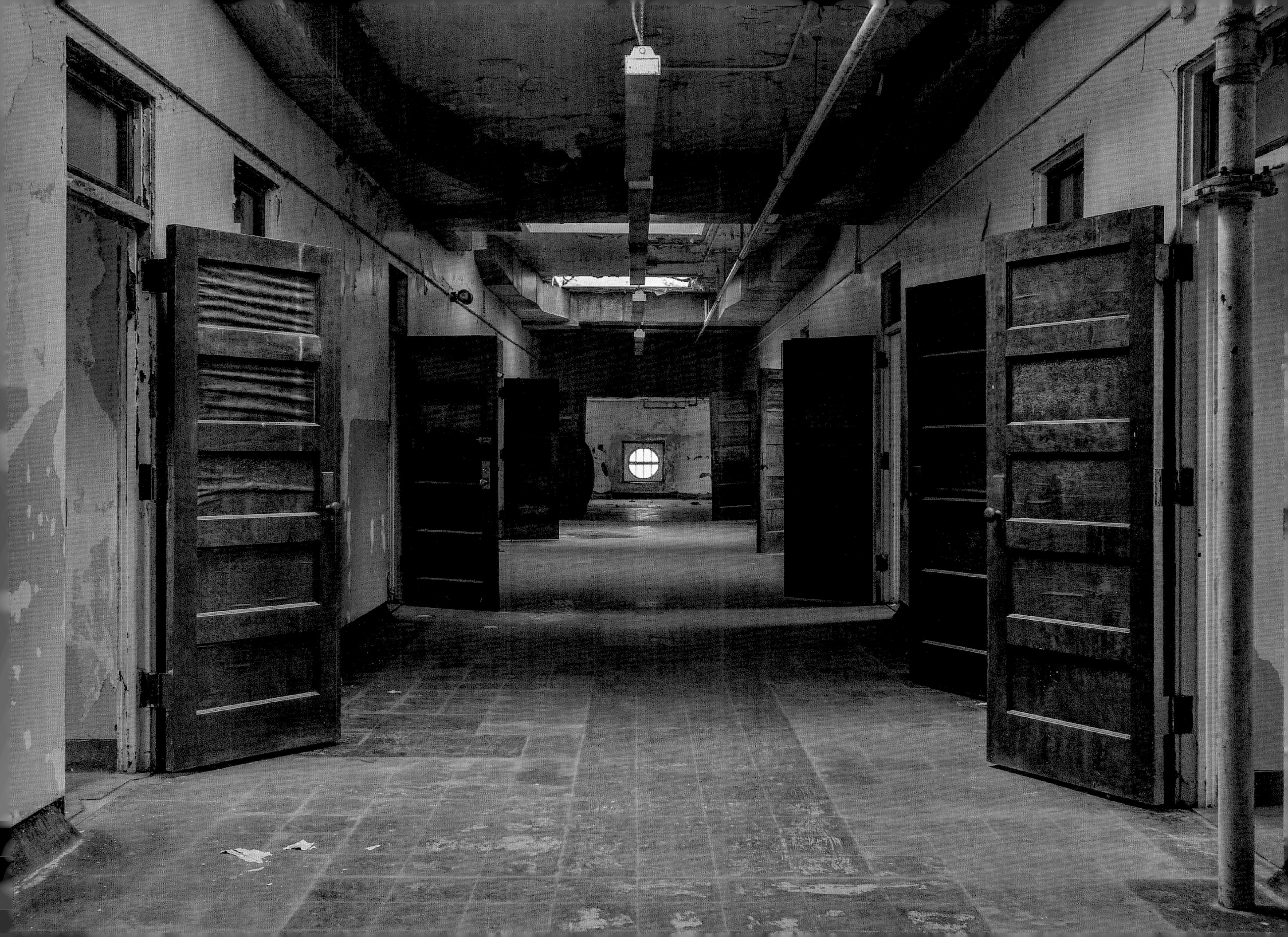

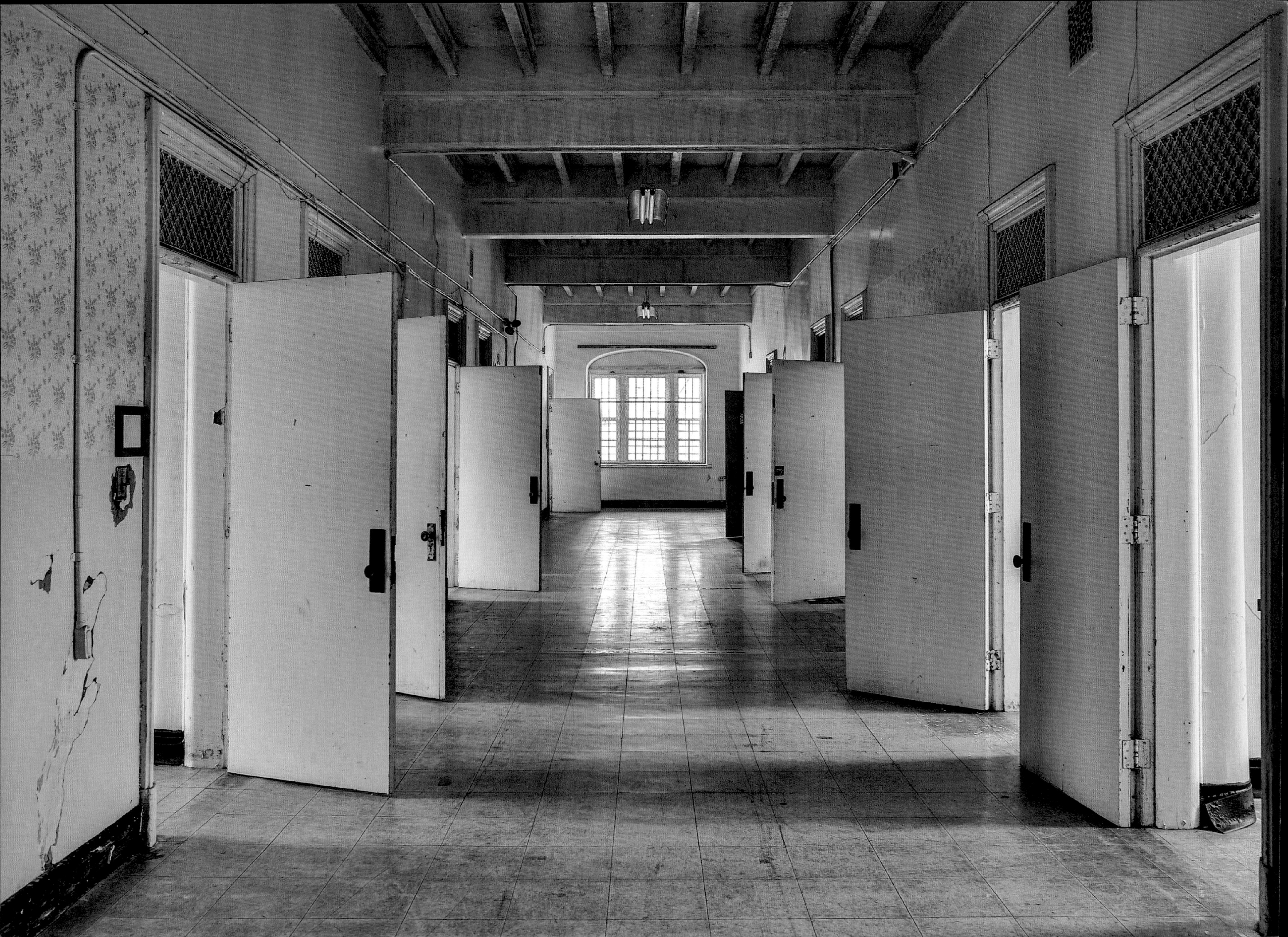

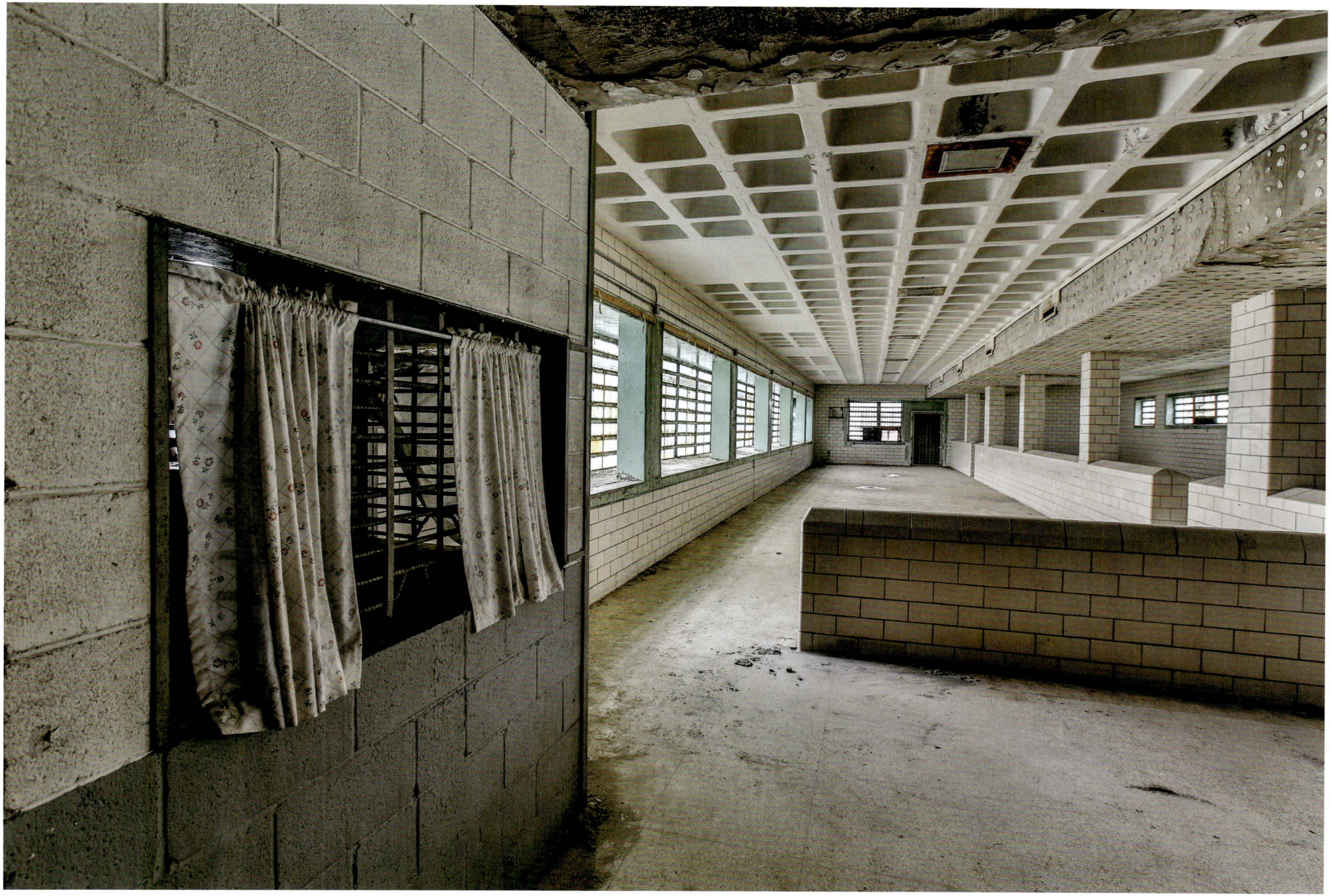

Forensics Building, Ward for the criminally insane with Nurse's security station

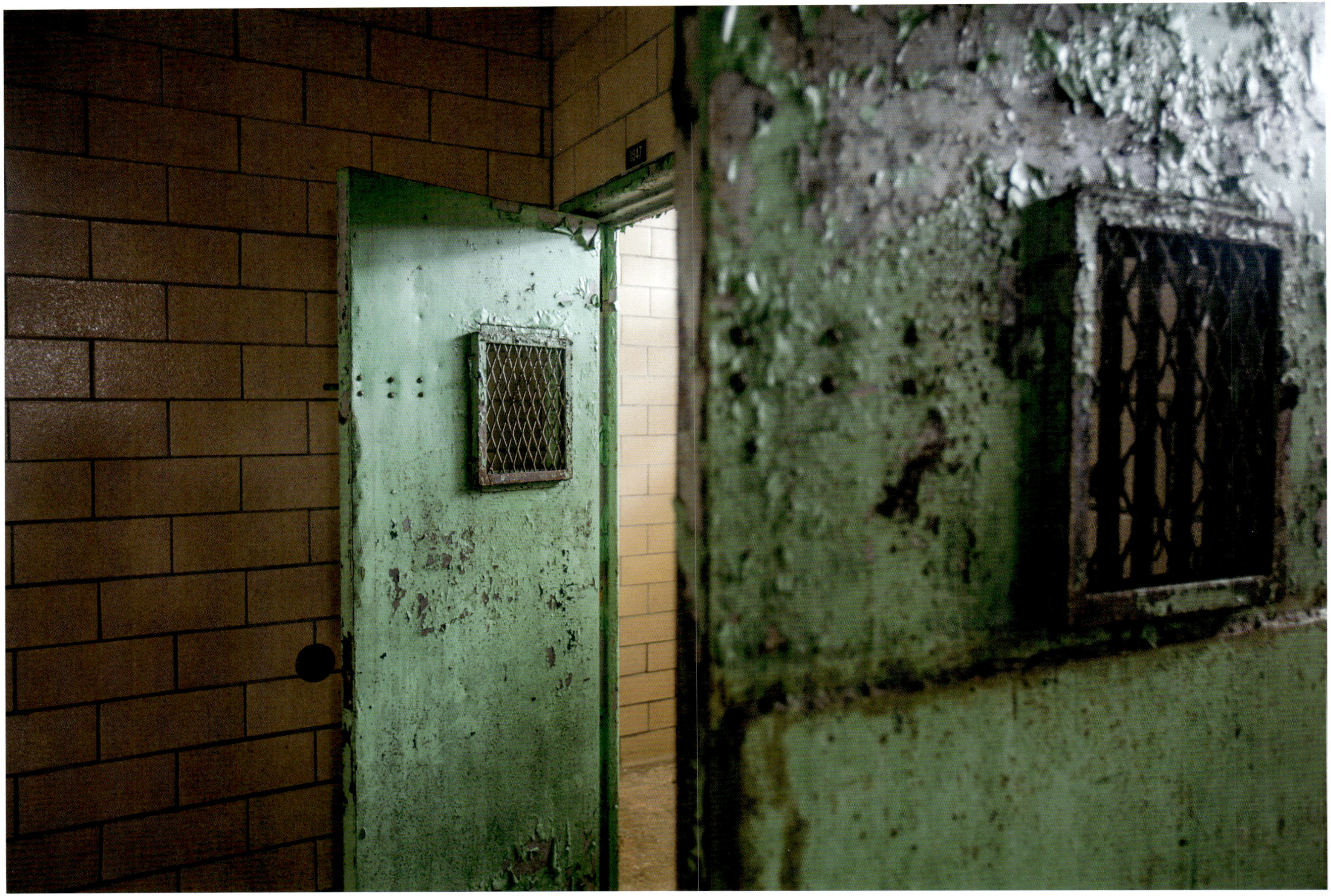

Solitary Confinement Cells

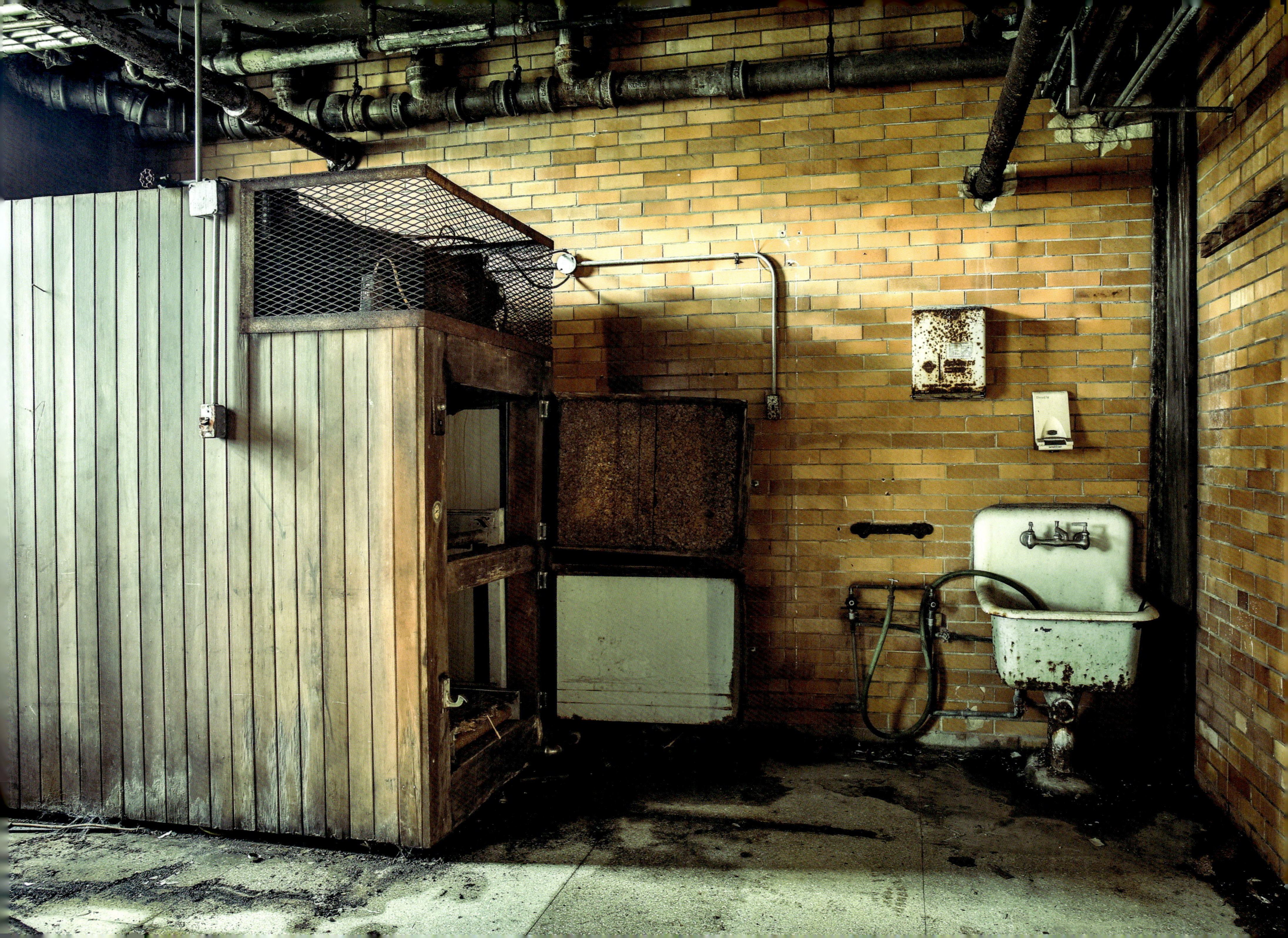

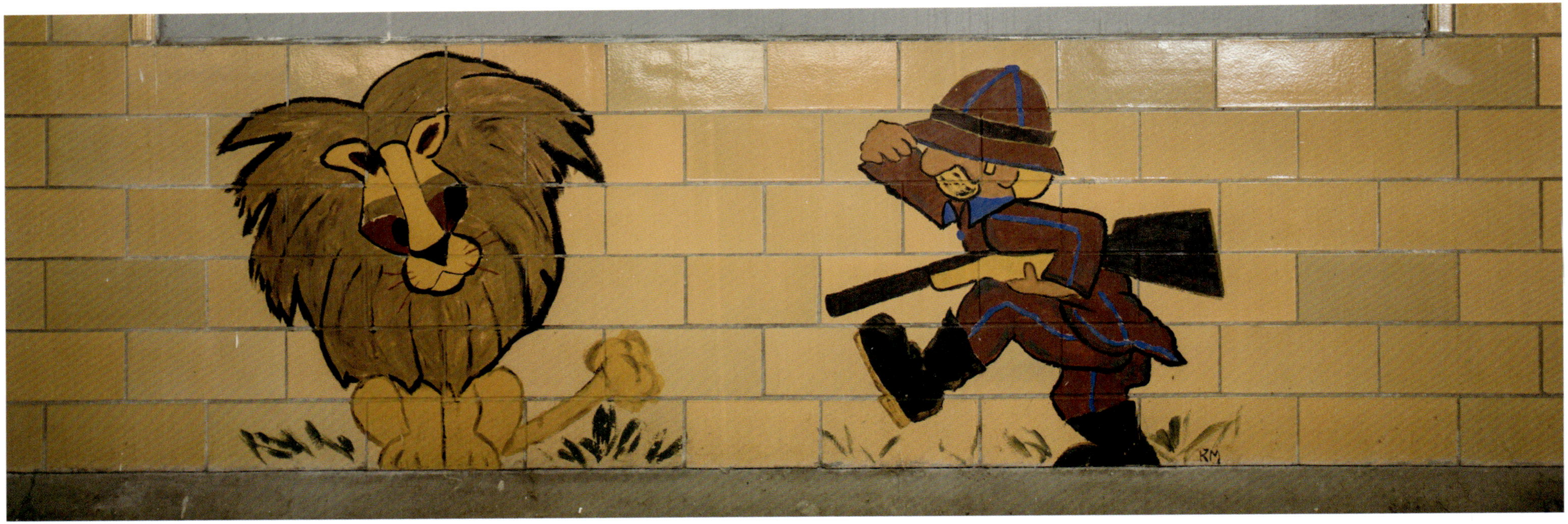

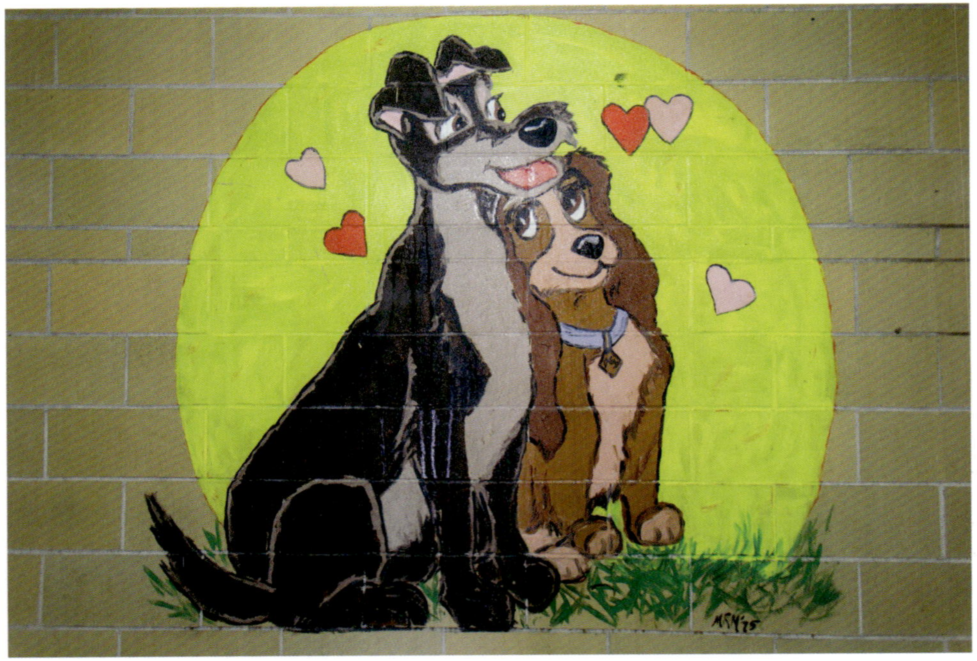

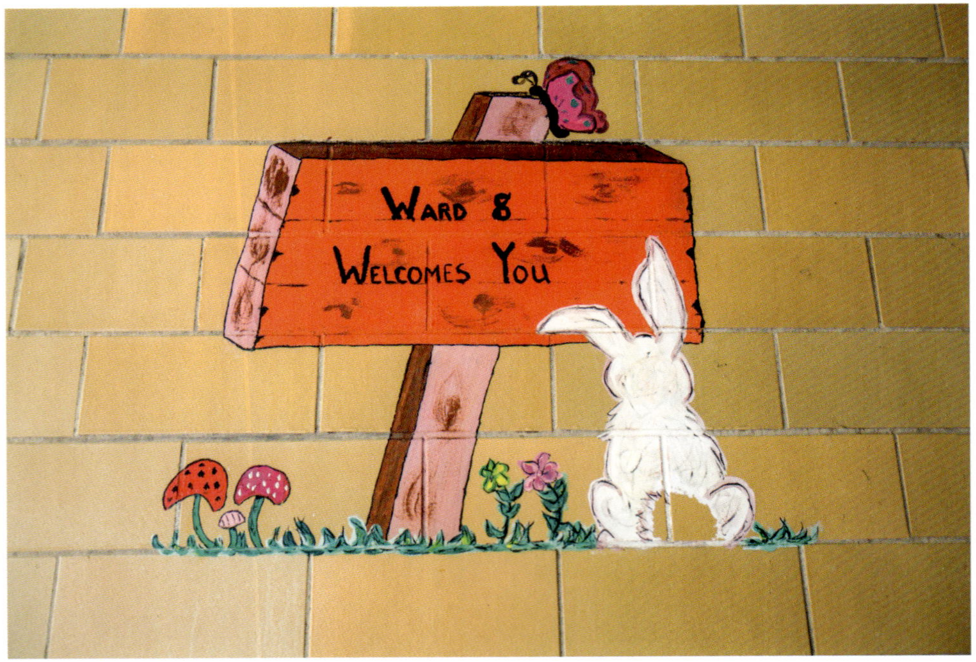

Ward murals hand-painted by patients

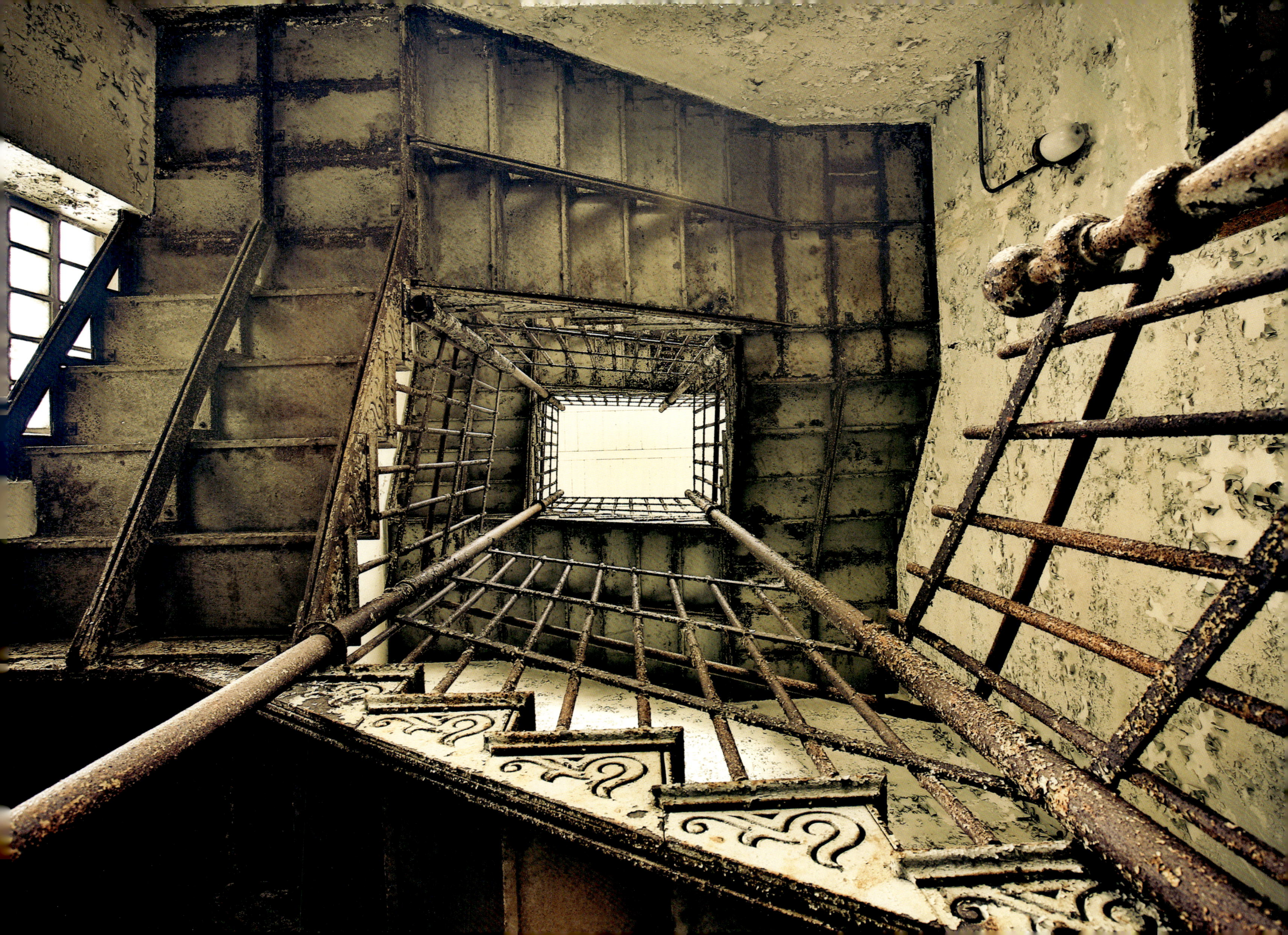

Willard Asylum for the Chronic Insane & the Suitcases

Opened in October of 1869, the Willard Asylum for the Chronic Insane (later renamed the Willard State Hospital) had origins similar to other institutions of the era. Its creation was brought about through the state's assumed responsibility for the care and treatment of the insane; previously the care for such individuals remained at a local level. The insane, the feeble-minded, the inebriates, crippled, epileptics, beggars and societal outcasts of the time had been kept in almshouses, poorhouses, jails and, in some cases, hidden in cellars and basements. While these places provided an individual with shelter, they certainly did not offer medical treatment of any kind. The medieval 'treatments' one could expect at a poorhouse were flogging, pulleying, or hanging an individual by their thumbs until the desired disposition was achieved and behaviour had been corrected.

The need for an institution to treat the chronic insane was realised after the construction of the Utica State Hospital in 1843, which sought to treat 'curables' for a period of no longer than 2 years – at which point they were discharged either 'cured' or sent back to where they came from. New York State needed an institution to care for the 'incurable' or 'chronic' individuals who had no foreseeable means of recovery and were destined to be institutionalised for their entire lives.

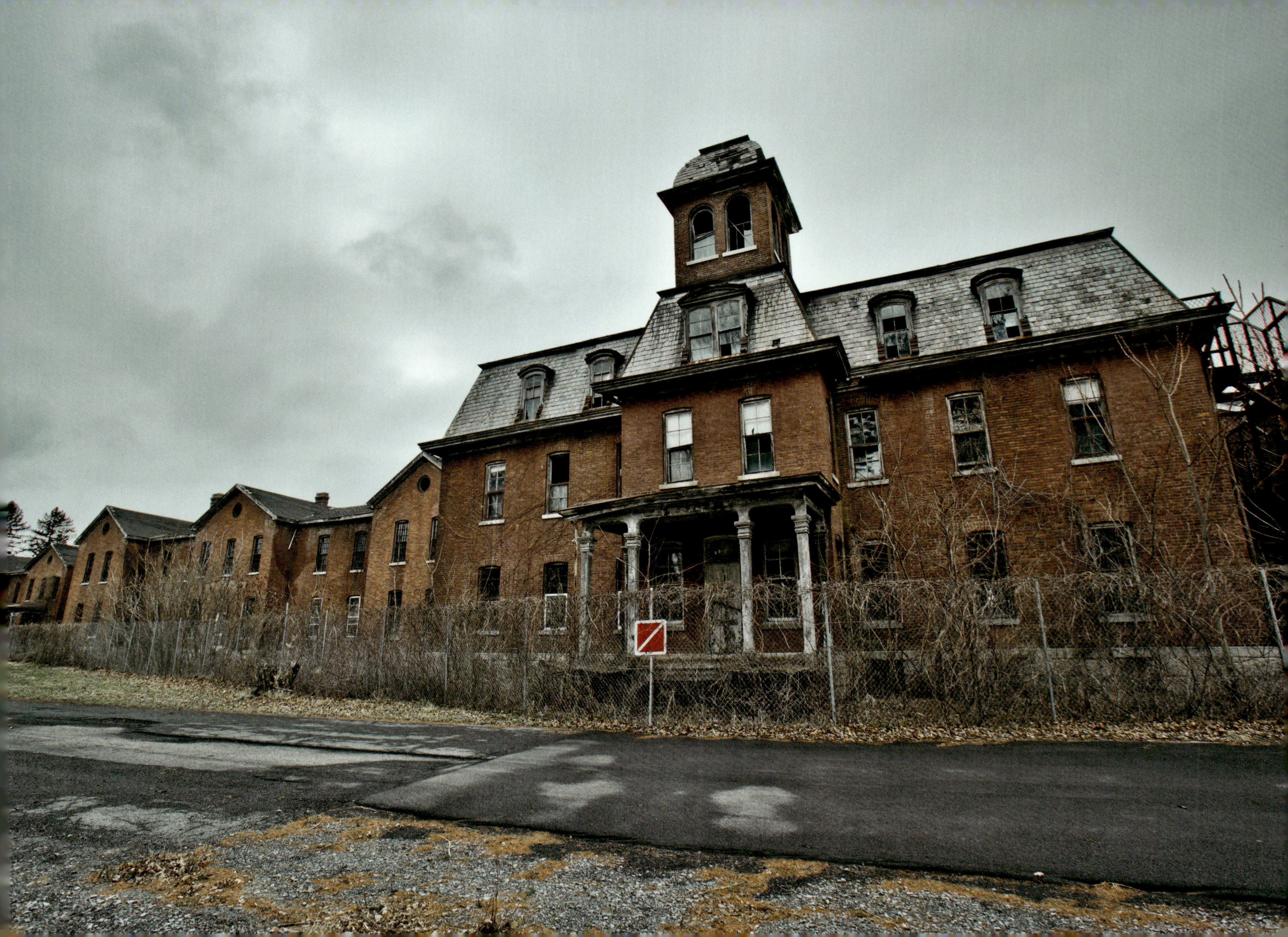

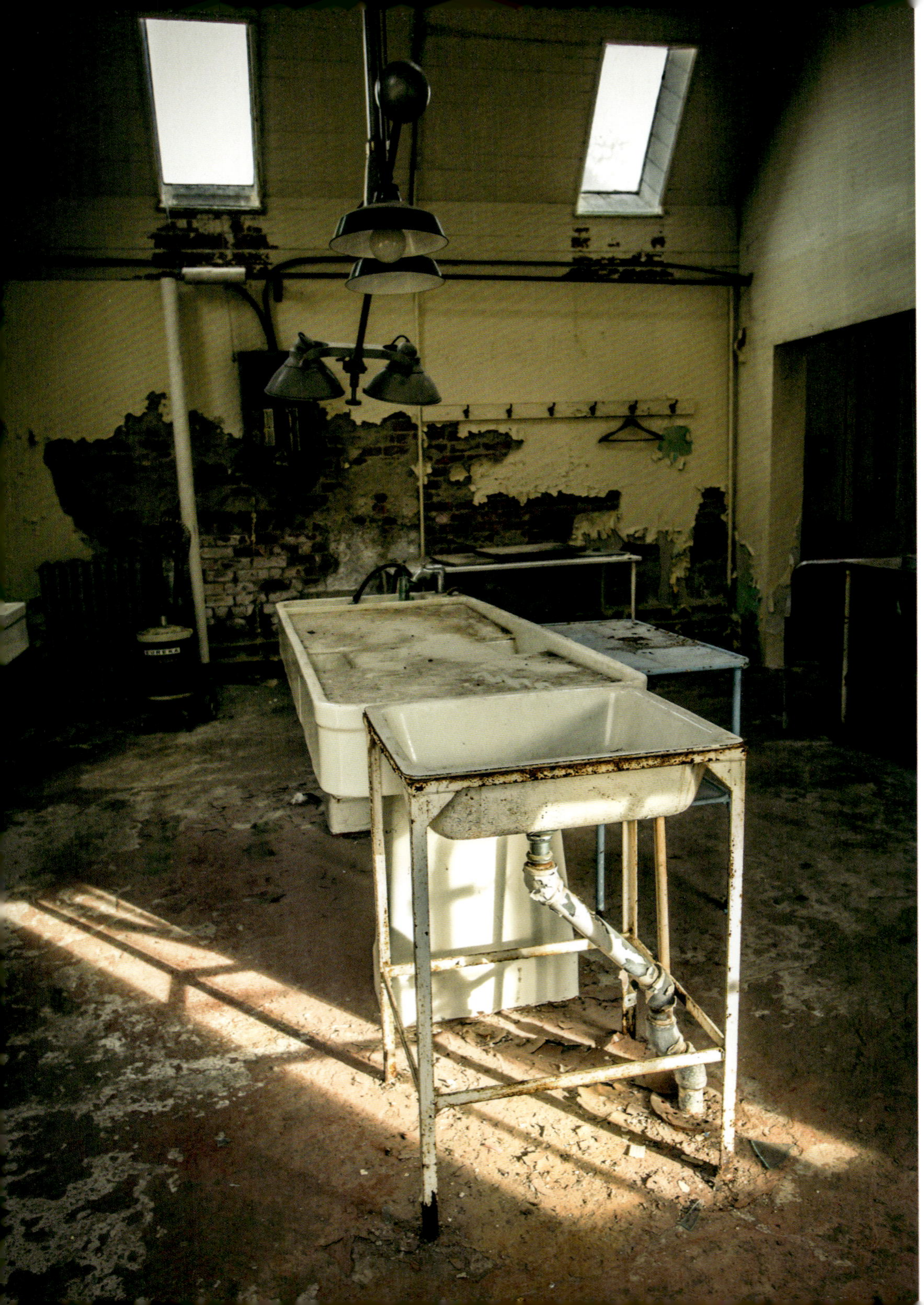

Upon the release of a report documenting the deplorable conditions at these almshouses, the governor put into legislation the 'Willard Law', stating that all chronic cases were to be directed to Willard. Nestled discreetly on almost 500 acres of Seneca Lake waterfront, Willard's serene views offered comfort for those admitted there.

Willard's first patient, Mary Rote, arrived from the Columbia County Poorhouse on October 13, 1869. "Deformed and demented", she was carefully guided off a steamboat at Ovid Landing, a docking area on the asylum waterfront grounds. For 10 years prior she had been shackled naked in a basement with nothing more than a mat. Her arrival at the asylum saw her showered, dressed, well fed and given a warm bed. That same afternoon saw three males arrive shortly after – they arrived shackled in irons and confined to a chicken crate. Surely, Willard would offer them much more of a humane and dignified existence.

In an era of indifference, neglect and brutality, Willard (like other institutions at the time) was revolutionary; it offered patients kindness, gentleness and understanding. Unfortunately, it was not immune to overcrowding and consequently, Willard suffered a similar fate to the other asylums, ceasing most operations in 1995.

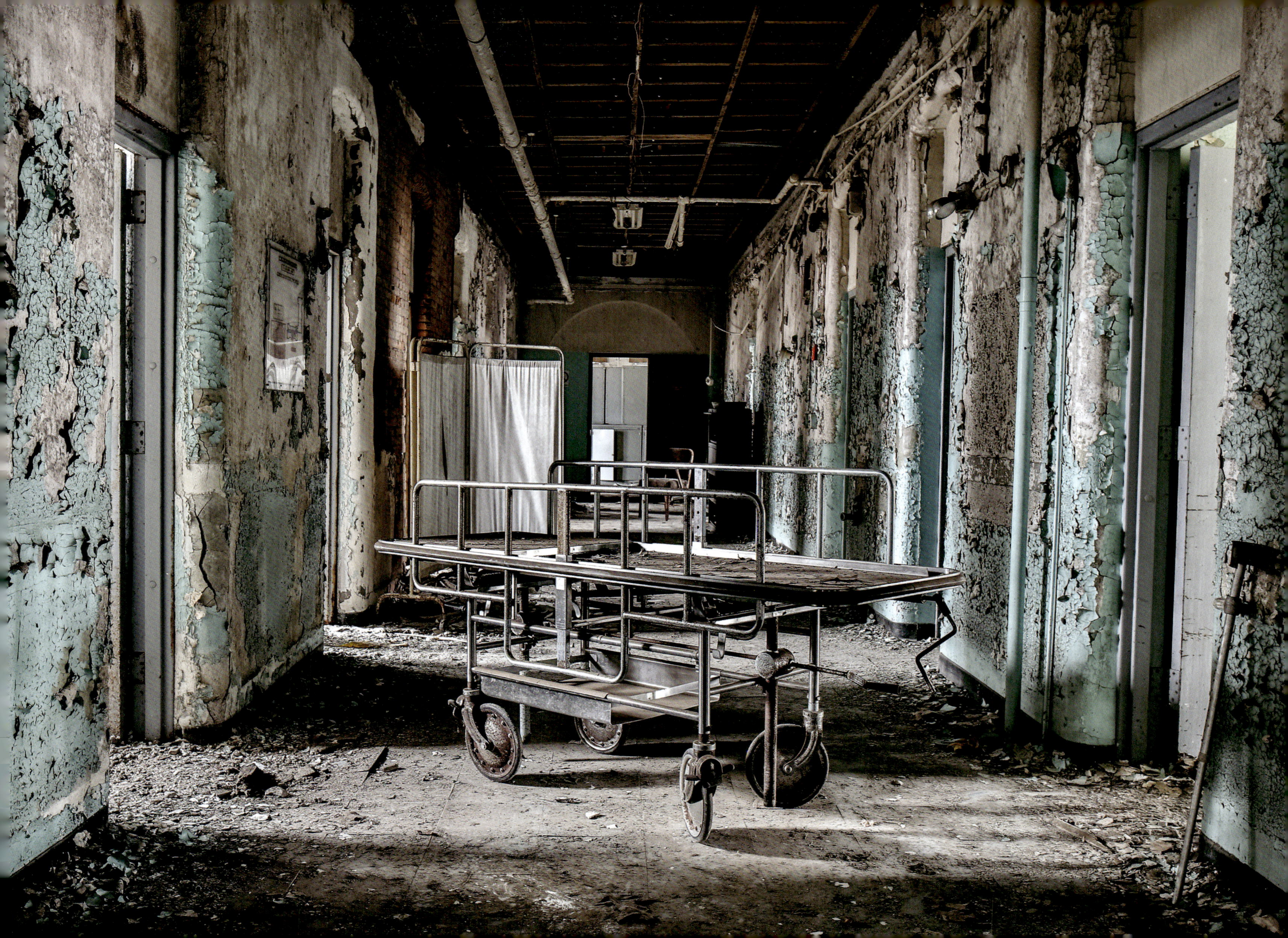

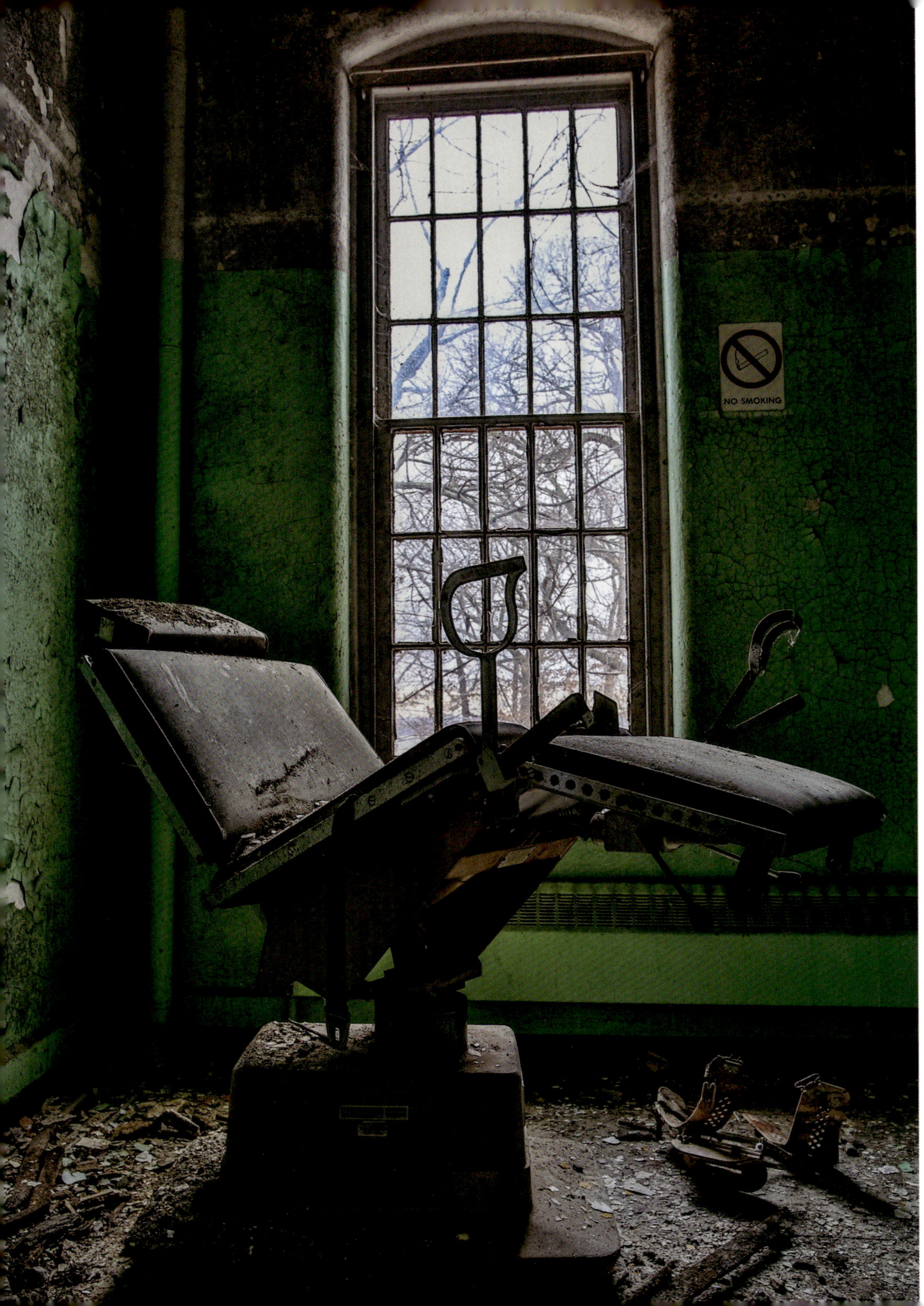

Not long after its closure, a discovery was made that would propel Willard into the spotlight, attracting much public attention and allure. Some 400 suitcases were found untouched in a locked and sealed attic. Each piece of luggage served as a time capsule of a period from approximately 1910 to 1960, offering a heartbreaking glimpse into the daily existence of Willard's patients.
Photographer Jon Crispin was commissioned to document each and every artifact found inside the cases and penned a book entitled *The Lives They Left Behind*. Crispin's photographs offer the curious an open window into the lives – and the minds – of so many that entered Willard, tragically never to leave. Upon their arrival at the asylum, all patients' belongings would be stored and never seen again.

In a suitcase owned by a patient and US Army Veteran named Frank, Crispin found a pristine military uniform, sewing and grooming kits, a toy pistol, food ration cards, and several photos of Frank and his family. Another suitcase owned by a woman named Anna revealed the memories of a socialite fond of attention. Her luggage included a pair of stylish heels, hats, sequined gold belts, brushes, combs and a written inventory cataloguing her glamorous clothing.

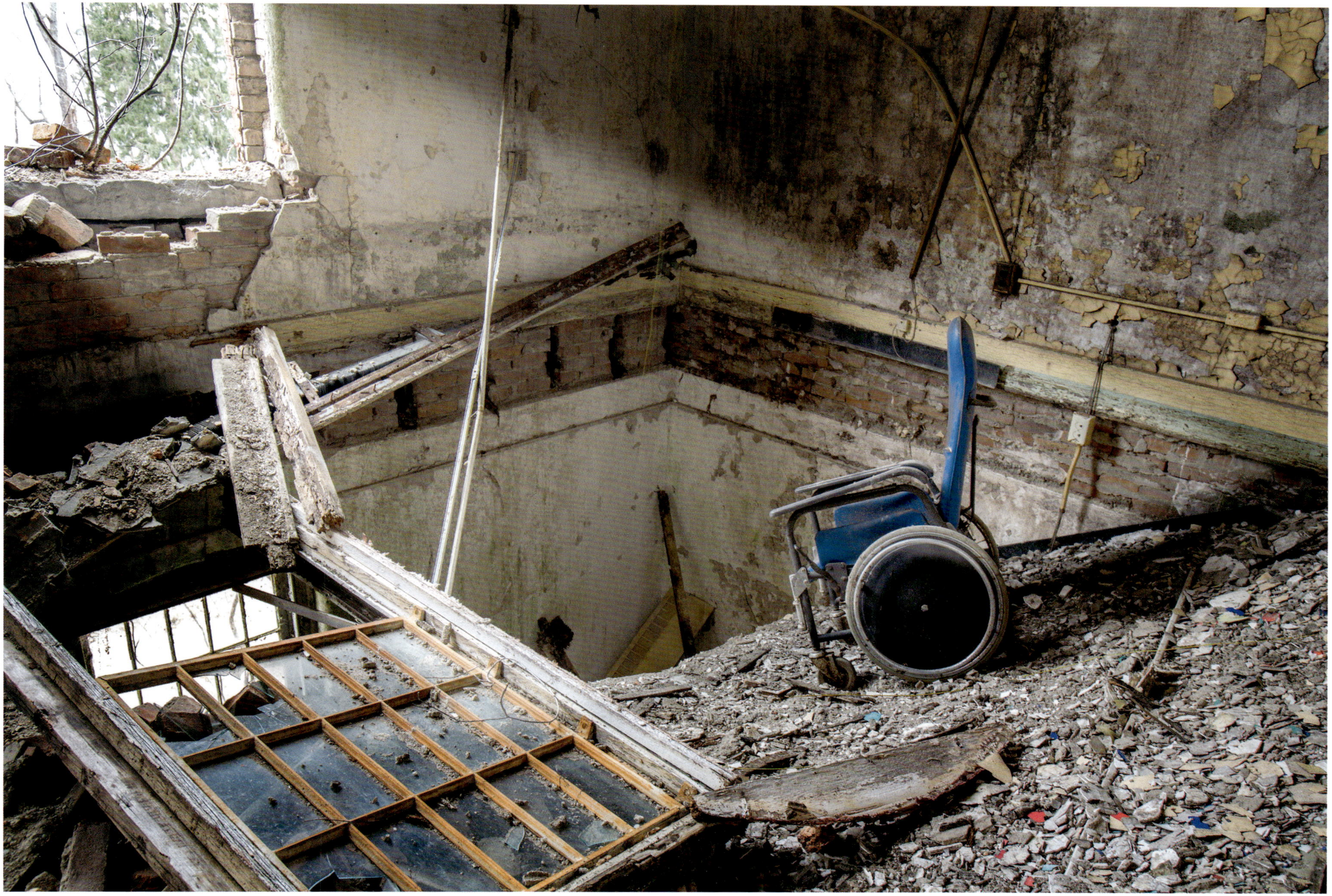

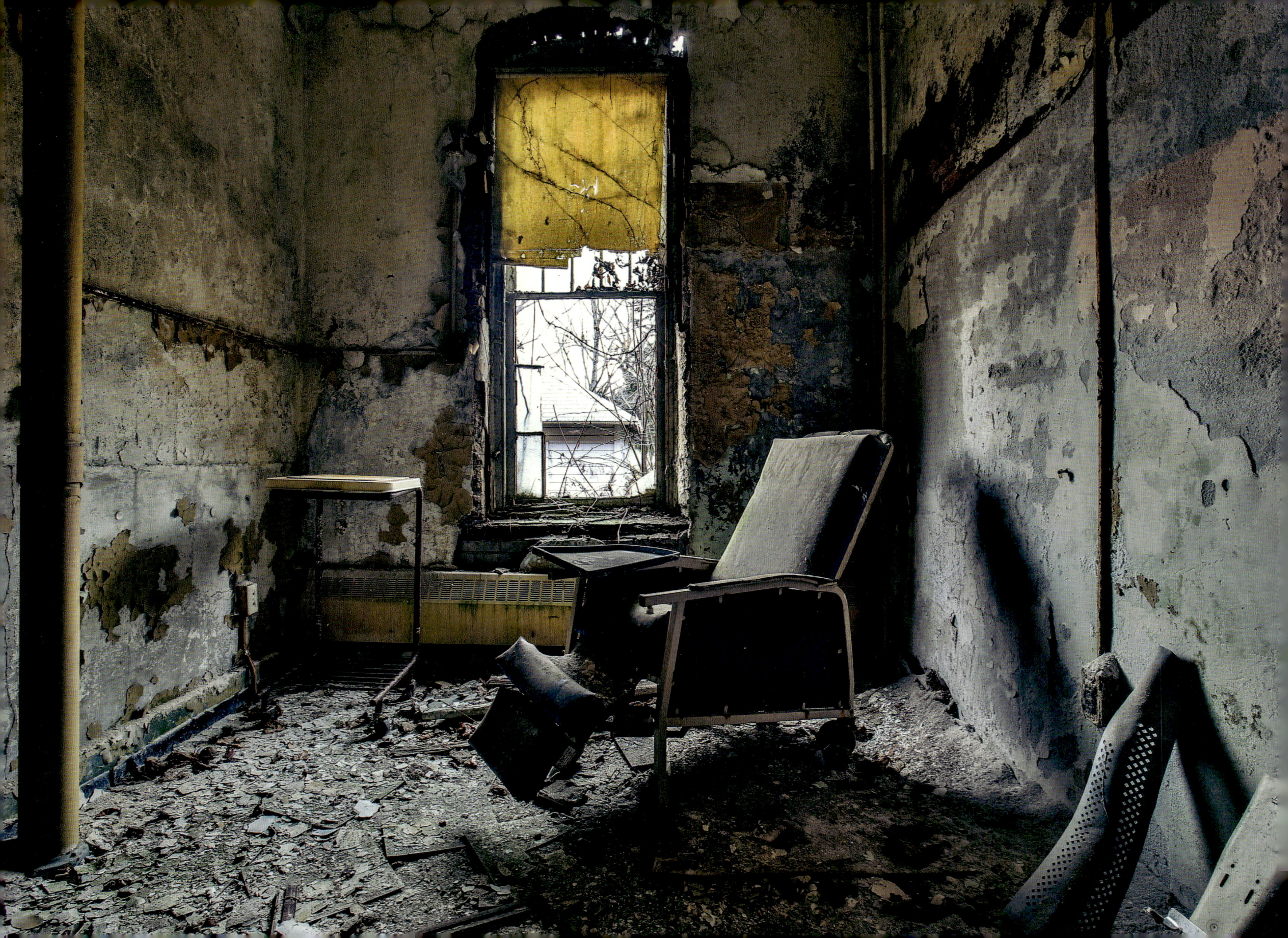

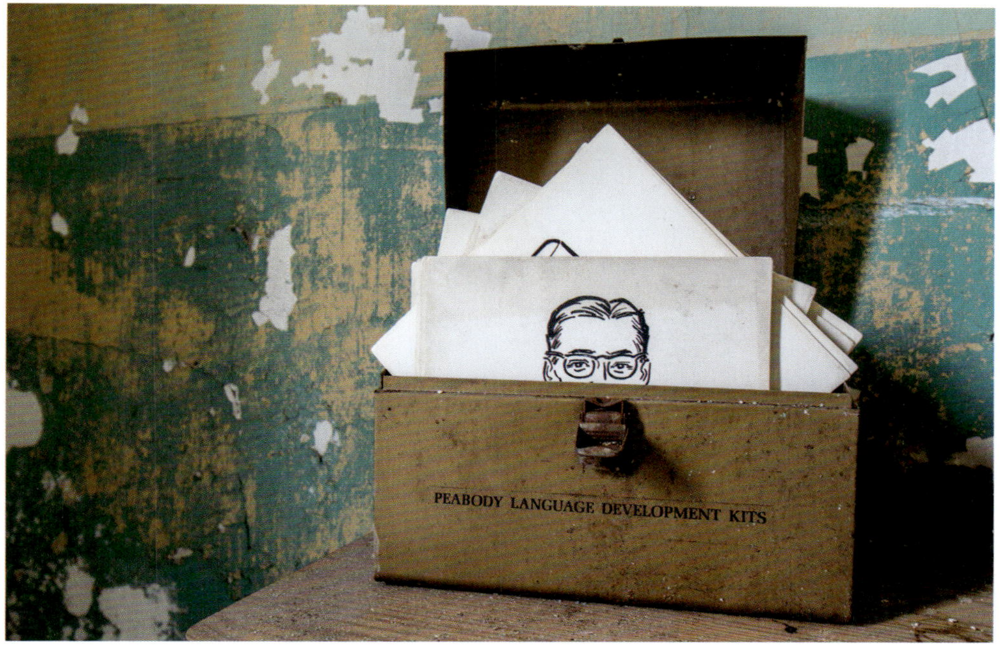

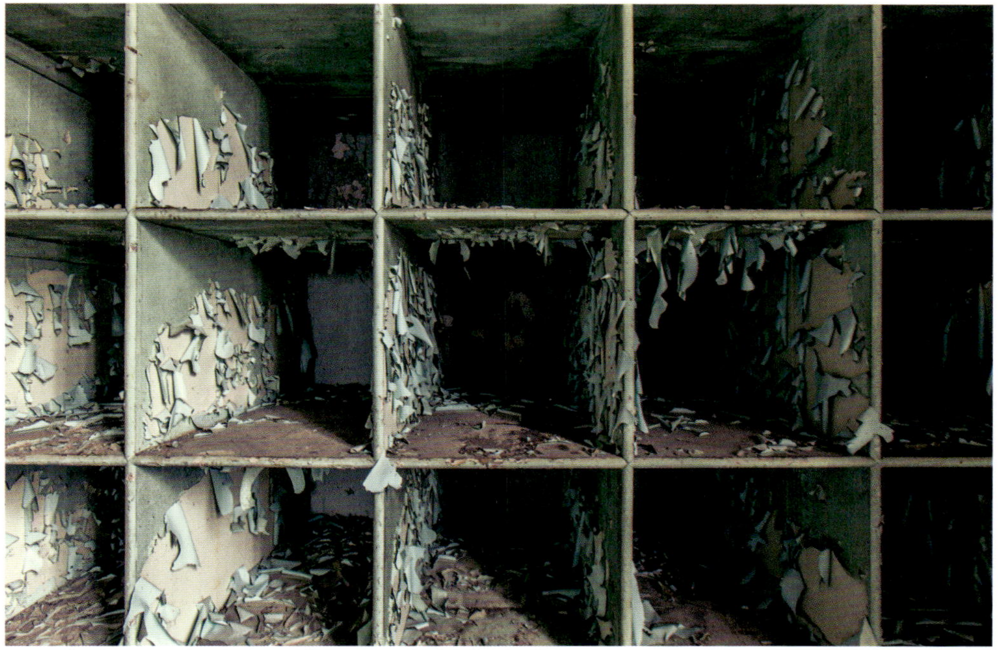

The suitcases evoke a strong human connection. They offer a face, a story and a heartbreaking portrait of the lives these individuals lived before they were institutionalised and ultimately reduced to an anonymous number on a grave marker. Jon Crispin's work in *The Lives They Left Behind*, documenting these incredible vessels of humanity, is invaluable to the fight against stigma. No one is immune to mental health issues; as haunting and elegiac as the photos of Willard are in this section, they are a timeless representation of the people who lived and died here.

In 2005 the suitcases became a travelling museum exhibit. However, as of 2015 the exhibit has found a permanent home in Buffalo, NY at the Museum of DisABILITY – the only museum of its kind in the United States – where the legacy of the suitcase owners lives on in a respectful and dignified way.

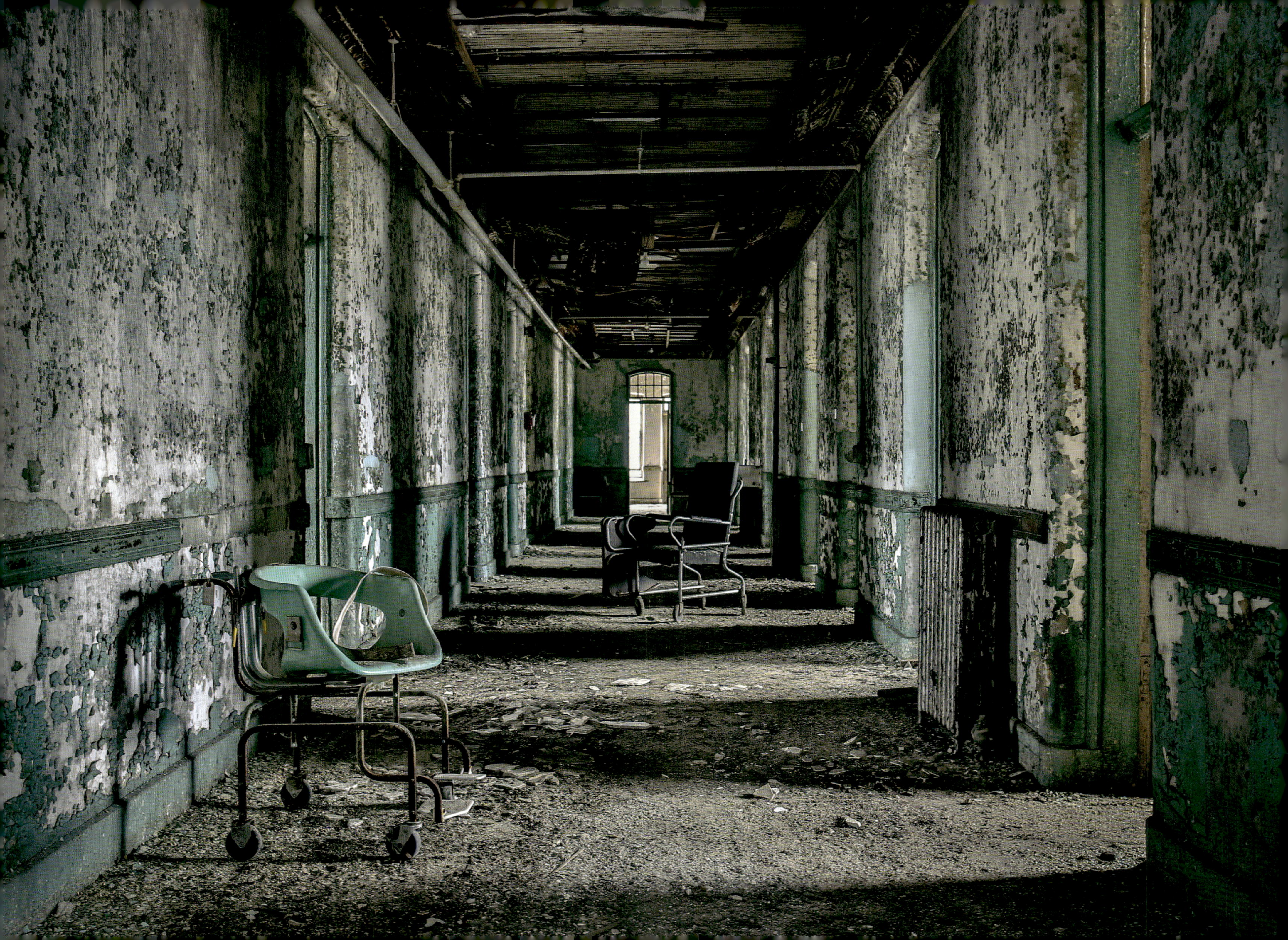

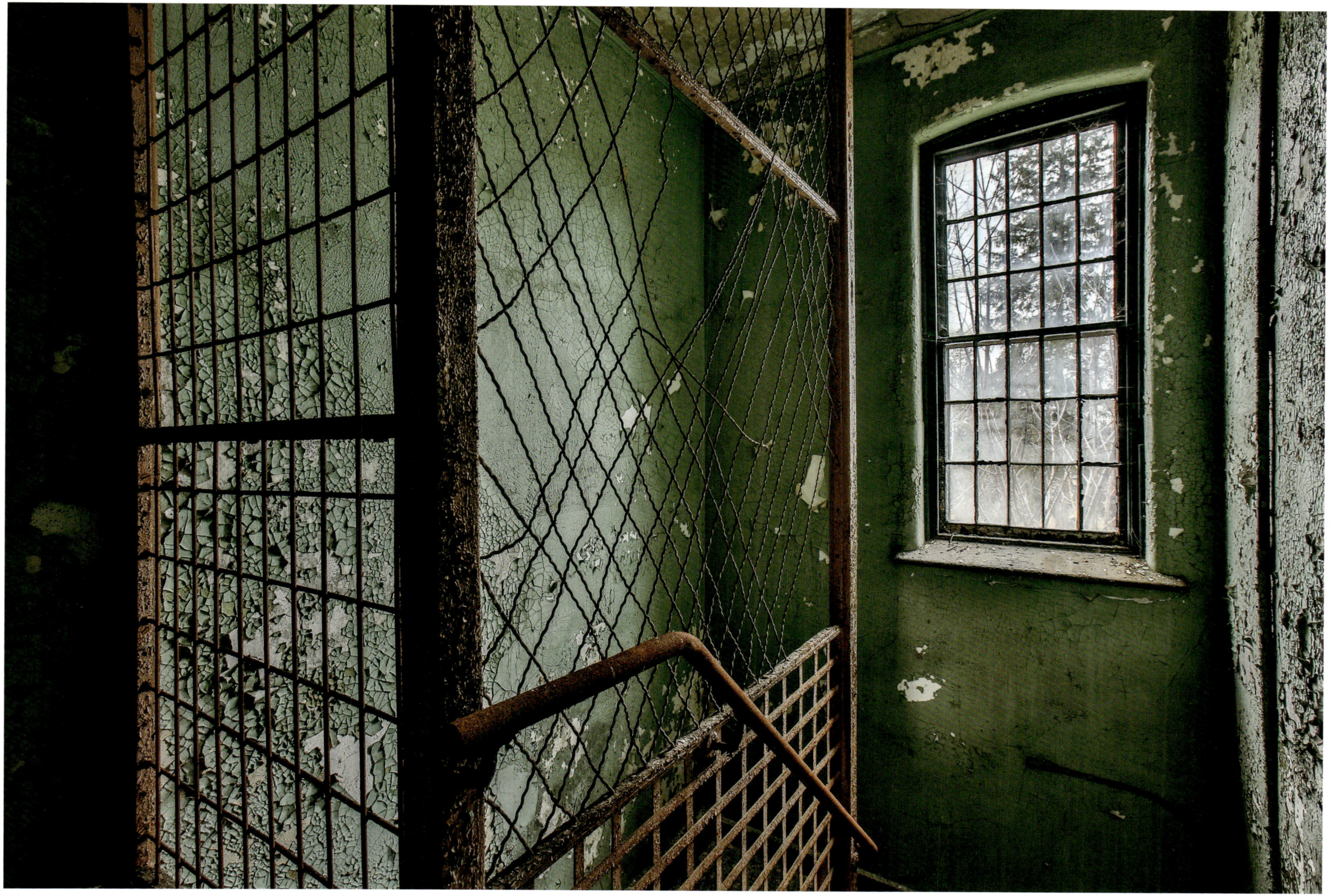

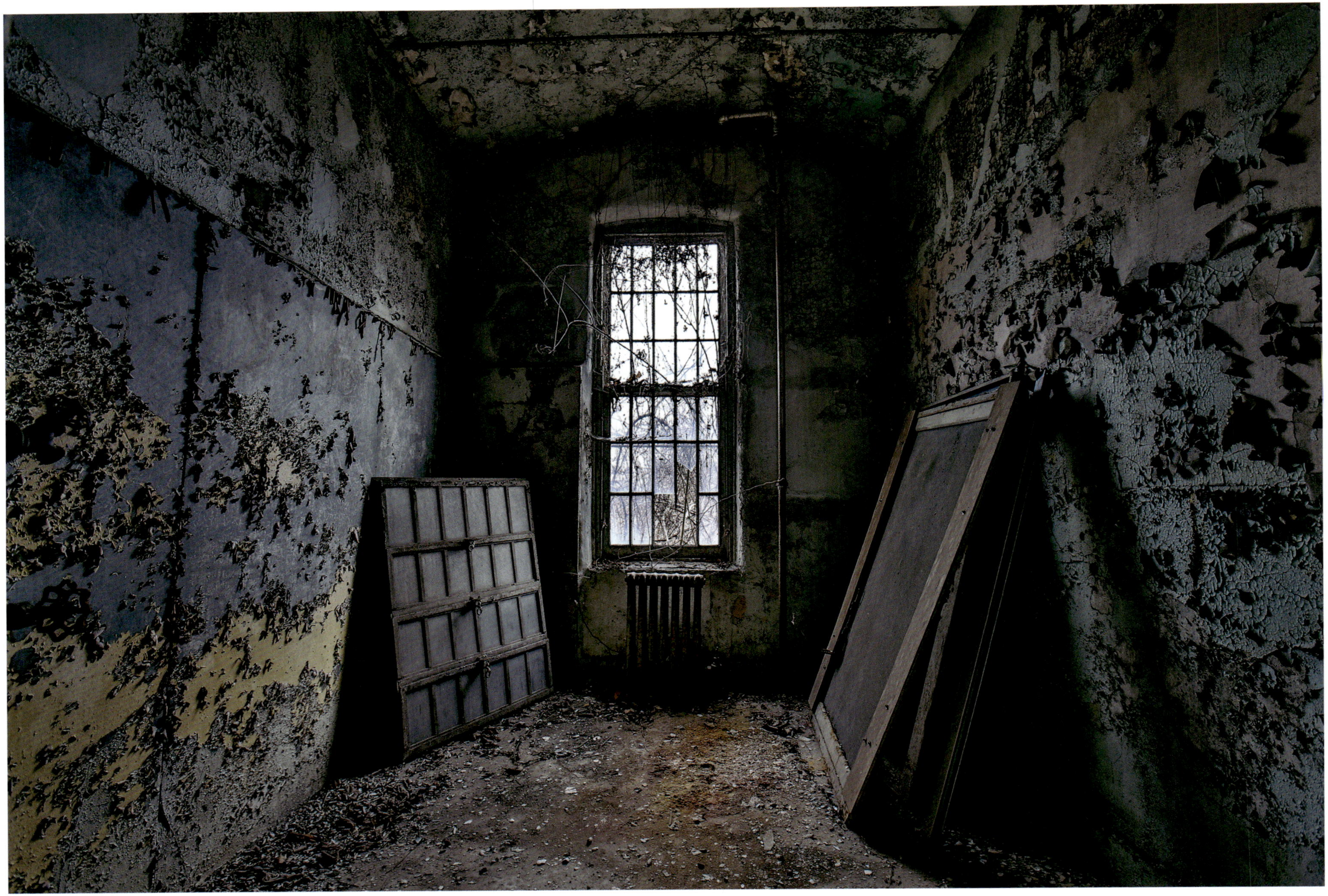

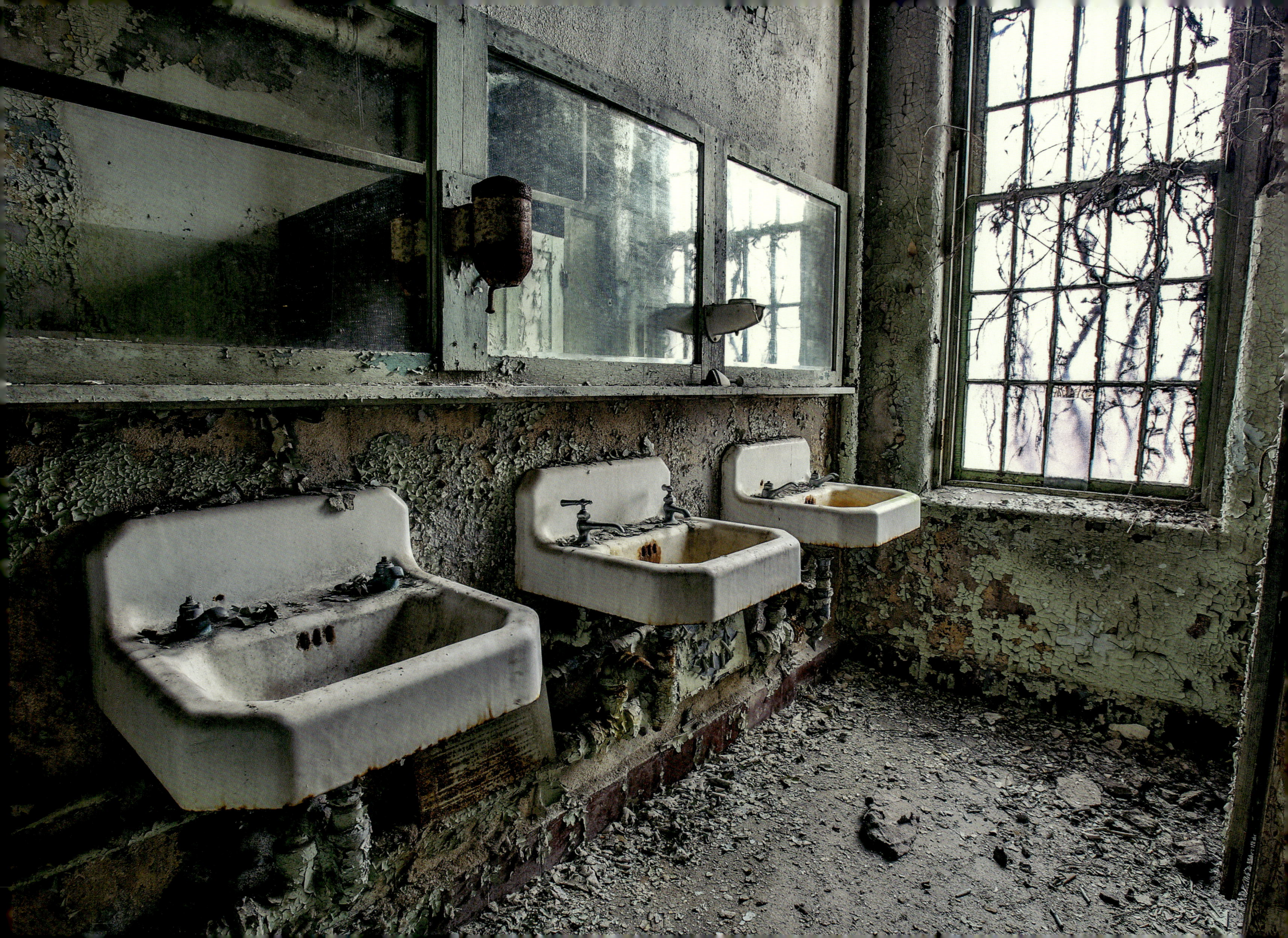

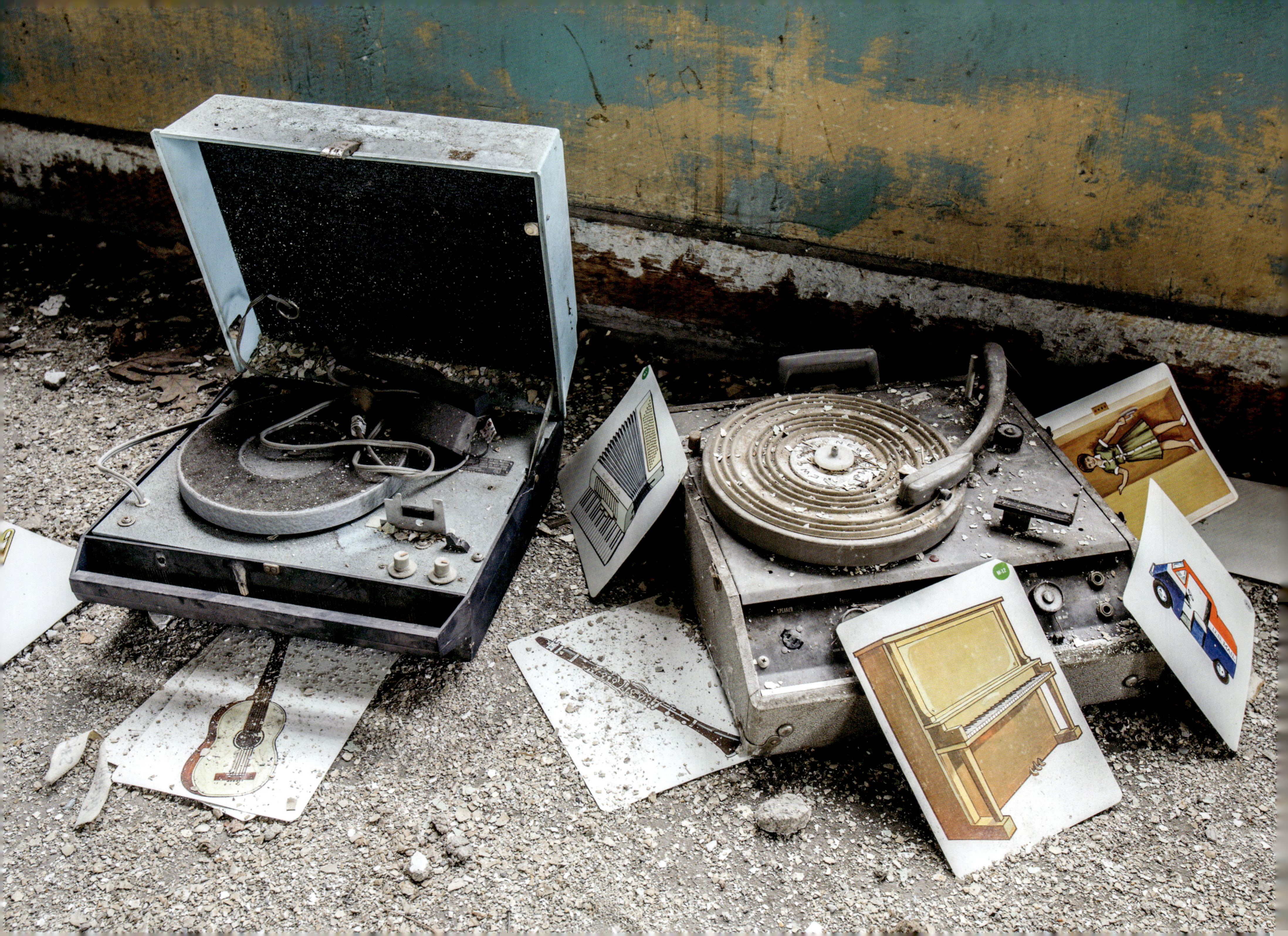

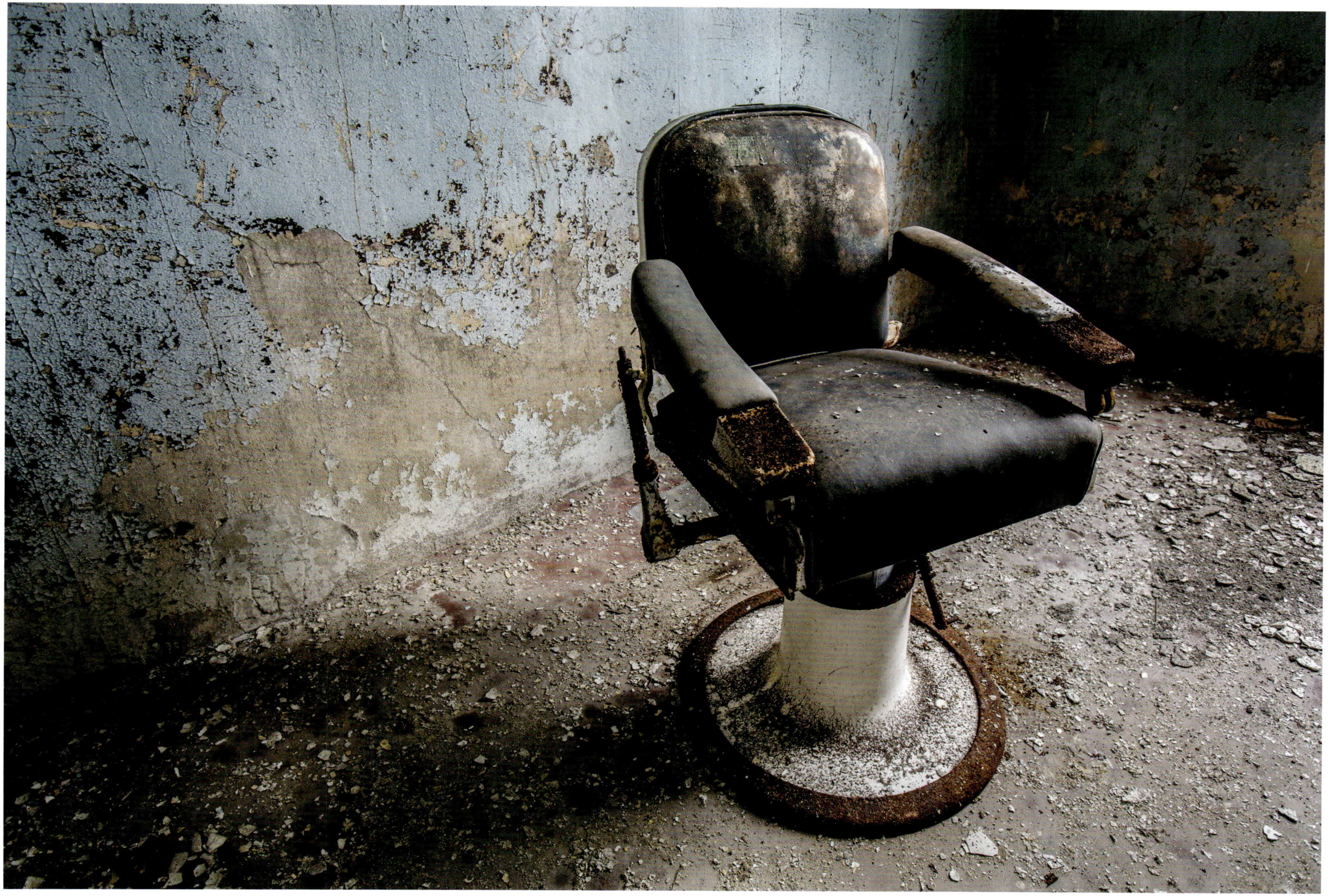

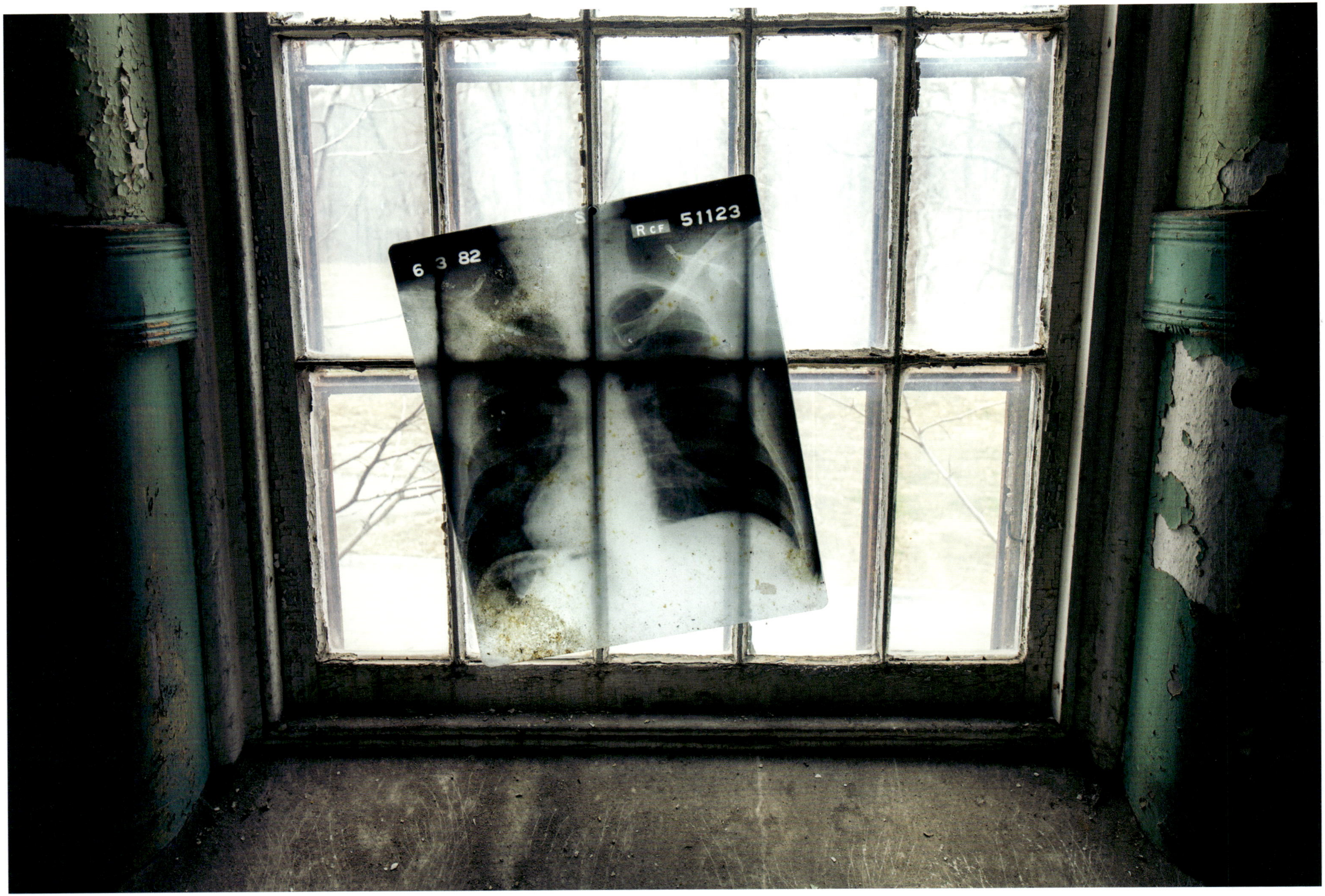
6 3 82
RCF 51123

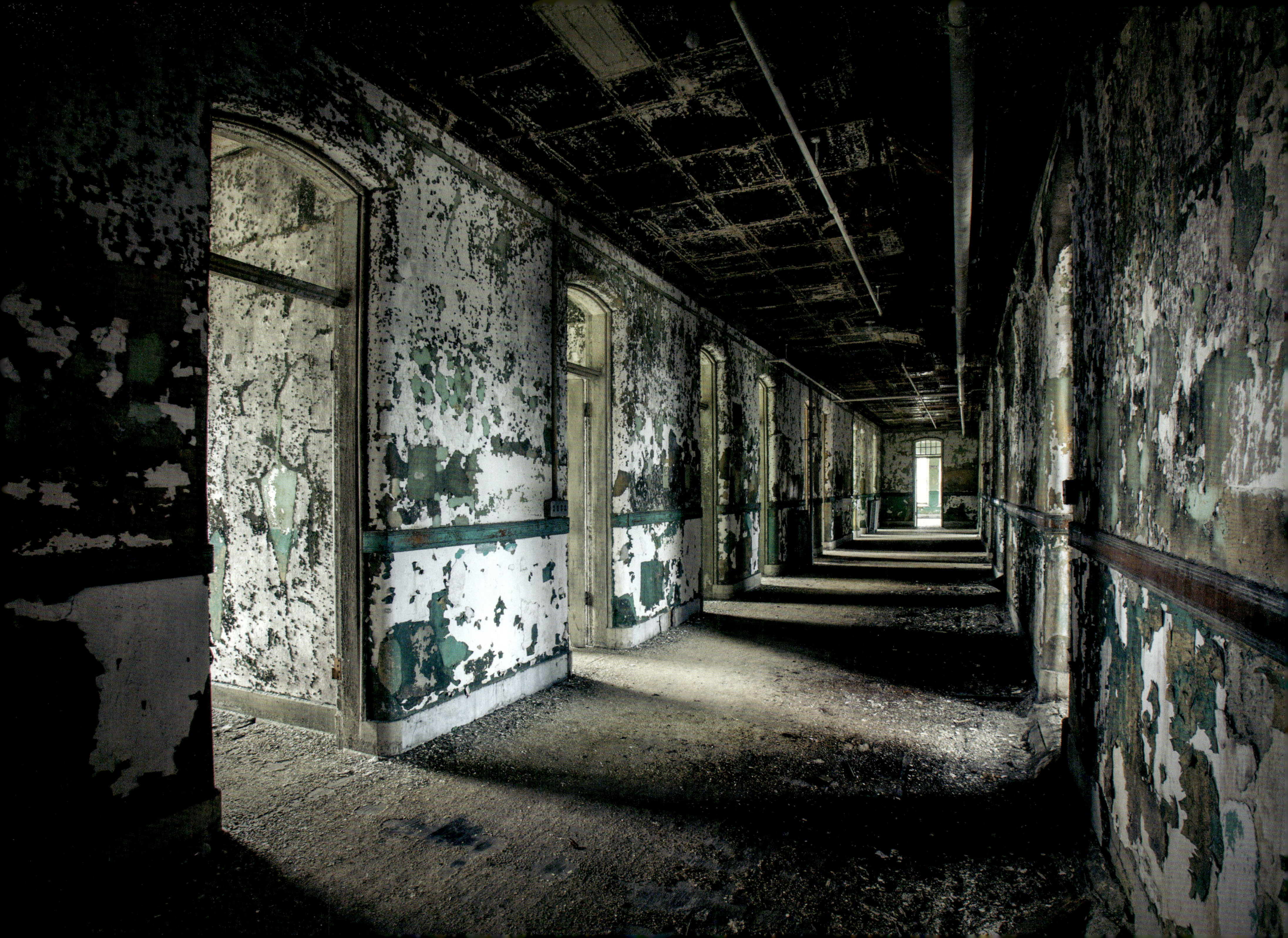

Hudson River State Hospital

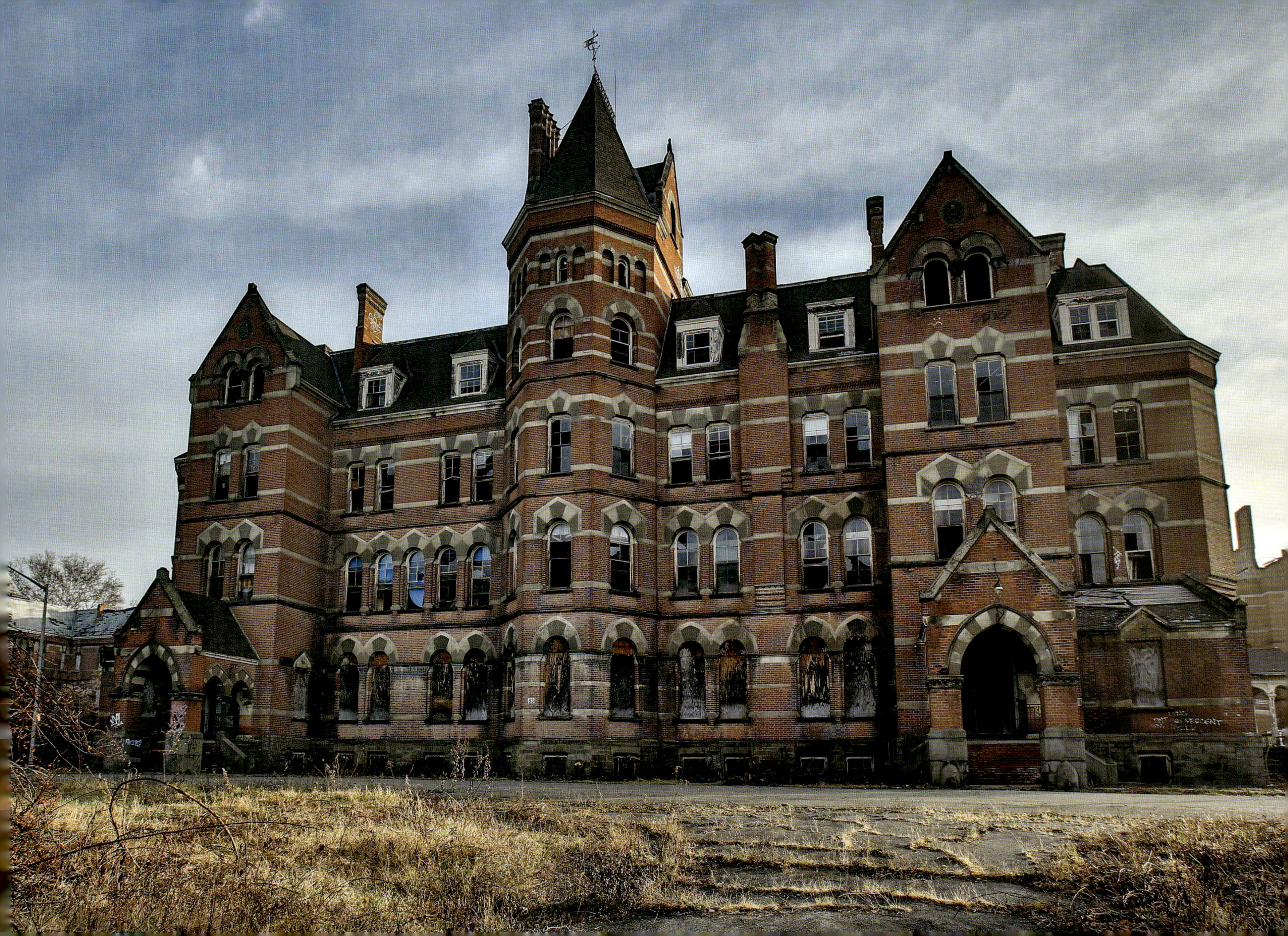

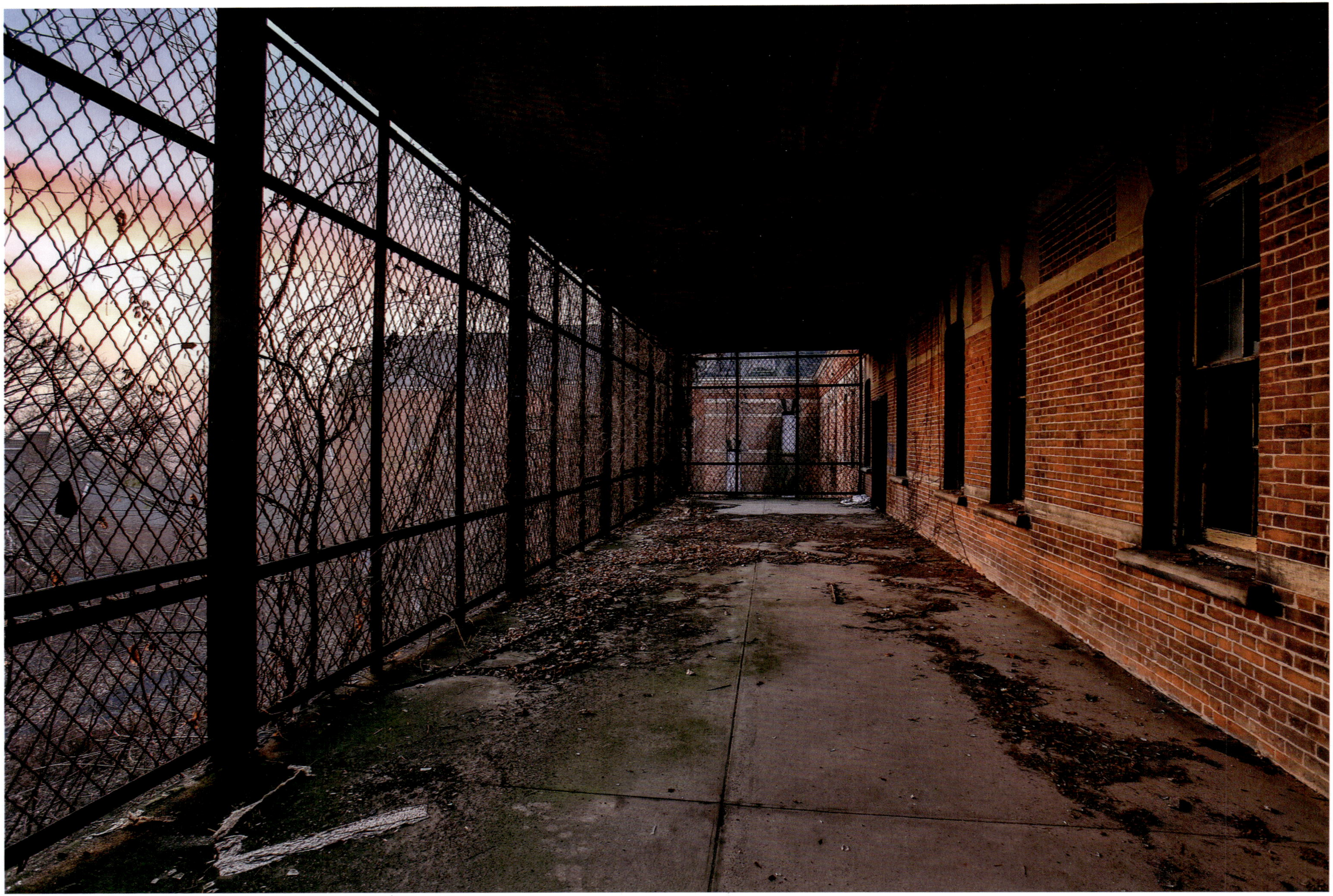

Patient Porch

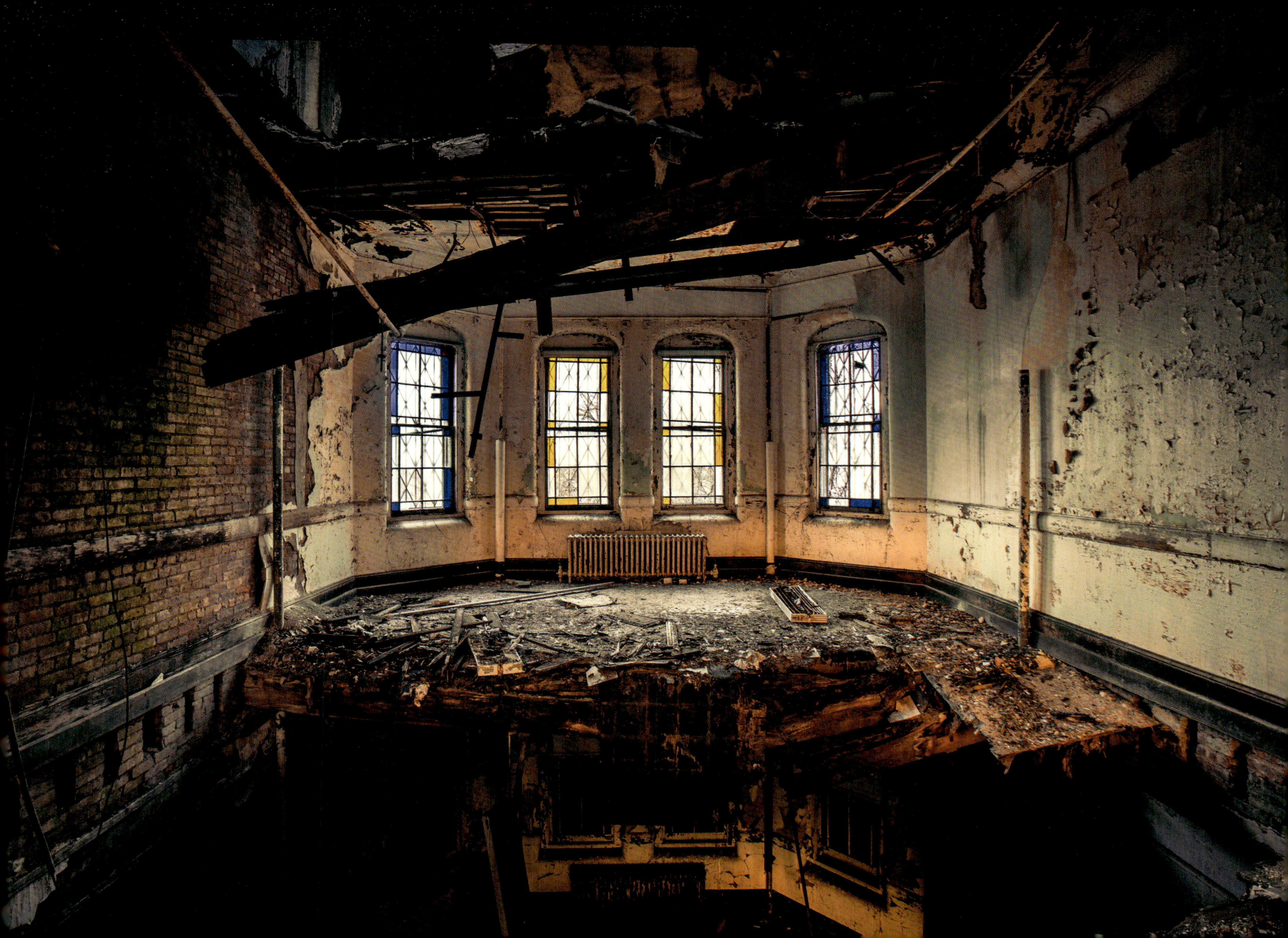

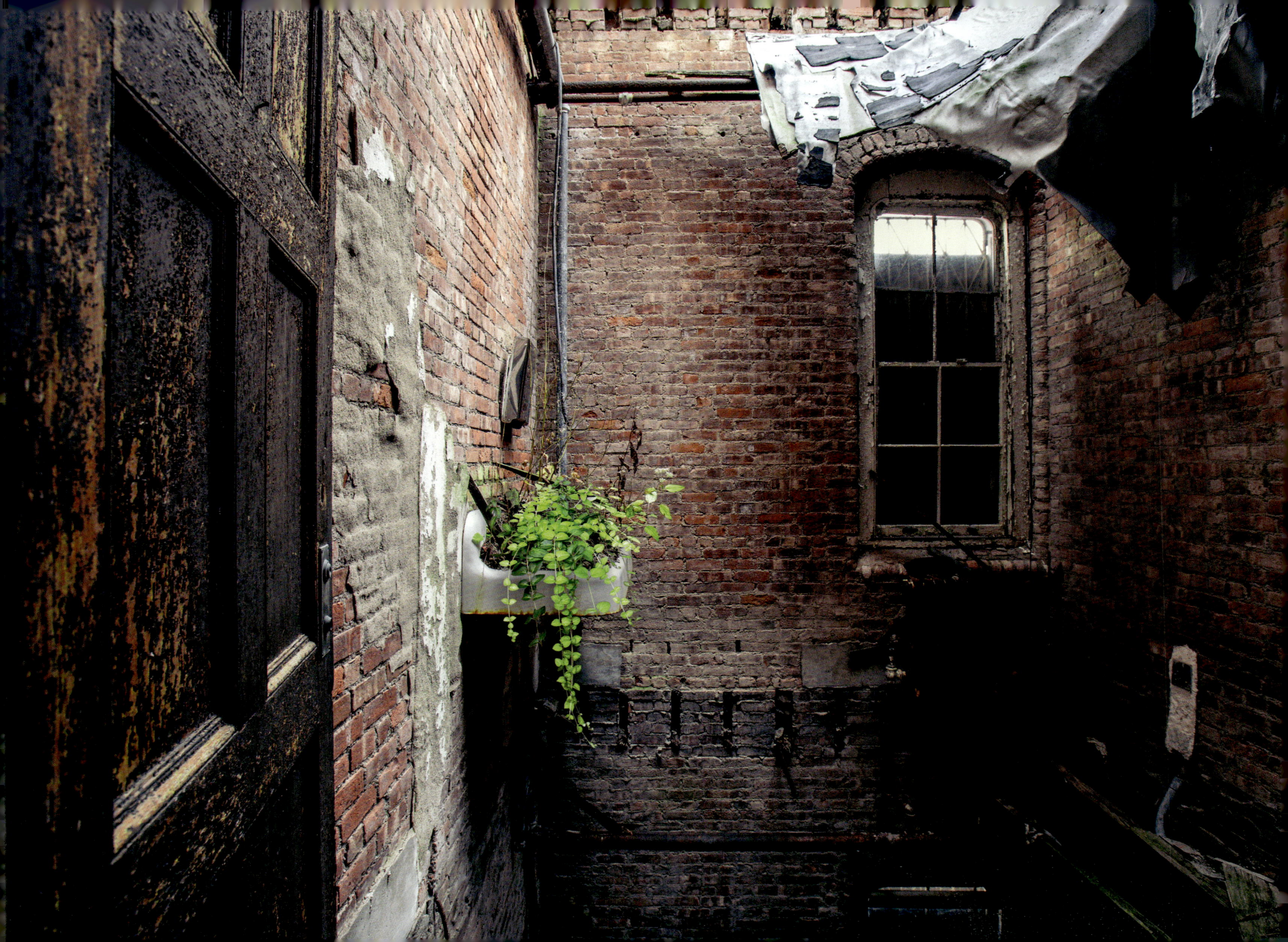

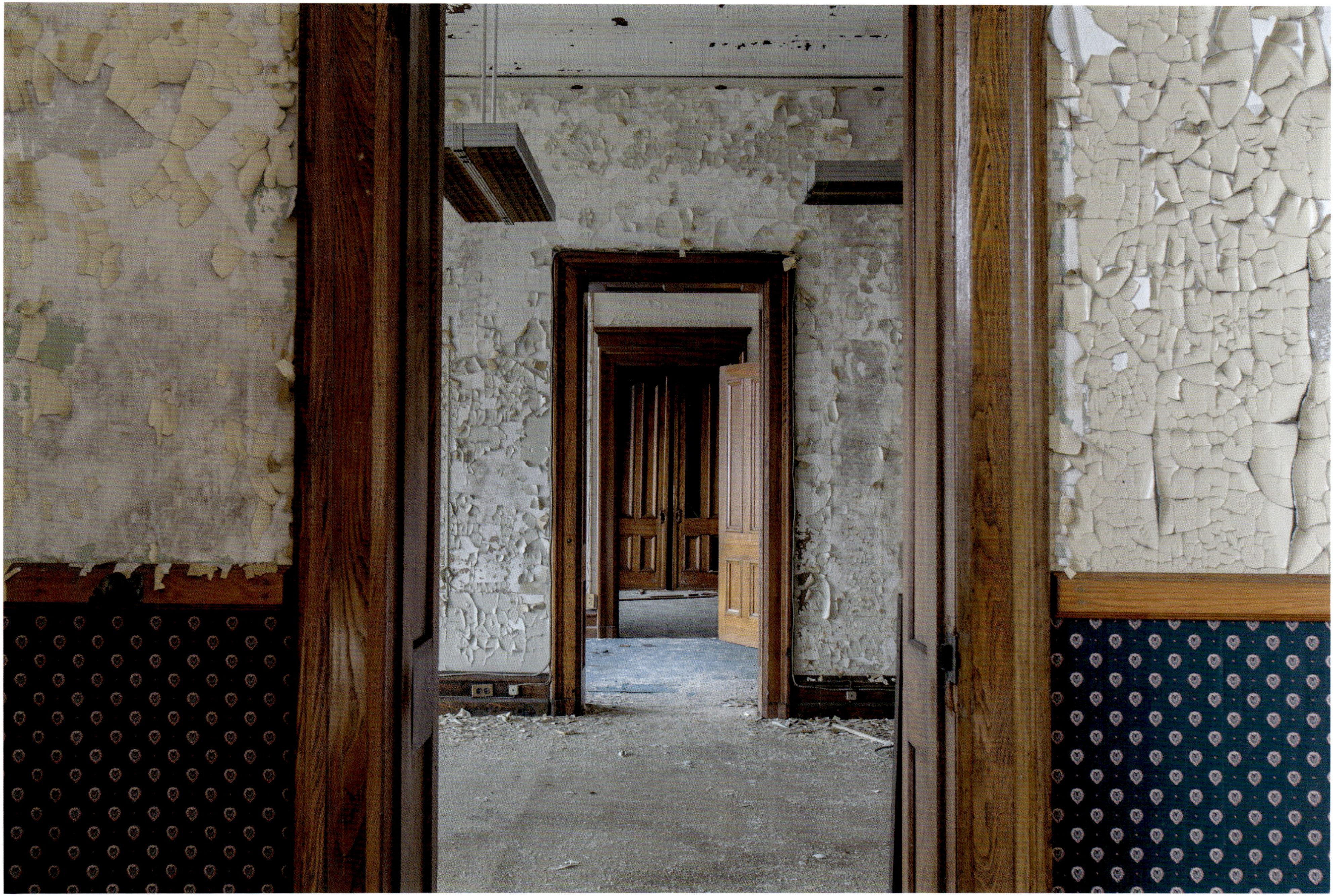

Superintendent's offices, Administration building

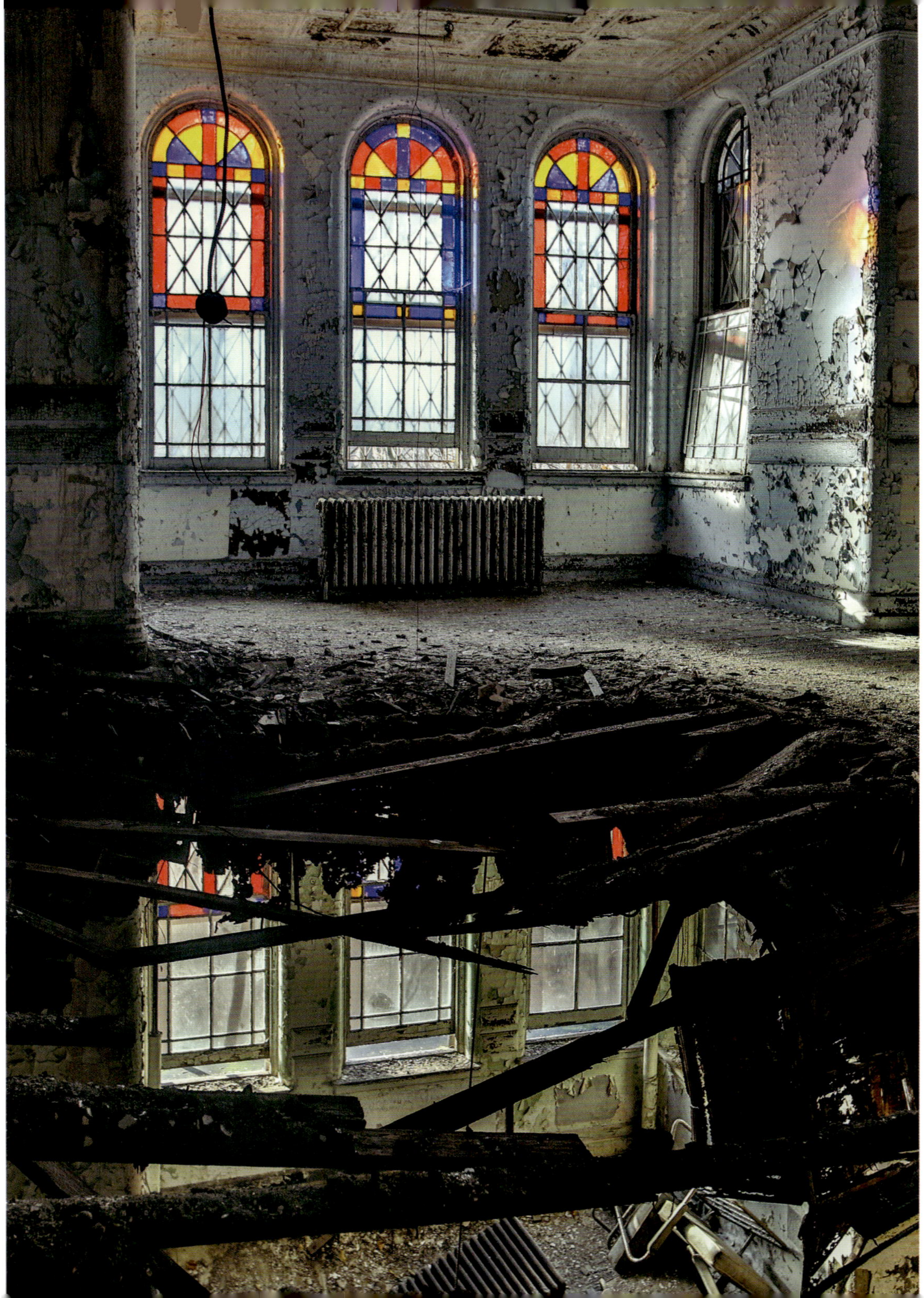

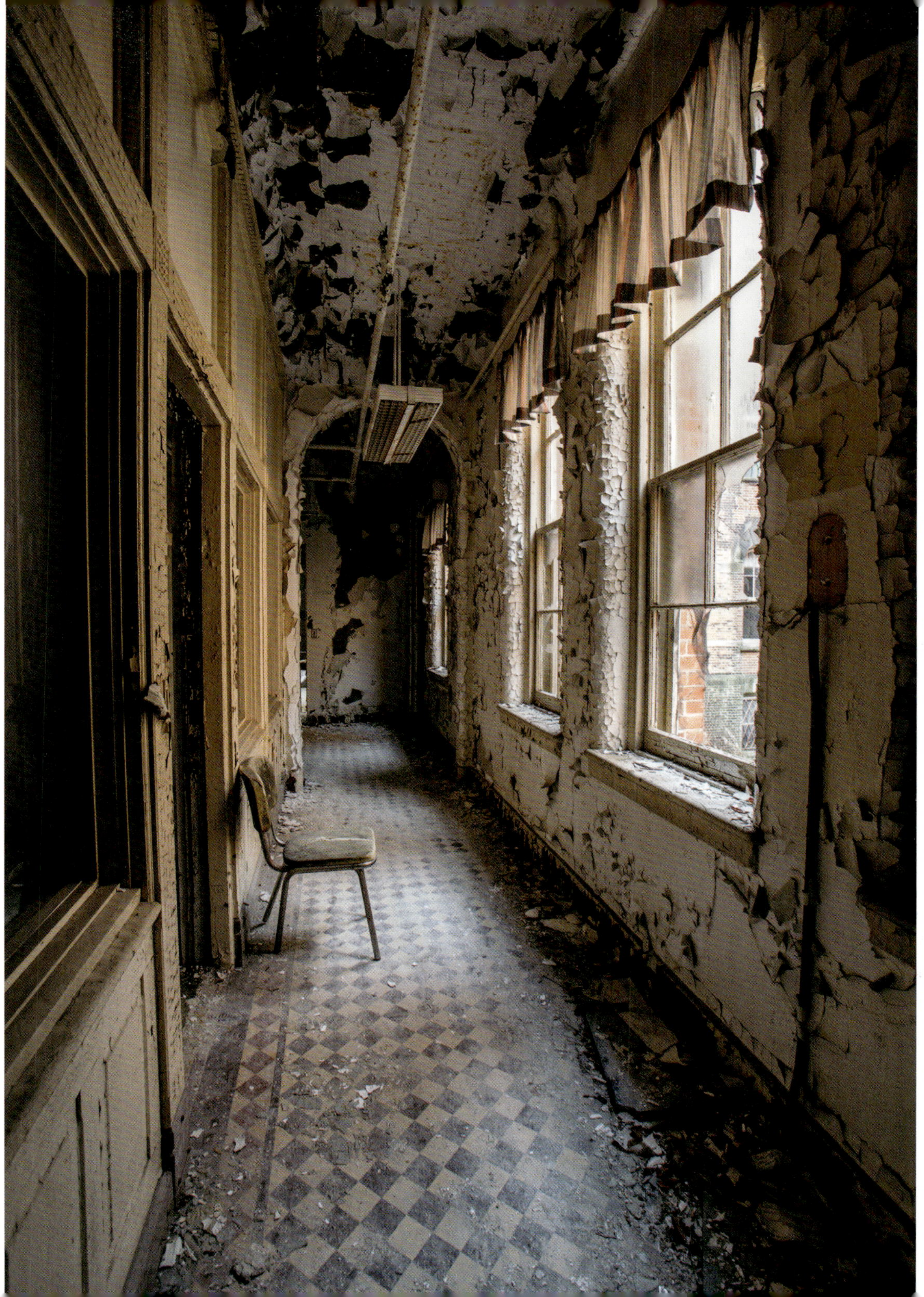

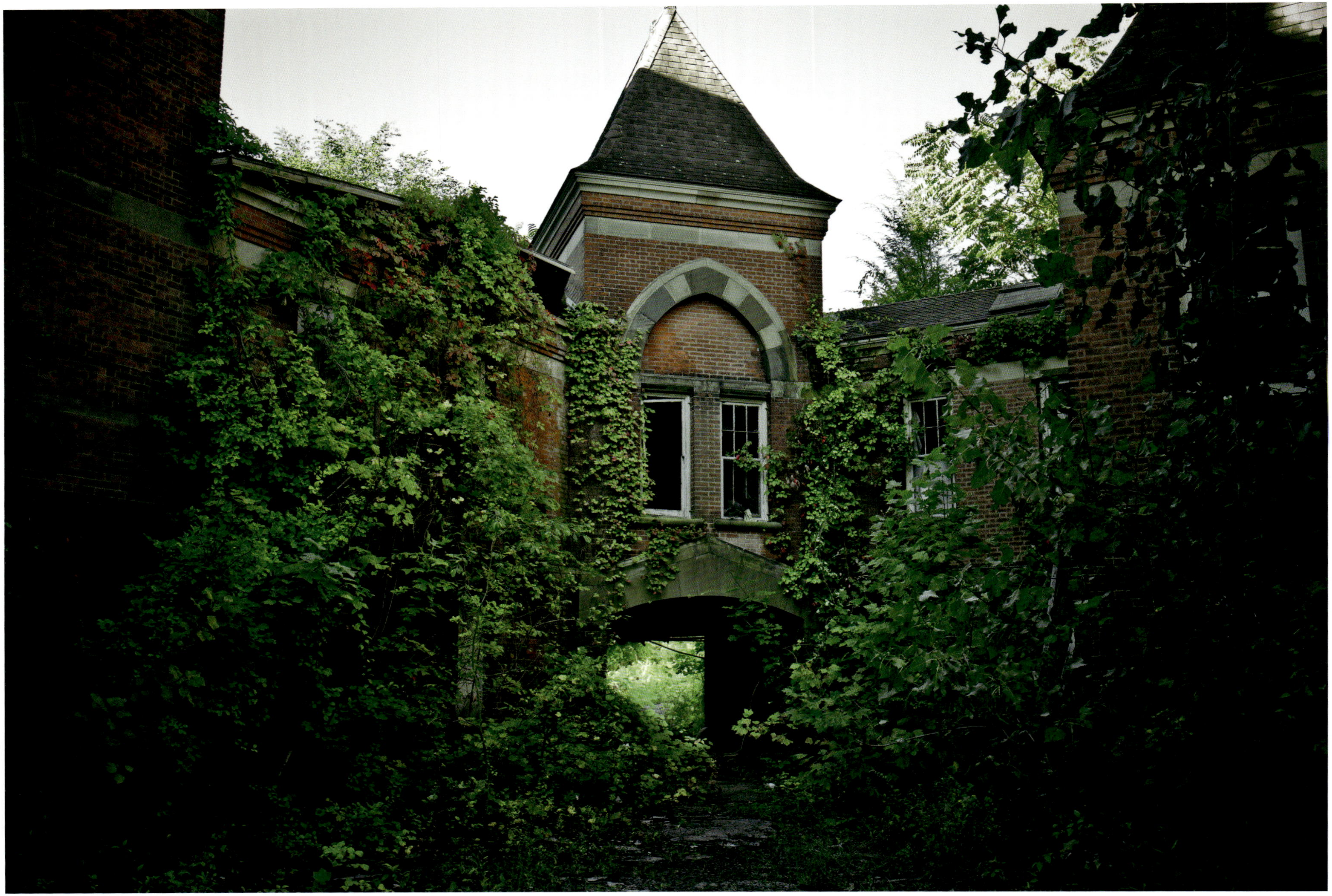

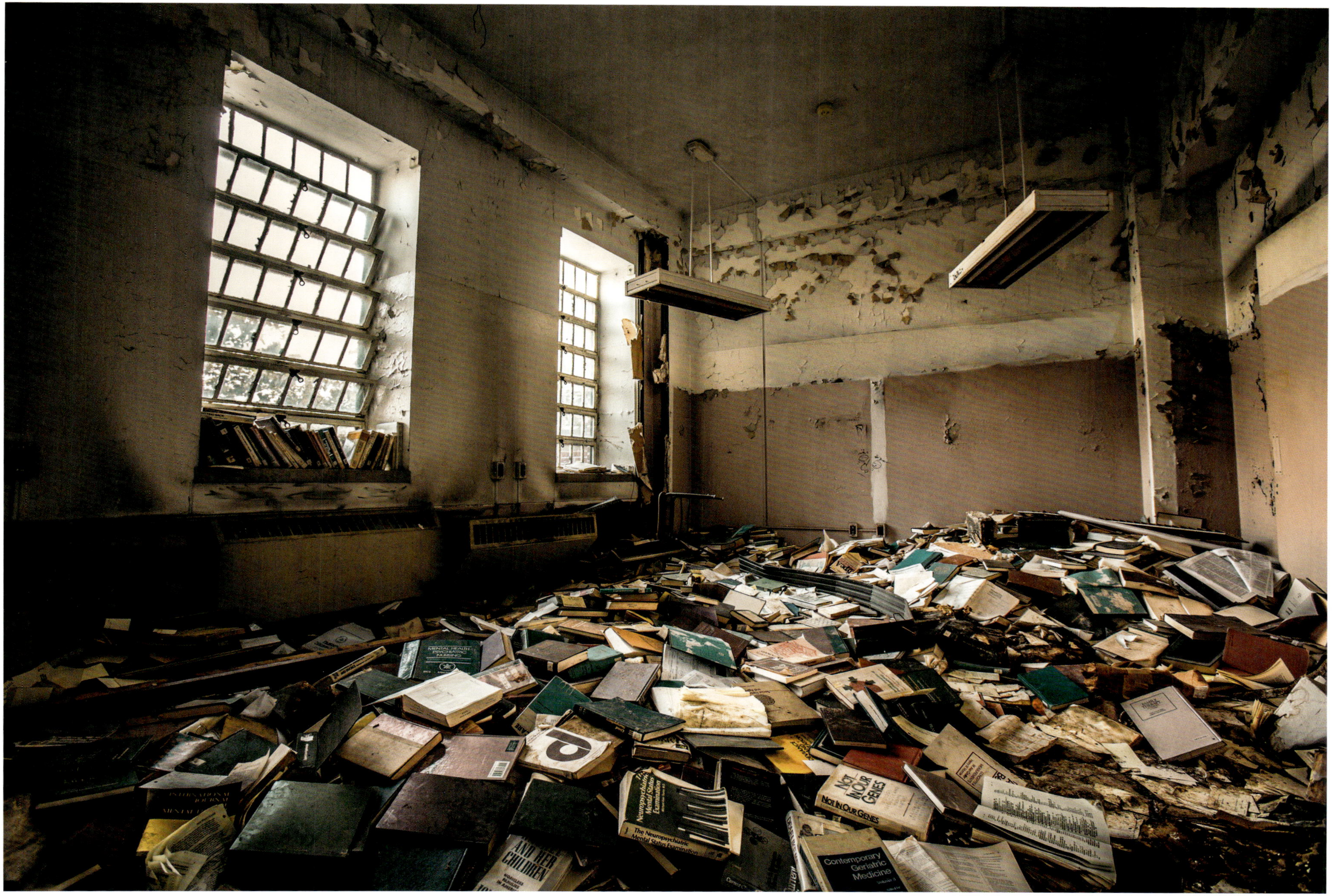
NOT IN OUR GENES
Contemporary Geriatric Medicine
The Neuropsychiatric Mental Status Examination
AND HER CHILDREN

Library

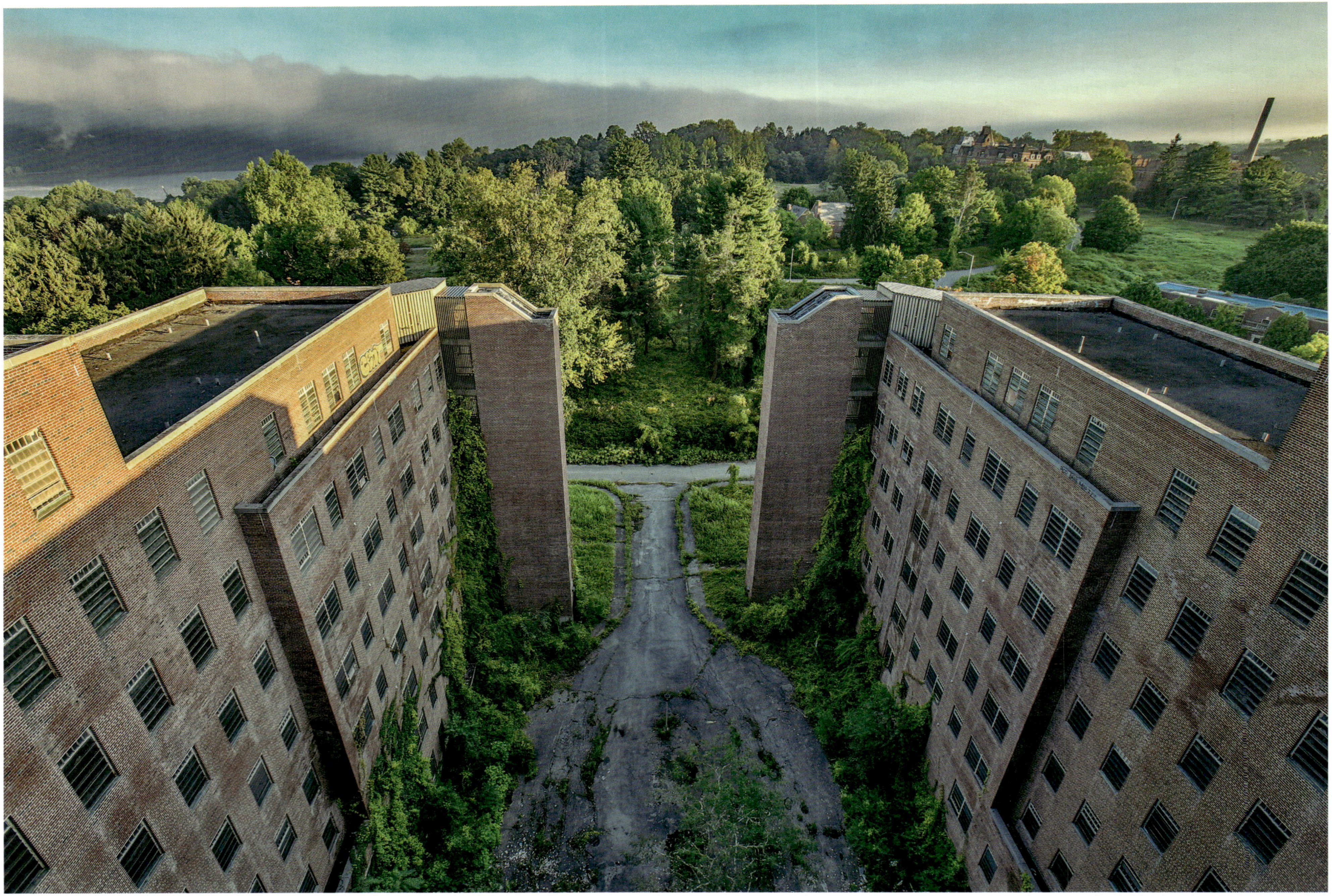

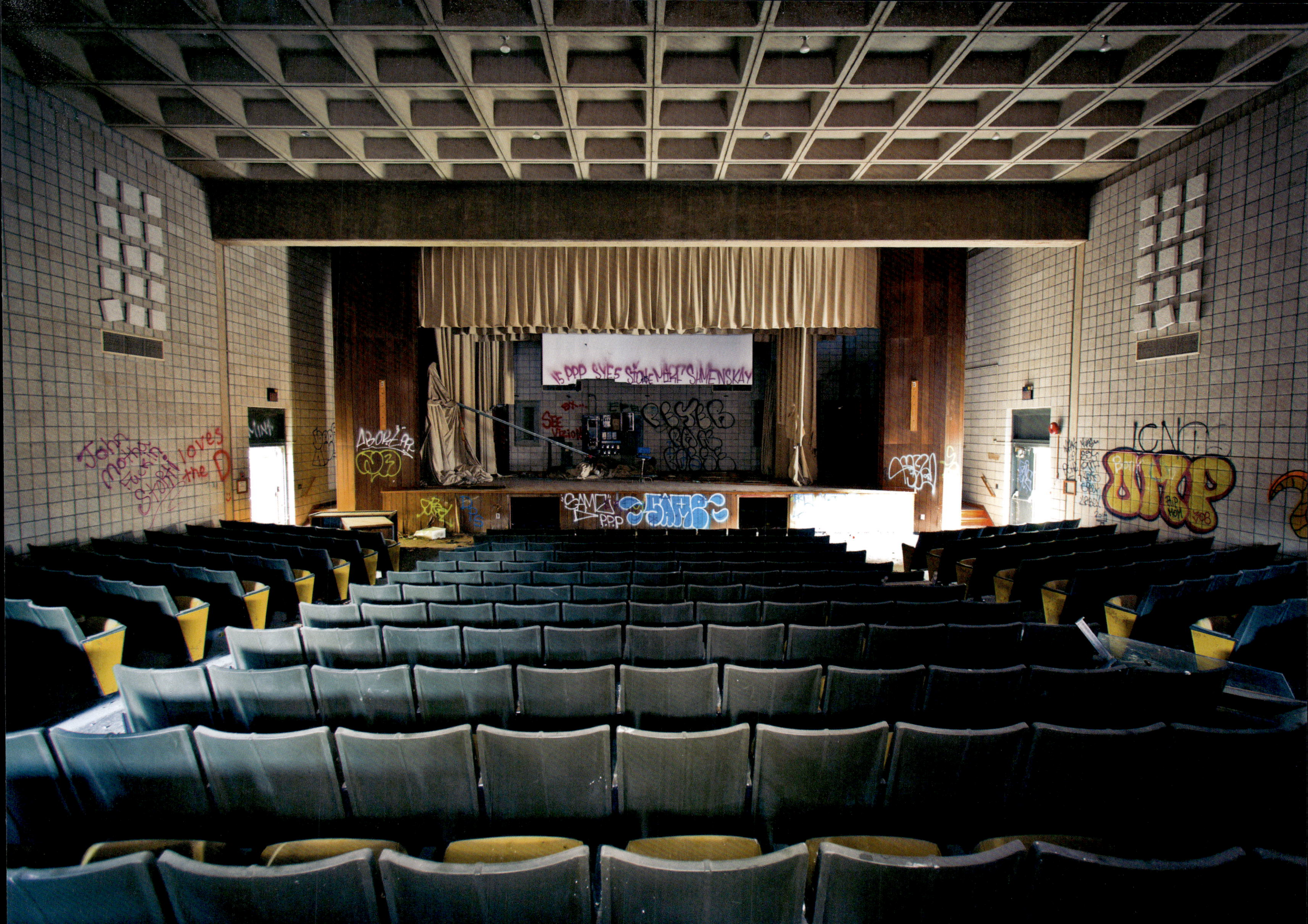

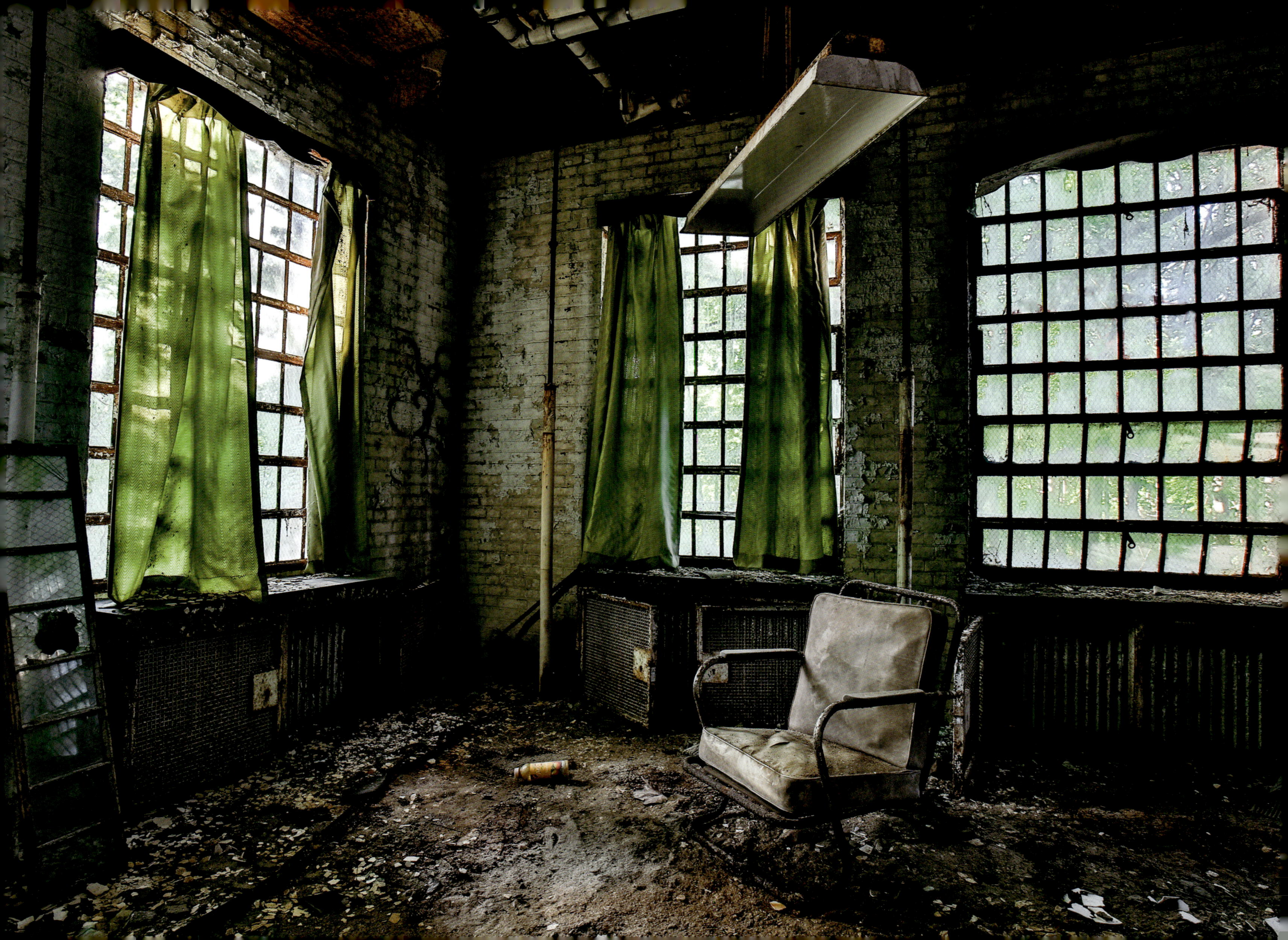

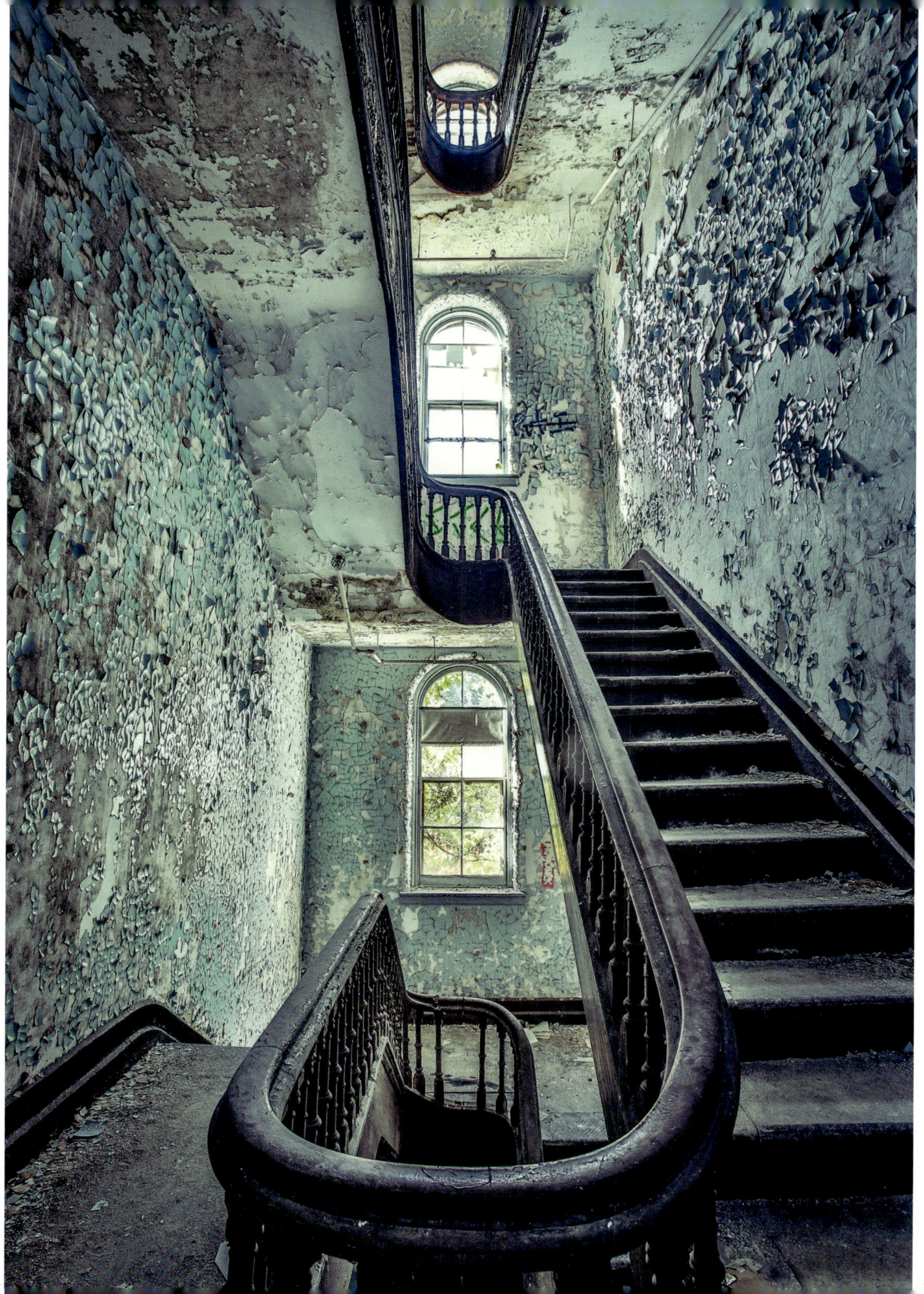

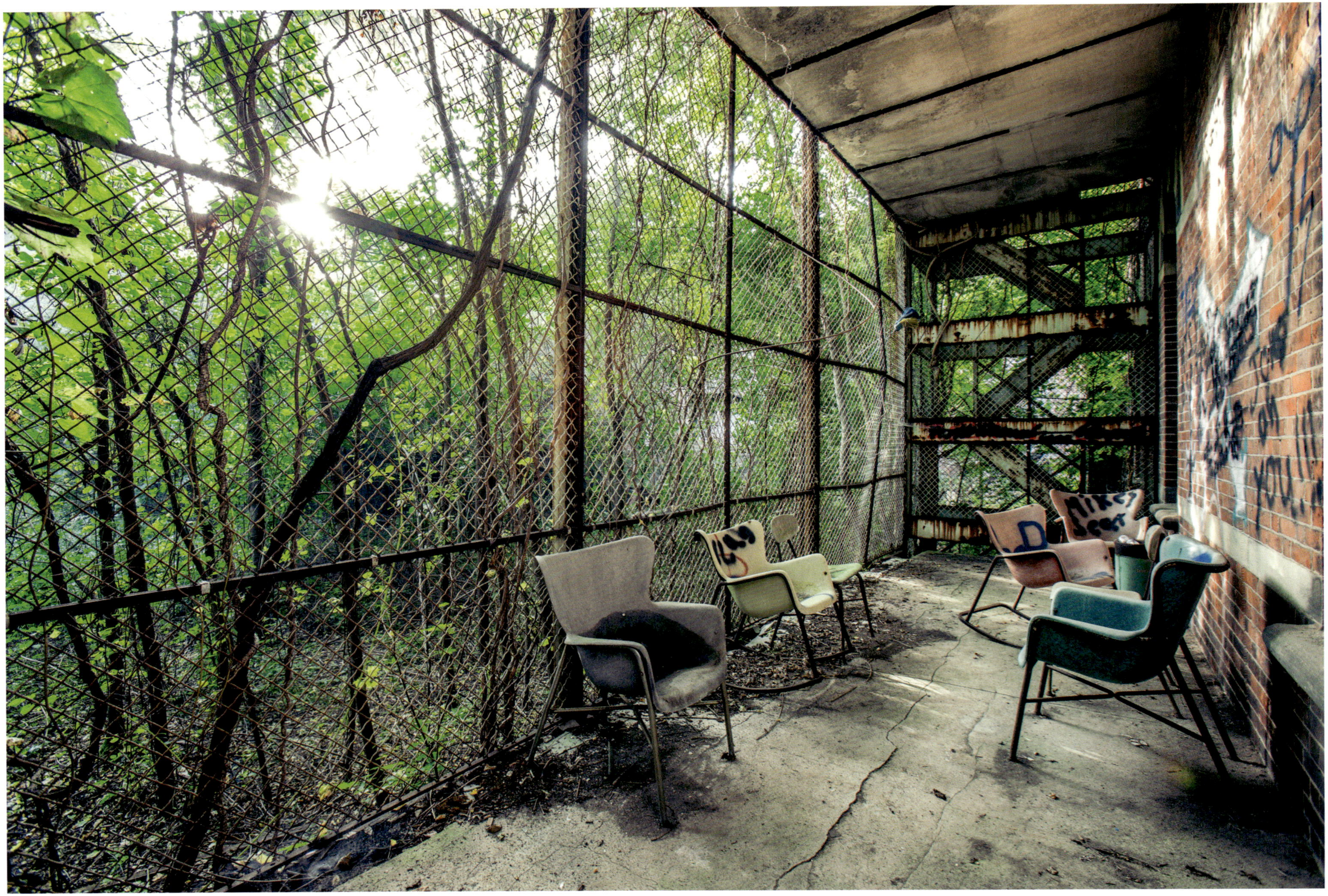

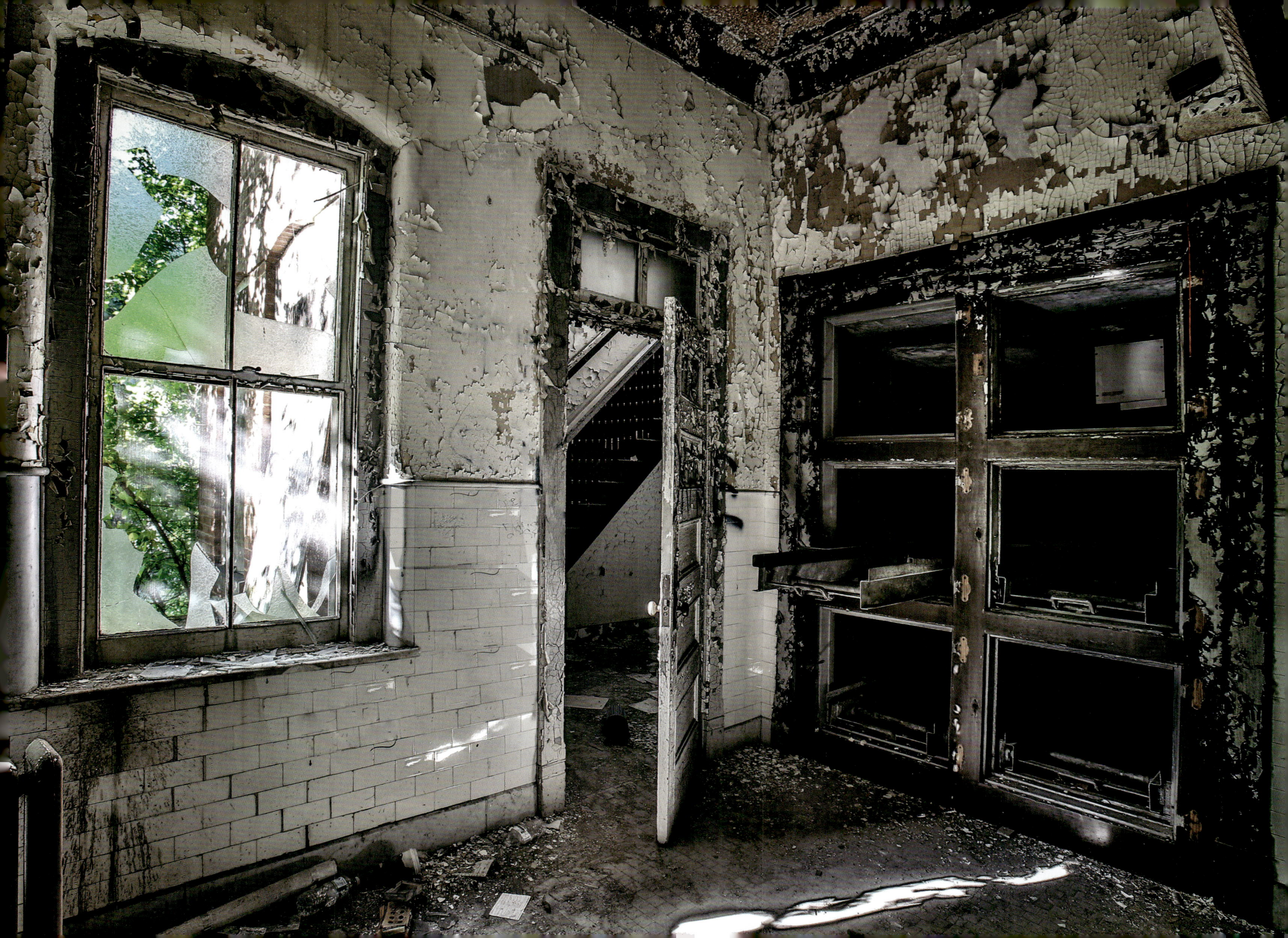

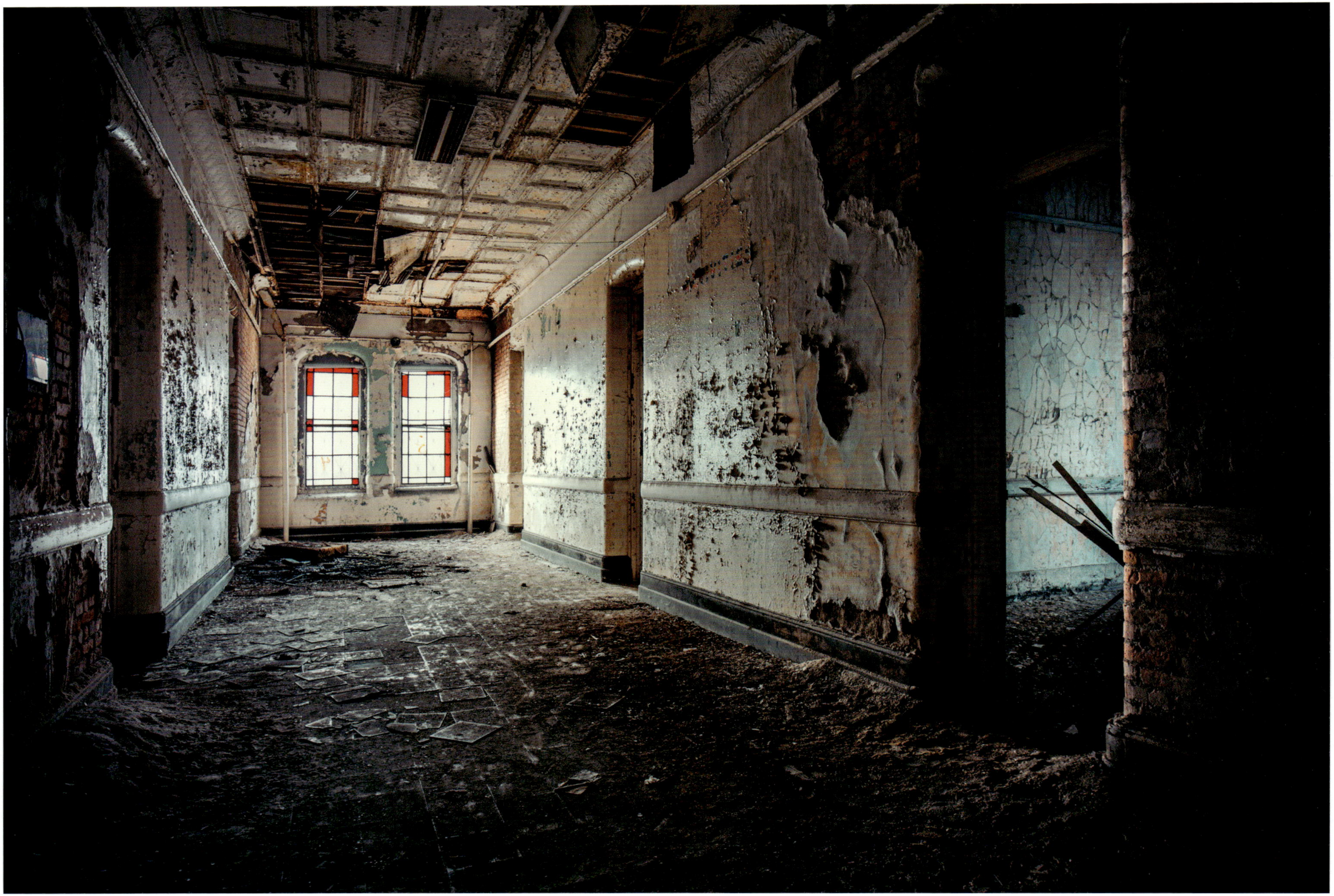

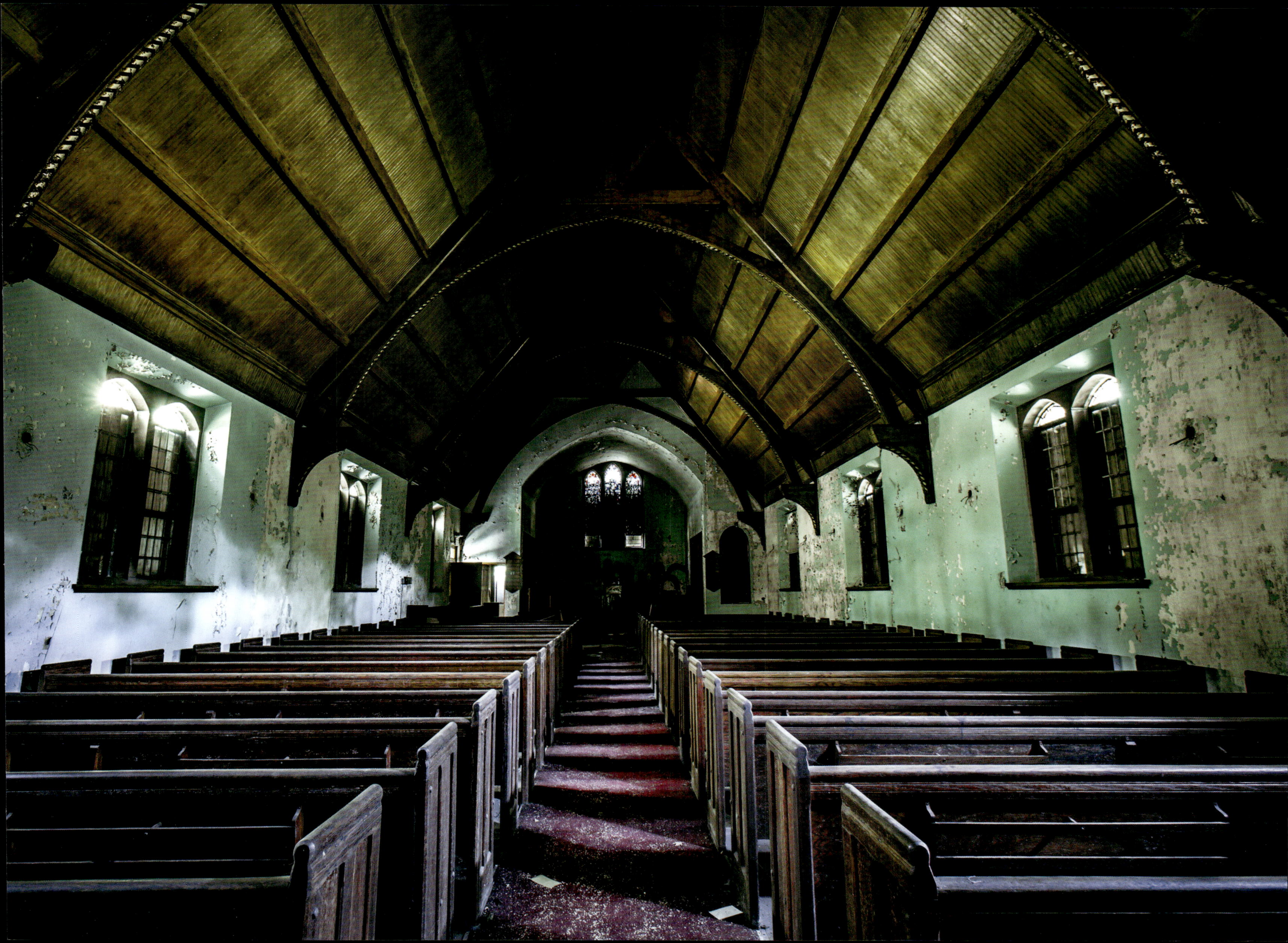

Westborough State Hospital

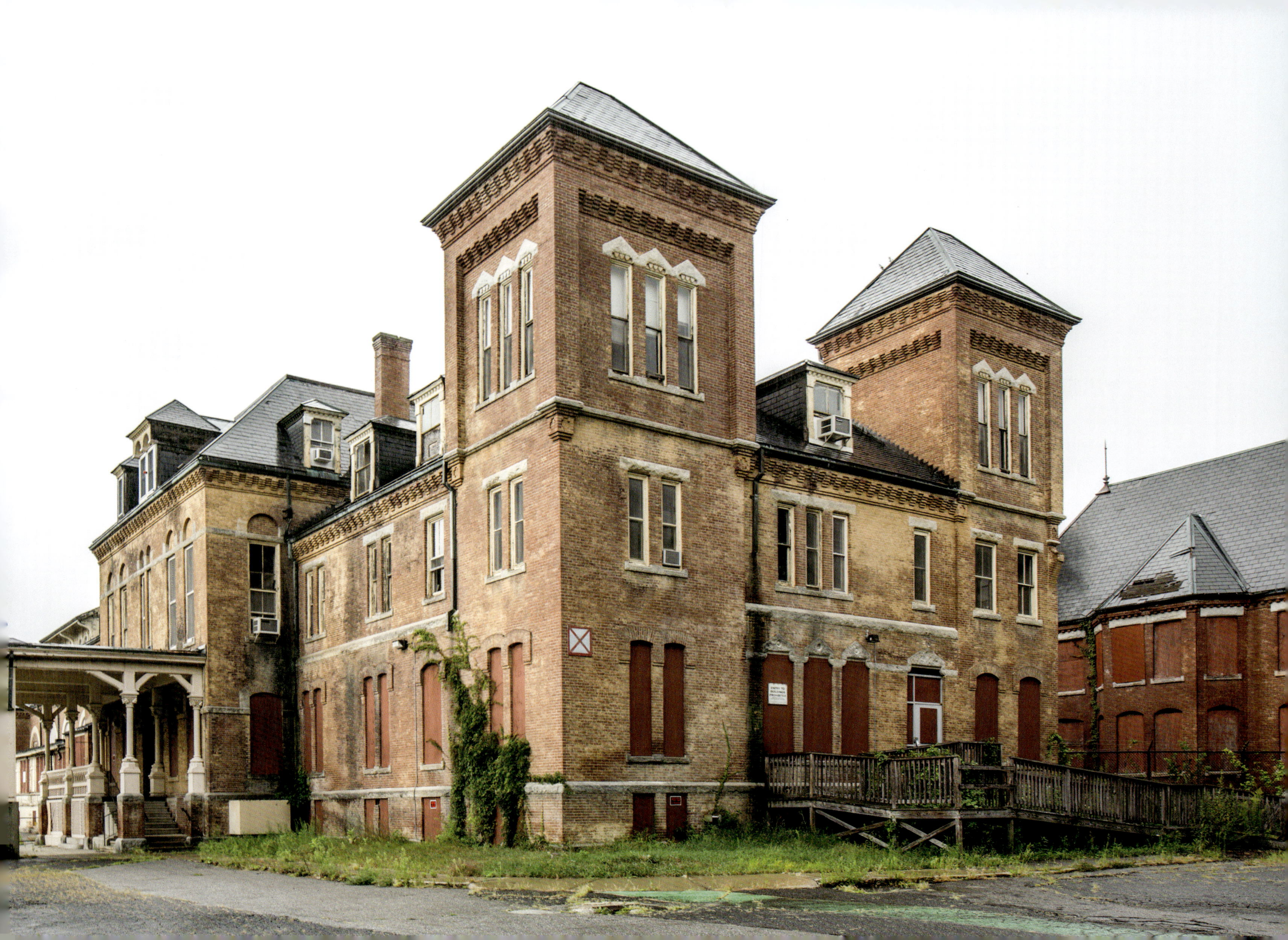

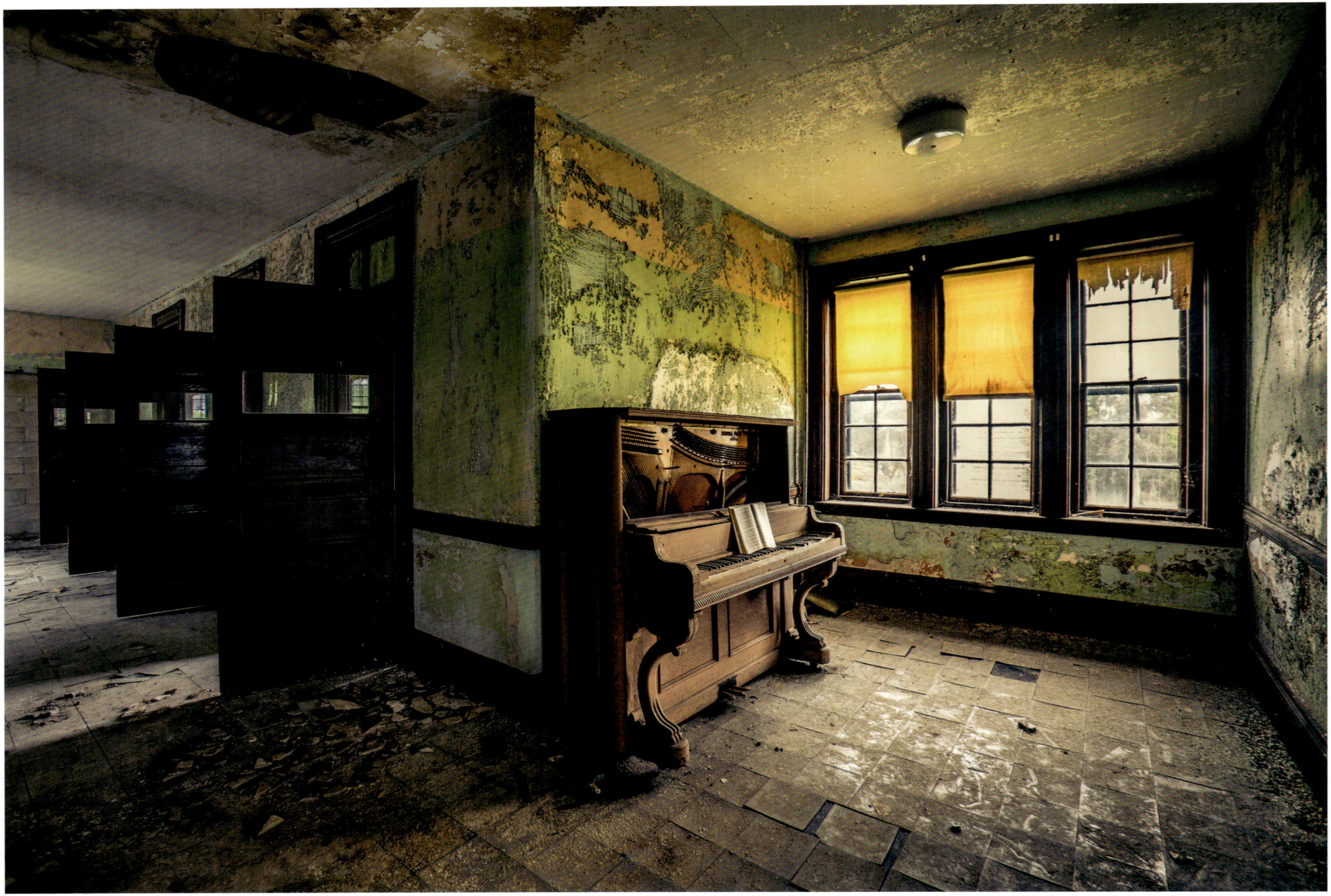

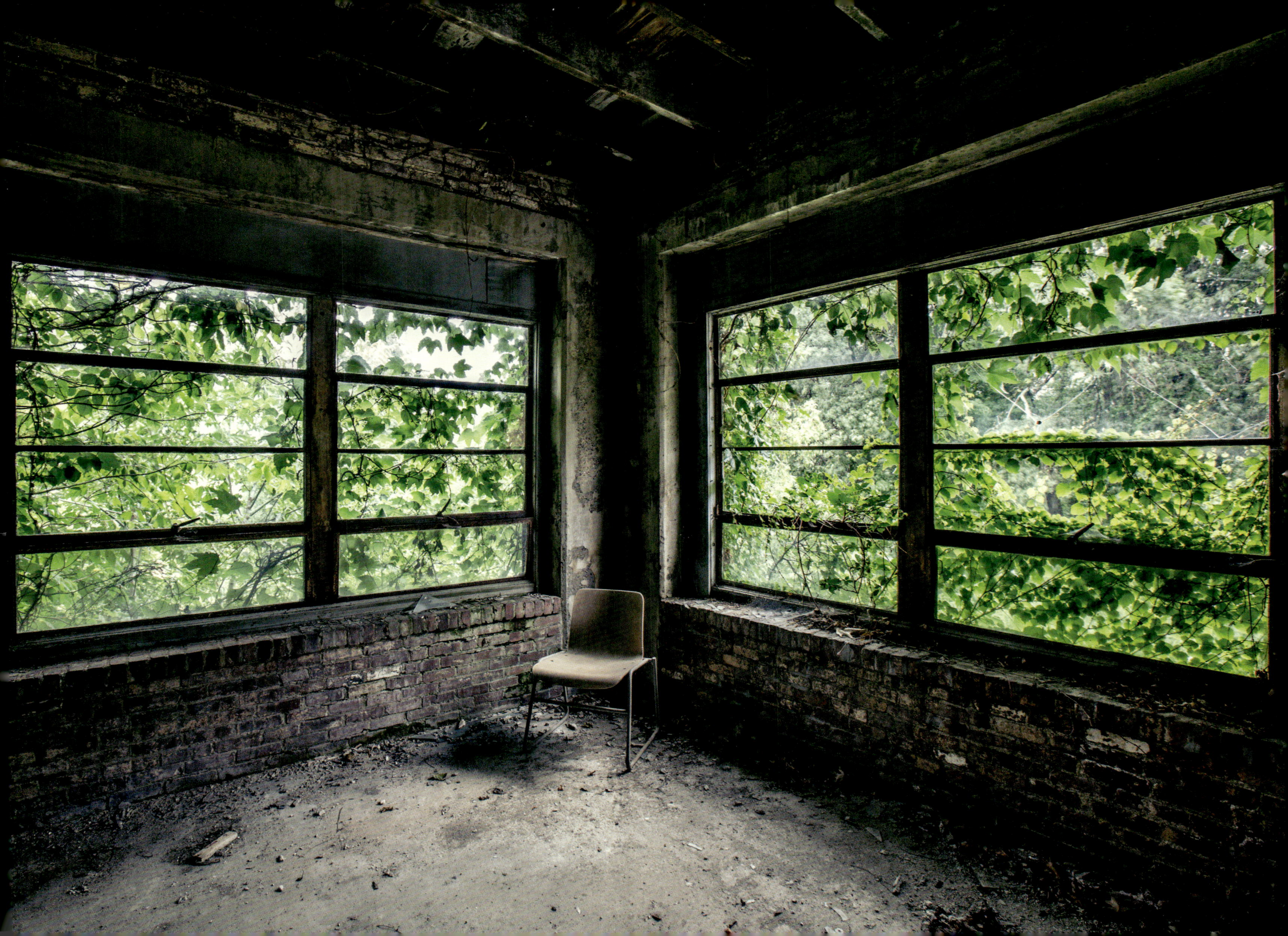

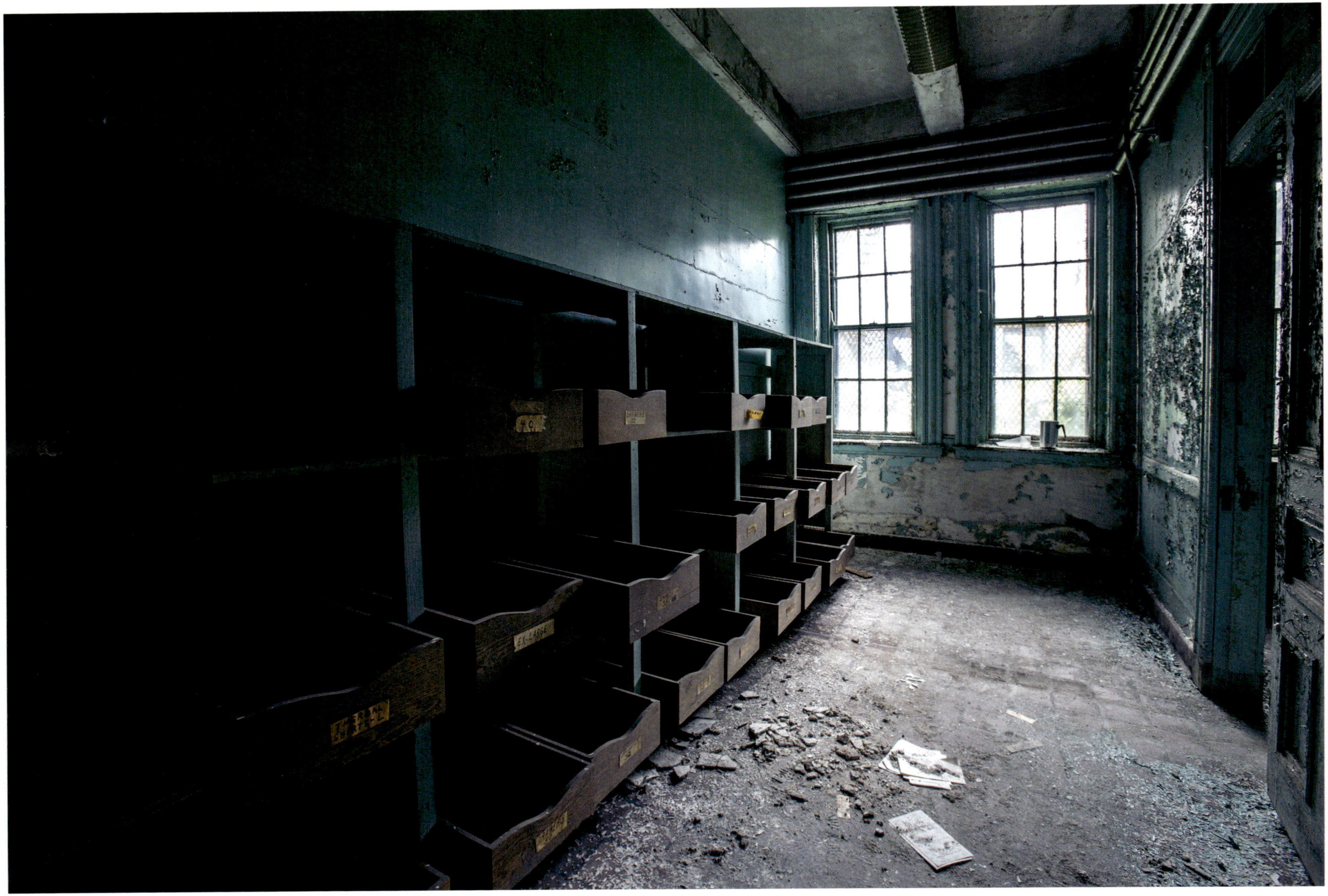

Patient Clothing storage

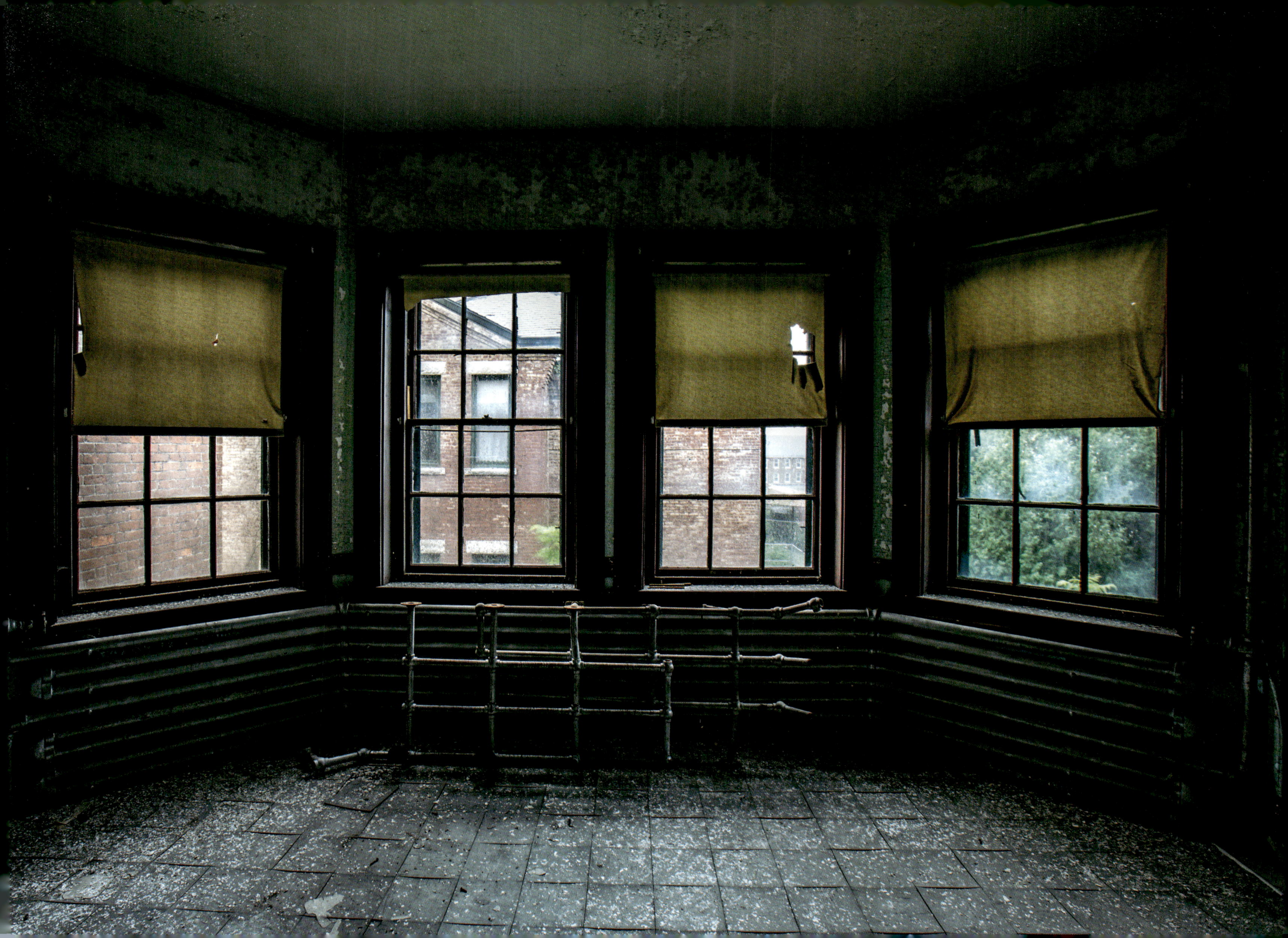

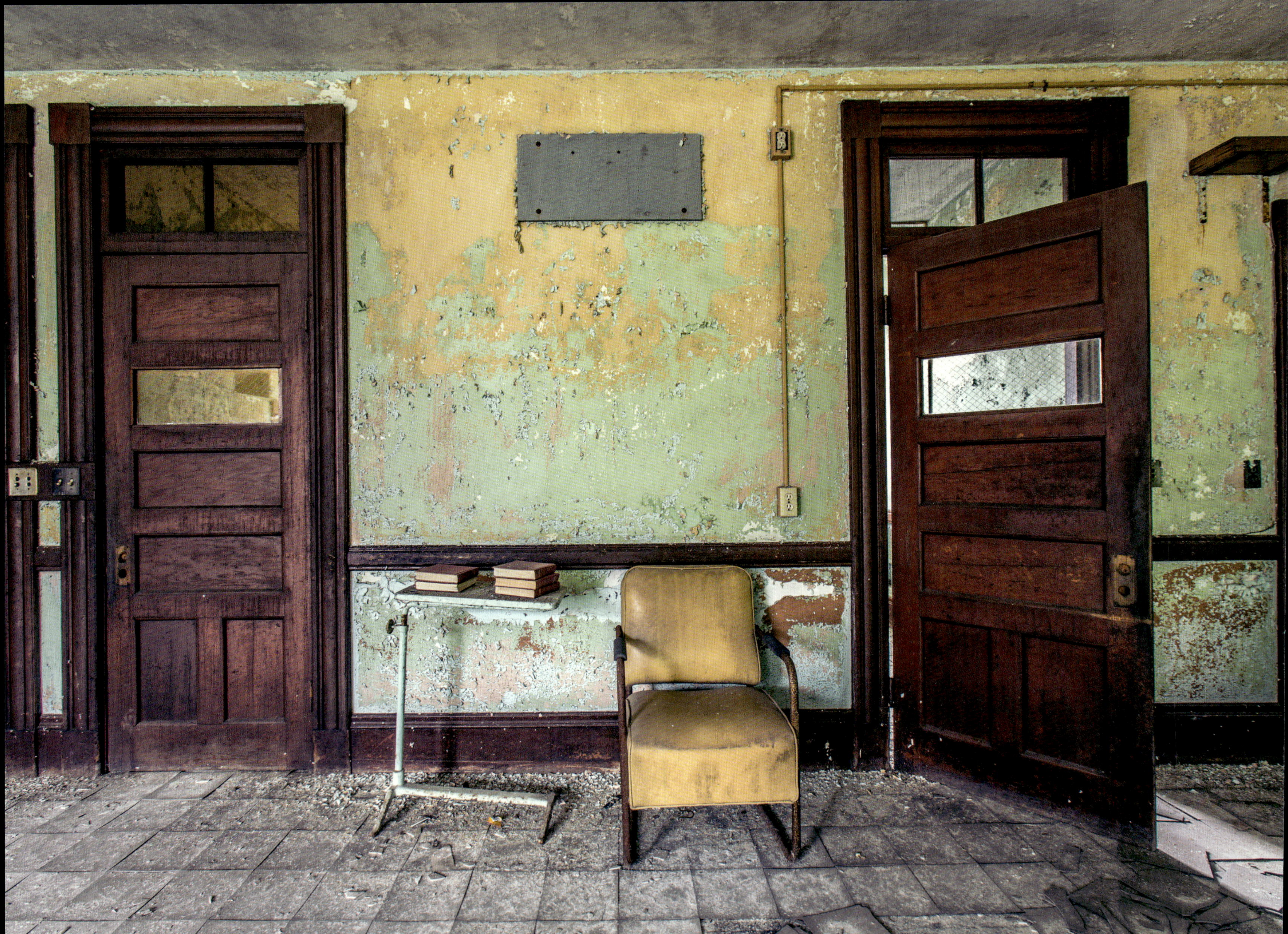

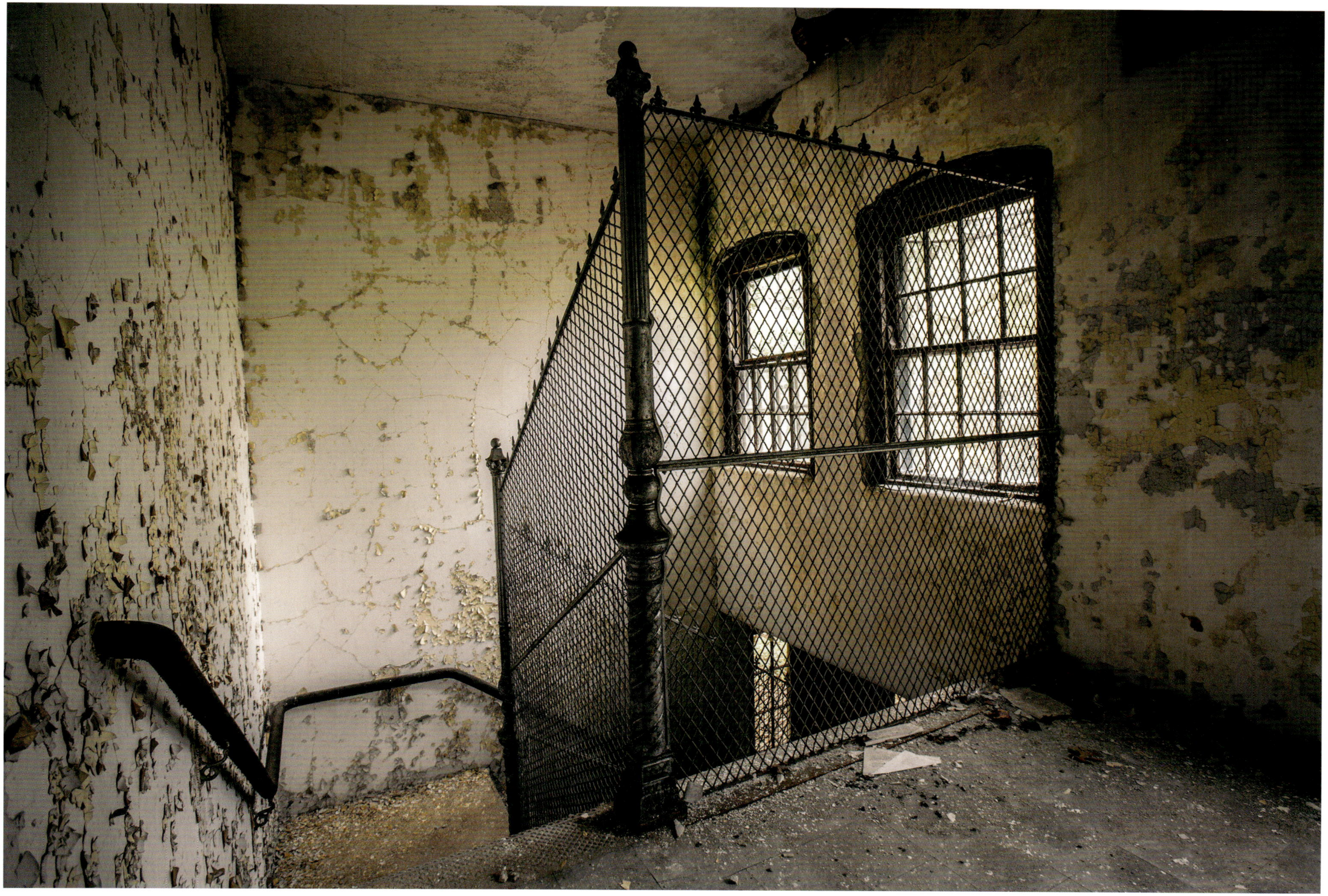

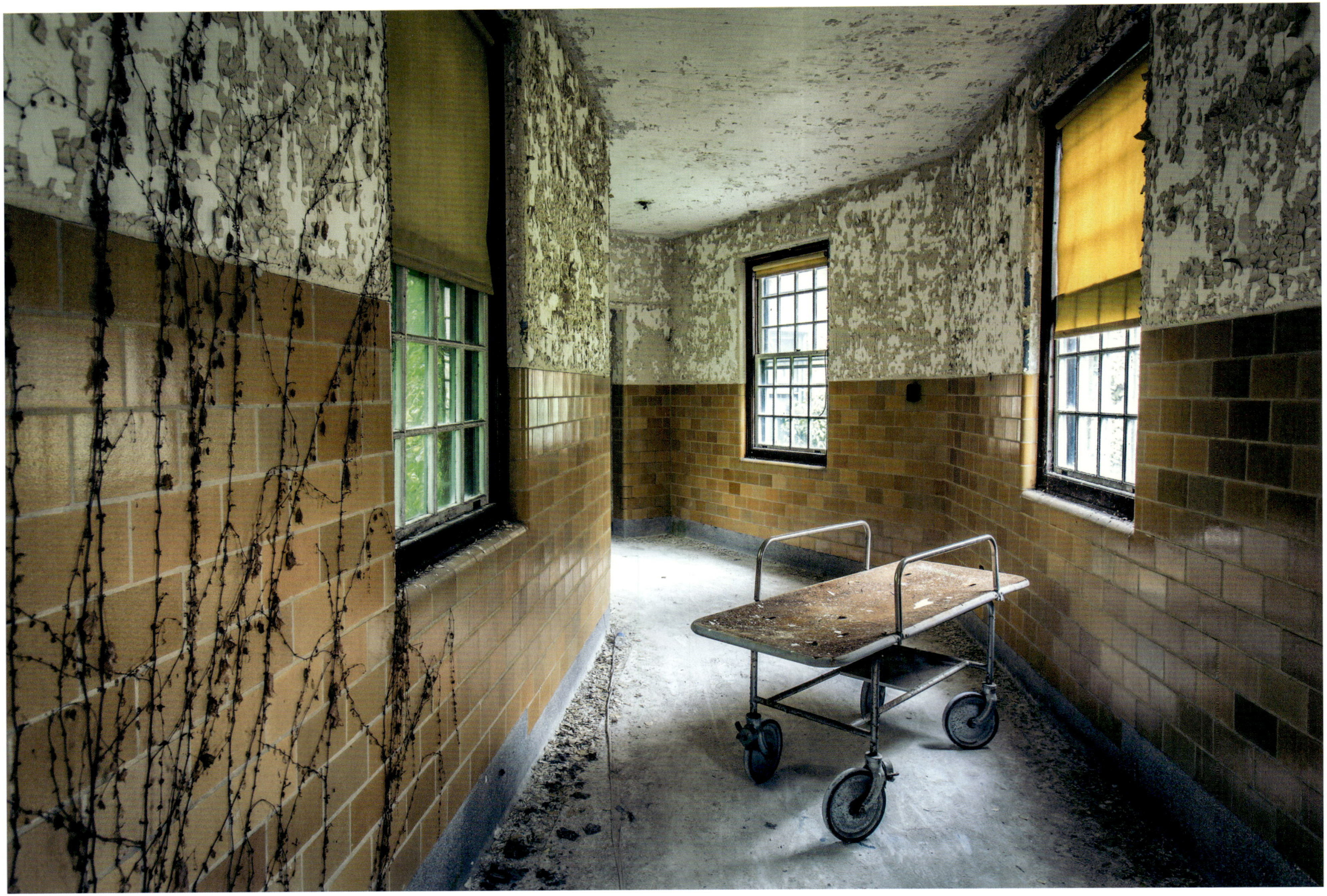

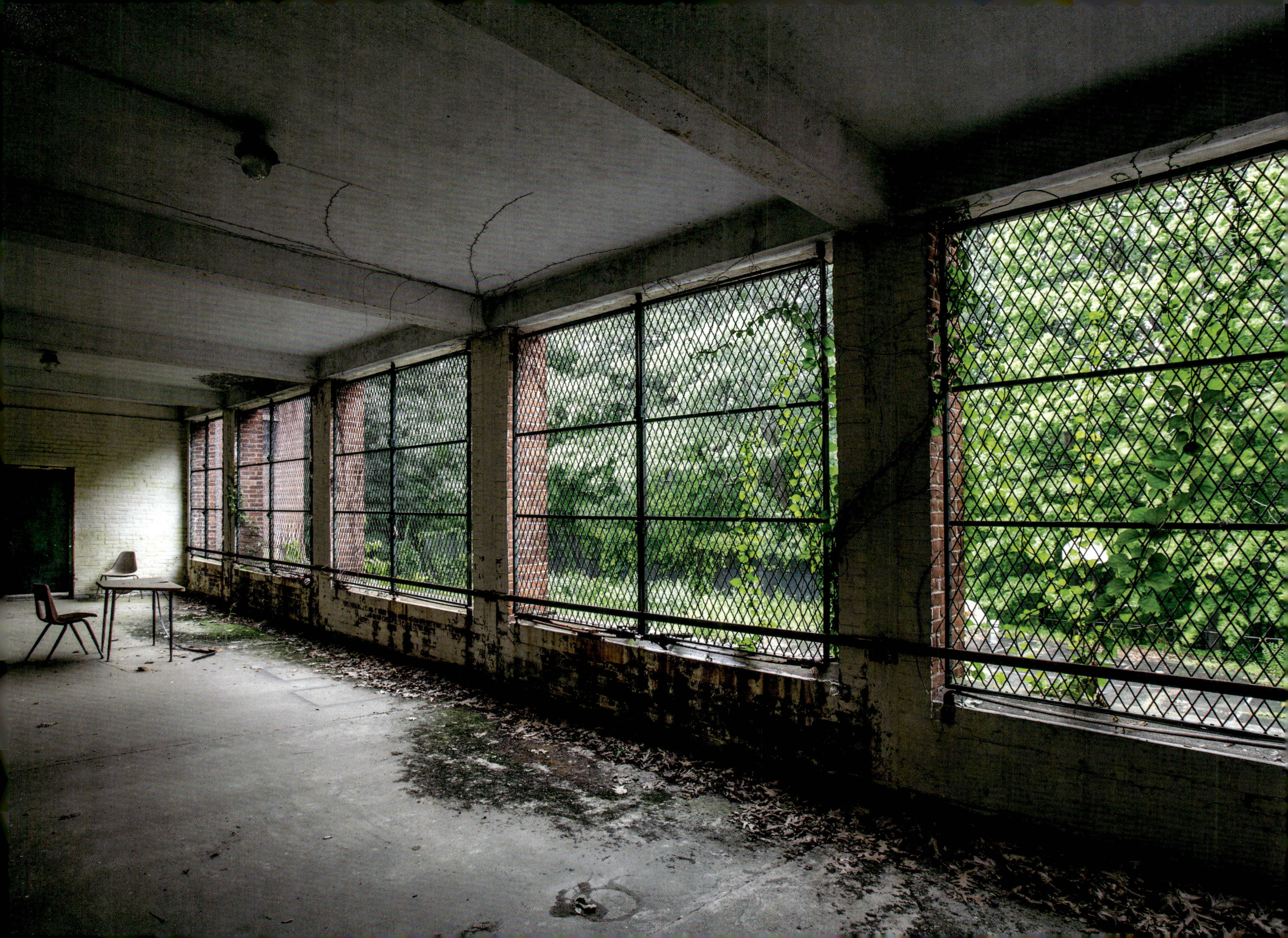

Hagedorn Psychiatric Hospital and Sanitorium

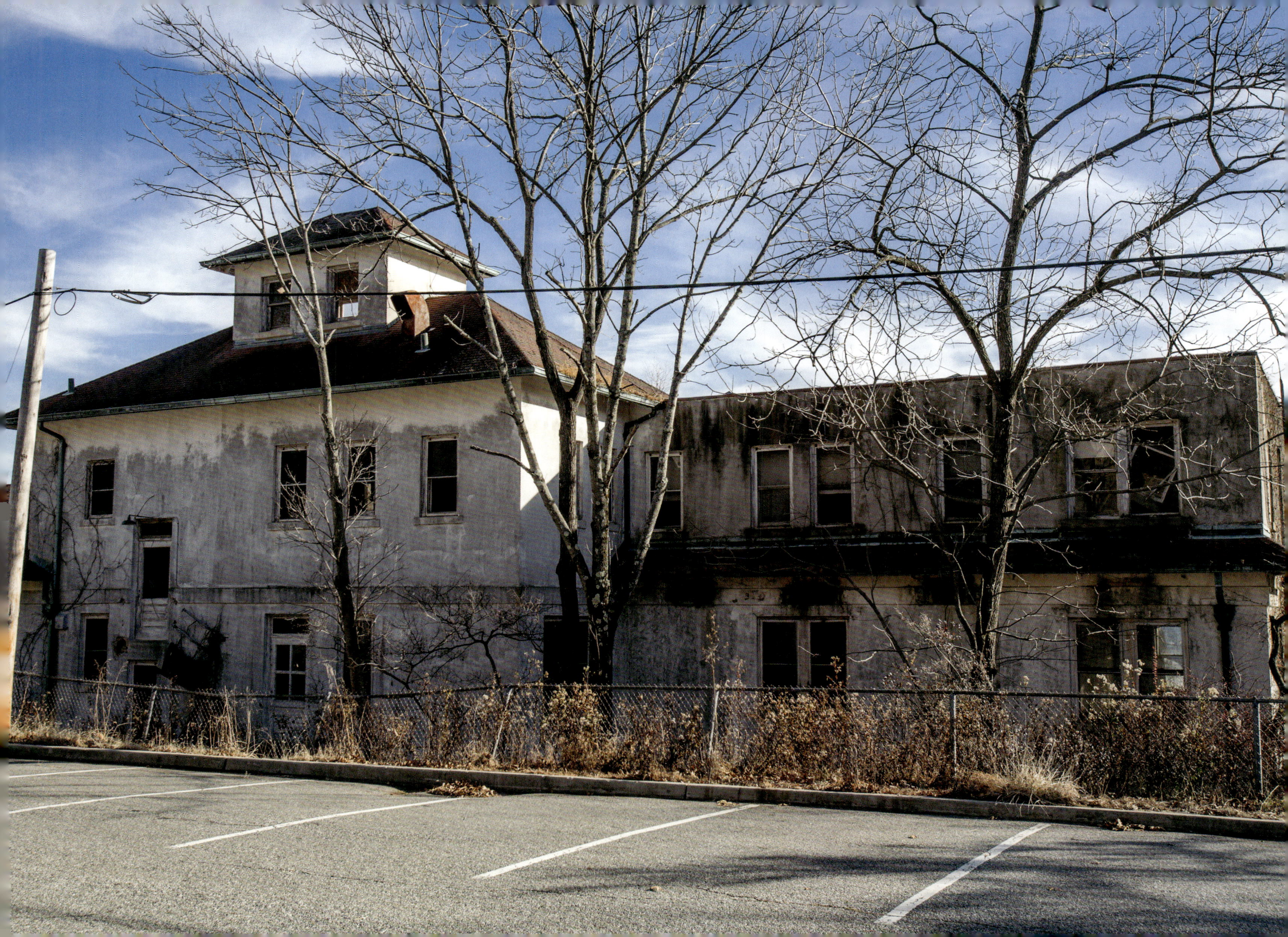

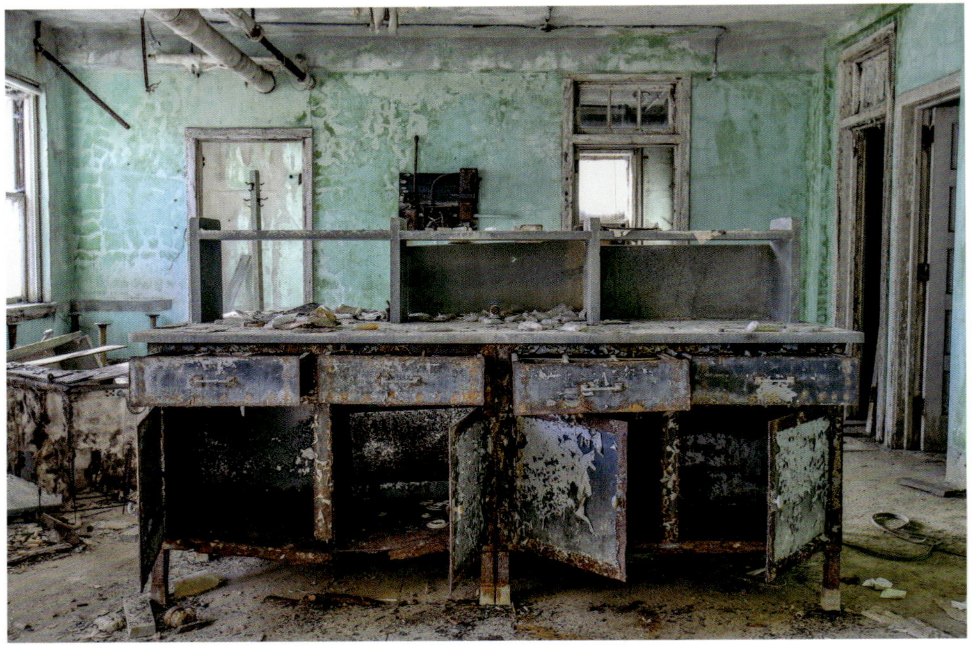

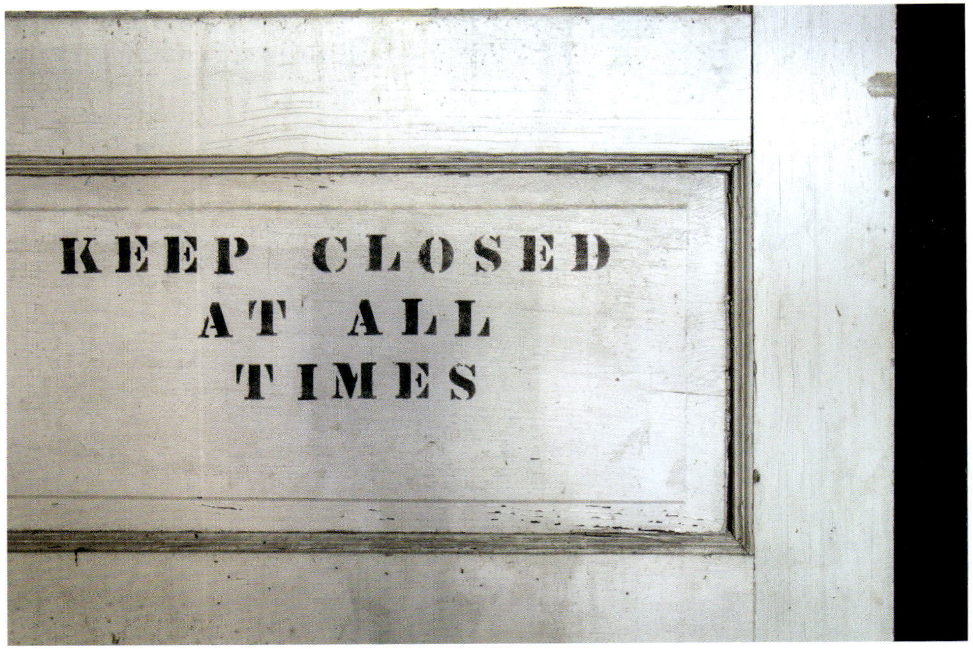
KEEP CLOSED
AT ALL
TIMES

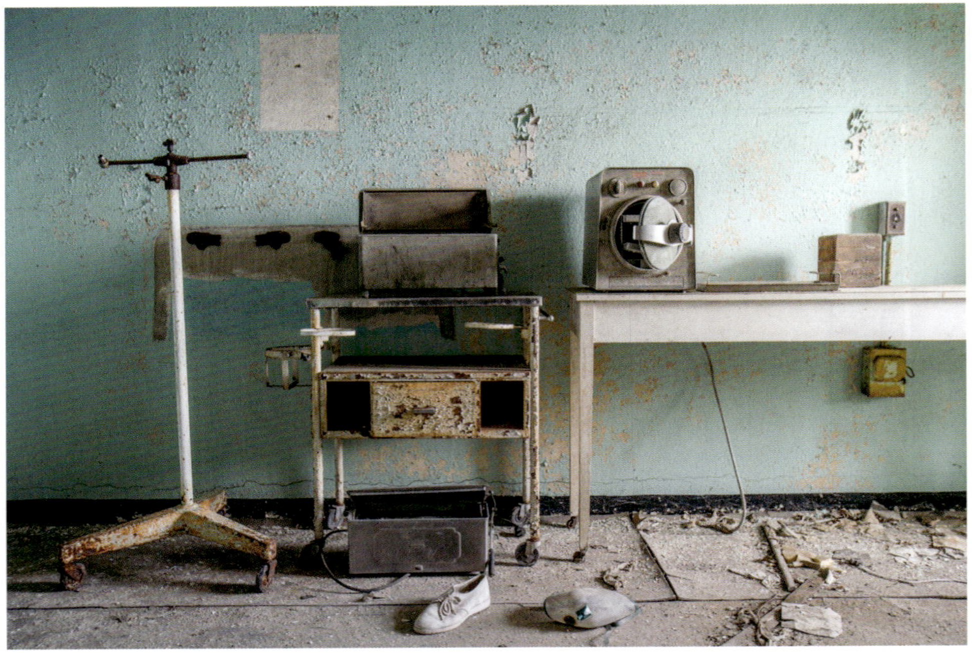

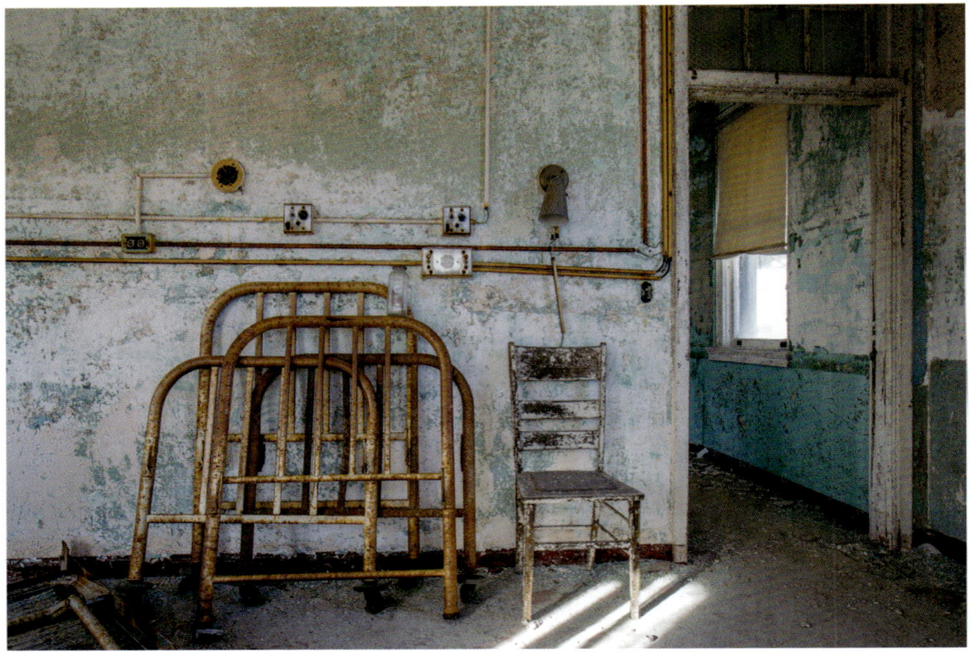

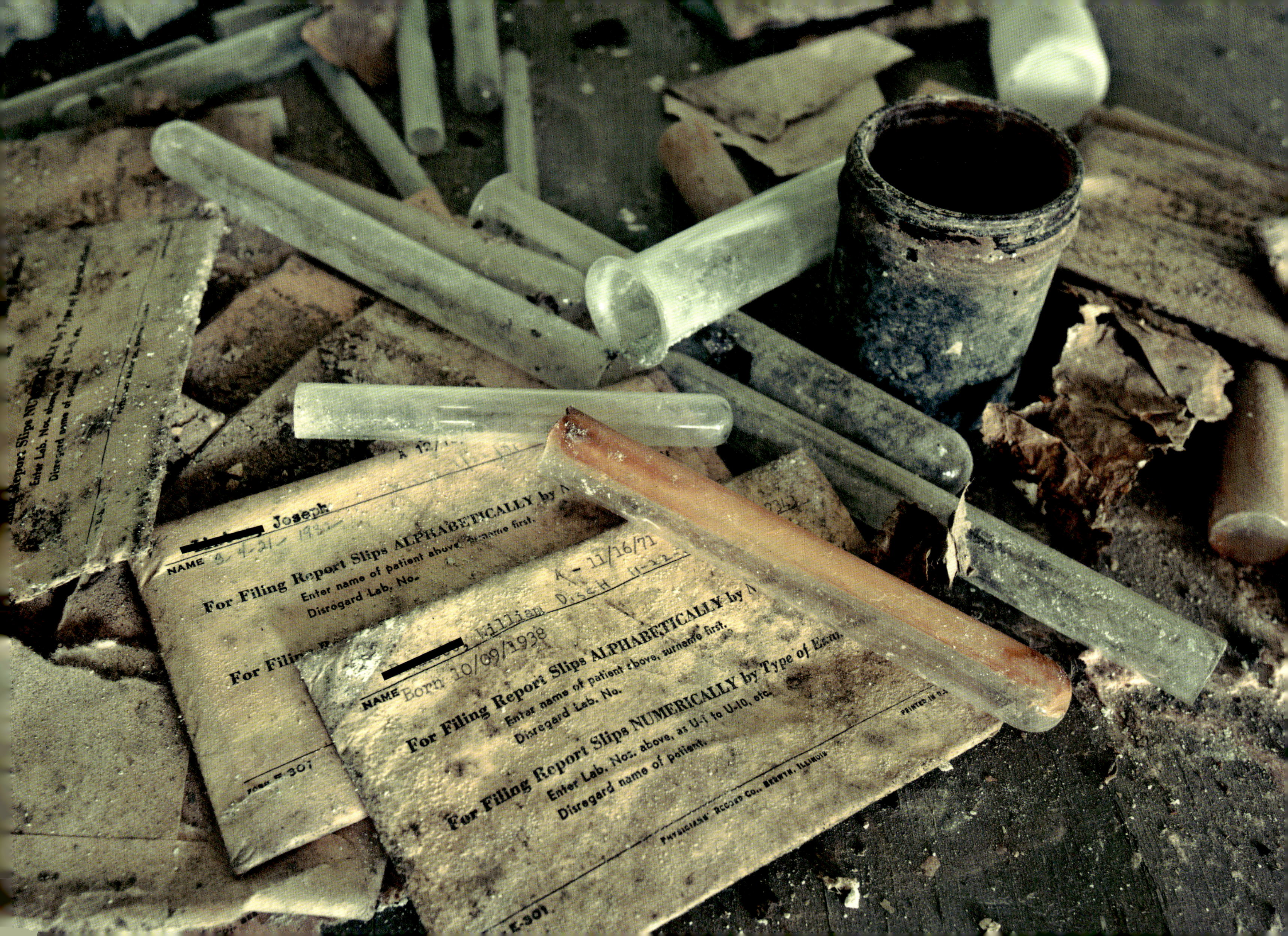

Joseph
NAME
For Filing Report Slips ALPHABETICALLY by
Enter name of patient above, surname first.
Disregard Lab. No.
A - 11/16/71
William
NAME Born 10/09/1938
For Filing Report Slips ALPHABETICALLY by
Enter name of patient above, surname first.
Disregard Lab. No.
For Filing Report Slips NUMERICALLY by Type of
Enter Lab. Nos. above, as U-1 to U-10, etc.
Disregard name of patient.
PHYSICIANS' RECORD CO., BERWYN, ILLINOIS
E-301

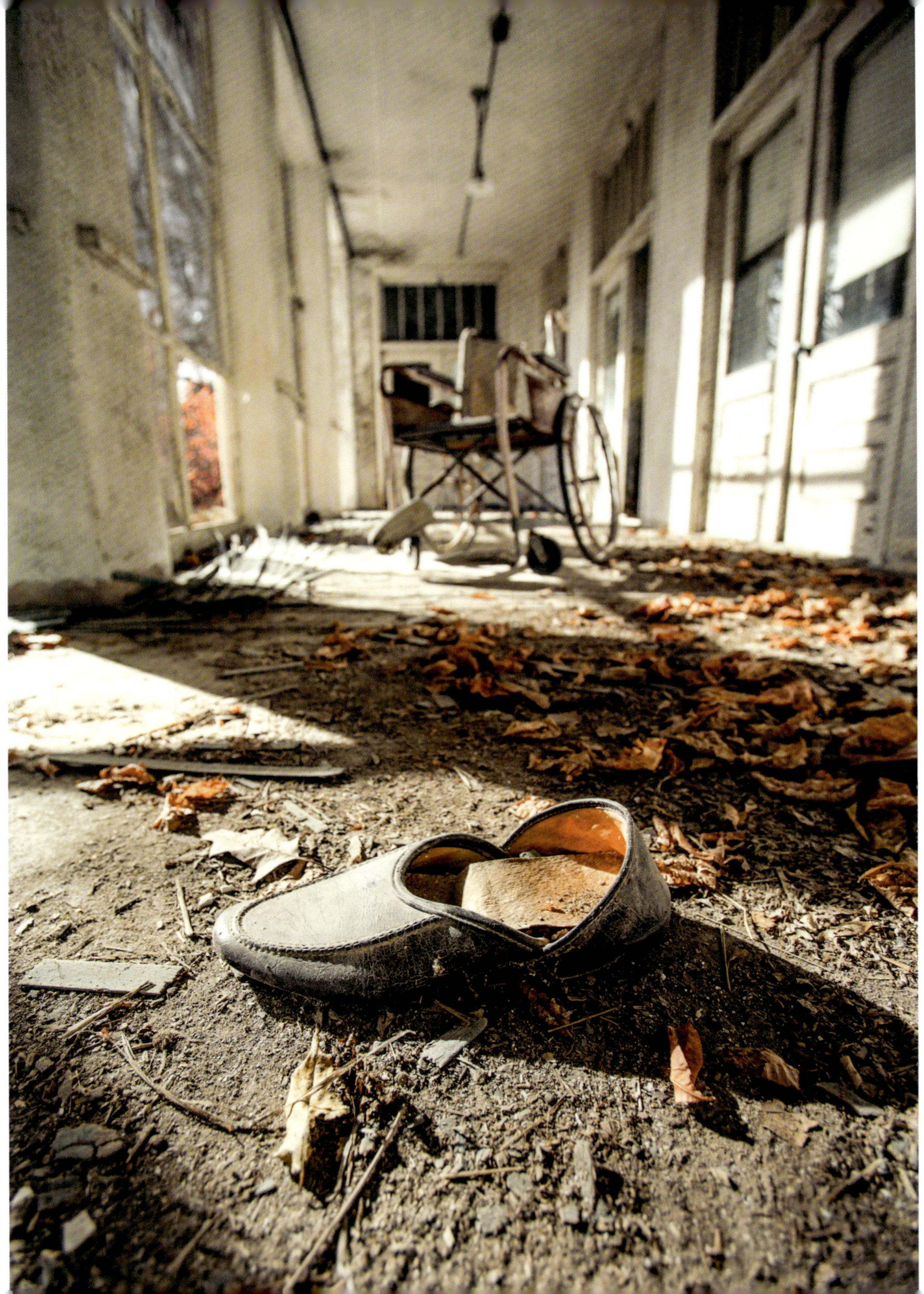

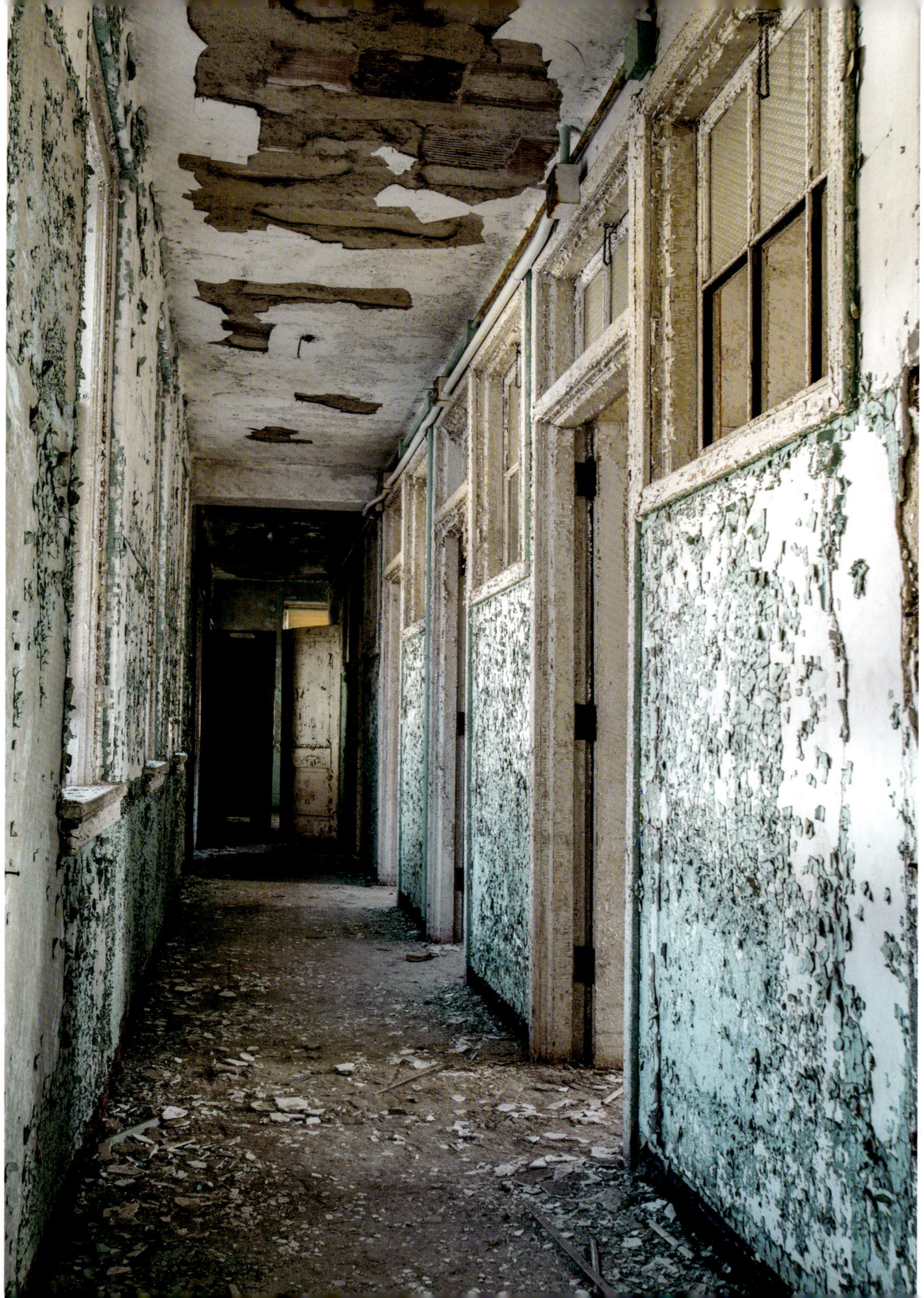

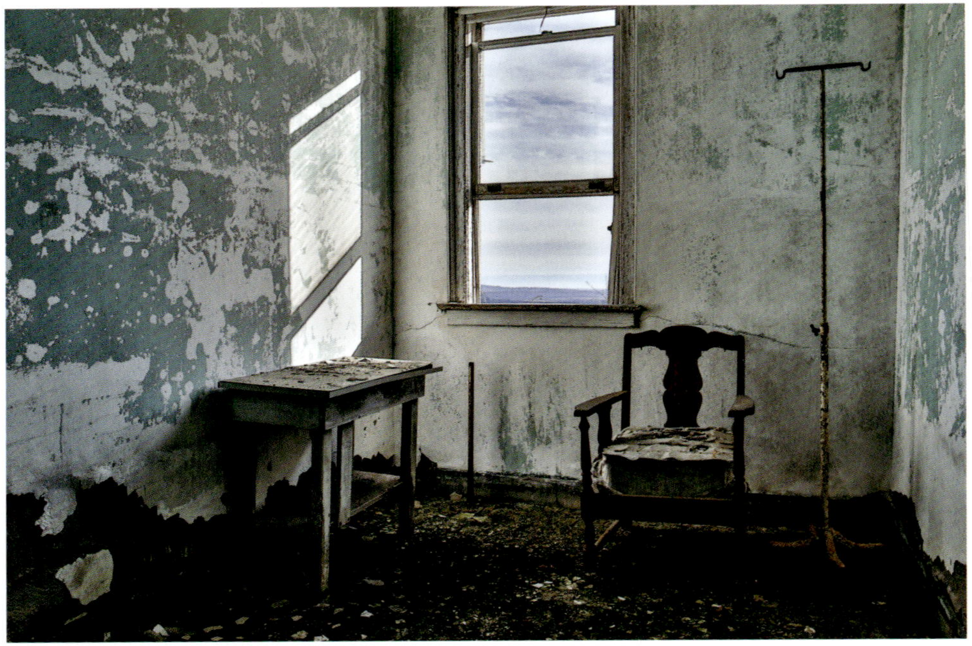

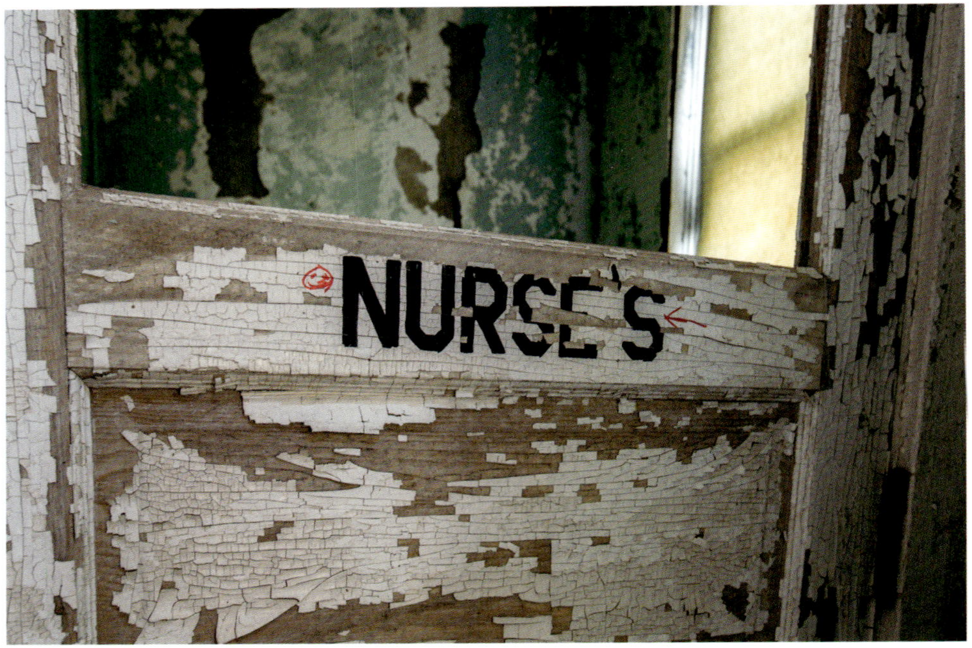
NURSE'S

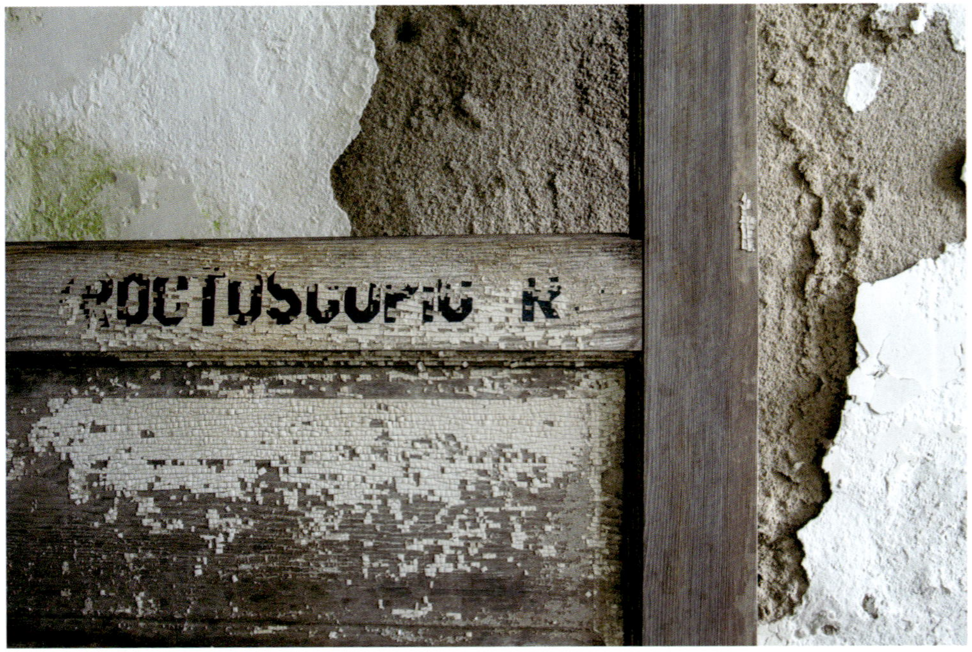

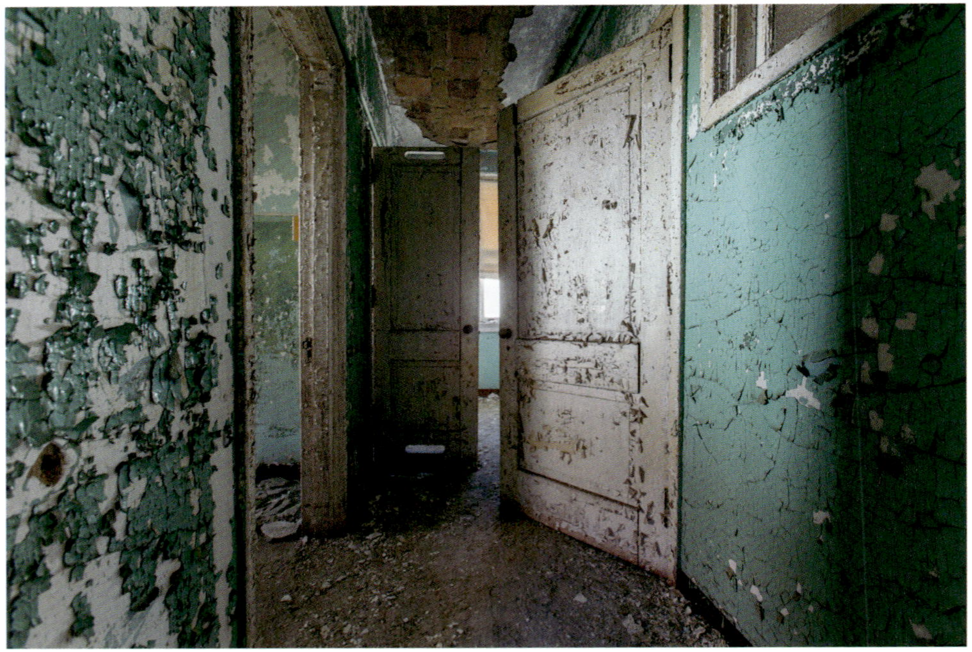

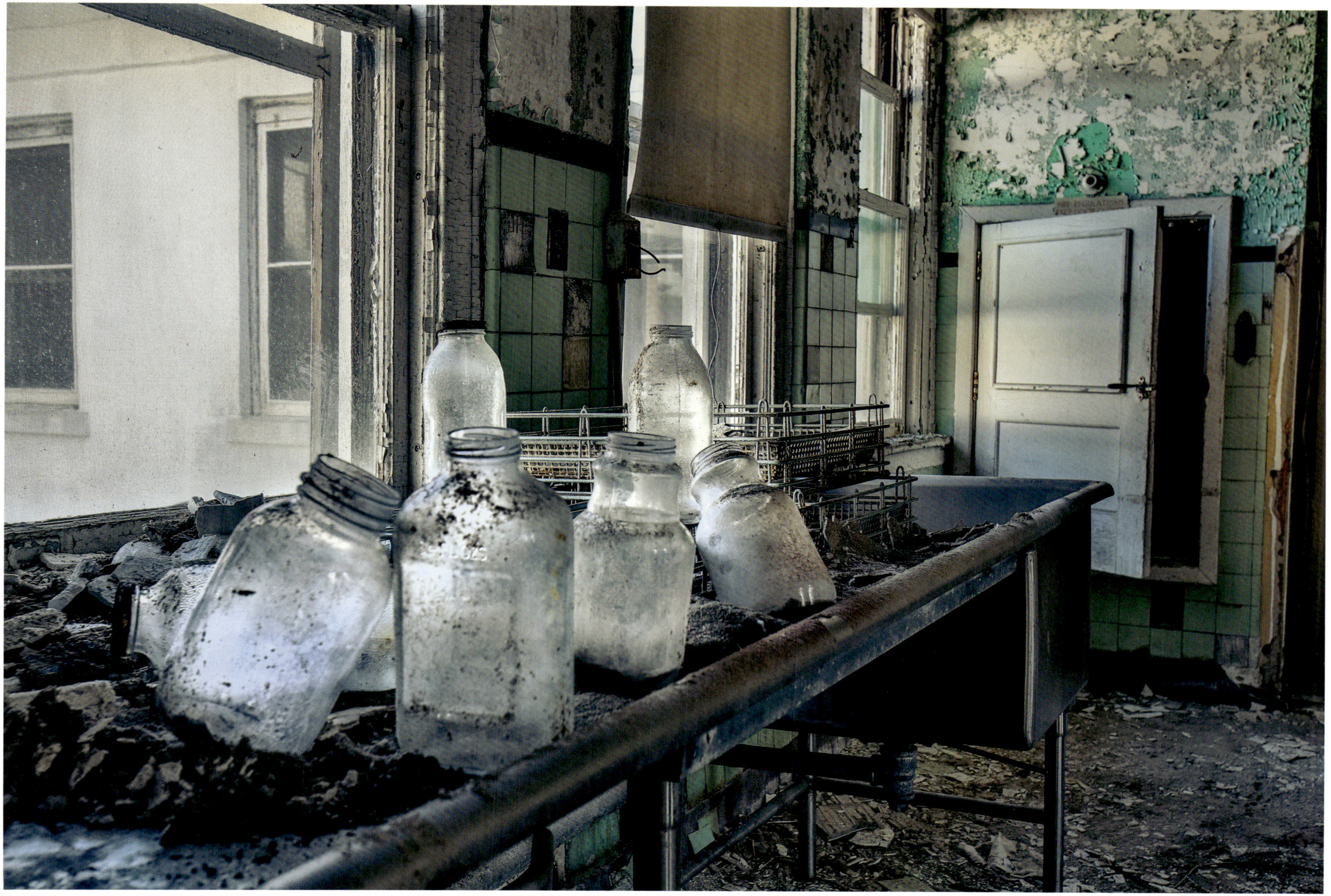

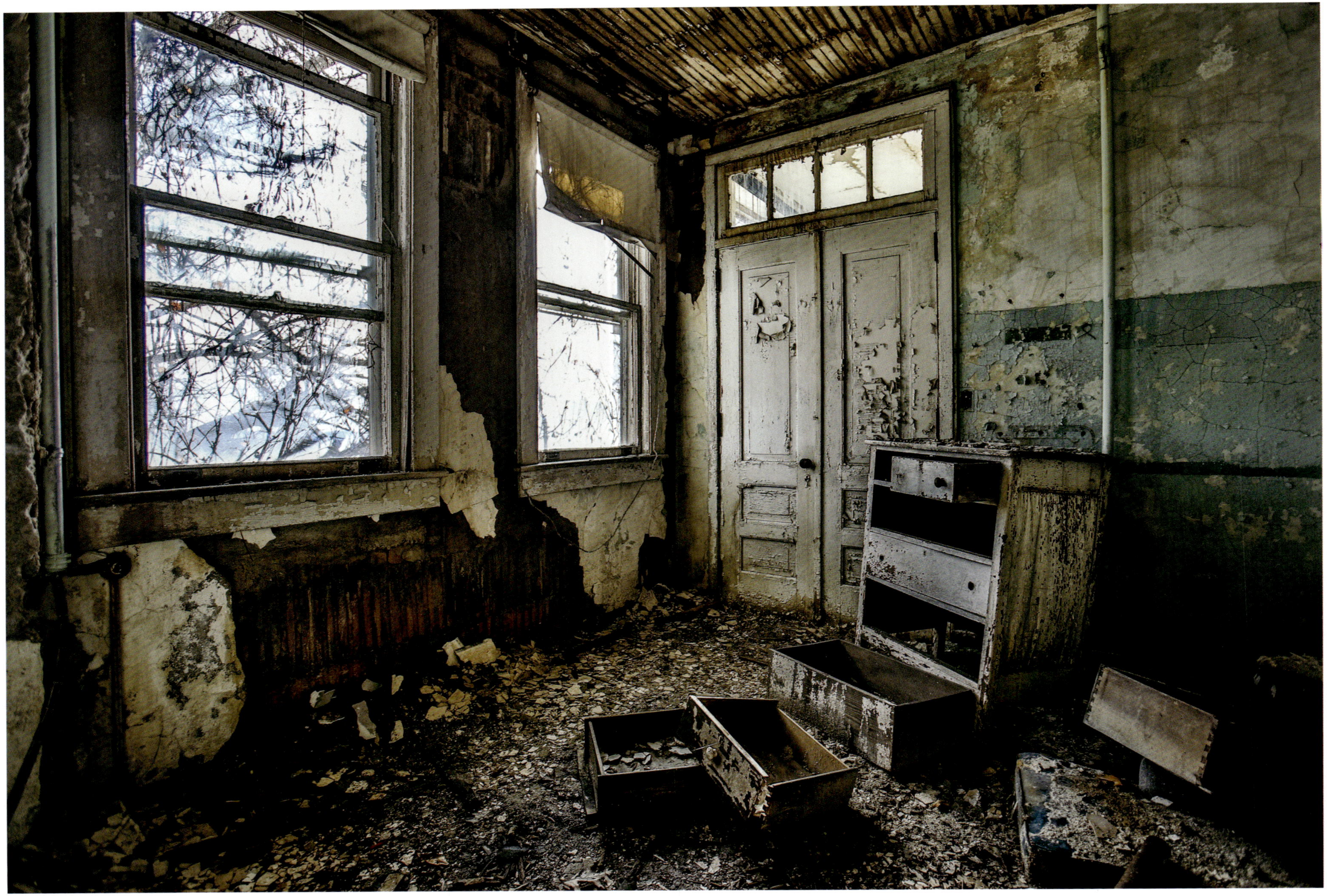

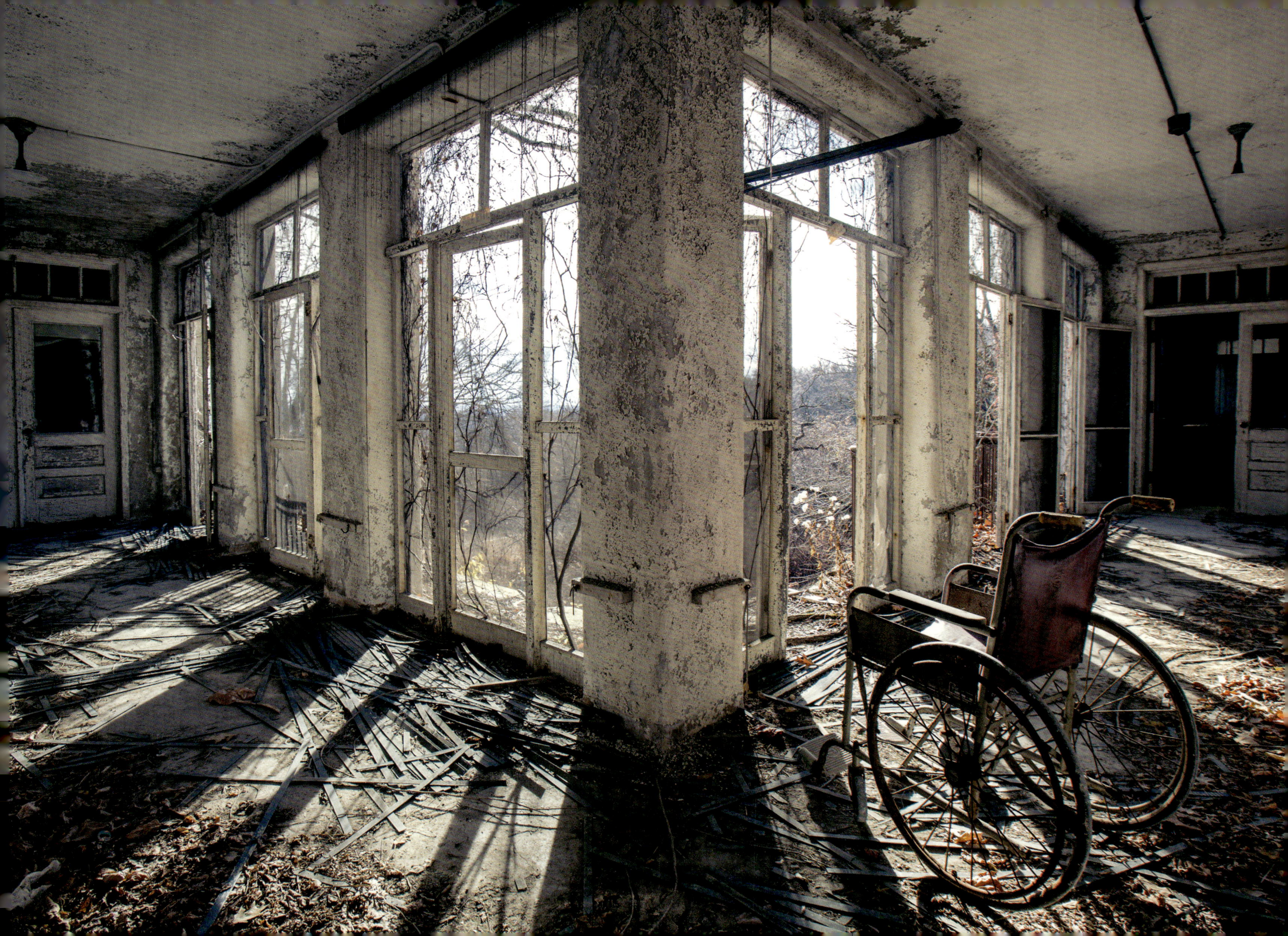

Craig House Hospital

Craig House Hospital is a picturesque, Civil War-era Gothic mansion set deep in the mountains. The 350 sprawling acres of professionally landscaped property include an indoor swimming pool, a gymnasium, a private golf course, a library and facilities for horseback riding. Among the exotic trees replanted from around the world are weeping beech, oak and endangered gingko; there are also sprawling vineyards. The property has a compelling history, with characters whose tragedies and eccentricities are unique even by today's standards.

At first glance, it seems to be an estate of the ultra-wealthy. But that's only half the truth: in 1915, it was transformed into "Craig House"– the finest psychiatric hospital in the country and possibly the world, providing celebrities and the wealthy with a place of refuge in times of mental despair. Although official records are hard to come by, it has long been said that Craig House was a safe haven for Zelda Fitzgerald (wife of acclaimed writer F. Scott Fitzgerald); Frances Ford Seymour (Jane Fonda's mother, and wife of Henry Fonda); the "Hidden Kennedy", Rosemary Kennedy; Marilyn Monroe; Jackie Gleason; and Truman Capote. The most famous inmates, however, were Frances Ford Seymour and Rosemary Kennedy.

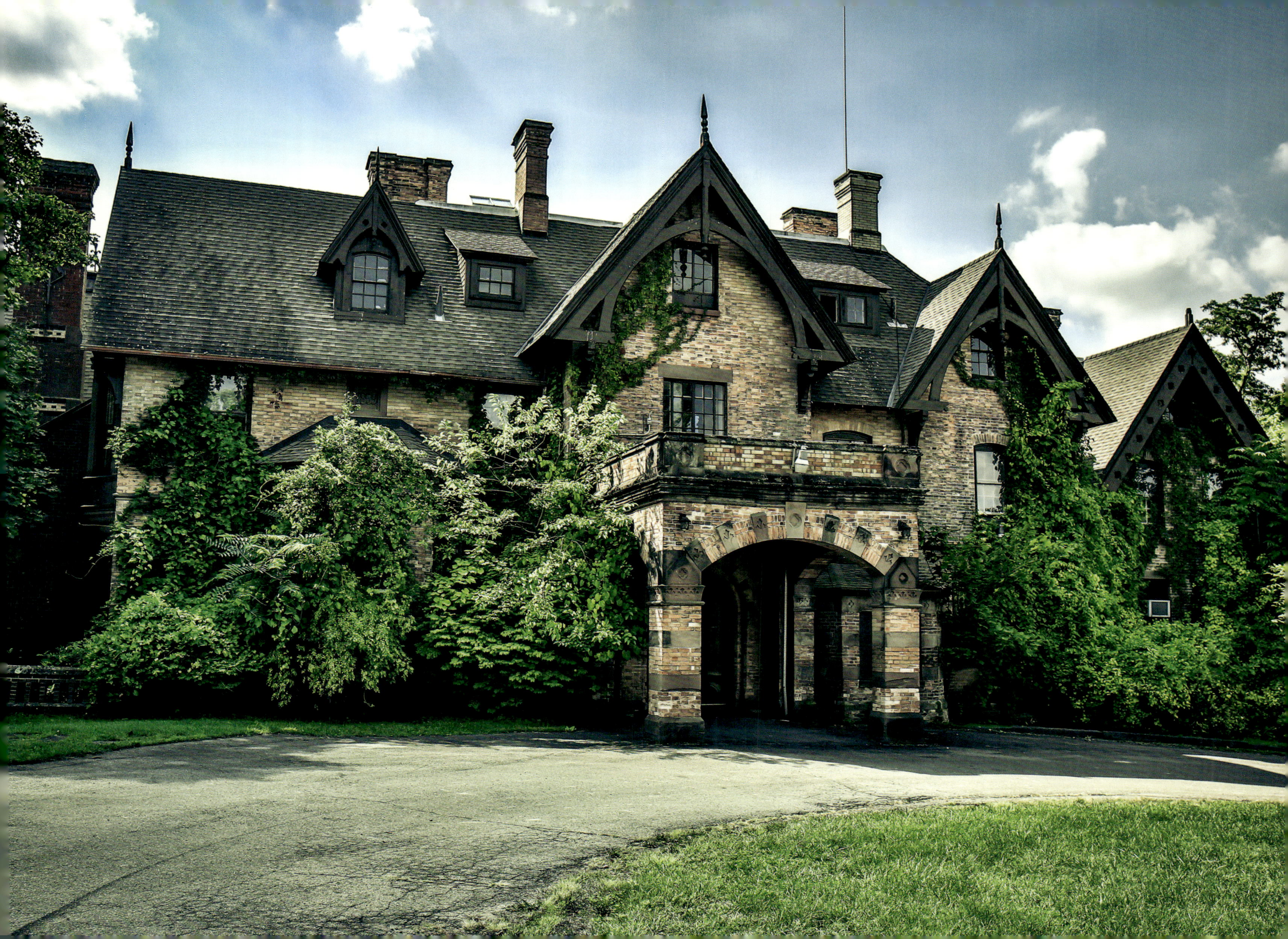

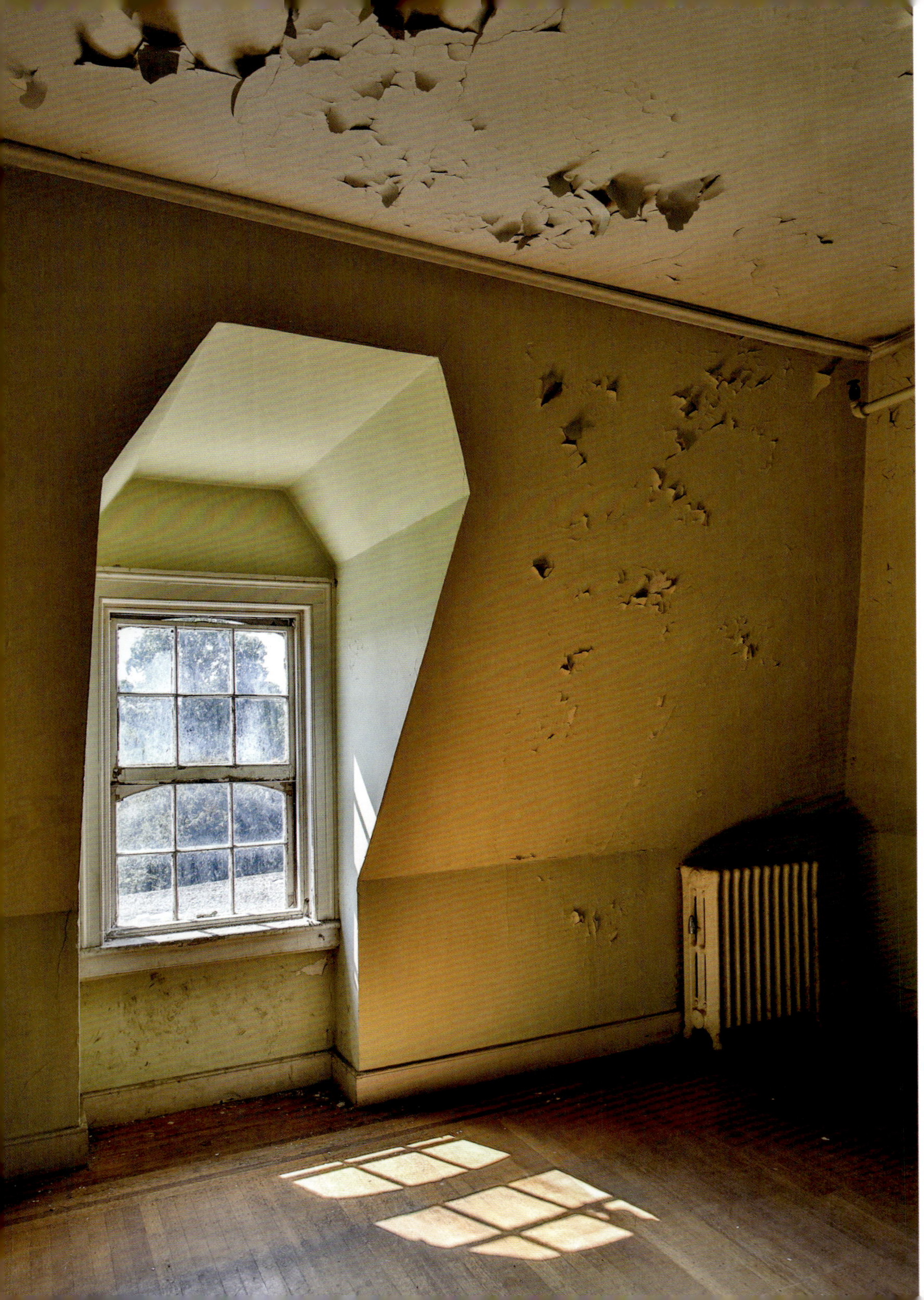

The house was designed and built in 1859 by Frederick Clarke Withers (architect of the Hudson River State Hospital) for the Civil War general, Joseph Howland; it was christened the Tioronda estate. Howland, who was born into a prominent merchant family, had lived a relatively unremarkable life until the outbreak of the Civil War in 1861. He quickly rose through the ranks, and as a commander at the Battle of Gaines's Mill in the Peninsula campaign, was struck in the leg by a Confederate bullet while directing his men. The wound did not deter him and he refused to leave the fight, staying with his men until the end of the battle. Due to his courageous actions, he was awarded the rank of general; however, the wound spelled the end of his military career. In the post-war years, Howland became involved in politics. He played a key role in plans for the Hudson River State Hospital and also fought for the humane treatment of people with mental health problems.

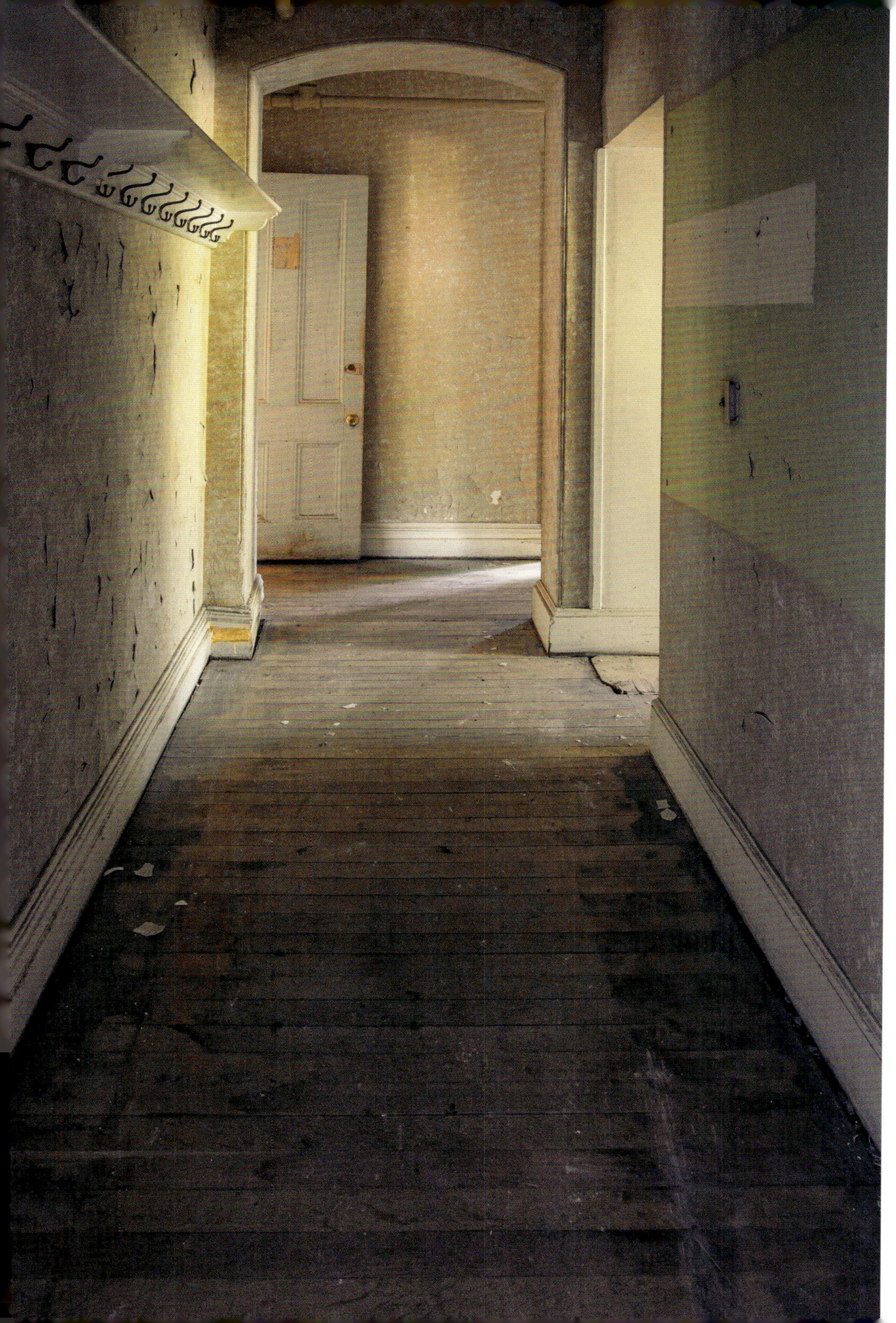

In 1915, some twenty years after Howland's death, the Tioronda estate was sold to Dr Clarence Slocum and rechristened "Craig House" in tribute to a progressive psychiatric facility in Scotland. Dr Slocum's aspirctions for Craig House were similarly progressive – he believed that patients could be cured through intensive talking therapy partnered with fine dining, leisure activities and recreational pursuits. He didn't believe in psychoanalysis, and instead focused on positive patient-doctor relationships, hydrotherapy, and occupational therapy based around arts and crafts, woodworking and weaving. There were no locked doors and no bars on the windows. Patients were free to socialize and to come and go from their private quarters (which had their own bathroom and living room); they had meals alongside the private nursing staff. Today, the only external evidence that the property was once a private hospital is a rusted metal-worked caduceus still visible on one of the brick chimneys.

Rosemary Kennedy arrived at Craig House in 1941 after a botched lobotomy had left her partially paralysed; her head tilted, frozen to her shoulder; and the fingers of her left hand had become gnarled and unresponsive. The twinkle in her eyes was gone; all that she'd once been was lost. She has since been dubbed the "hidden Kennedy" and the "first tragedy of the Kennedys". Abandoned by her family, she was treated as though she did not exist so as not to tarnish the almost "royal" reputation of America's favorite family.

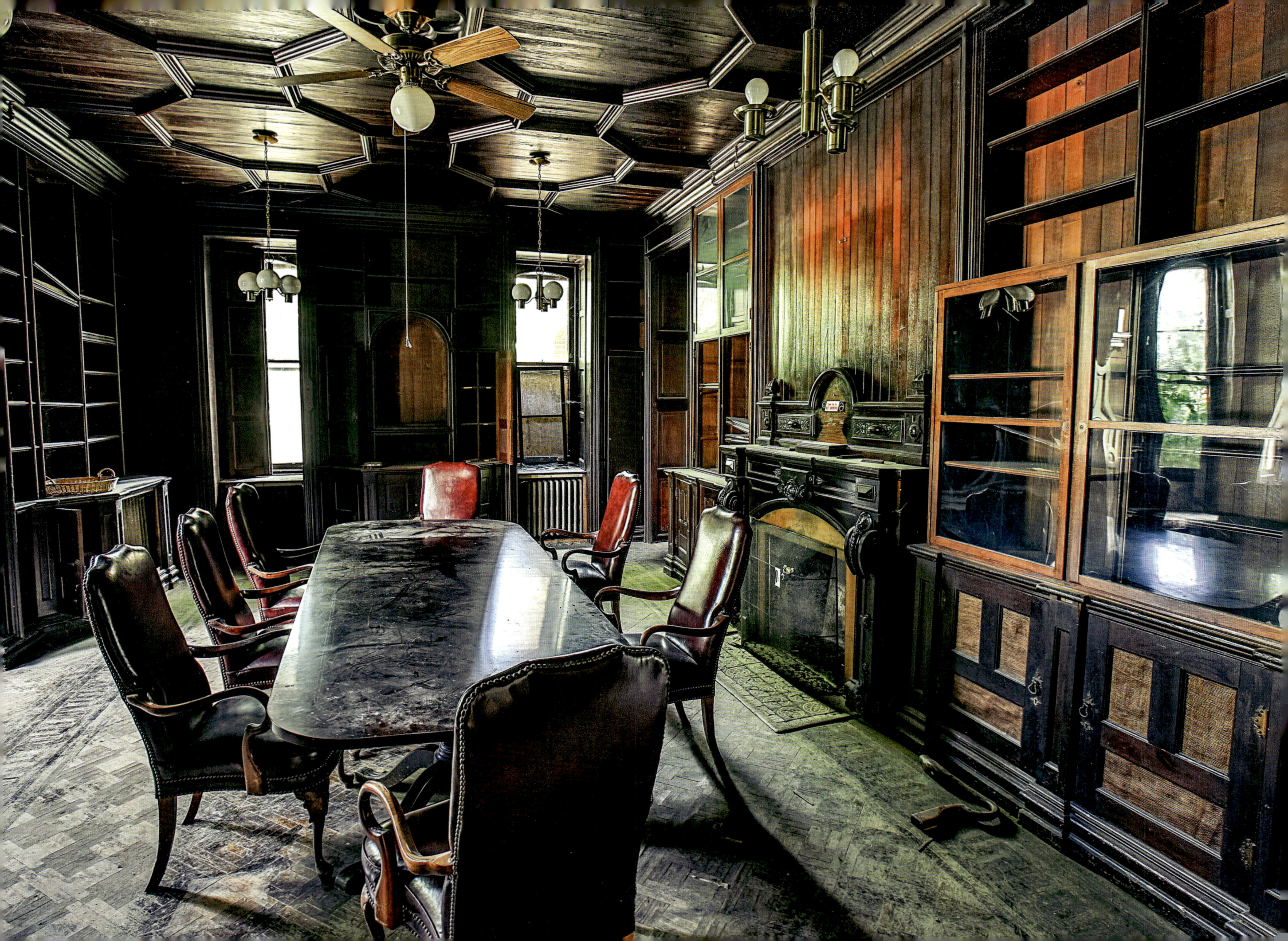

One Kennedy family biographer has described Rosemary as "absolutely beautiful", with "a gorgeous smile". At 20, she was "a picturesque young woman, a snow princess with flush cheeks, gleaming smile, plump figure, and a sweetly ingratiating manner to almost everyone she met". However, she suffered from behavioral problems and fell behind in her studies; her siblings outshone her in sport. Rosemary had an IQ of 60 or 70 (attributed to a nurse, who, during the birth, waited too long to call a doctor, thus depriving the baby of oxygen). Throughout her early life, her ailments were kept secret. And it wasn't until her post-pubescent promiscuity and rebelliousness that Joseph P. Kennedy Sr sought a lobotomy in the hopes it would calm her mood swings and stop her occasional violent outbursts. The procedure was performed in secret; not even Rosemary's mother was told or consulted.

The lobotomy went terribly wrong and, as a result, Rosemary's mental age was that of a 2-year-old child. She could not walk or speak intelligibly and was incontinent. She was then institutionalized and hidden away until the end of her life. None of the Kennedys – not even her siblings or her mother – ever came to see her, with the exception of Joseph, who visited several times during her stay at Craig House. Rosemary's treatment plus extras were said to cost $2,400 a month, in addition to the annual fee of $50,000. This included Rosemary's extra attendants and aides, private nurses, laundry, hairdresser, druggist, stationer and tailor.

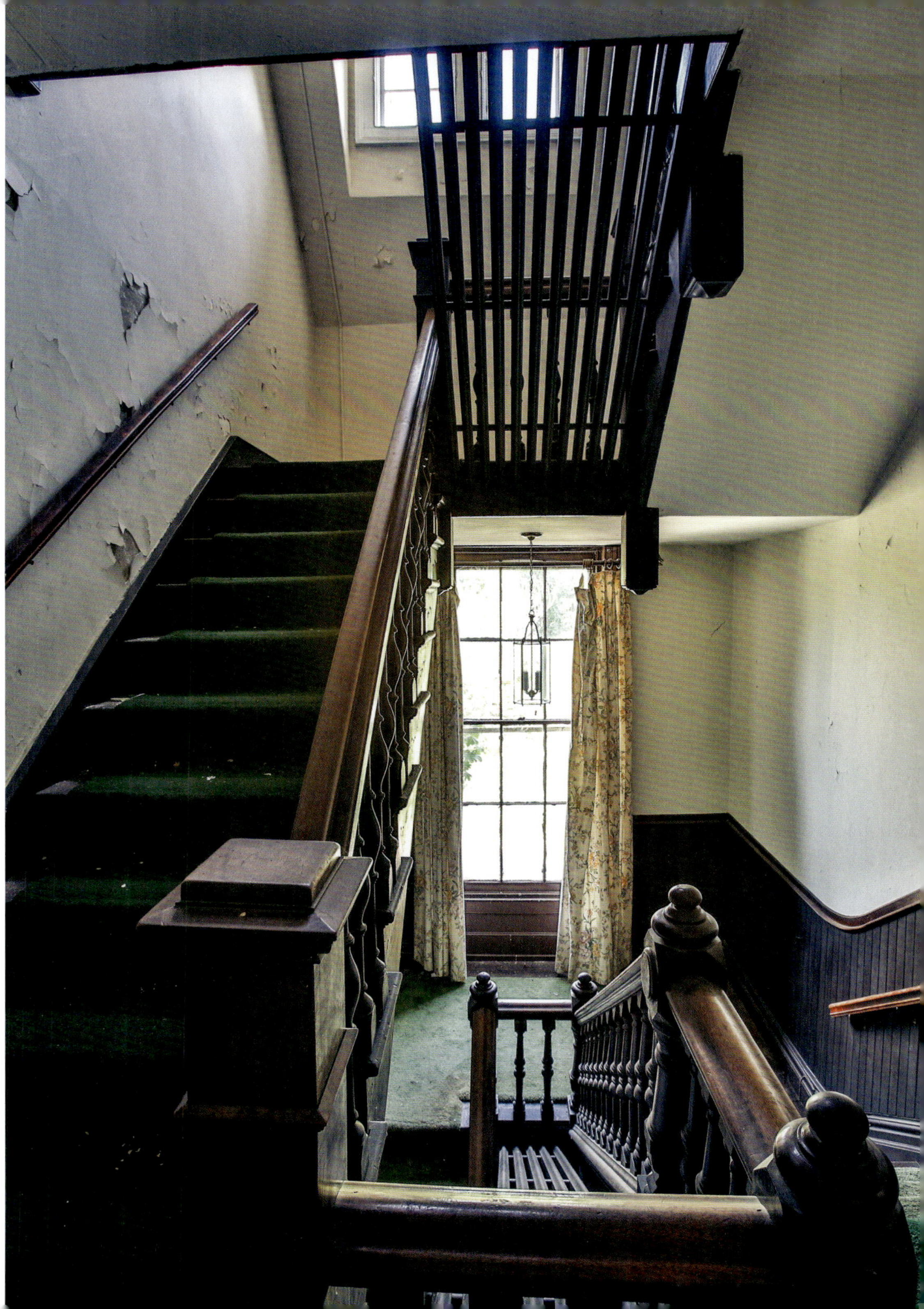

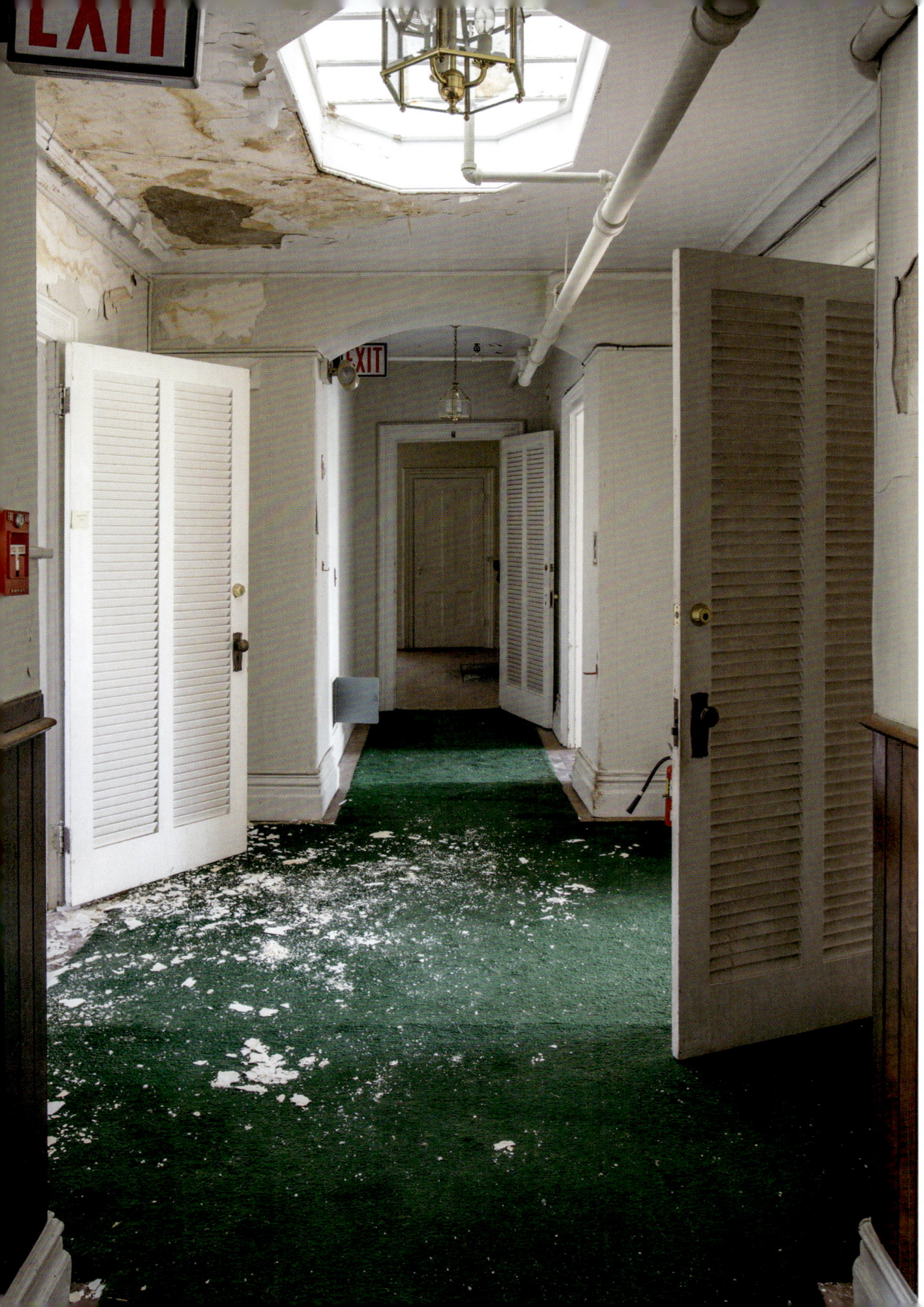

Zelda Fitzgerald arrived at Craig House in the mid-1930s: her time there was just as tragic. Like Rosemary Kennedy, Zelda was noted for her beauty and high spirits. F. Scott Fitzgerald dubbed her the first American "flapper". Diagnosed with schizophrenia, and possibly suffering from bipolar disorder, her correspondence with her husband while institutionalized became the inspiration for Nicole Diver, the beautiful, doomed heroine of *Tender Is the Night*. The couple's marital difficulties were also well publicized, and Zelda's mental problems are often said to have been the direct consequence of an overbearing husband. Their marriage was plagued by wild drinking, infidelities and bitter recriminations.

Unfortunately for Zelda, no cure was to be found among the sloping lawns and green fairways of Craig House. The fees became too much for Scott, so he arranged to have her moved to a more affordable institution, the Highland Hospital in North Carolina. But the last letter Zelda ever wrote to Scott would be from Craig House: "Whenever you are ready to make the change, I will be ready to go. I am awfully home-sick in spite of the beauties of this place." Tragically, on the night of March 10, 1948, a fire broke out in the Highland Hospital kitchen and Zelda succumbed, unable to escape from her locked room.

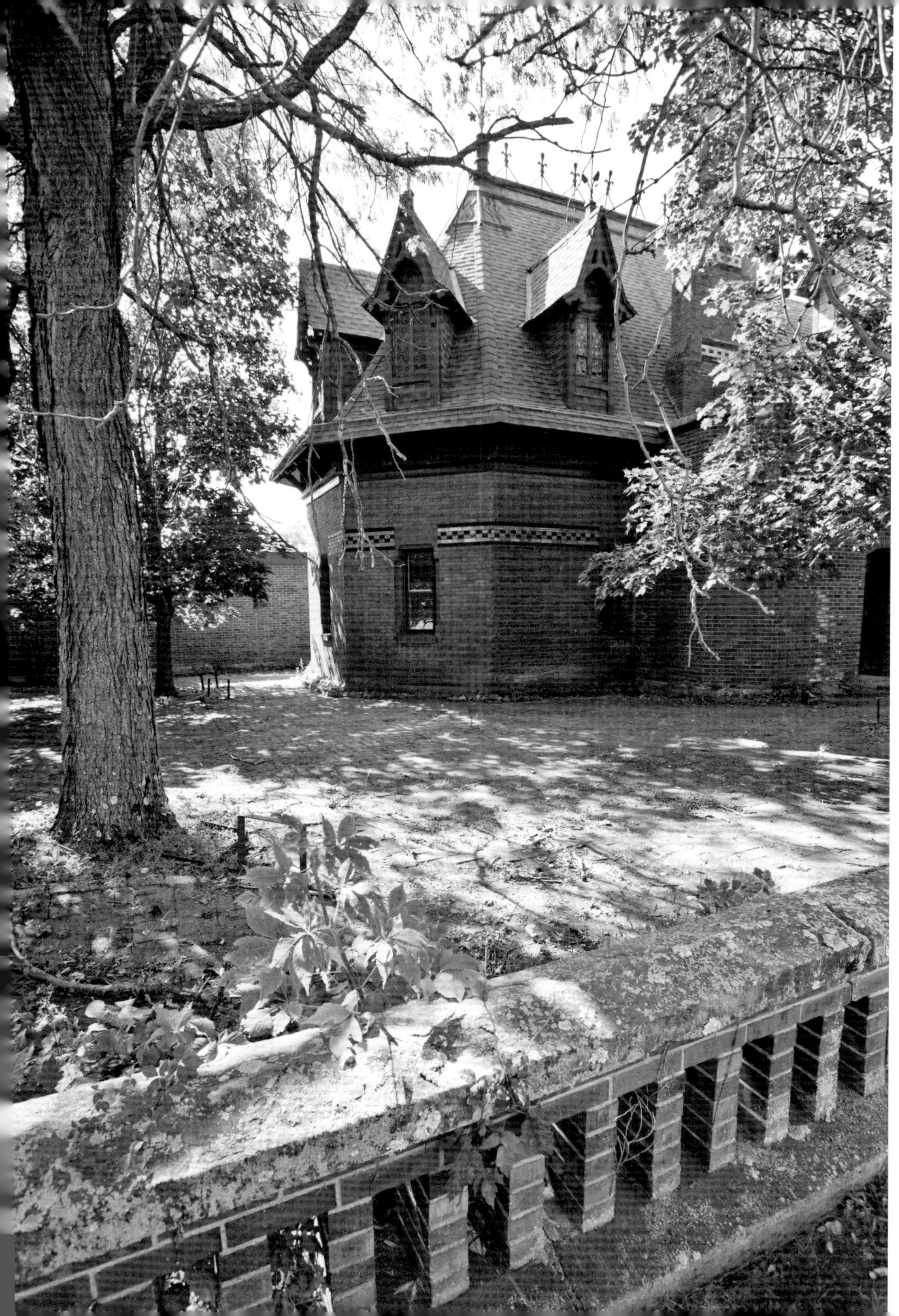

The tragedies continued with Frances Ford Seymour, who committed suicide at Craig House after years of alleged sexual abuse: she cut her throat with a razor in one of the turrets in 1942.

As times changed and state-of-the-art private institutions opened up throughout the United States, the hospital failed to evolve. Prospective patients sought treatment locally, unwilling to relocate to Craig House. The once exclusive hospital closed in 1999. In 2003 the mansion was bought by Robert Wilson, a Wall Street hedge fund manager. In December of 2013, aged 87 and recently having had a stroke, he jumped to his death from the window of his Upper West Side apartment.

As Zelda Fitzgerald at her most troubled wrote to her beloved husband, "The sense of sadness and of finality in leaving a place is a good emotion; I love that the story can't be changed again and one more place is haunted – old sorrows and a half-forgotten happiness are stored where they can be recaptured." After a series of demolitions in 2011, the property again sits silent and waits to be saved.

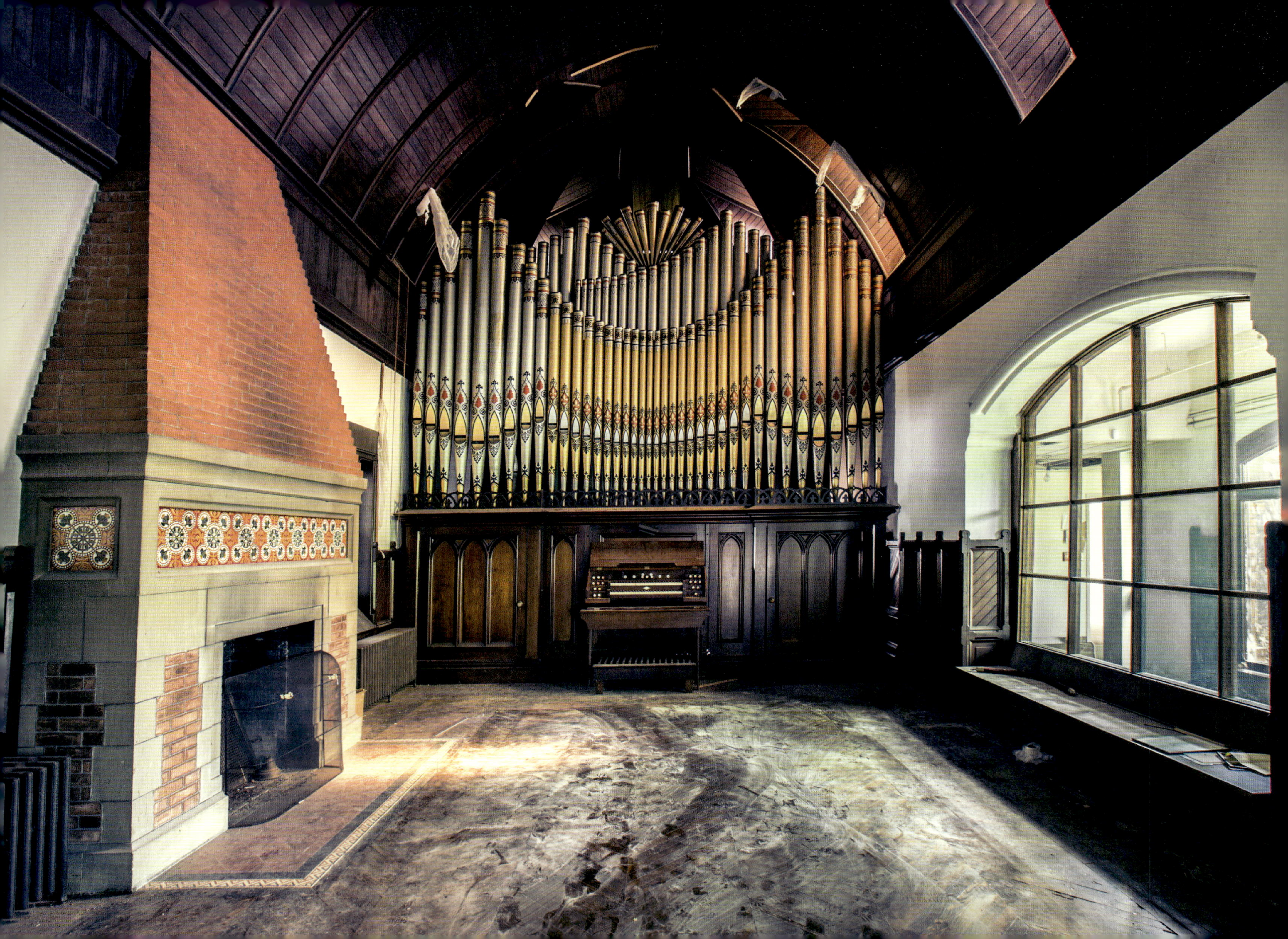

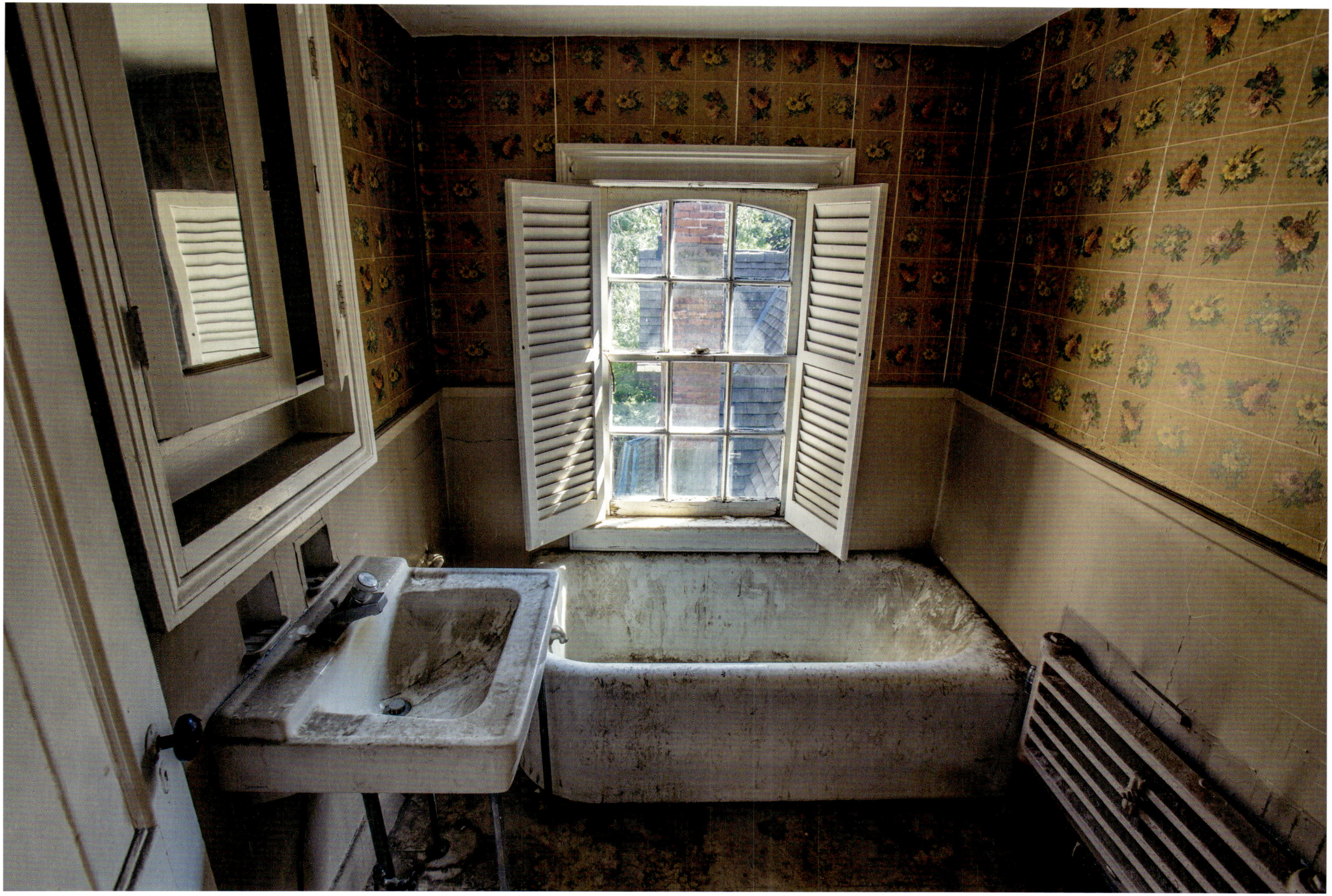

Western State Hospital, Virginia

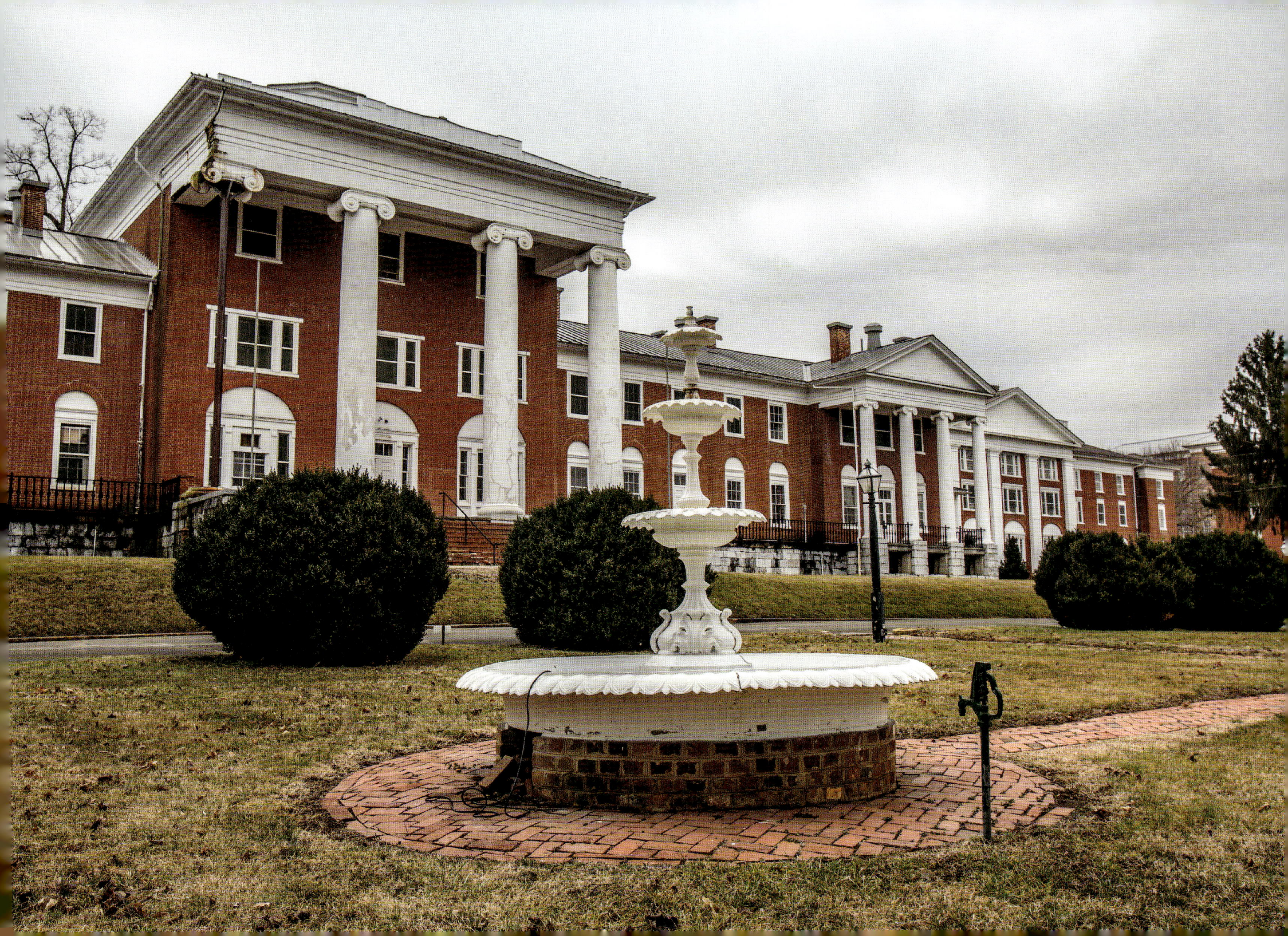

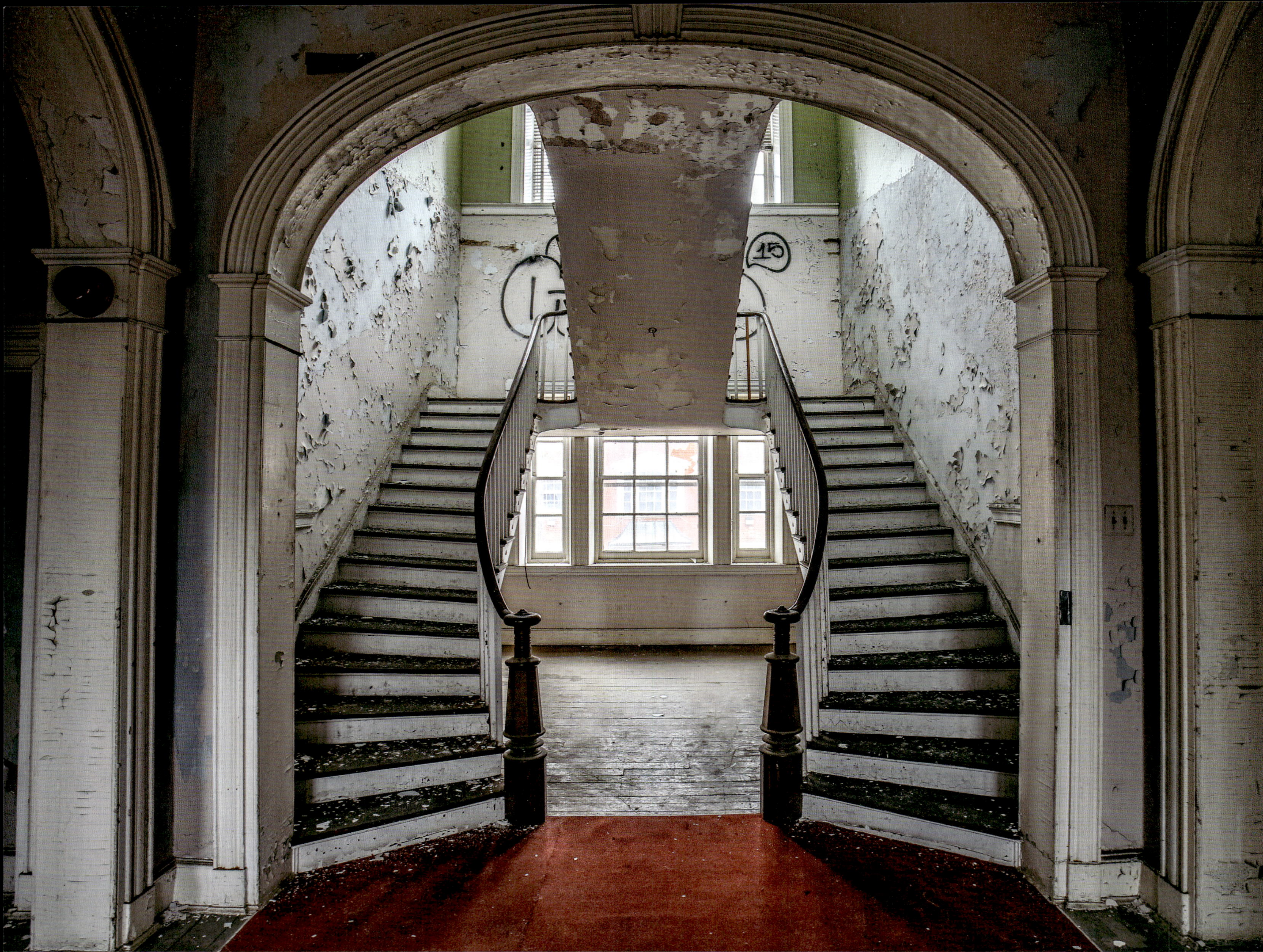
15

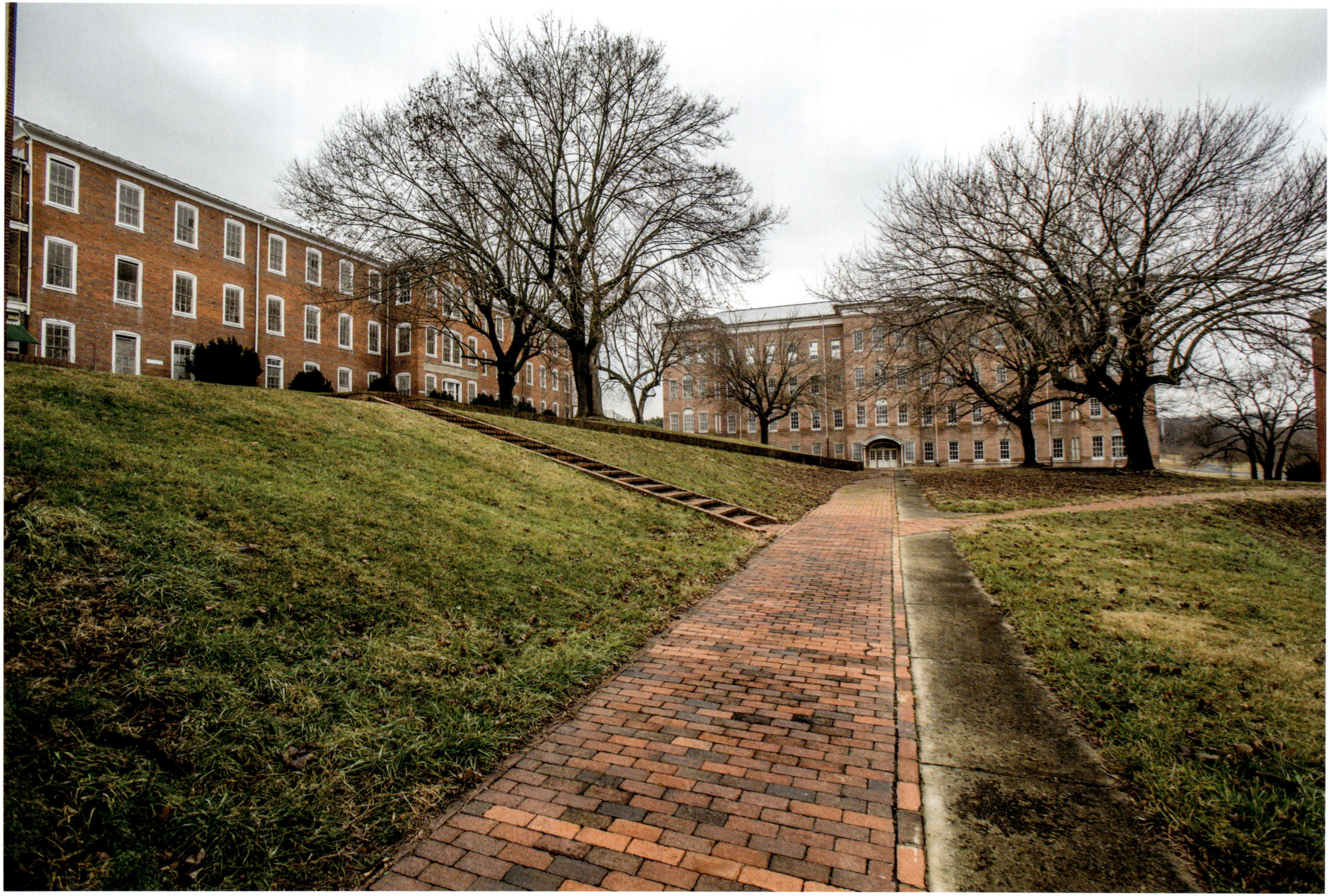

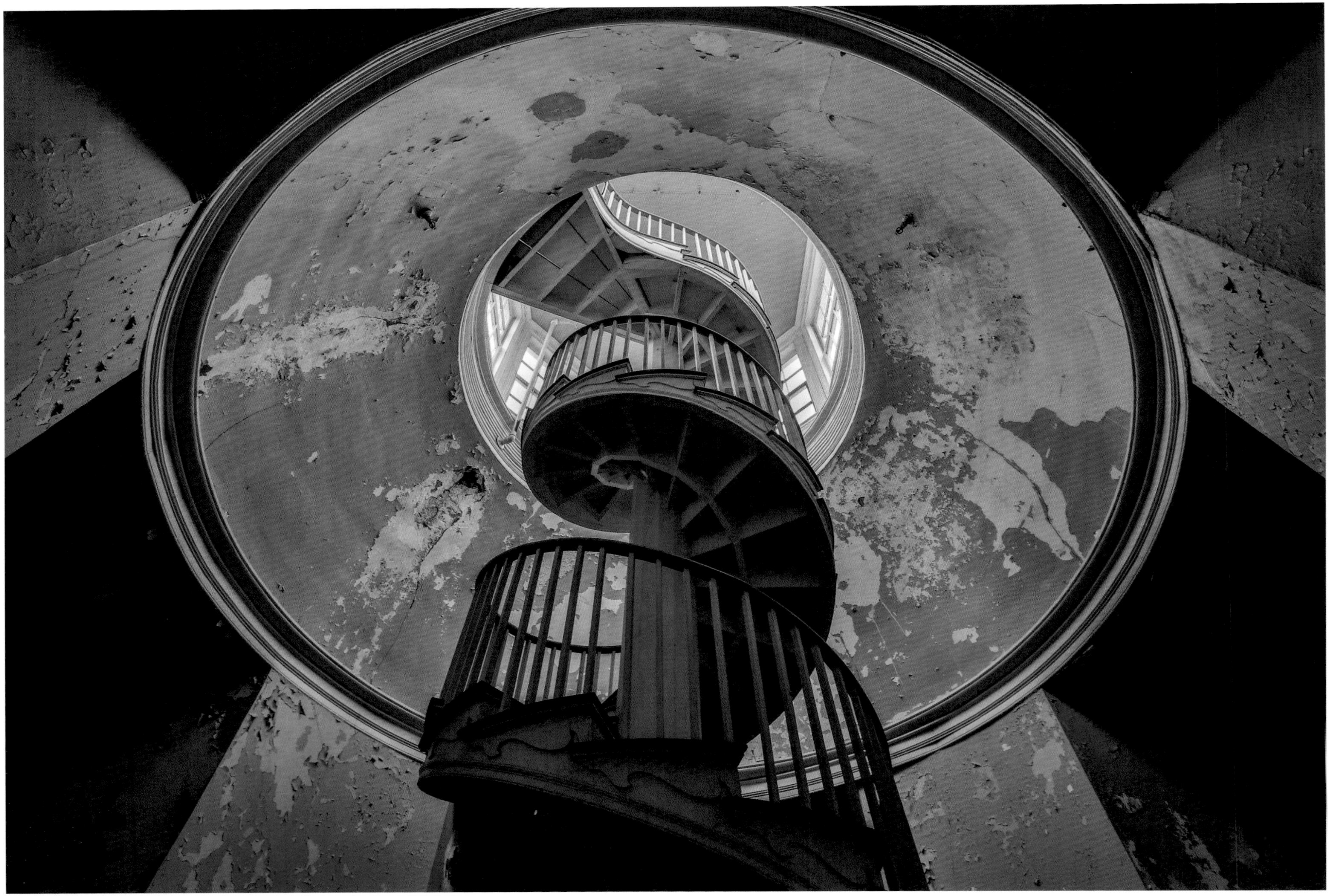

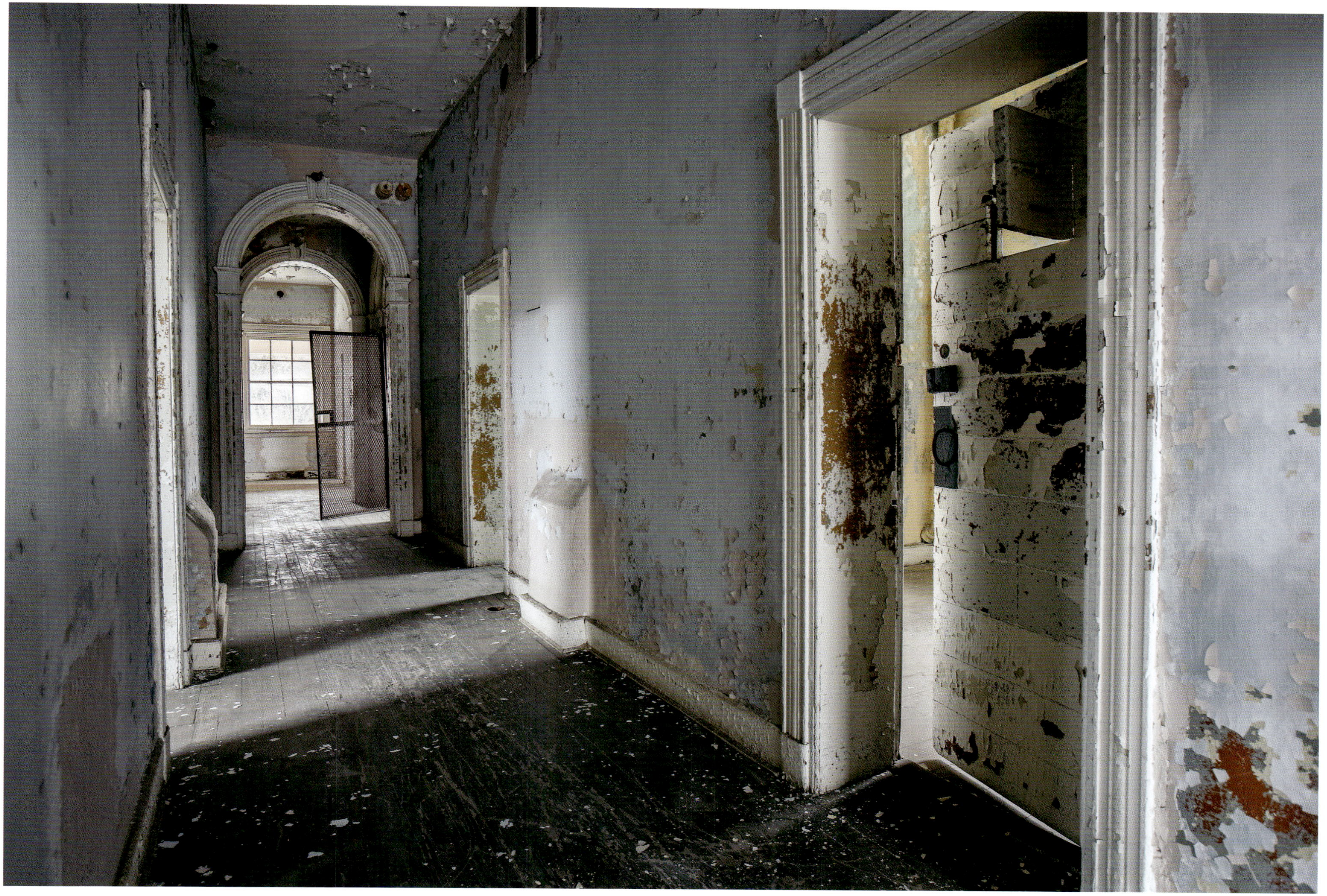

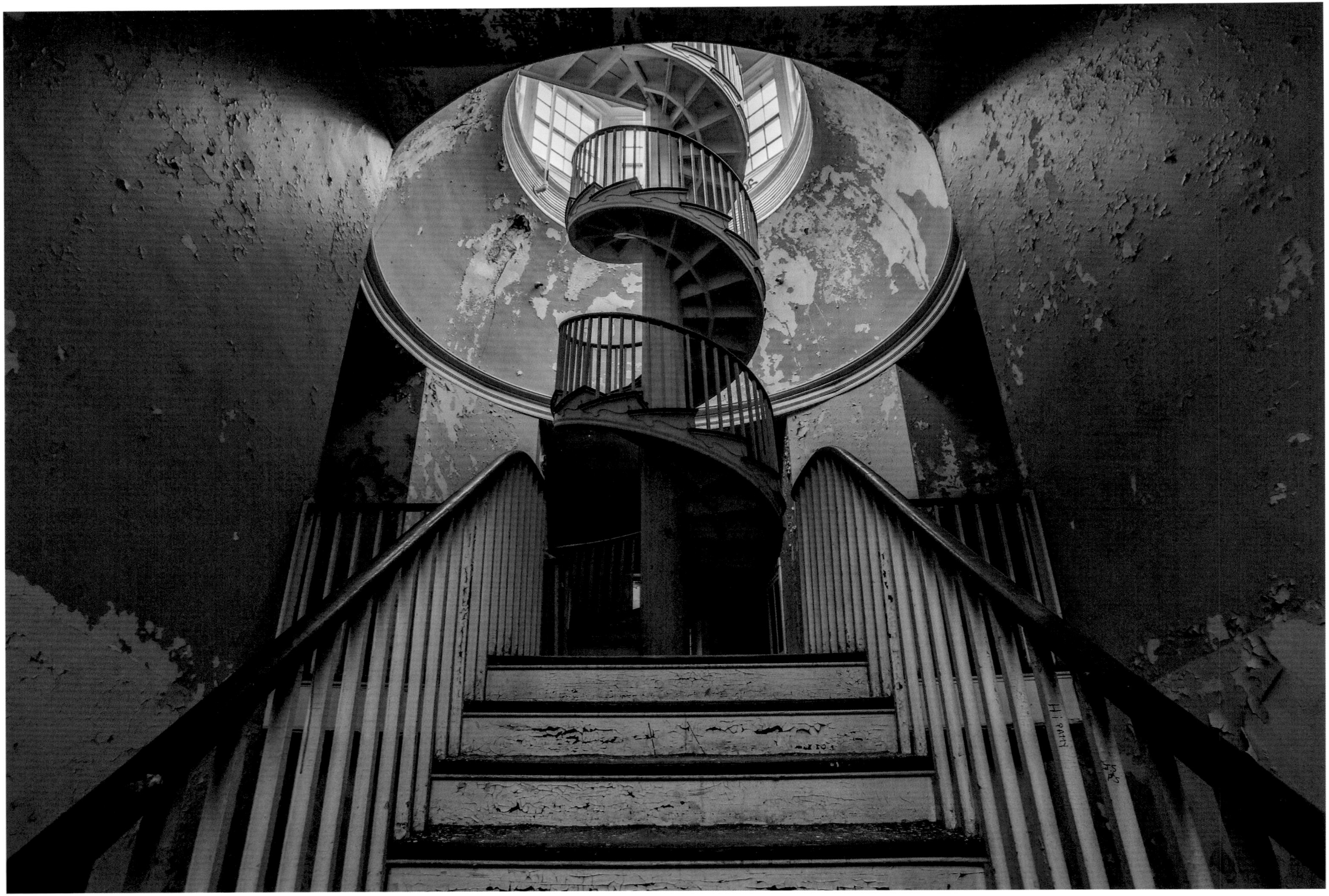

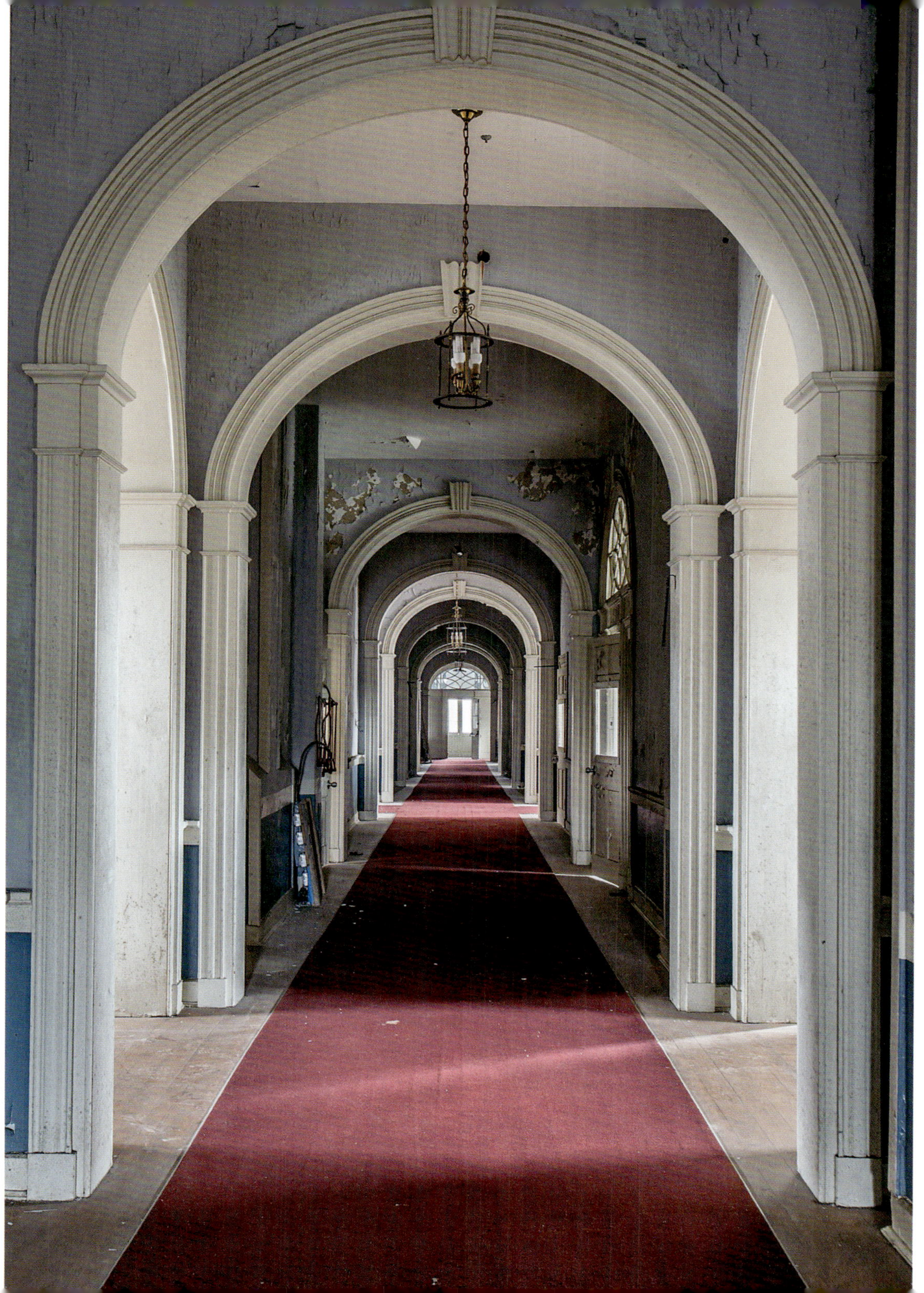

Rochester State Hospital

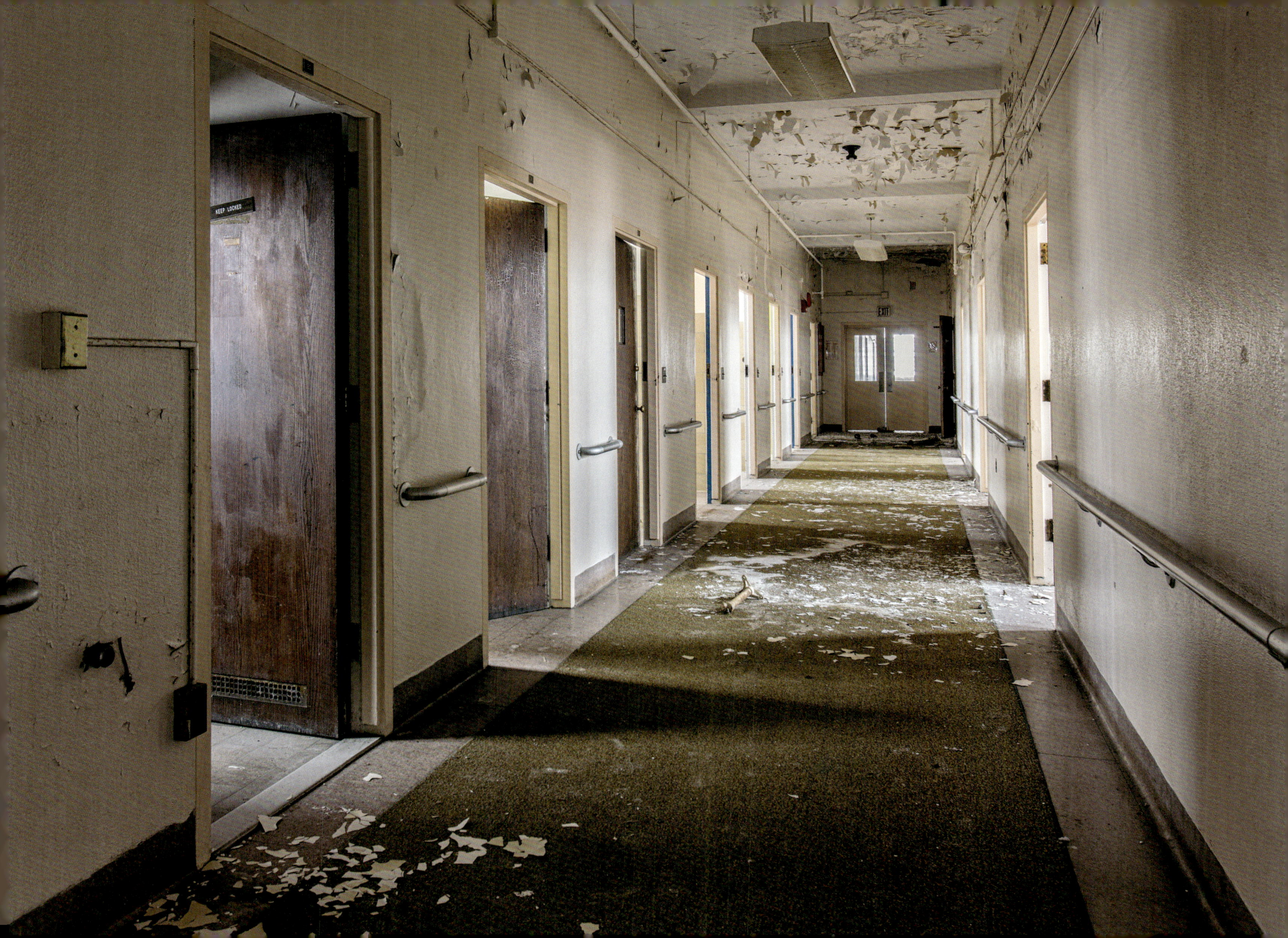
KEEP LOCKED

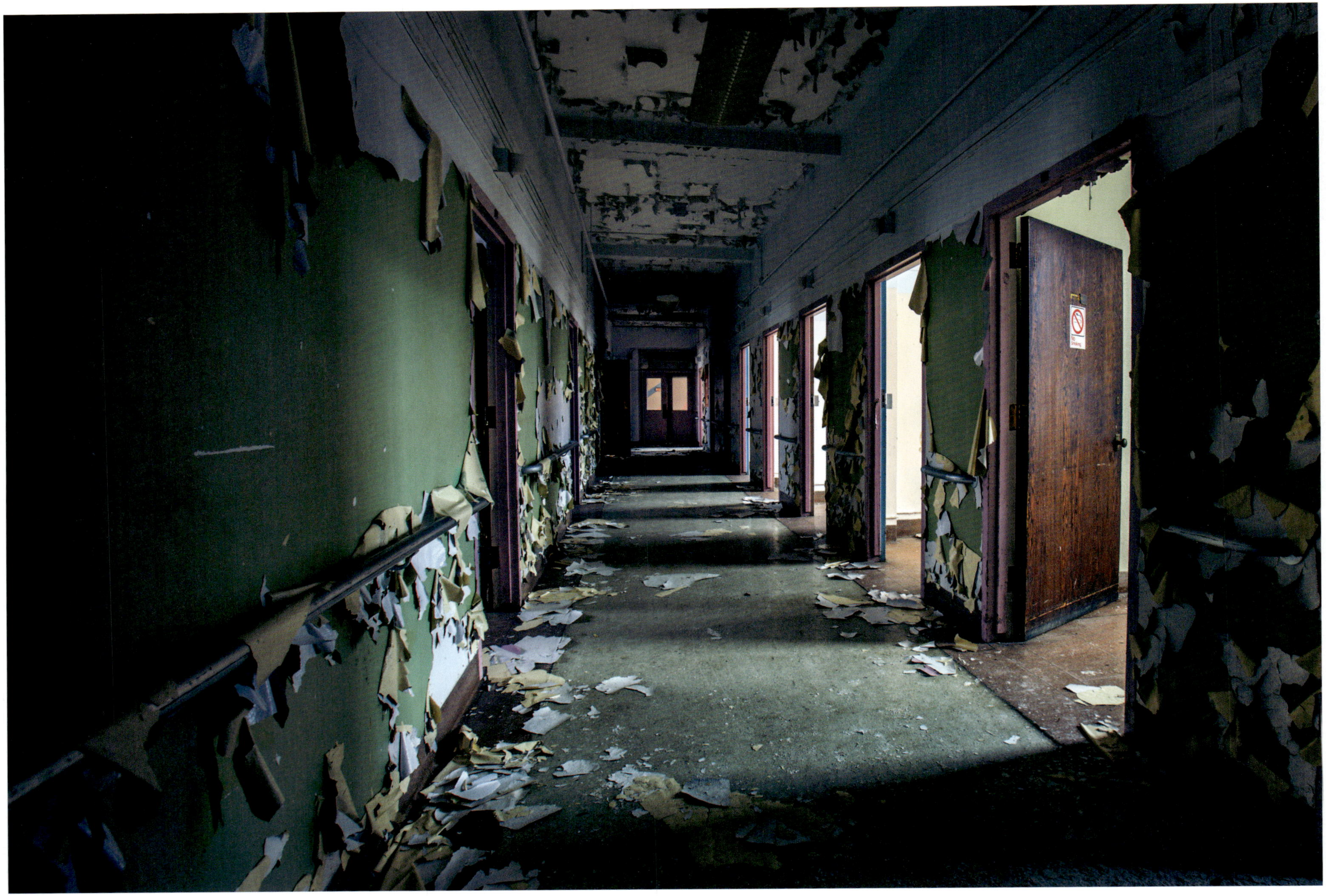
No Smoking

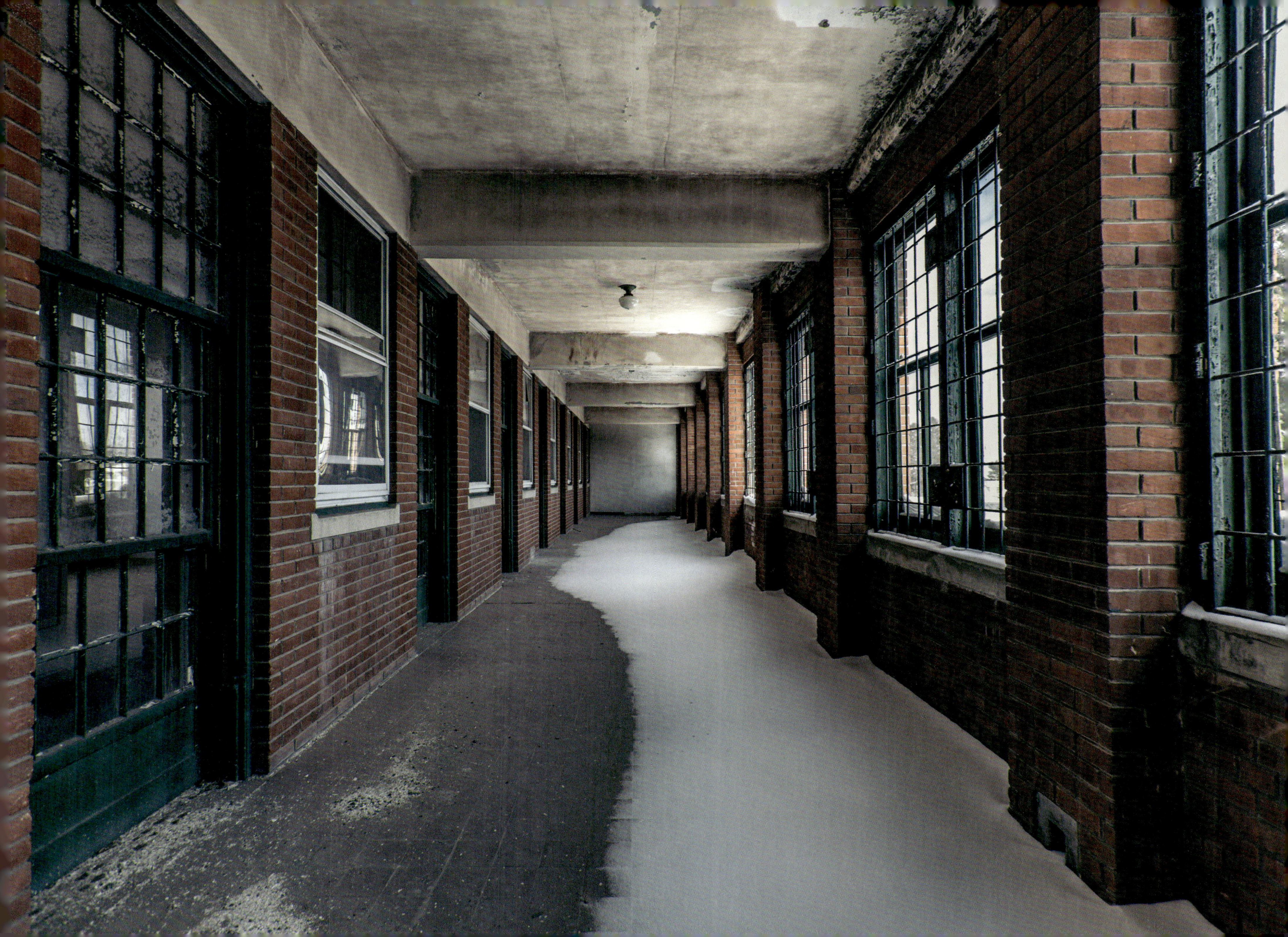

Morgue Laboratory and Autopsy Chalkboard

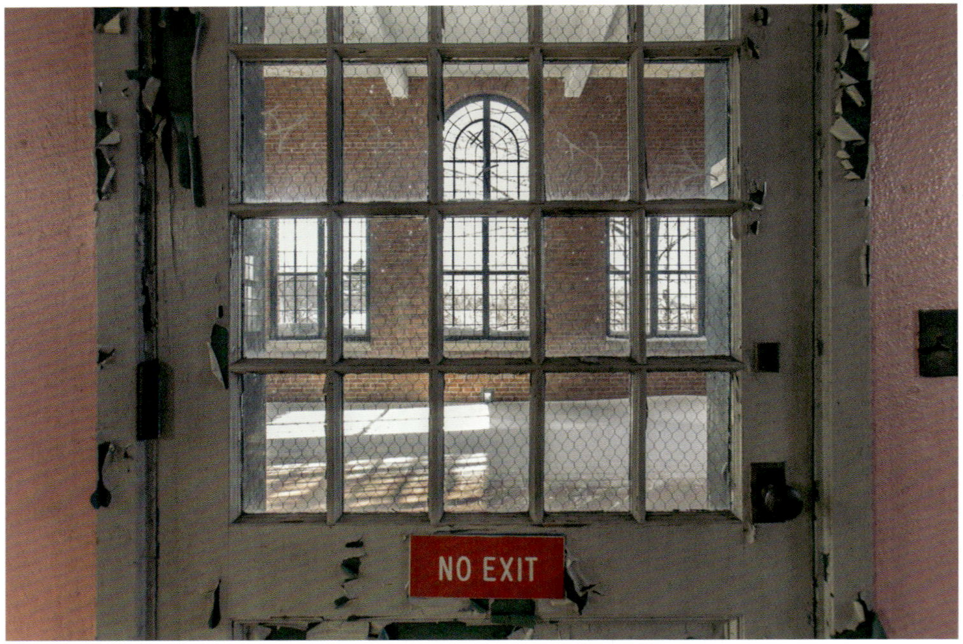

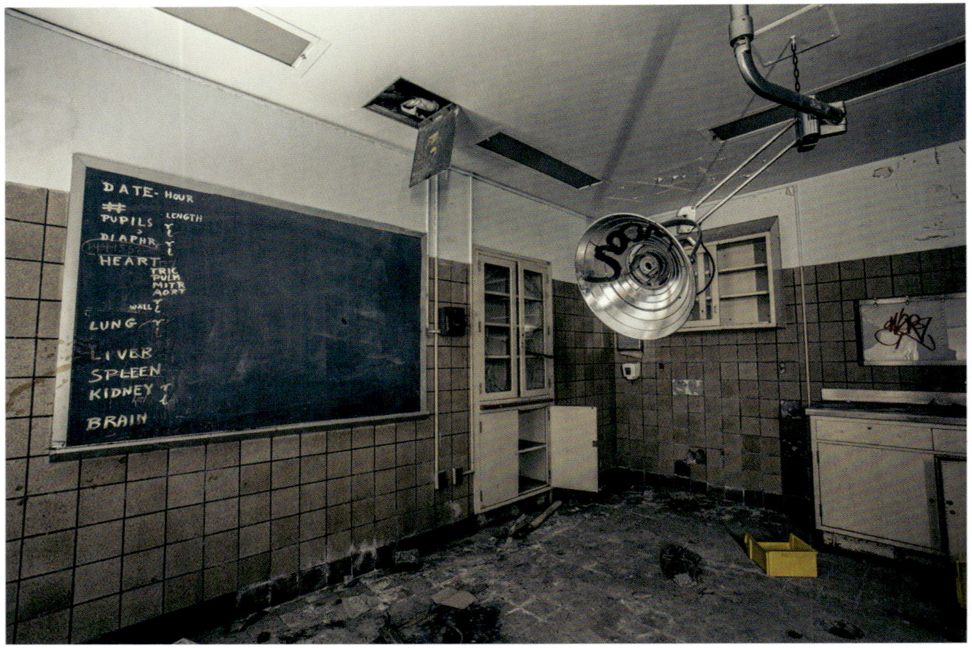

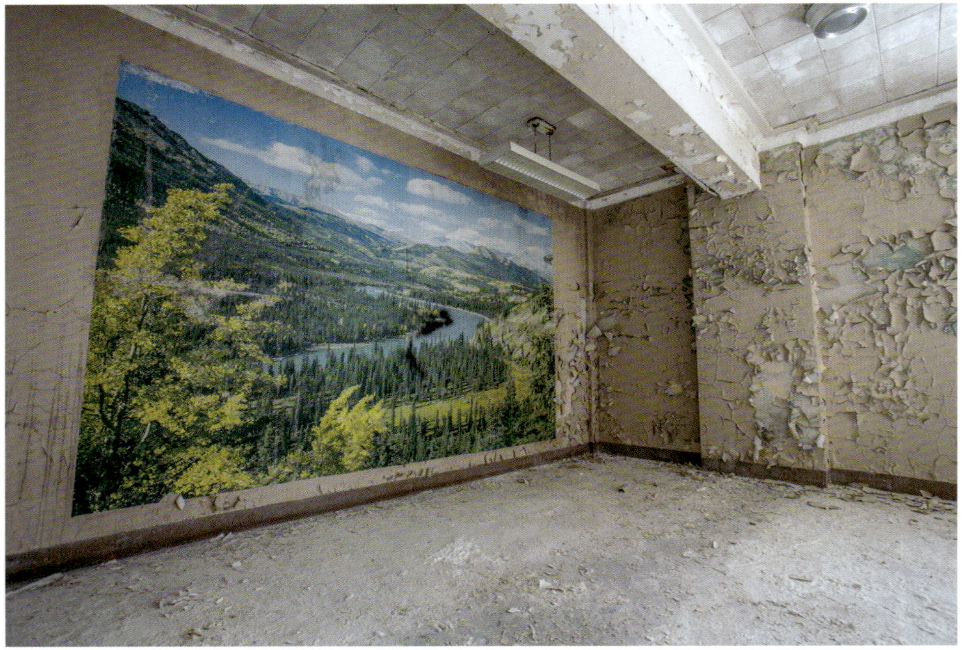

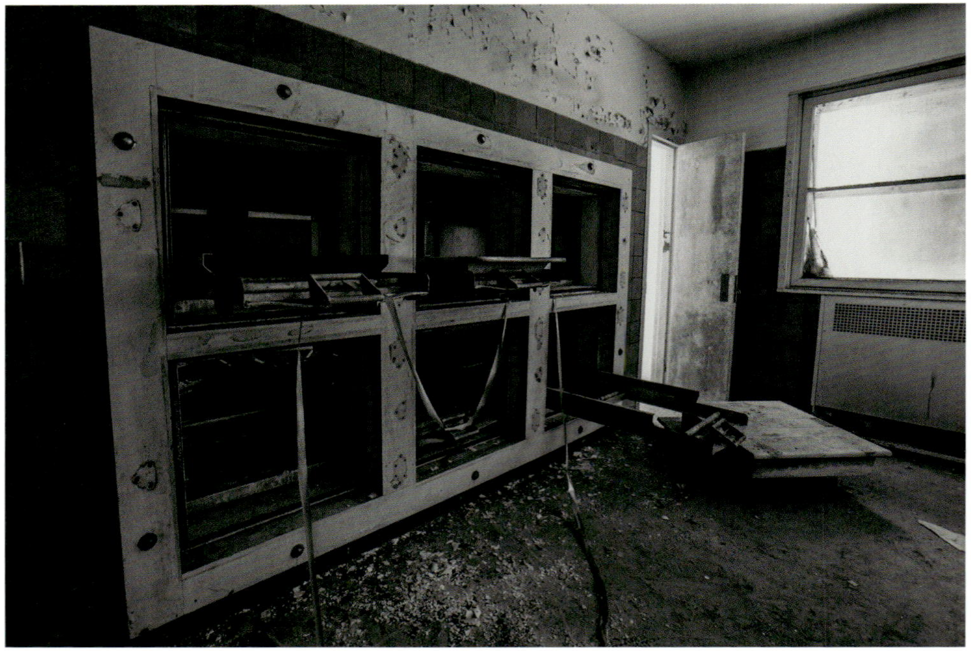

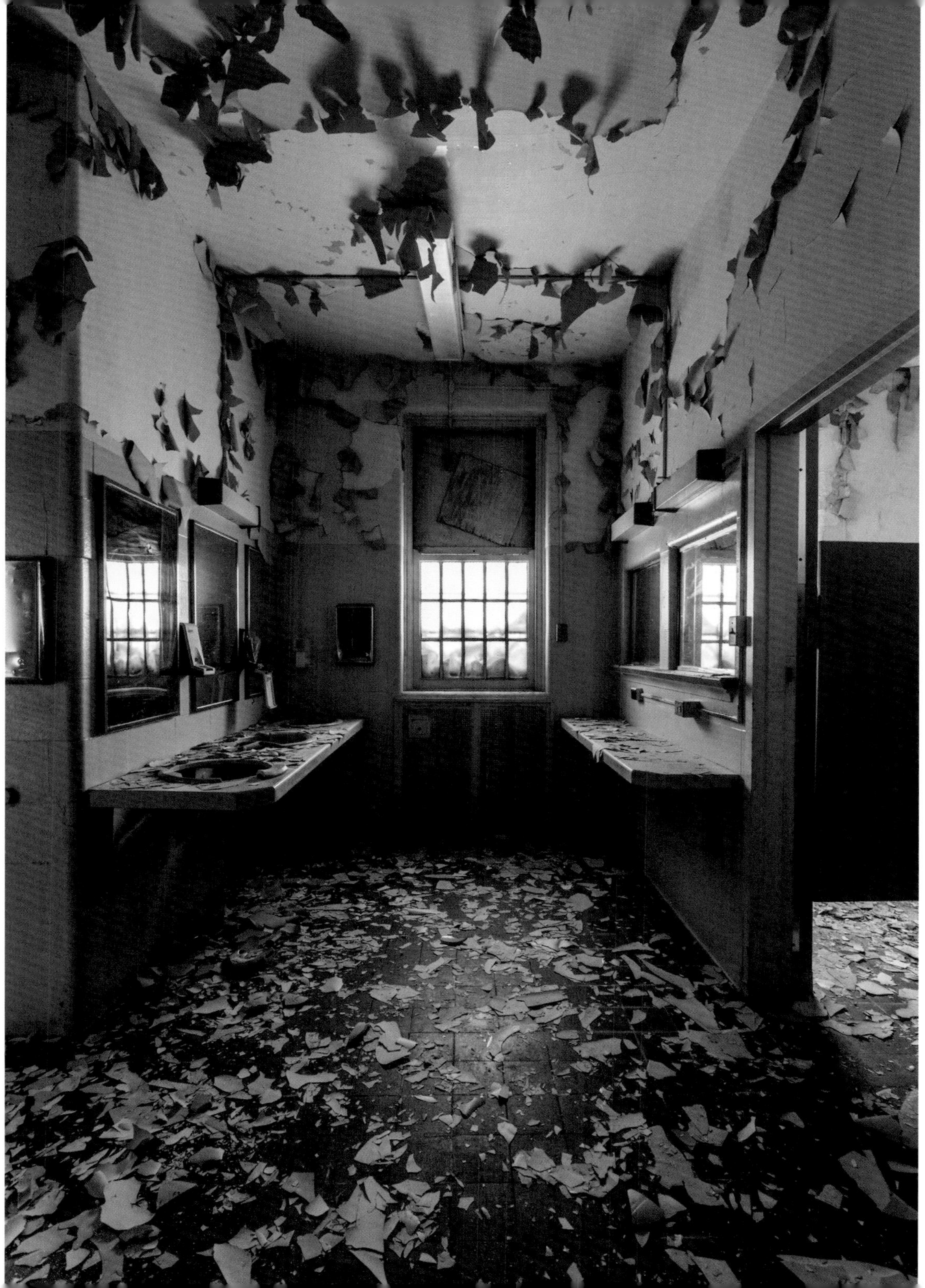

Fairfield Hills State Hospital

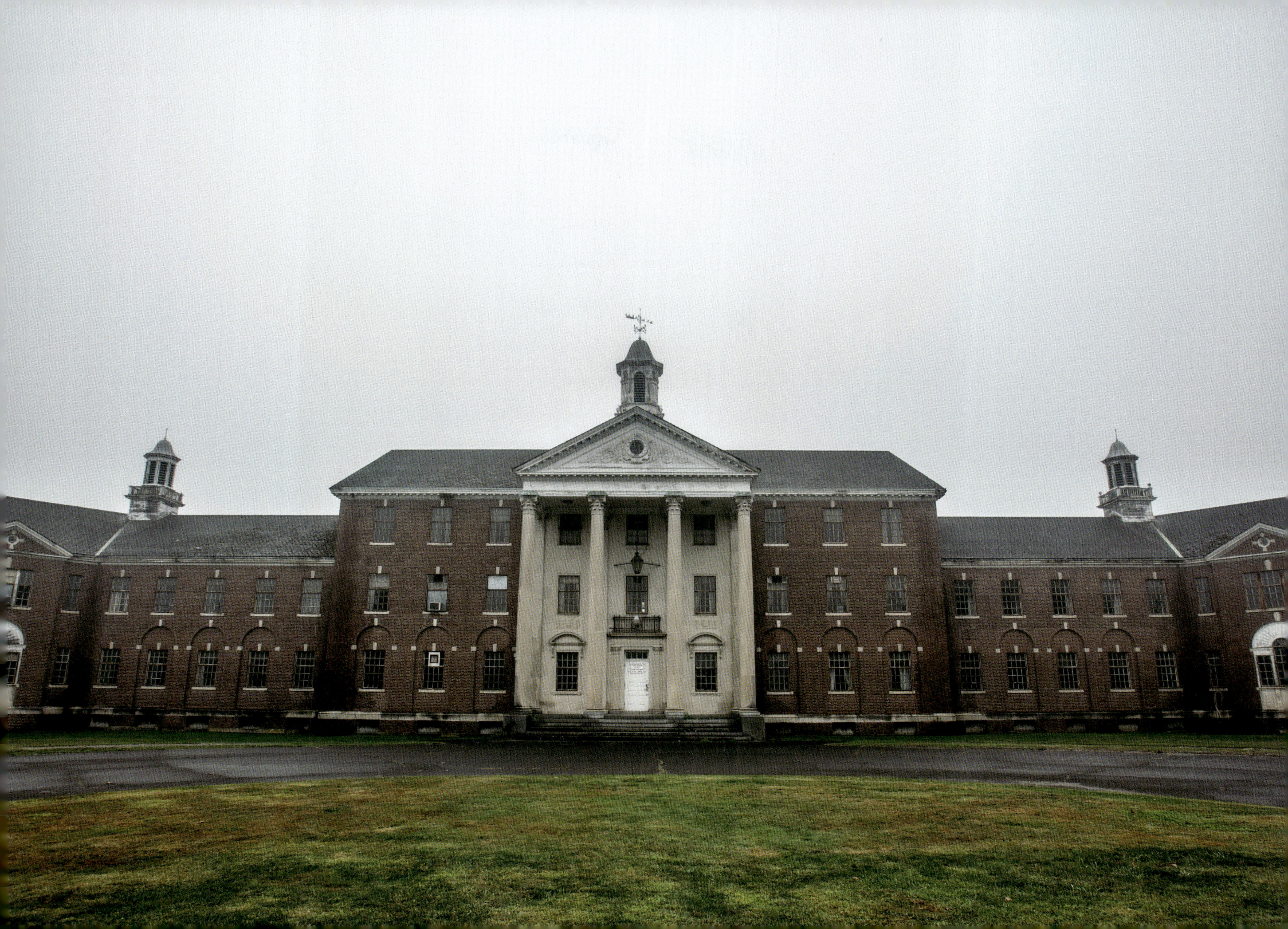

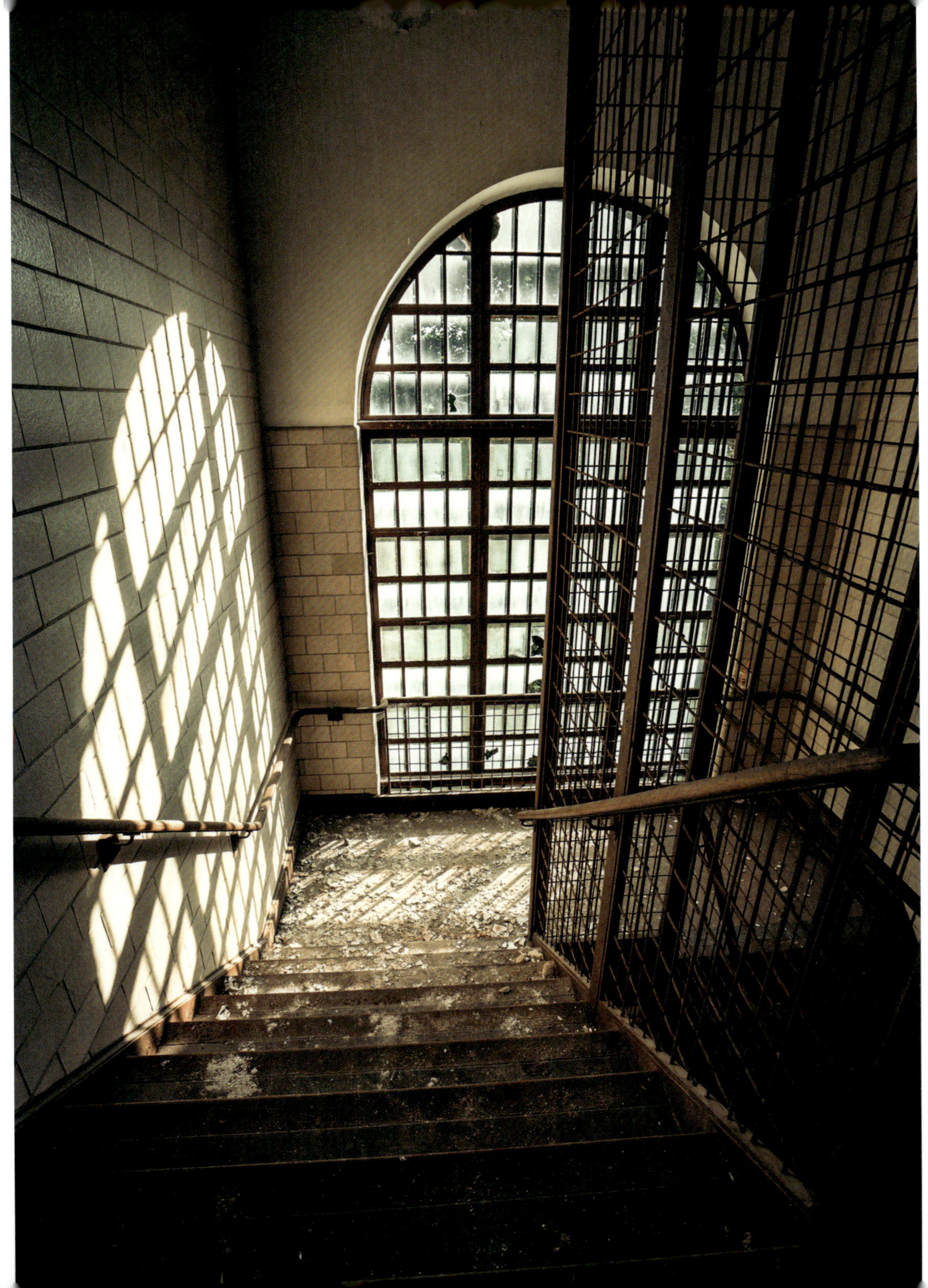

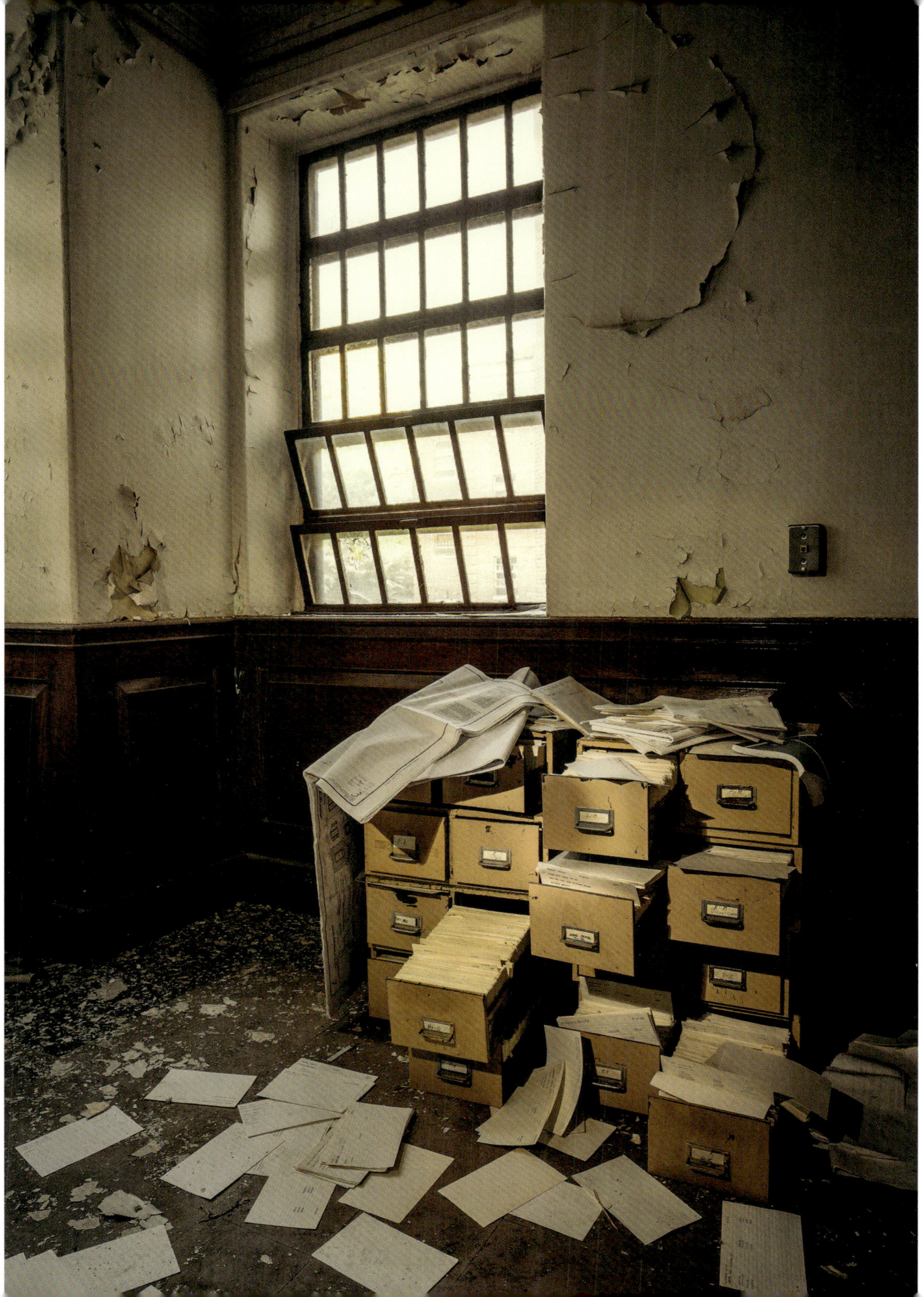

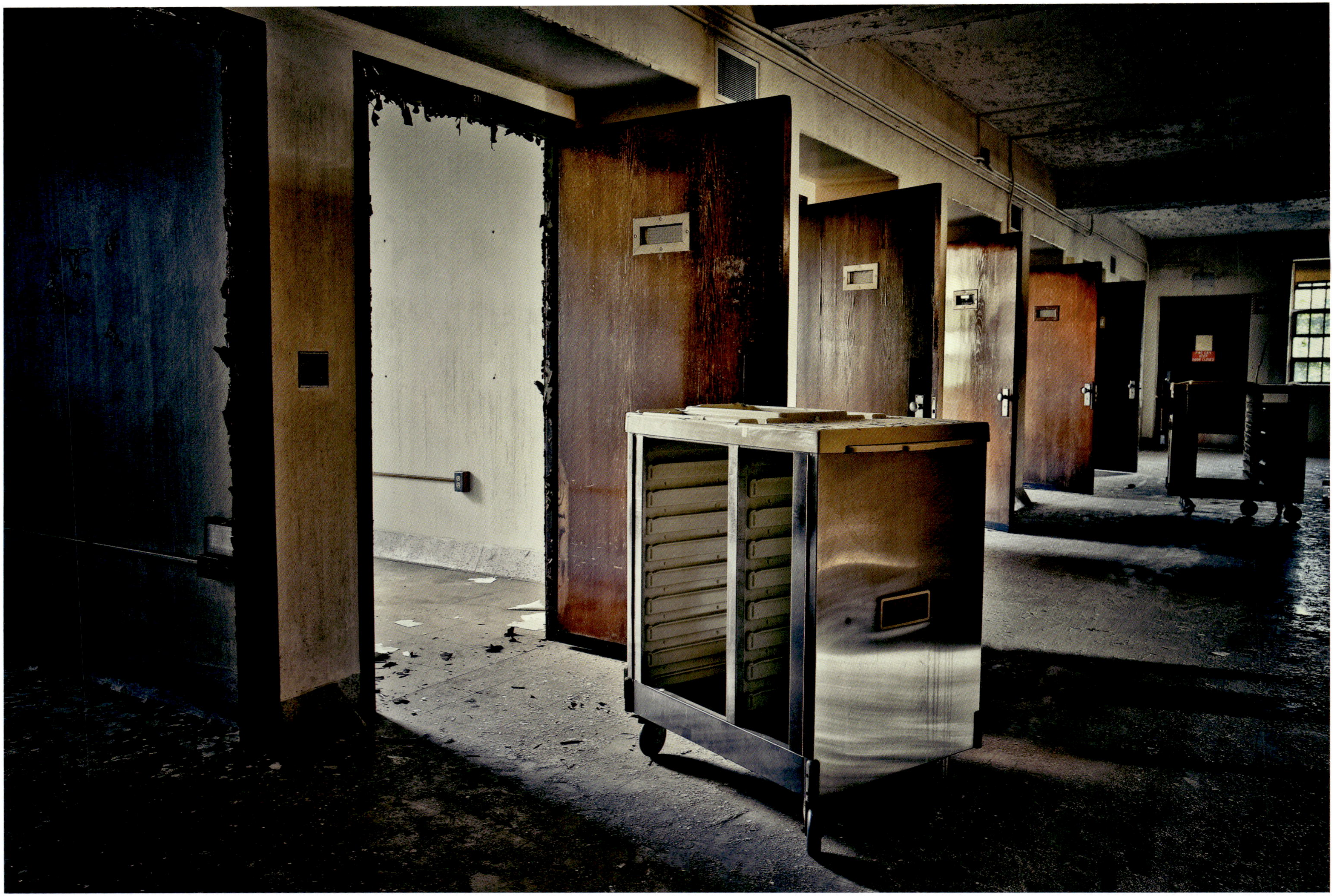

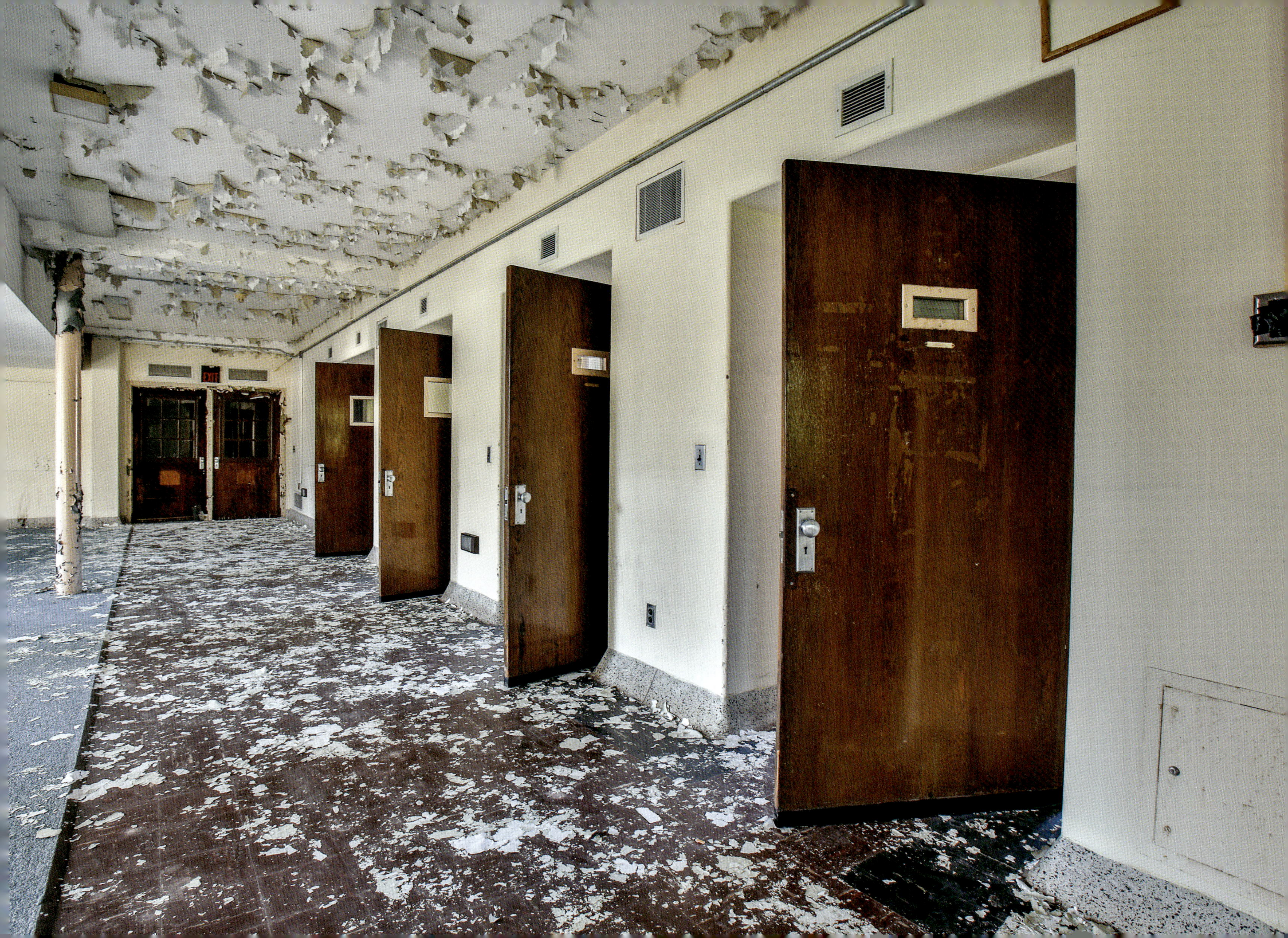
EXIT

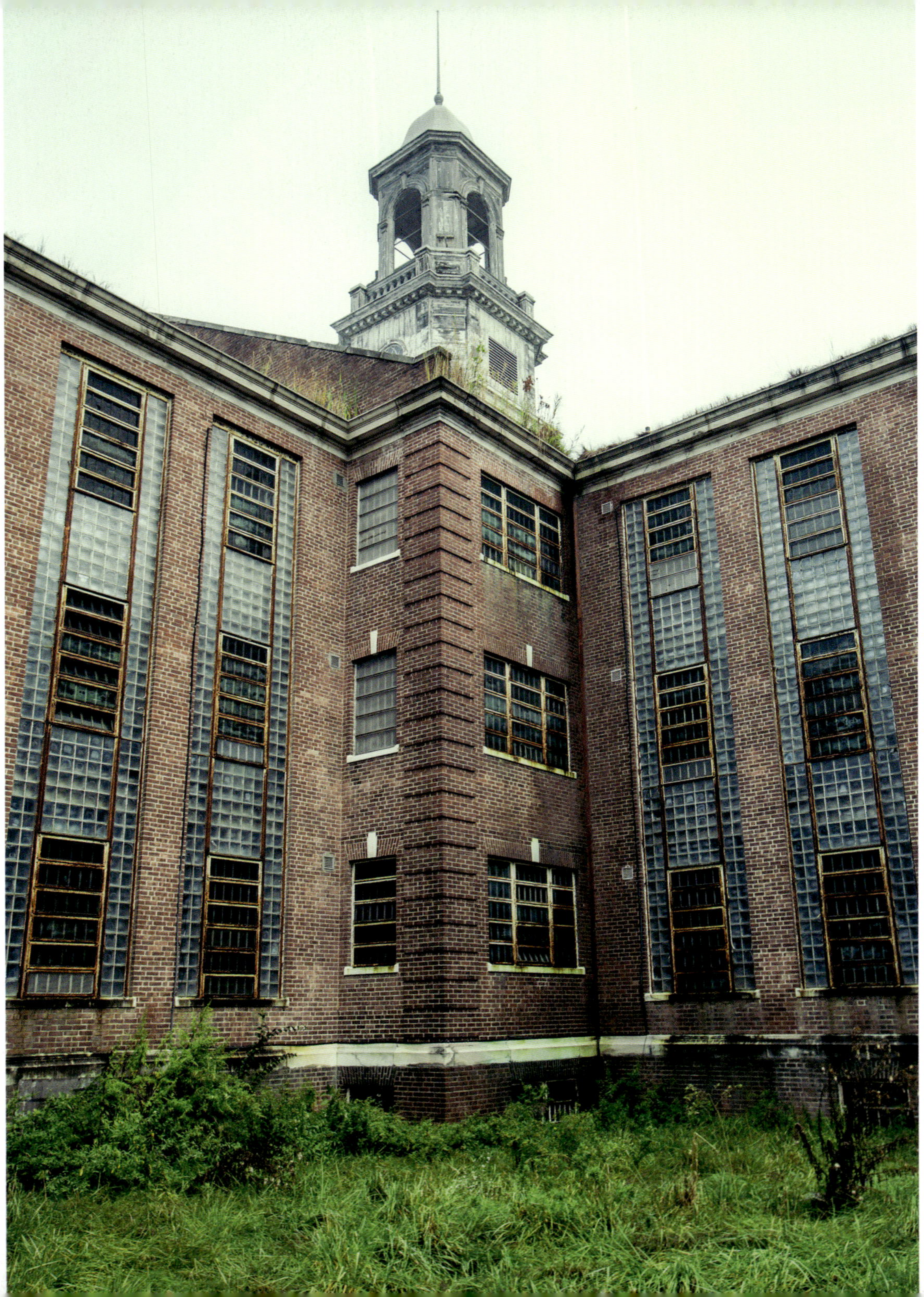

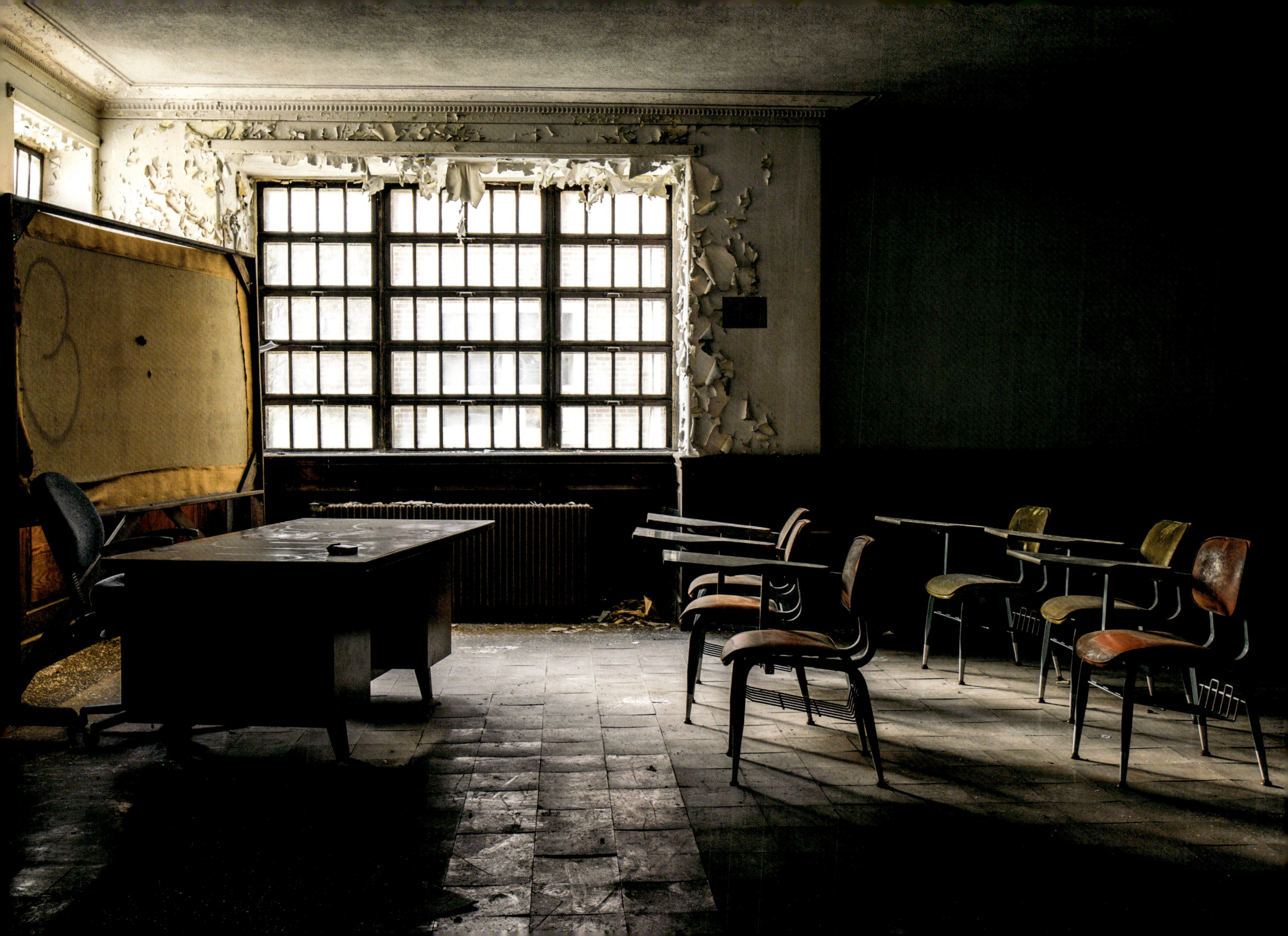

The Tragedy of the State Schools

As the United States began to transition from the pastoral way of life to a period of industrialisation in the early to mid-1800s, social reformers of the era identified a new class of people who presented a new array of challenges, those who would become known as the 'feeble-minded'. Whereas traditional asylums housed a plethora of patients – from the poor, to the criminal, to the 'lunatics' – it was determined that the feeble-minded required an institution of their own.

Although not politically correct by contemporary standards, the rather insensitive terms that arose at the turn of the century – retardation, feeble-mindedness, idiocy, imbecile, moron – were considered to be a precise psychiatric classification. Today we address such individuals as intellectually, physically, or developmentally disabled.

In 1908, however, feeble-minded was defined in a report by the British government's Royal Commission on the Care and Control of the Feeble-Minded (1904–1908) as the following:

Persons who may be capable of earning a living under favourable circumstances, but are incapable from mental defect, existing from birth or from an early age: (1) of competing on equal terms with their normal fellows, or (2) of managing themselves and their affairs with ordinary prudence.

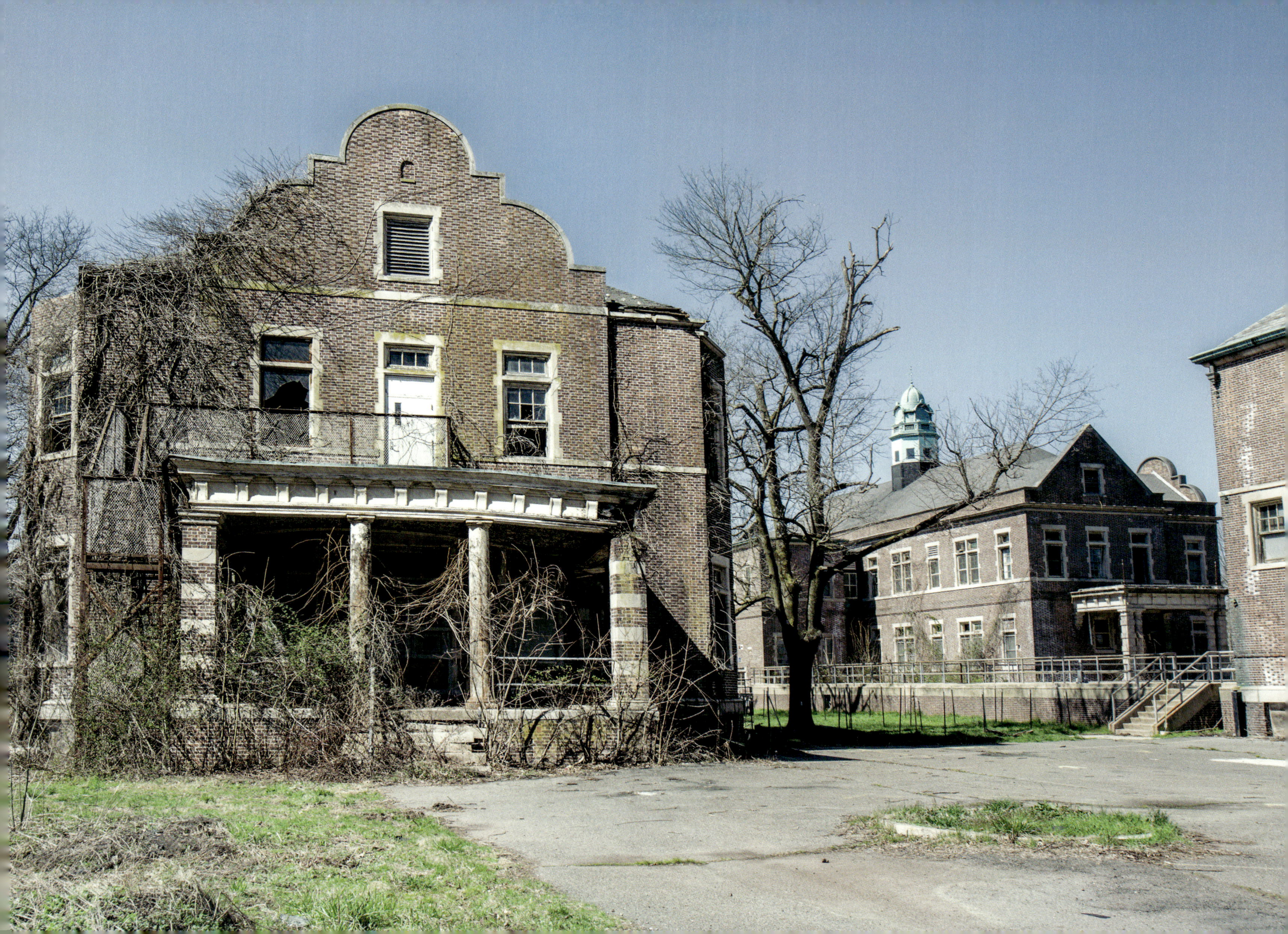

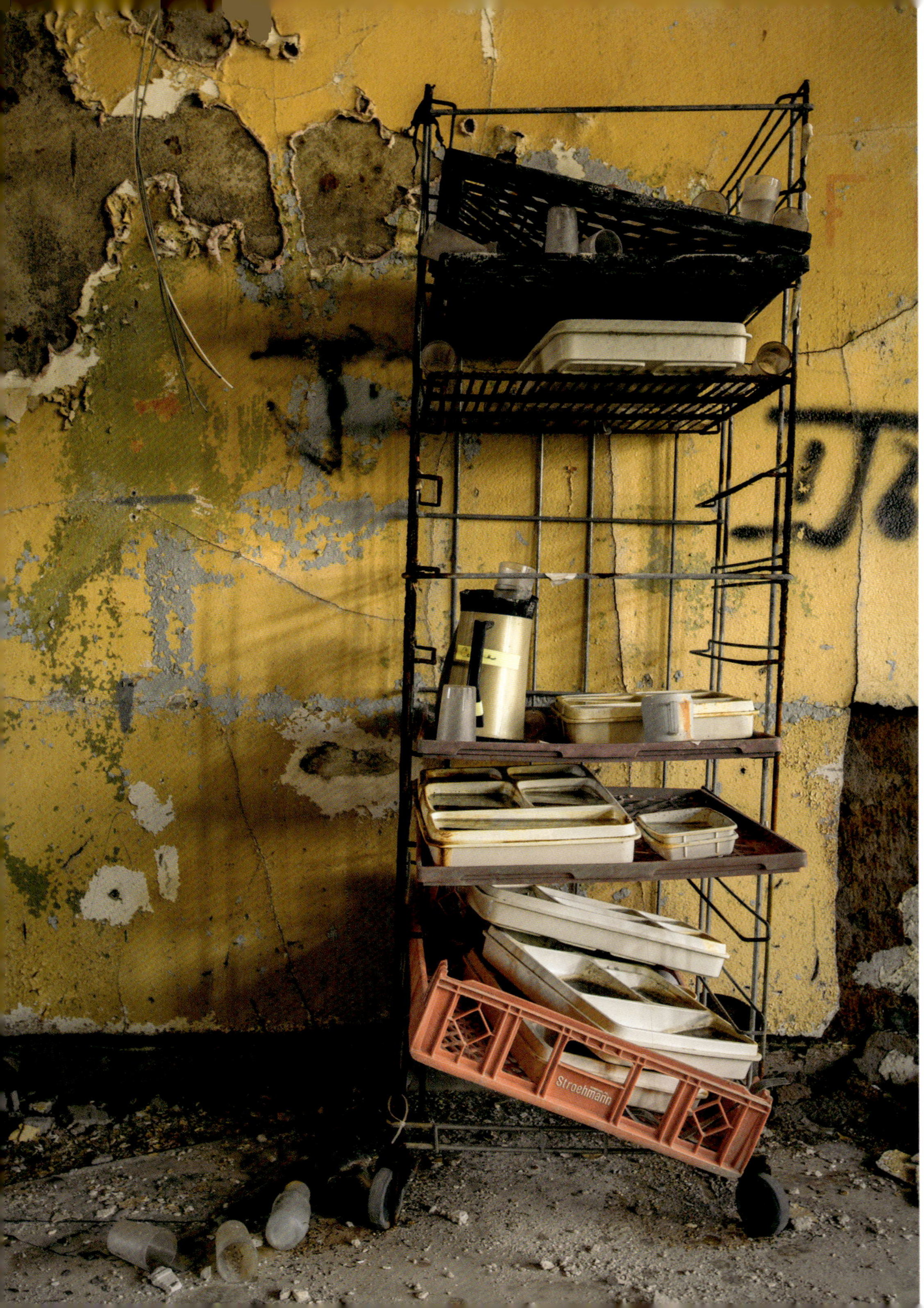

This new classification and the institutions that followed would lead to a dark period in eugenics and custodial care, proving that what is born through good intentions can quickly devolve through segregation and identification of persons who differ in any way from the majority. It is important to note however that the general mythos surrounding these institutions is that they were terrible places run by terrible people; this couldn't be further from the truth. Much of the staff operated day to day with the best of knowledge at the time, and for the most part, displayed a genuine care and concern for those they tended. But as a whole, it is society who is to blame. Society ultimately created a world separate for those we dehumanised and identified as 'not us'. We rendered an entire population virtually invisible, living a completely separate existence in overcrowded human warehouses. Institutions like Pennhurst State School & Hospital (known previously as the Eastern Pennsylvania Institution for the Feeble-Minded & Epileptics), Letchworth Village and Forest Haven to name a few, would inevitably all be wrought with controversy, legal disputes, and forced closure after almost a century of neglect, malpractice and inhumane conditions. Originally constructed to treat 500 to 1000 children and young adults, it's no surprise that the consequences of such a system would soon come to a head, as after only two decades of operation the populations were swelling to 4000 individuals.

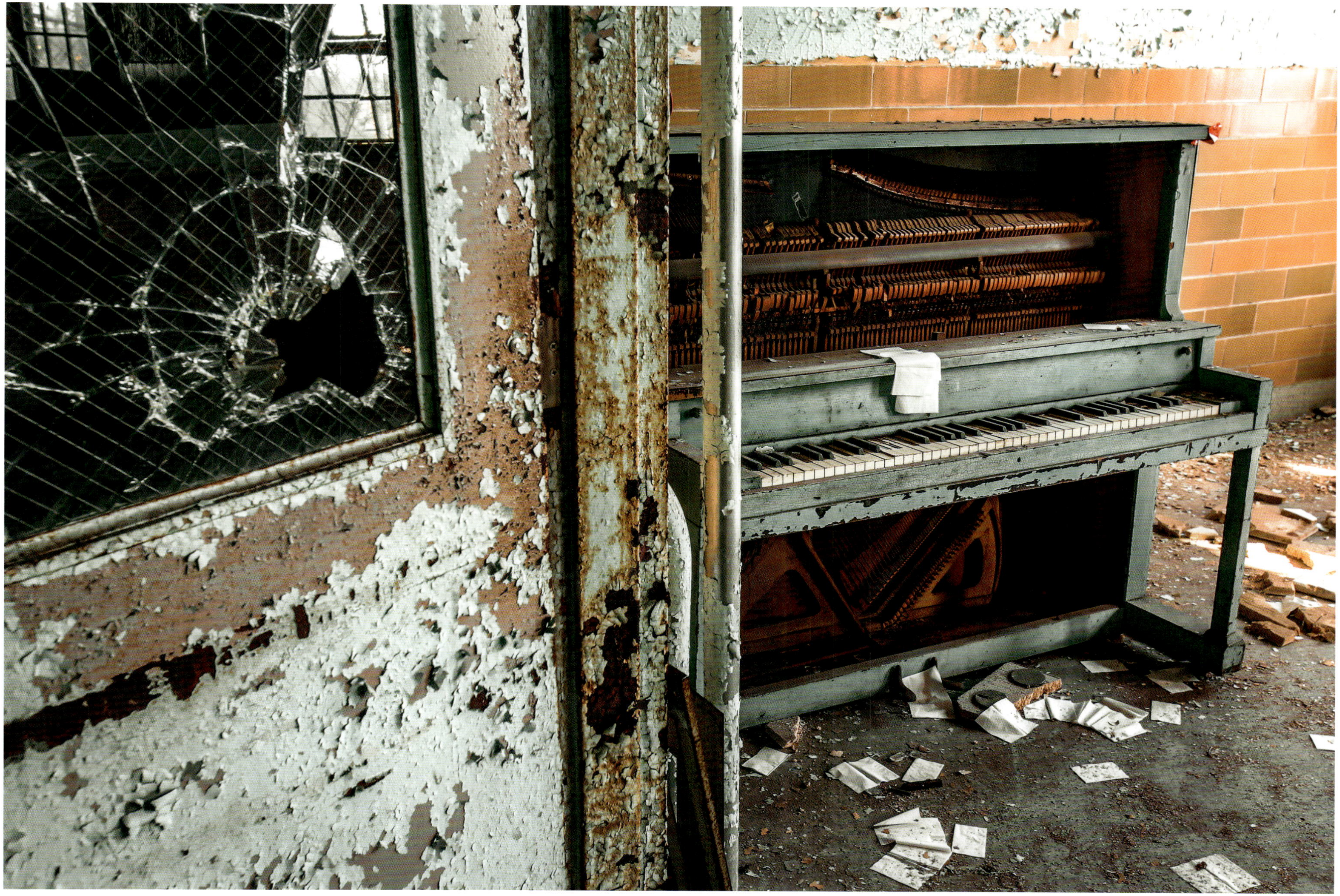

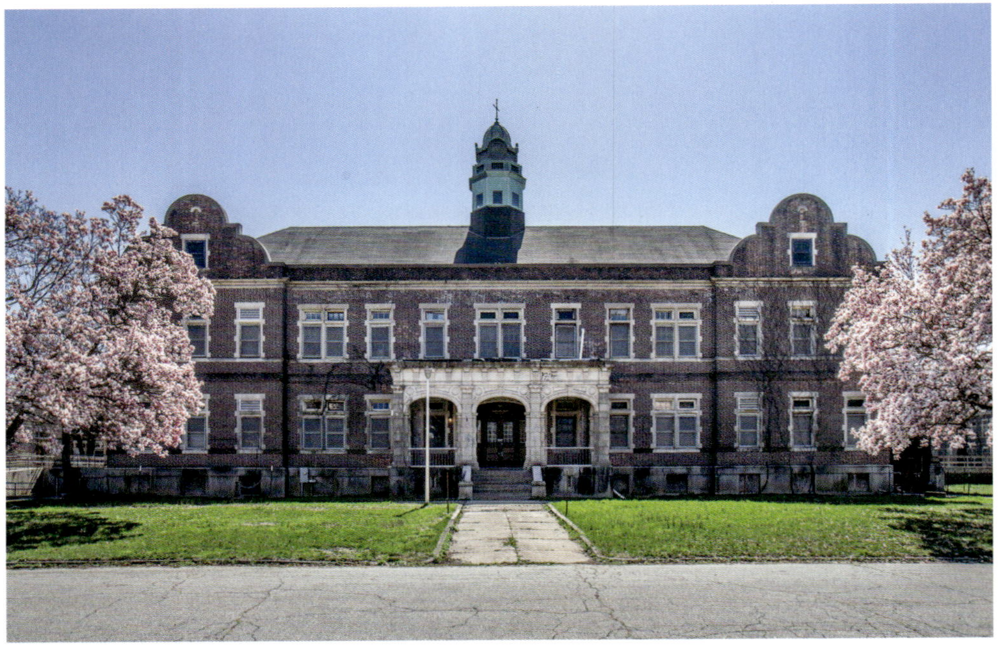

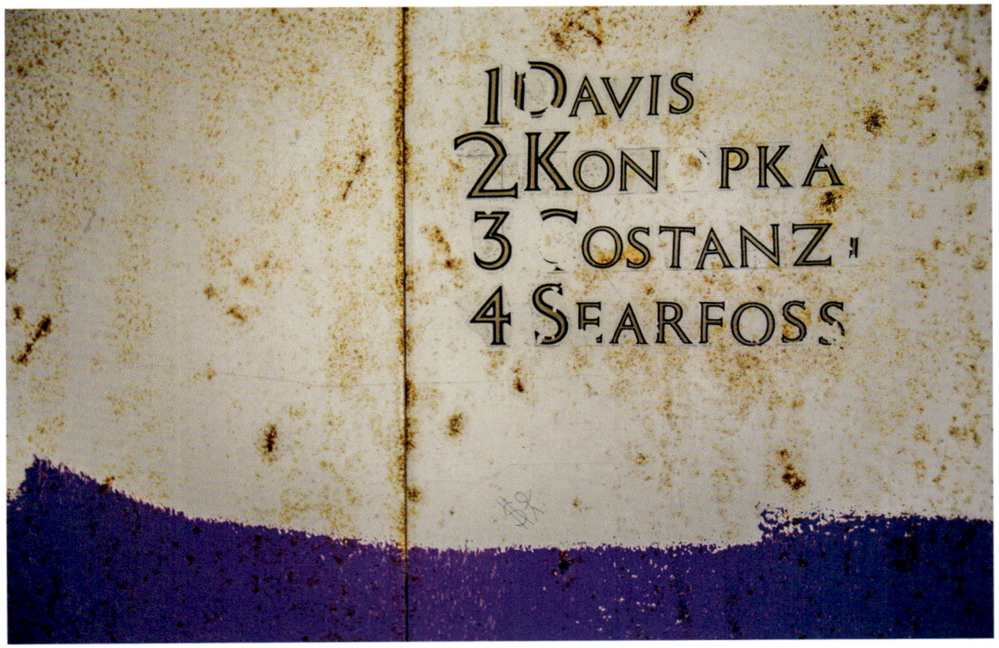

An exposé by NBC News investigative reporter Bill Baldini in 1968 entitled *Suffer the Little Children* took cameras inside the institution and documented the horrendous conditions. What the world saw was a cramped, filthy, understaffed warehouse for children. 'Patients' on the first floor of a low-grade cottage known as 'Quaker Hall' or 'Building Q' had their vibrating limbs physically restrained and tied to cribs; flies covered their emaciated bodies. More mobile and physically able children were housed on the second floor. A constant moaning echoed throughout the building as children paced their communal quarters, which reeked of faeces and waste; others lay in various states of awkwardness on the bare floor, some in a foetal position.

One boy from Quaker Hall ('Johnny', with an IQ of 69) was interviewed by Baldini. It was revealed that he had been punished by Dr. Jesse Fear for unacceptable behaviour. The punishment? Downgrading him to a ward with children who have an IQ of just 10-20. The interview clearly revealed just how inhumane this kind of punishment was, but also that the institution created to help these children was actually making them worse. On August 15, 1968, not long after the exposé aired, the *Gettysburg Times* reported that Dr. Jesse Fear had been placed under suspension, necessitating his resignation from Pennhurst after forcibly injecting a 'difficult' child with a tranquiliser.

Patient Clothing

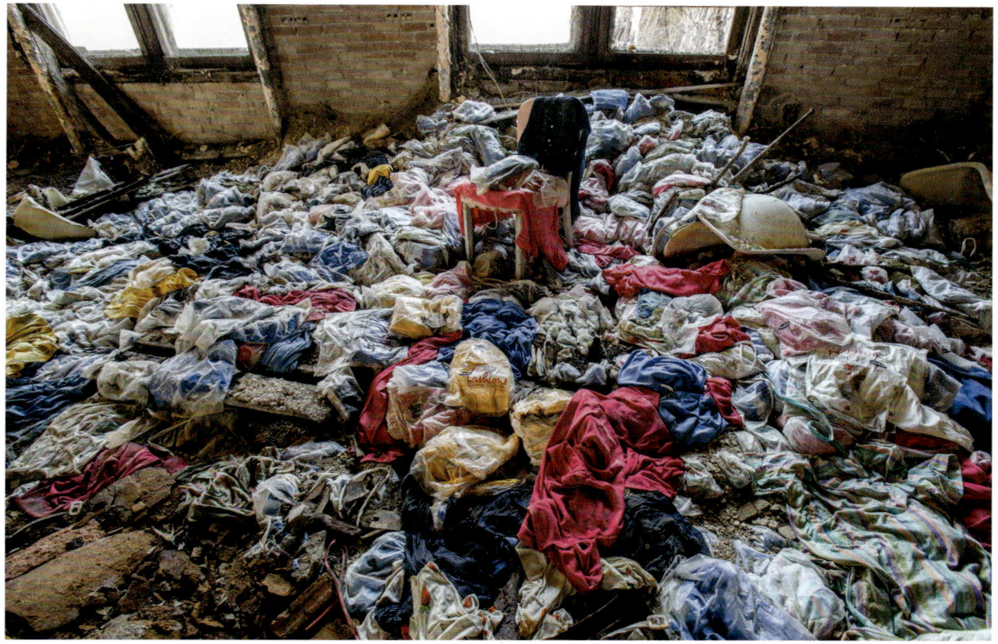

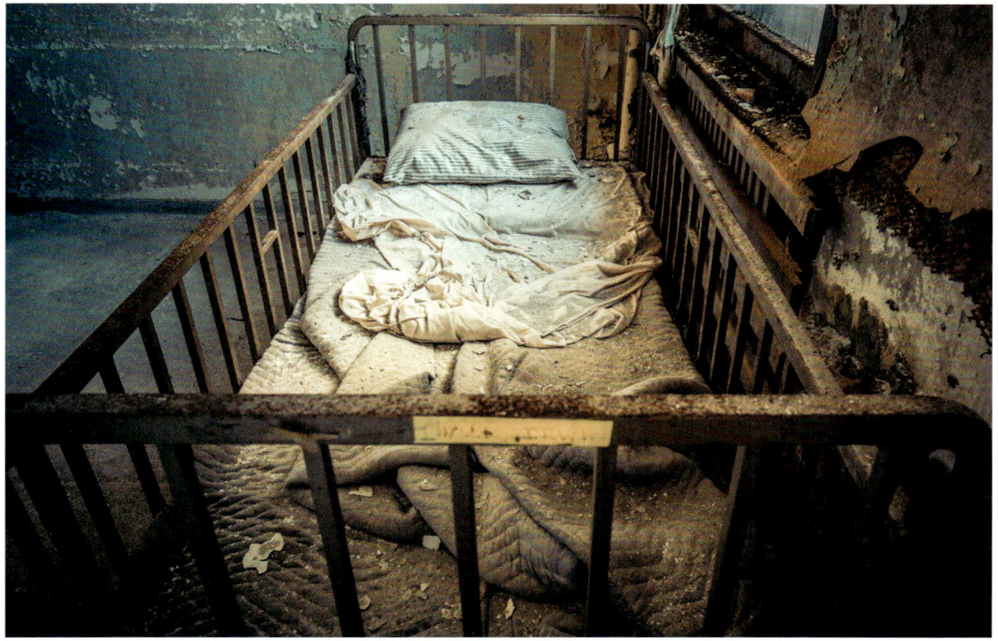

The fate of Letchworth Village – just like that of Pennhurst – was sealed by an investigative report. Just four years after Baldini's exposé of Pennhurst, a young Geraldo Rivera exposed the conditions at Letchworth, which were in his own words "the worst I have ever seen…ever. One attendant for perhaps 50 severely and profoundly retarded children – laying on the floor naked and smeared with their own faeces. They were making a pitiful sound… a mournful wail that it's impossible for me to forget. It smelled of filth… it smelled of disease… and it smelled of death". Rivera went on to conclude that "when there are 40-50 children for every nurse, the attendants are victims of the conditions at these institutions as much as the patients are – and the treatment of the 'retarded' is the last big social disgrace".

Atrocities and inhumane conditions aside, Letchworth's legacy is not completely negative. It served as one of the first institutions to successfully test a live-virus polio vaccine in 1950. Two years earlier, Koprowski would develop a witchy concoction of blended rat brain and spinal cord, as well as a carefully cultured sample of the highly infectious viral disease. Little did he know at the time, but Hilary Koprowski would change the world for the better with nothing more than a household blender as he opened his mouth and poured the "thick, cold, greasy" solution down his throat, successfully inoculating himself against polio.

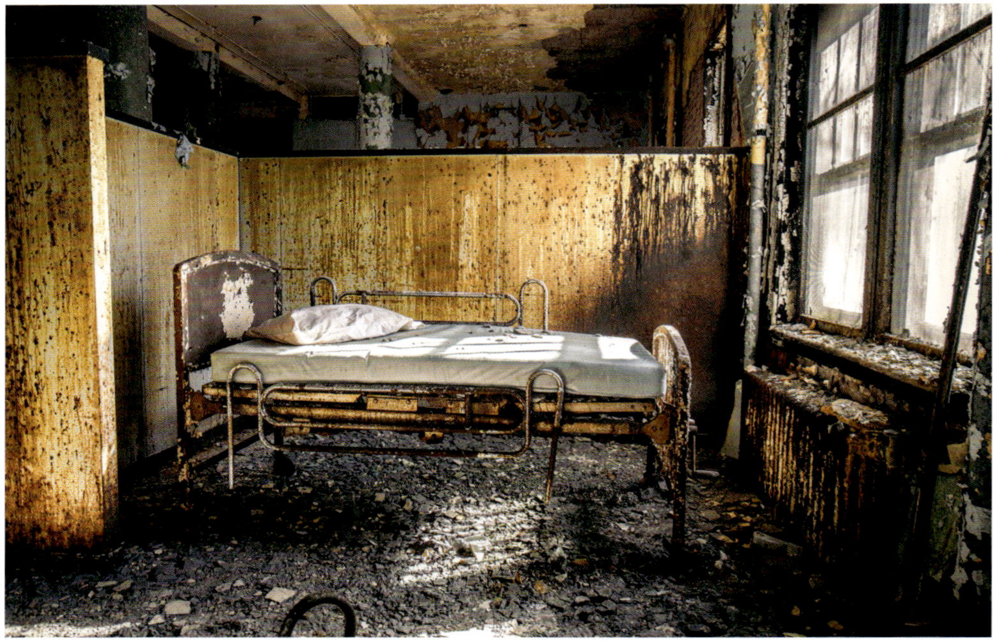

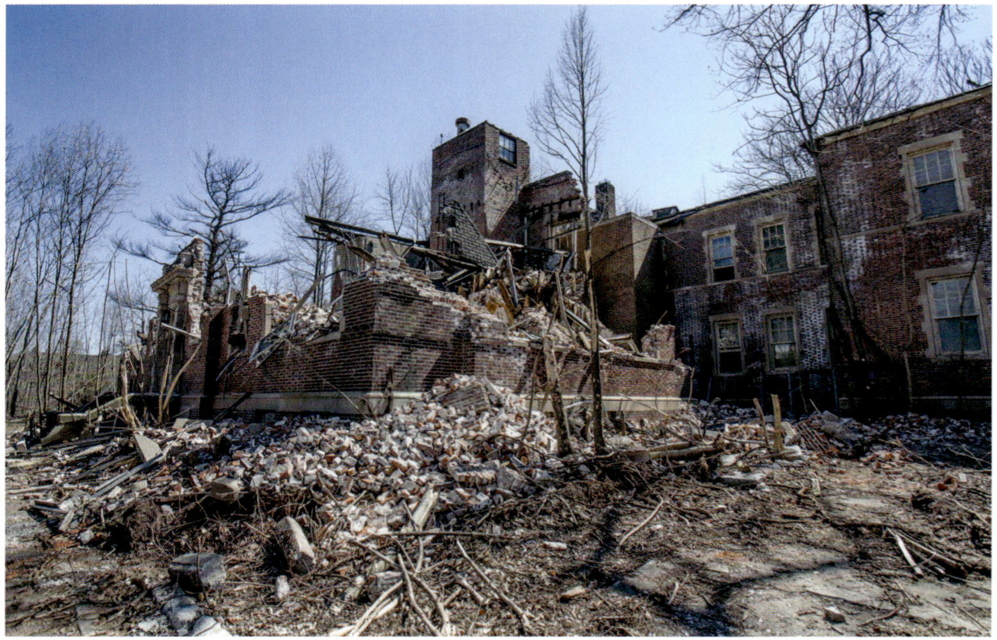

While historical record places the spotlight on Jonas Salk and Jonas Salbin as the forefathers of the polio vaccine, David M. Oshinsky's book, *Polio: An American Story,* refers to Koprowski as the "forgotten man" who deserves a place in that light. Unlike Salk's vaccine, which utilised dead viruses, Koprowski's live-virus advancement could be administered orally. Not only would it end up being cheaper and more accessible to the masses, its live-virus properties also allowed it to be spread within safe levels, to build immunity throughout households and the community.
Koprowski would go on to test his vaccine in 1950 at Letchworth Village after being kindly coerced by his friend, and then Letchworth laboratory director, Dr. George Jervis. Jervis saw the value of a vaccine in the realms of public safety and global health – and as faeces and human waste littered his wards, he knew it was only a matter of time before polio would decimate Letchworth Village. The patients at Letchworth were 'ideal' candidates in that they were "isolated, captive, easily studied and controlled".

The moral dilemmas inherent in Koprowski's tests are certainly a cause of polarity amongst historians and scientists alike. There is no written evidence that Koprowski sought out parental permission, nor did he notifty or seek permissions from the state of New York to perform his tests. Perhaps this is the reason behind his exclusion from historical record. During this time, live testing on human subjects was undoubtedly controversial in itself.

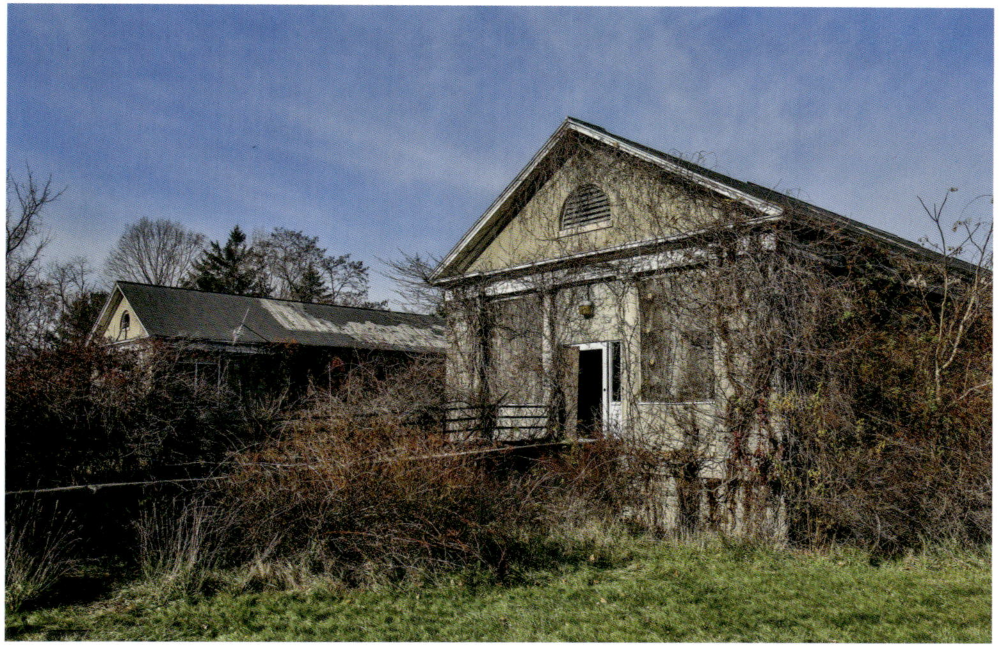

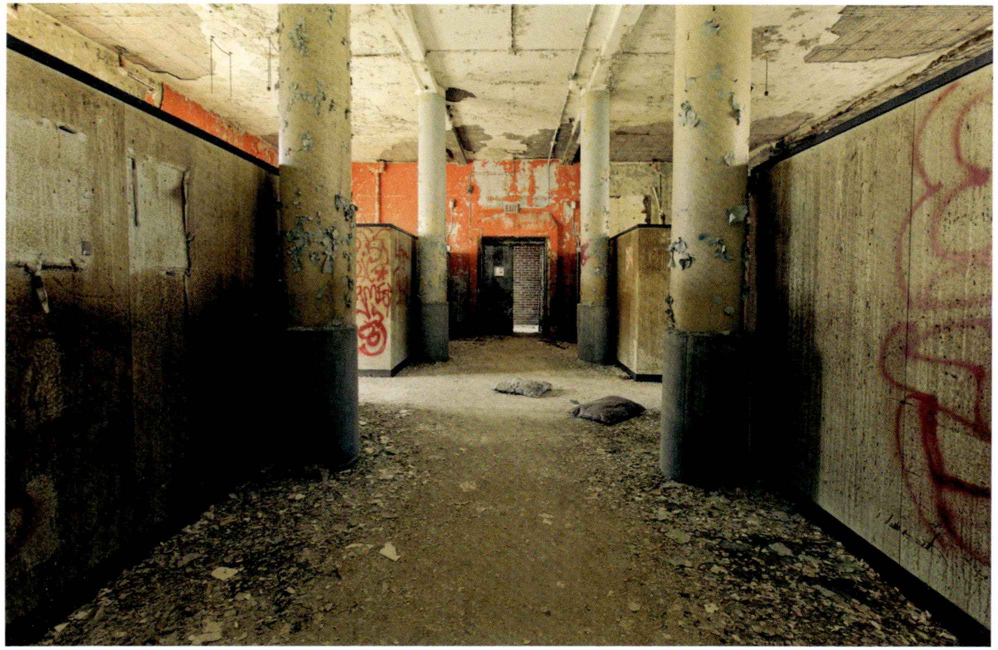

But proposing testing on developmentally challenged children surely would have had the doctor in hot water. Koprowski was insistent; he believed that the tests conducted at Letchworth, in secrecy or not, were well within the standards of scientific practice. Luckily, Koprowski's testing proved successful. All non-immune 'volunteers' developed antibodies and none showed any sign of the disease or its effects.

As the state schools shuttered under much controversy and governmentally forced closures, society as a whole had finally been made aware of the conditions behind locked doors, thanks to two budding investigative reporters. When the news broke, outrage ensued and in turn, attitudes on custodial care of the developmentally disabled began to change for the better. Budgets that were previously cut were reinstated, and the horrors of these institutions would influence adjustments and reform in social policy. Notably, *Halderman v. Pennhurst State School and Hospital* asserted precedence that the developmentally disabled in the care of the state deserved a constitutional right to humane care and education. The District Court decision was the first time that any federal court ruled that an institution must be closed based on a constitutional right to community services. The case drew huge attention and its proceedings birthed an important rule of law known as the 'Pennhurst Doctrine', which has been cited by state Attorneys General as binding precedent under United States constitutional law. It enforces the policy that States who receive federal funds for the treatment of the developmentally disabled must comply with federally imposed conditions.

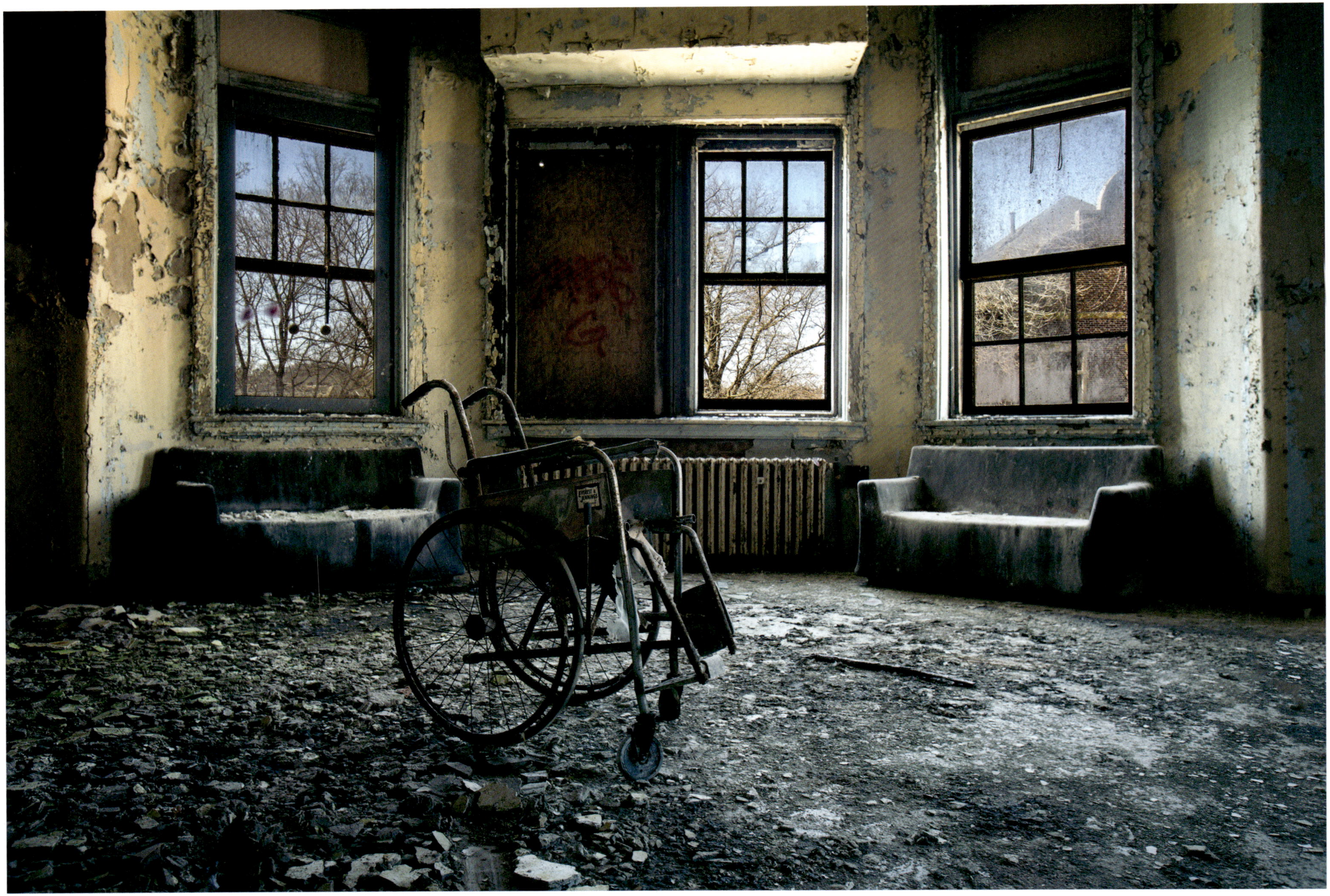

Pennhurst's Quaker Hall (Q2) unit for severely disturbed and intellectually disabled boys

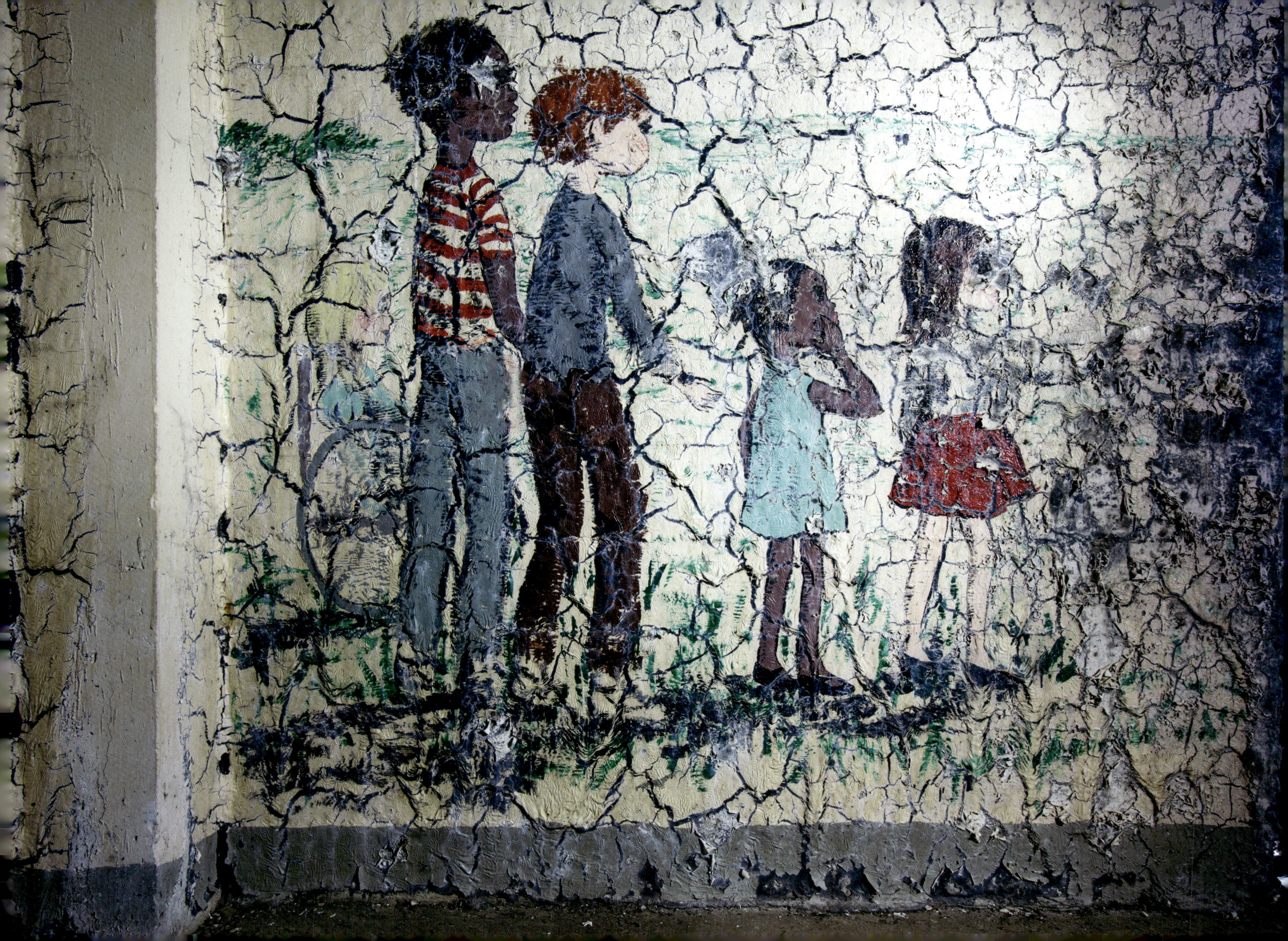

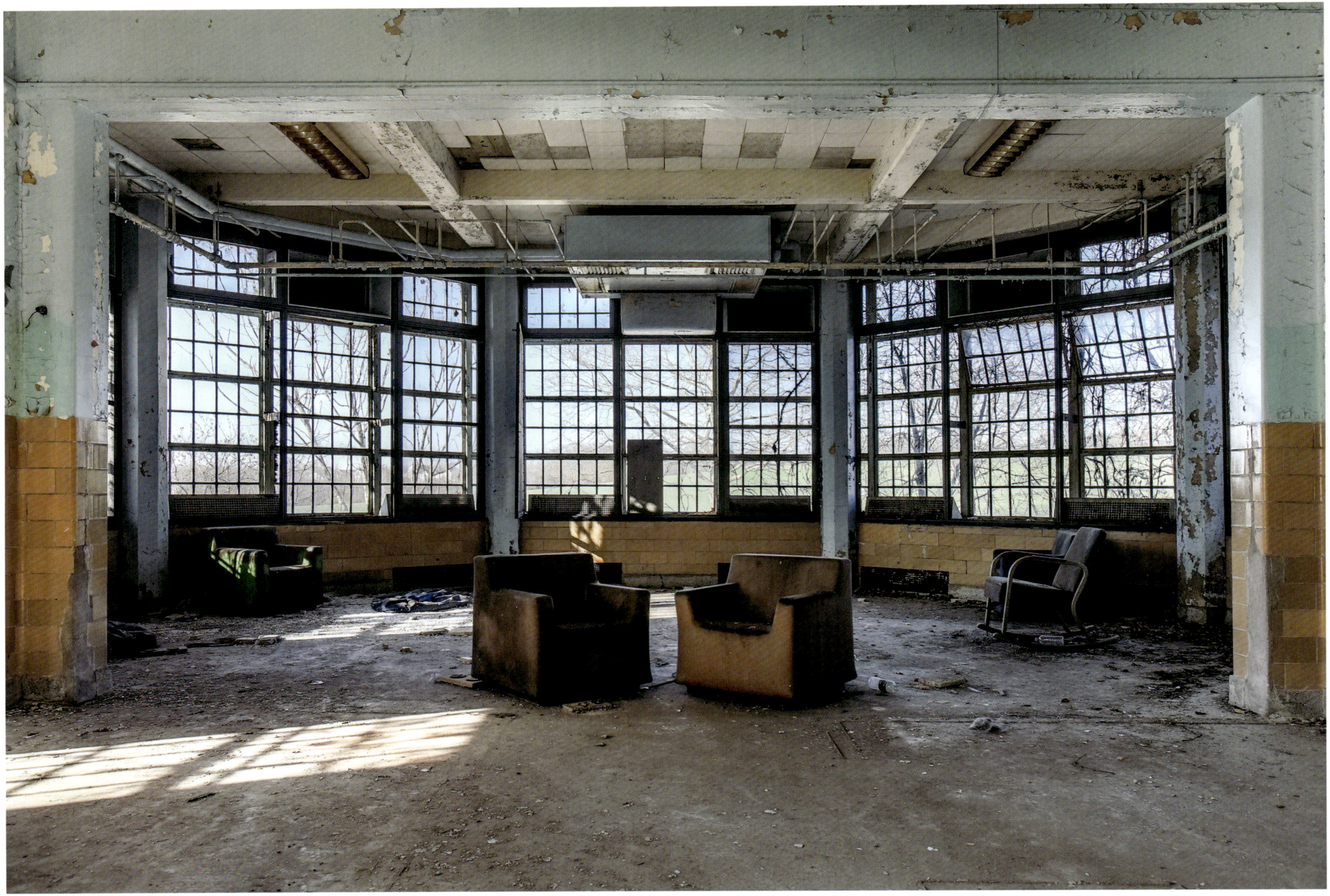

Rubber safety furniture

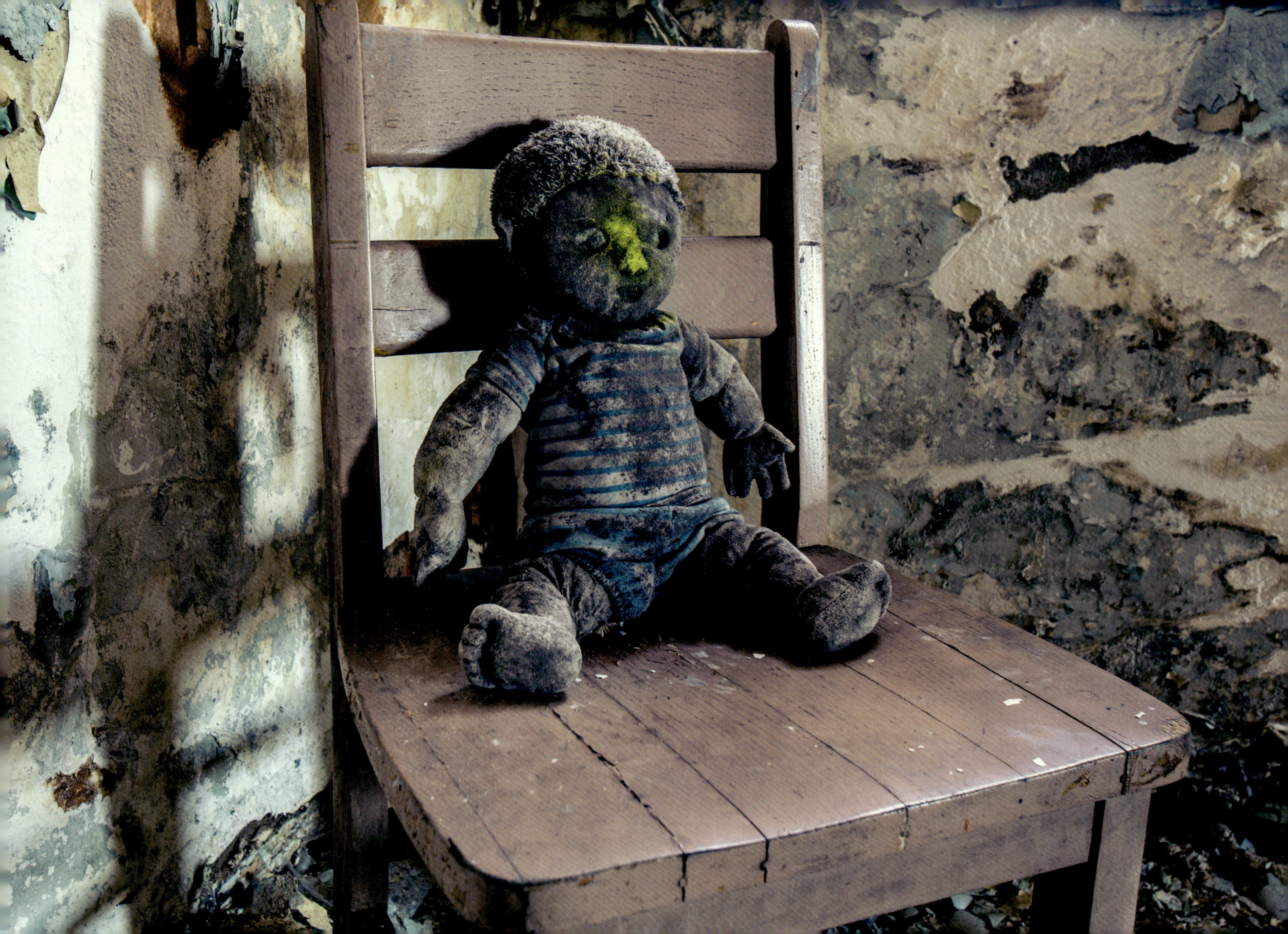

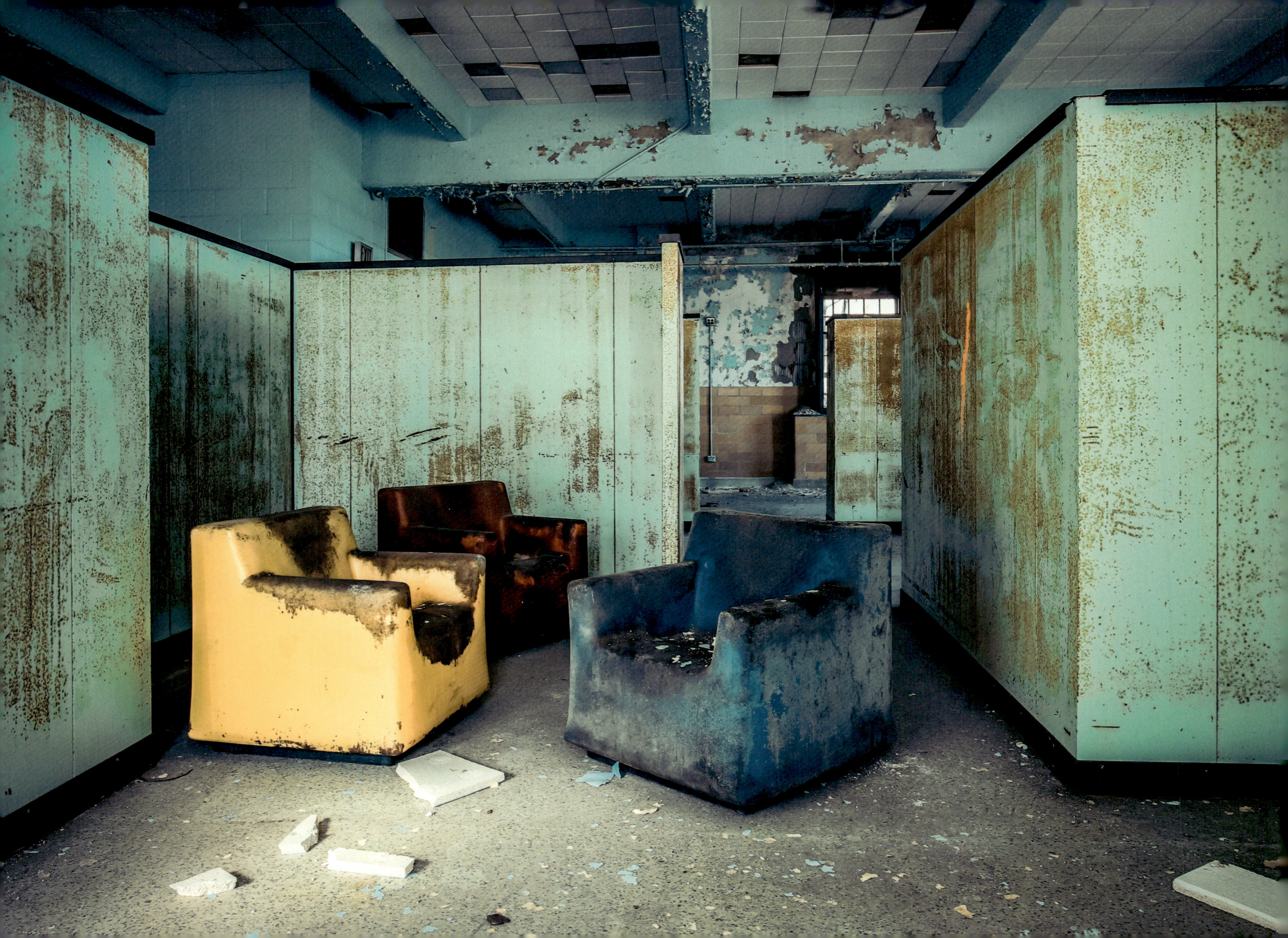

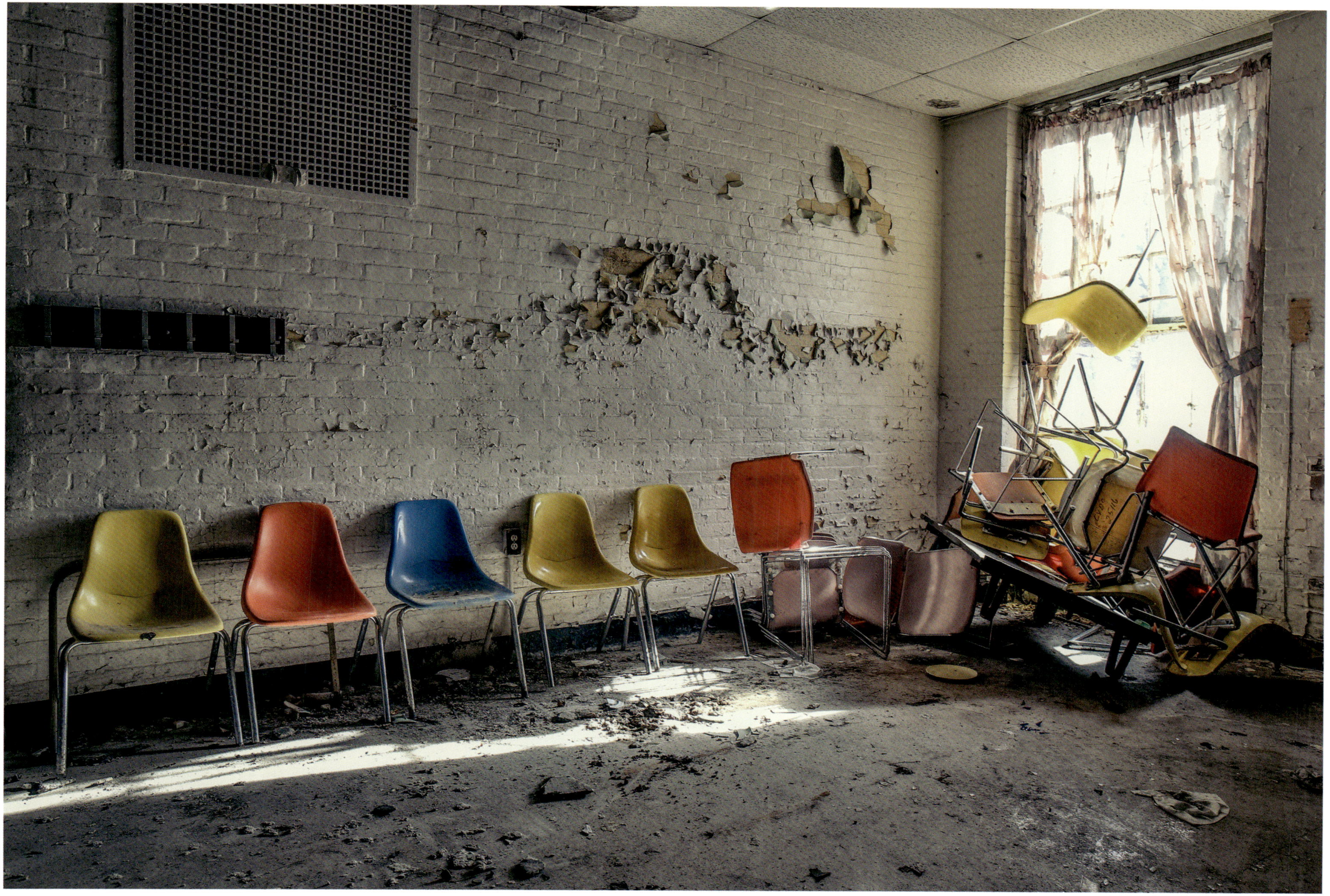

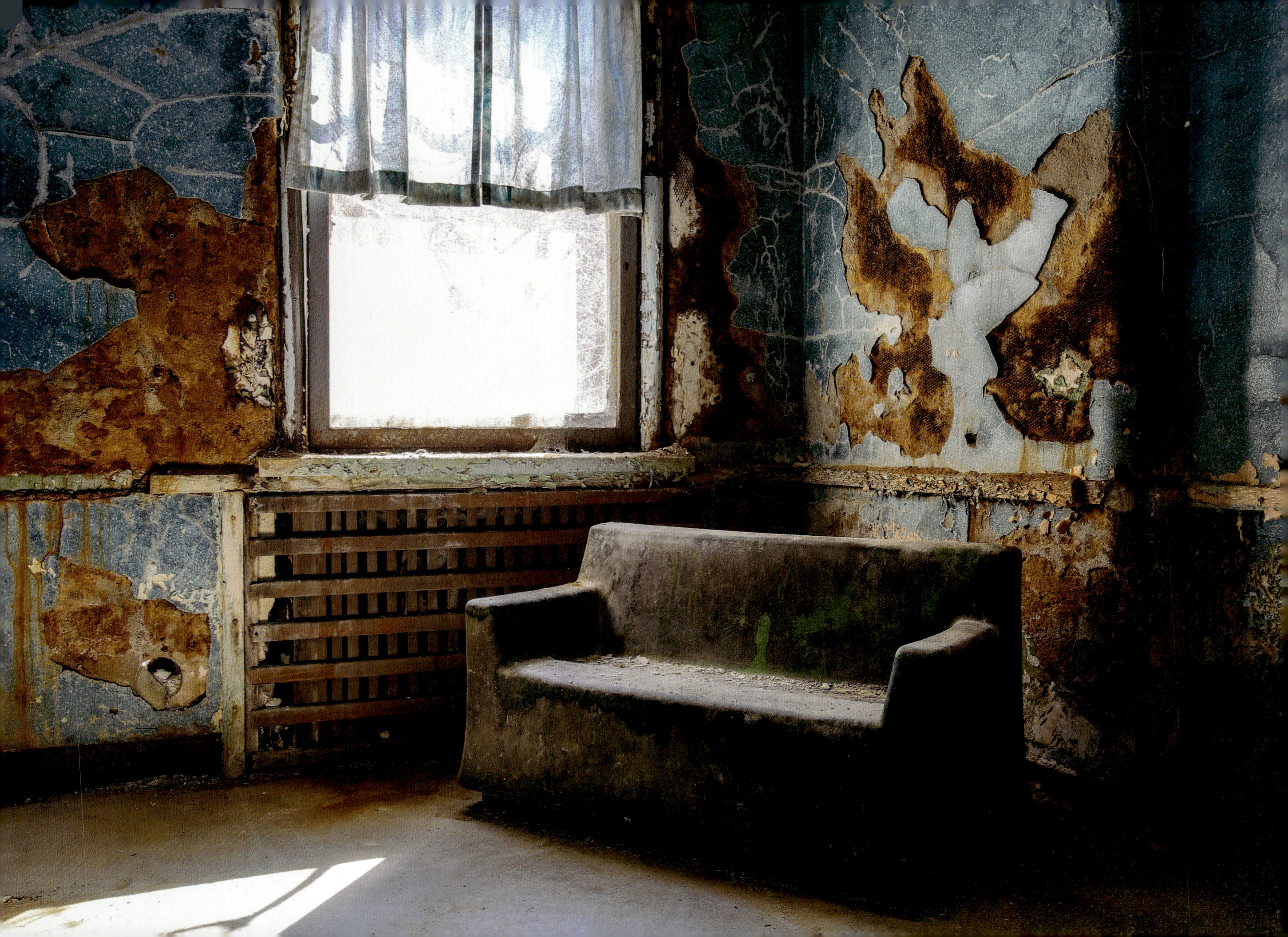

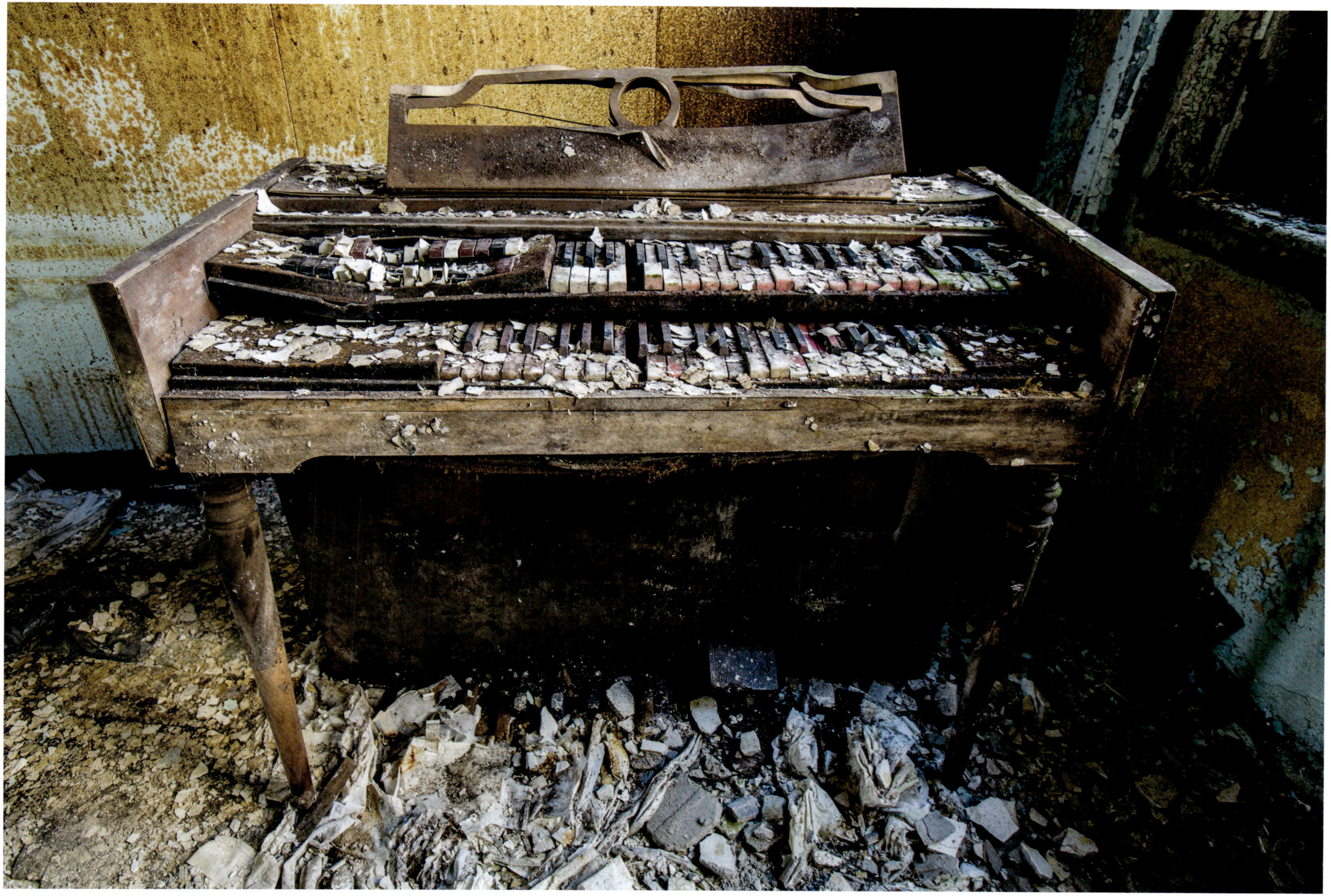

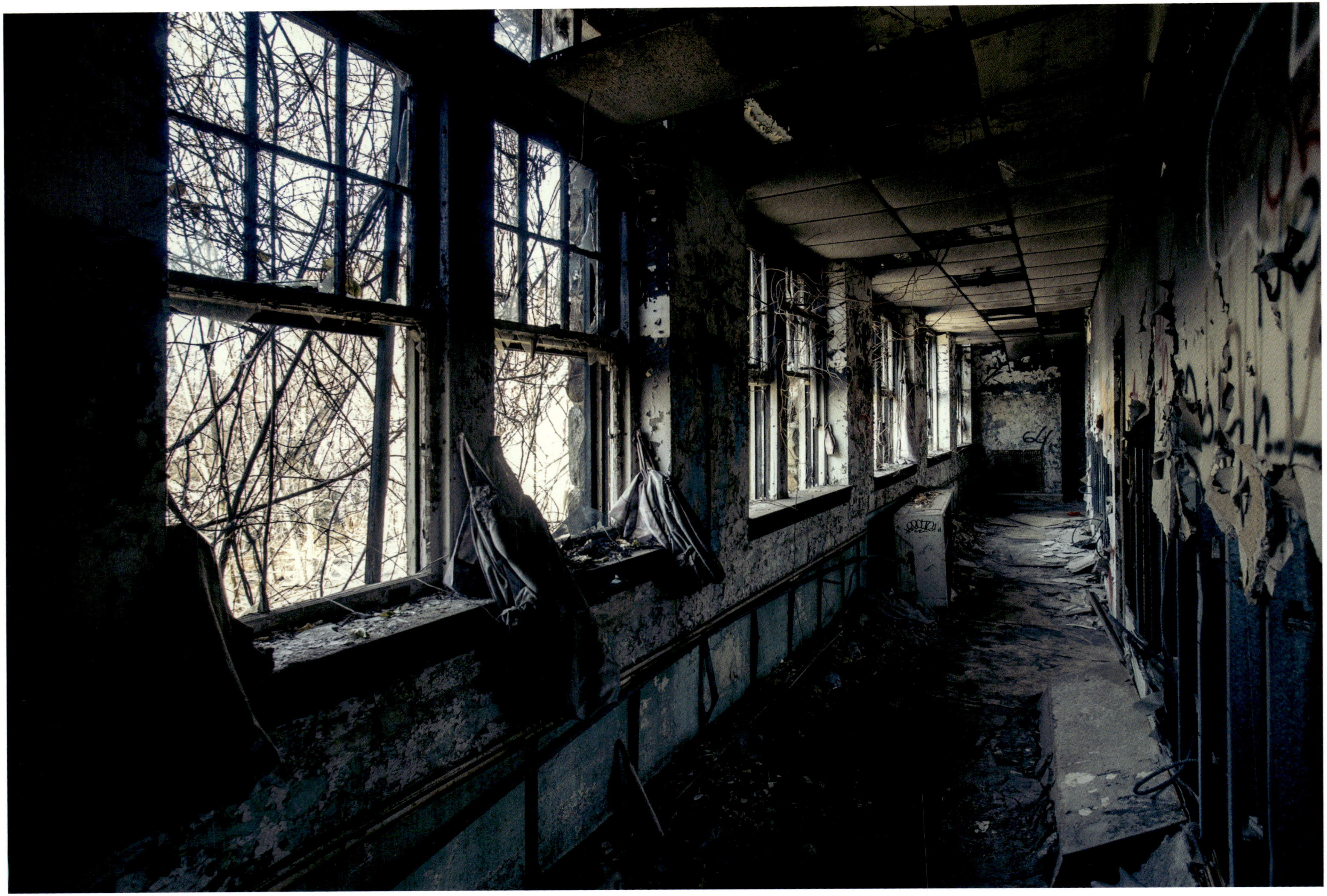

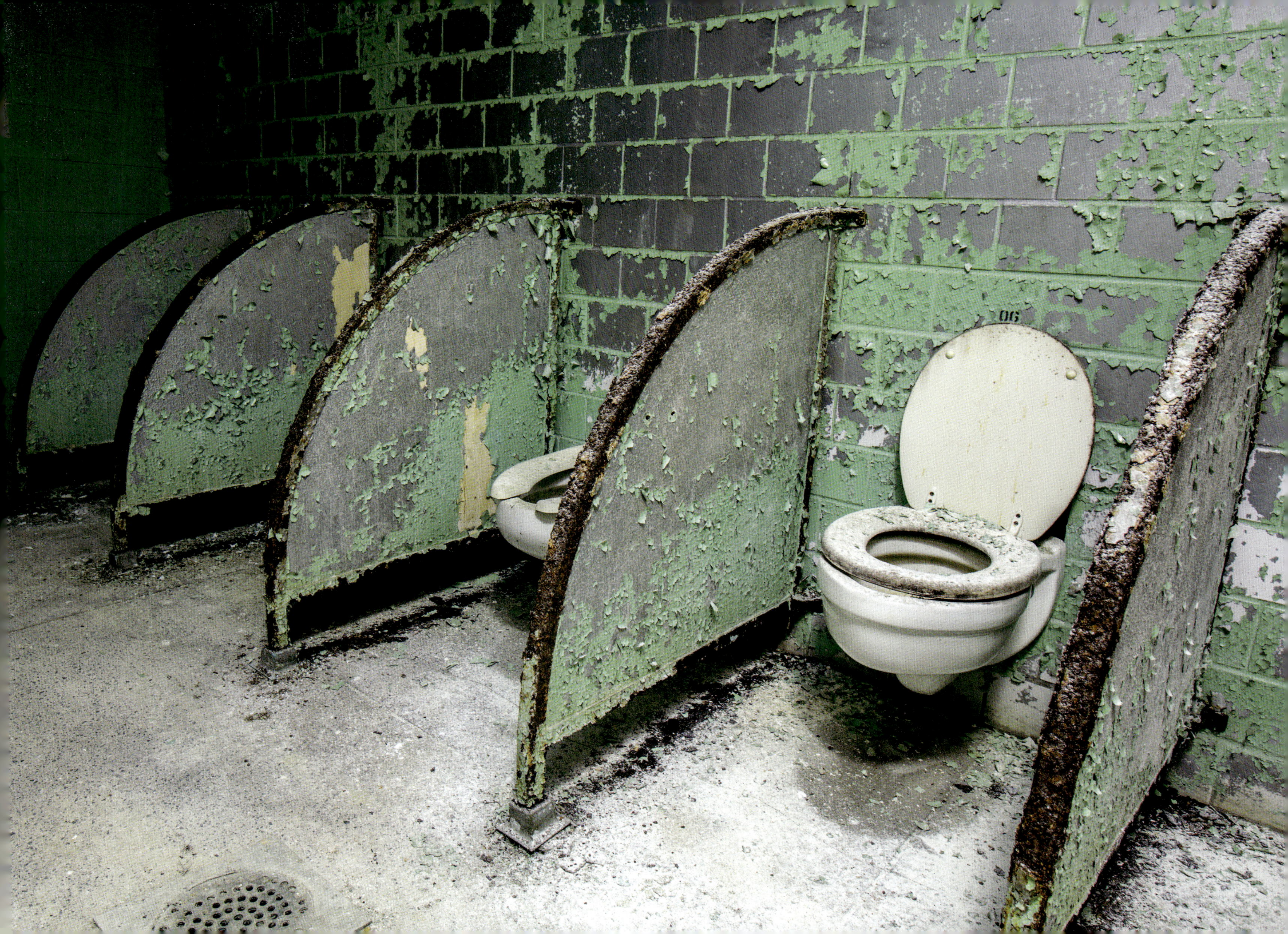
06

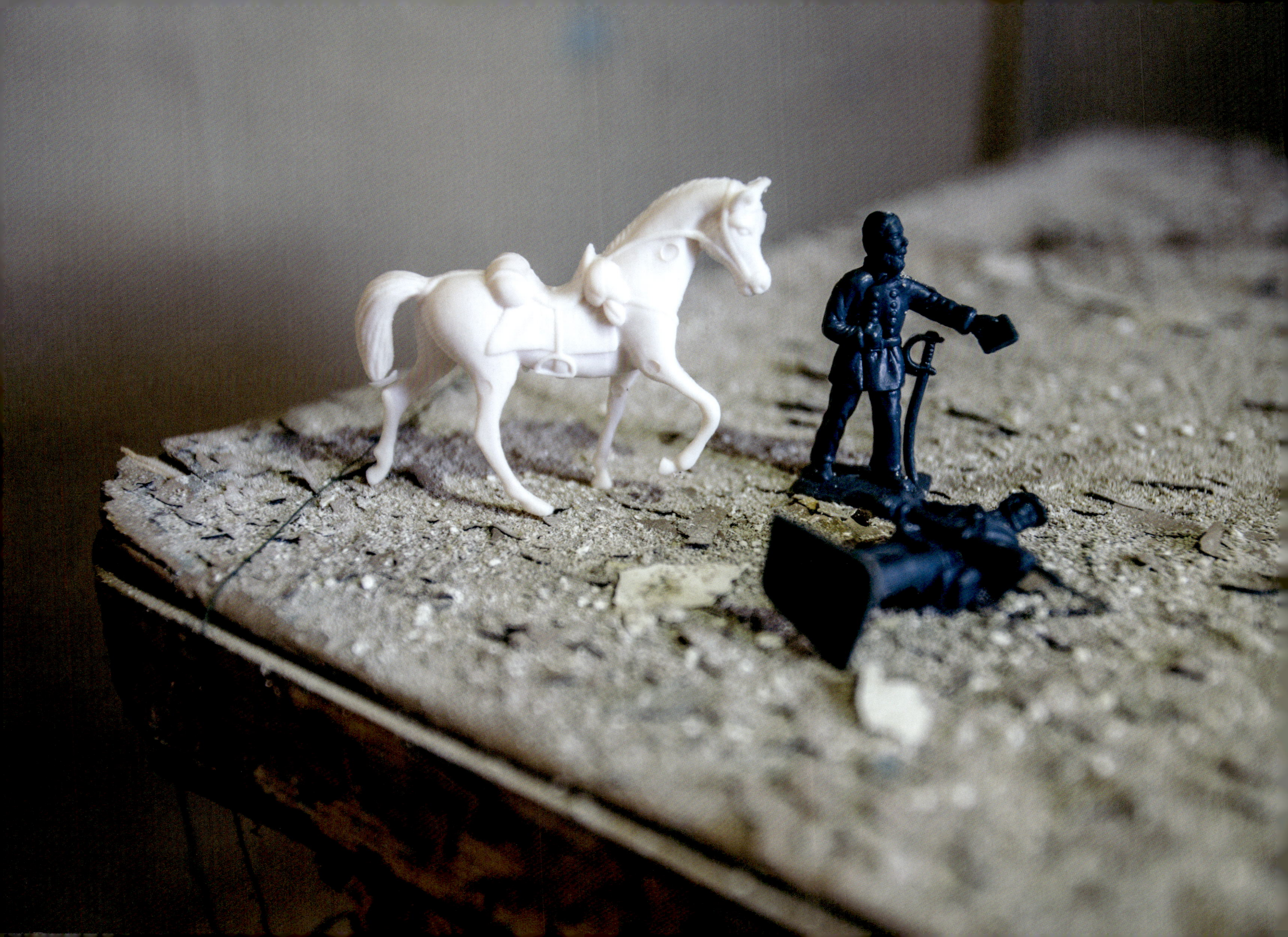

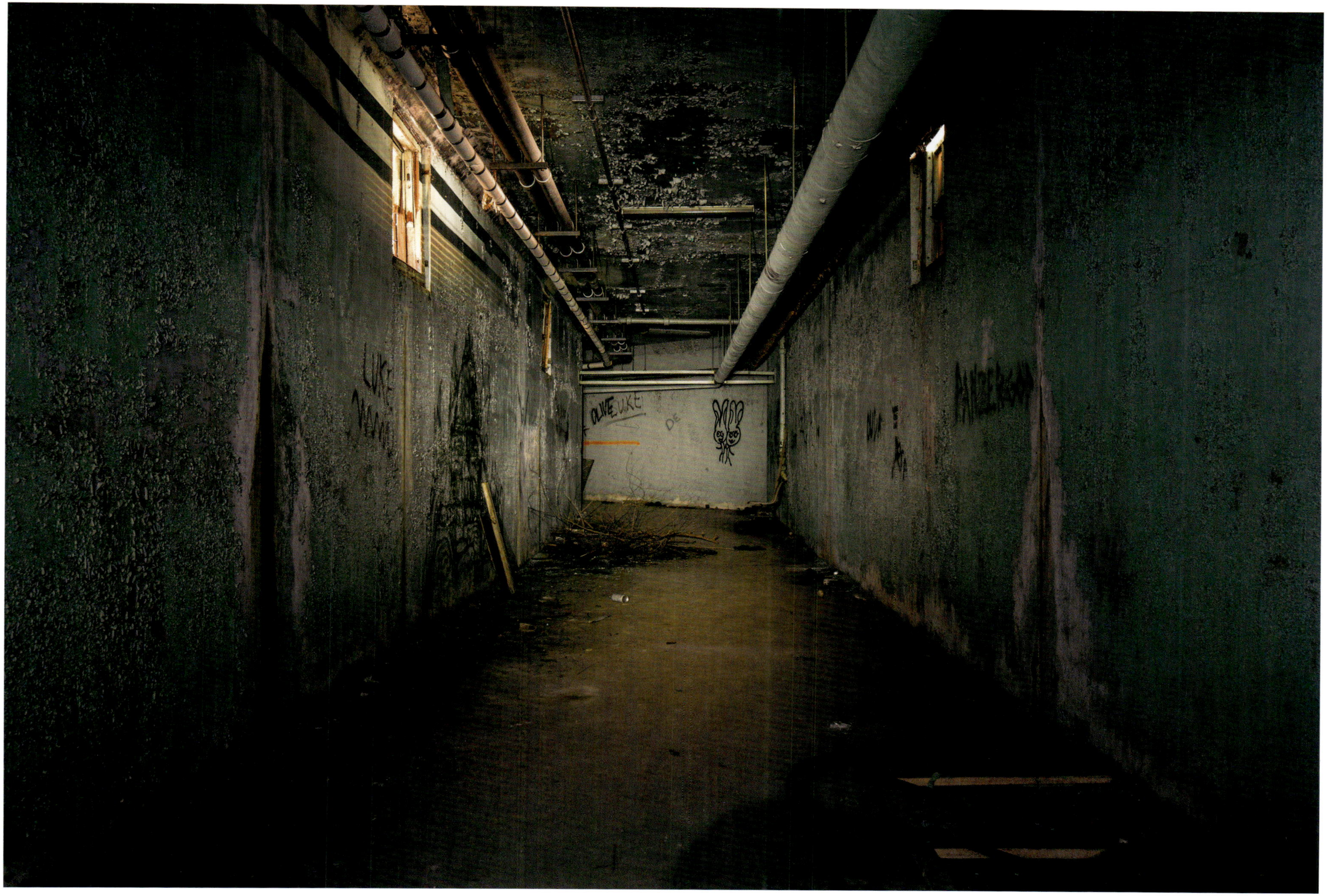

Pennhurst State School and Hospital tunnel system

Rockland State Hospital

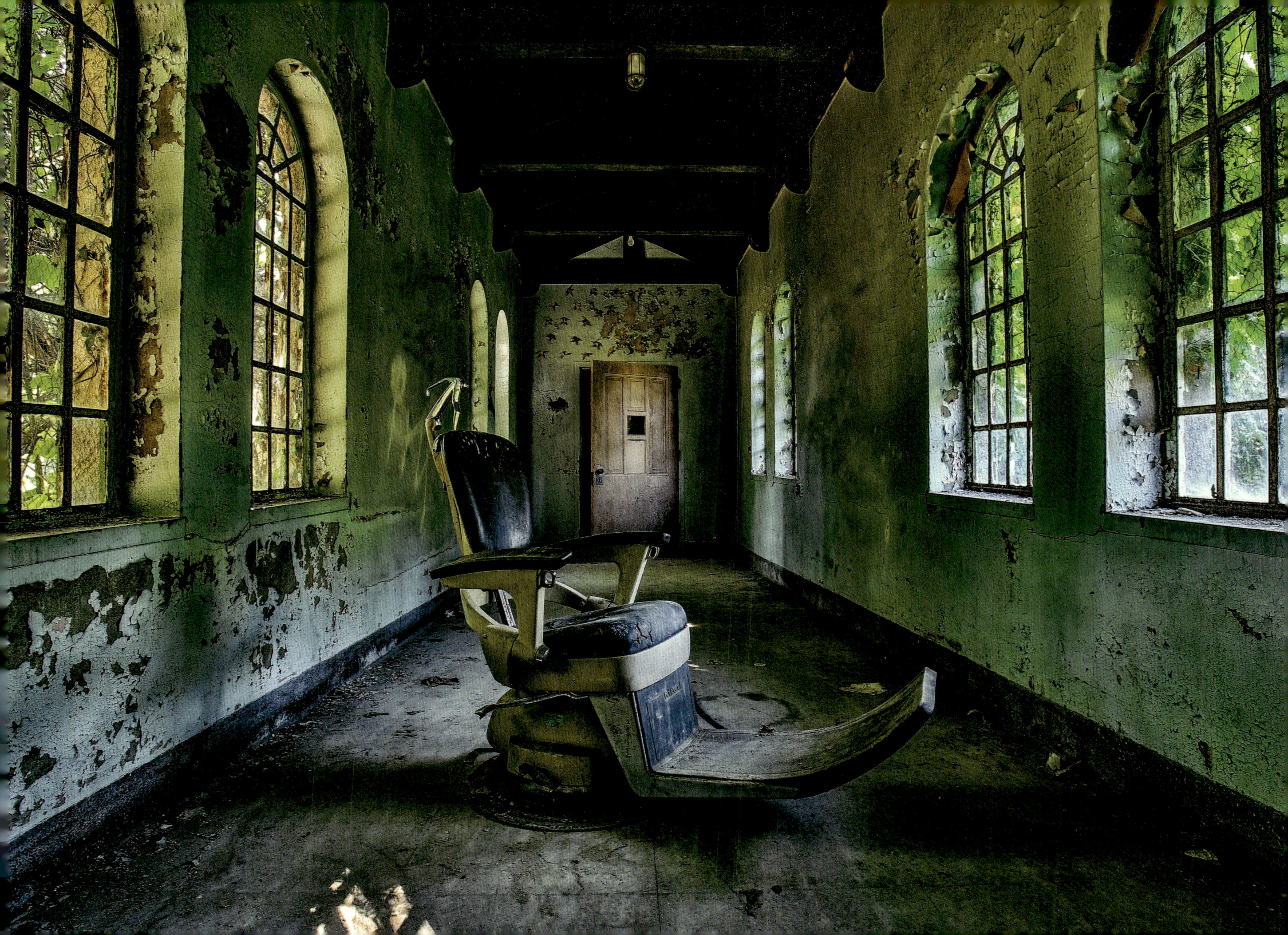

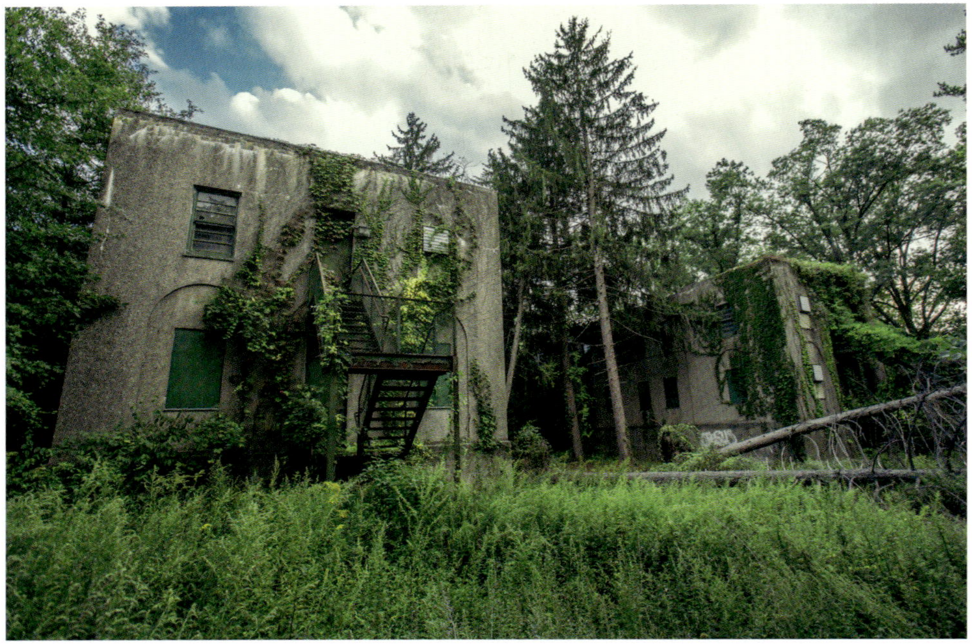
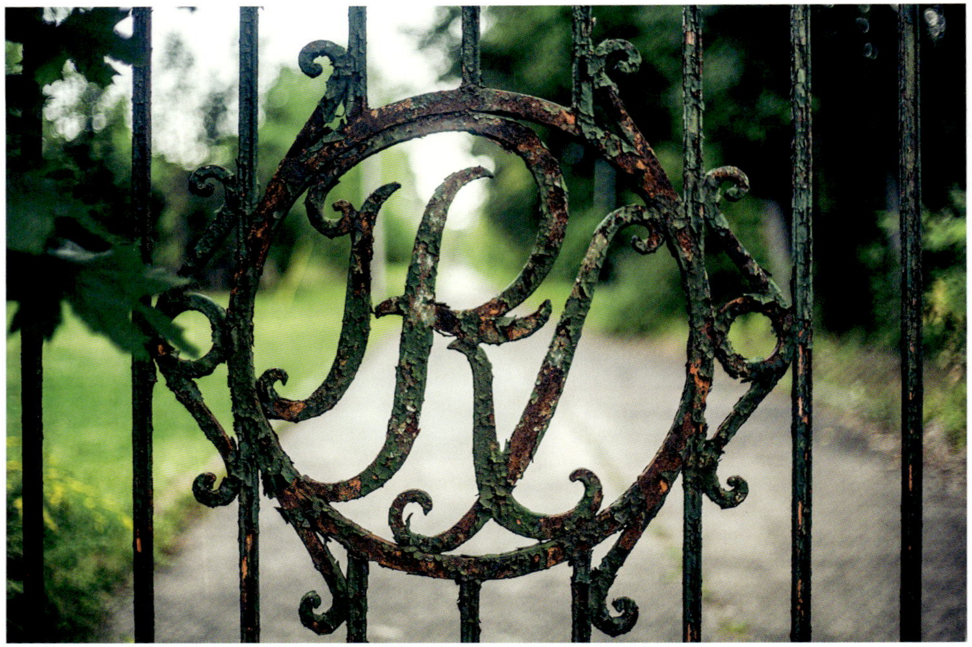
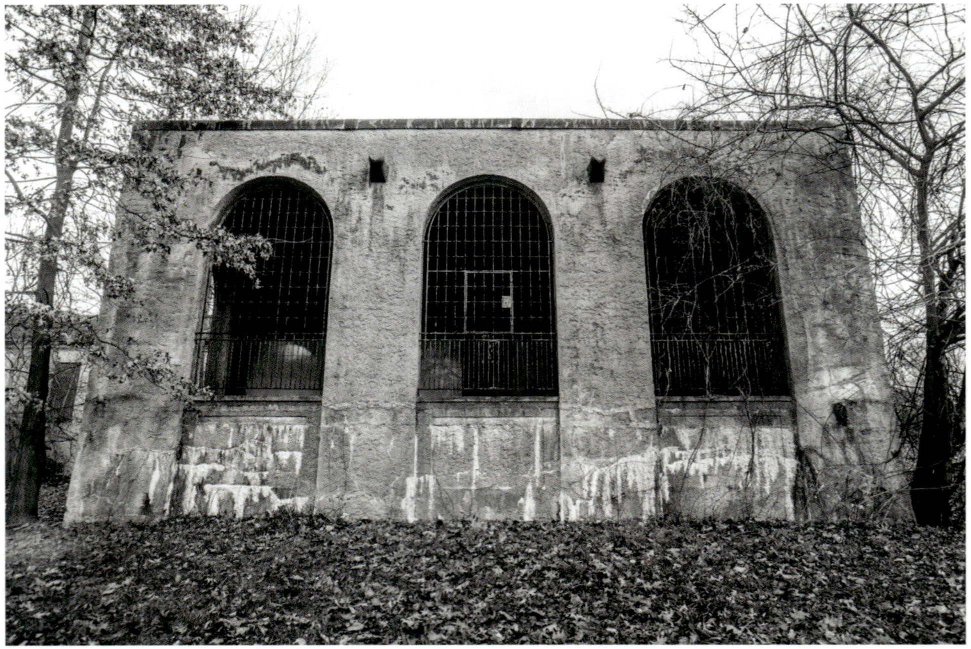
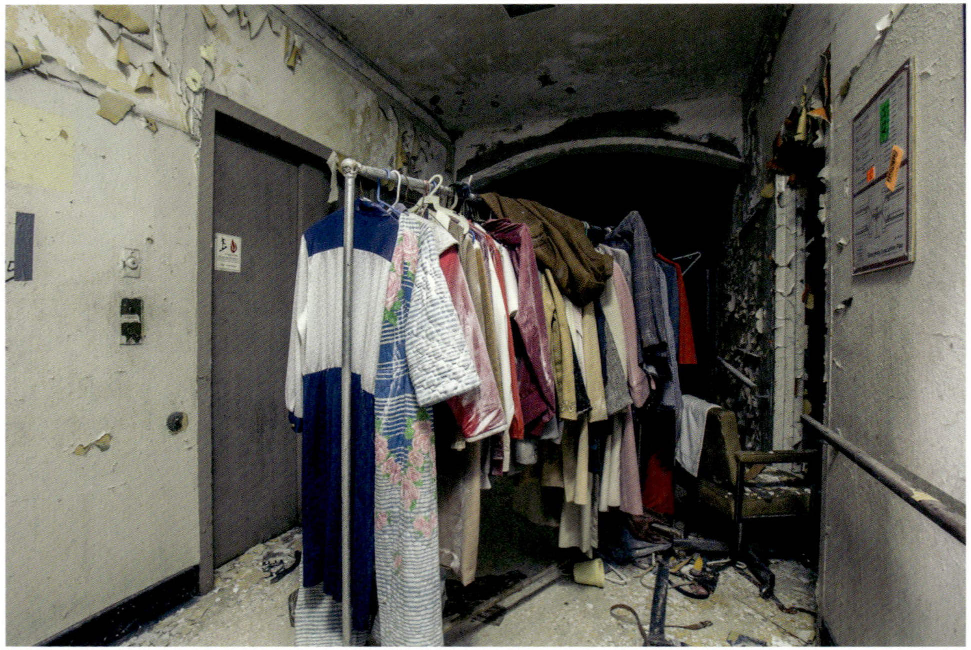

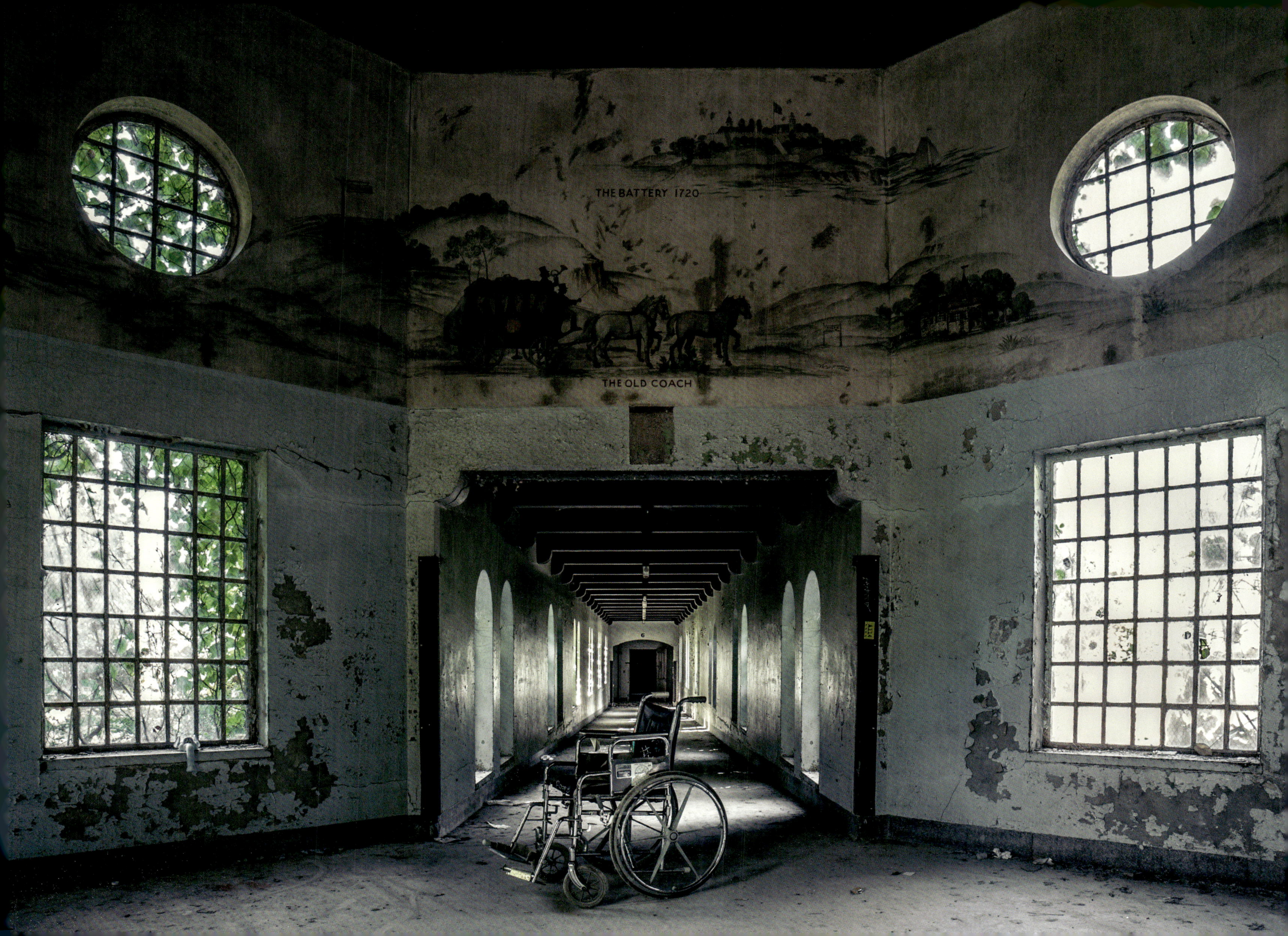
THE BATTERY 1720
THE OLD COACH

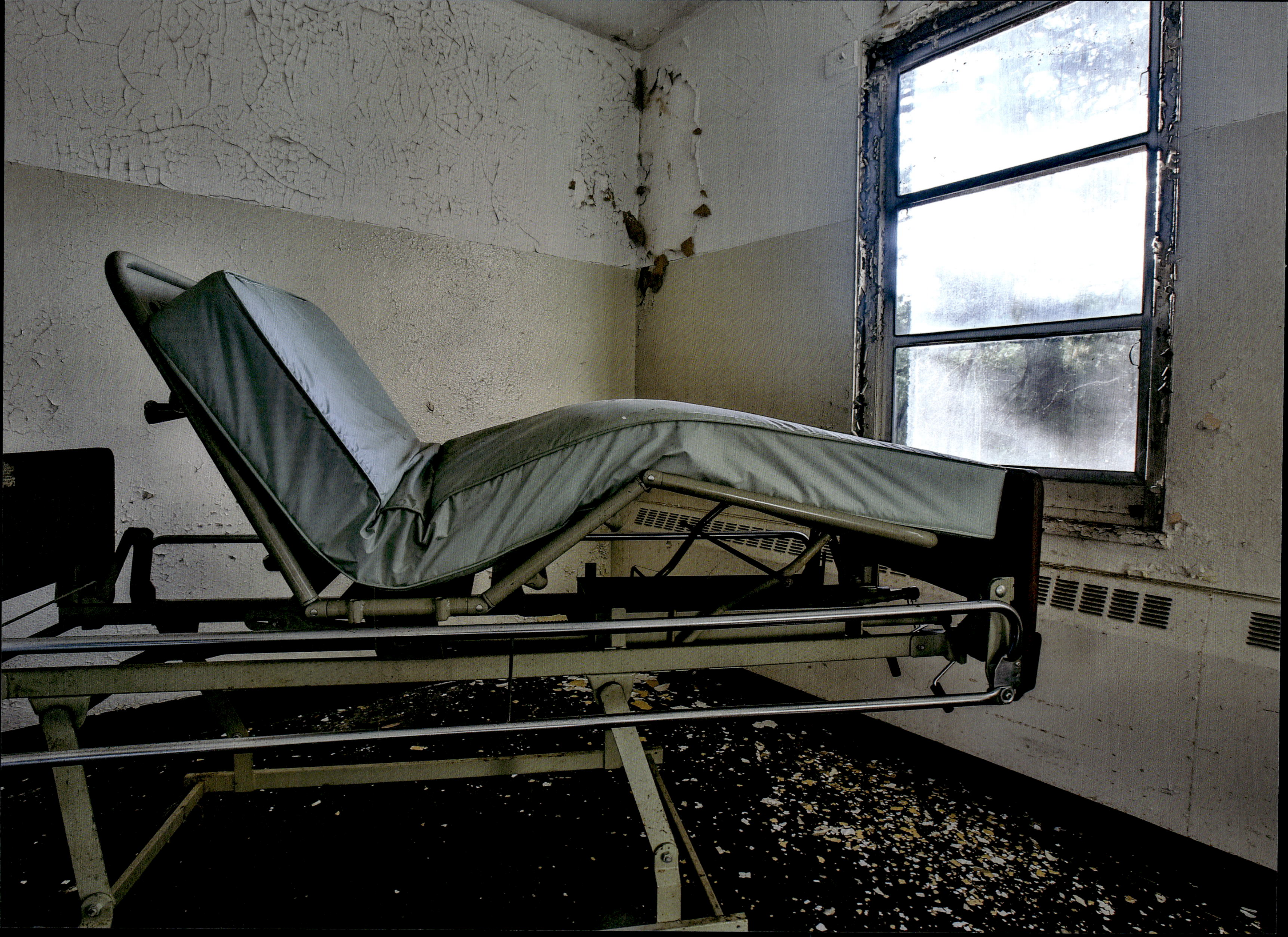

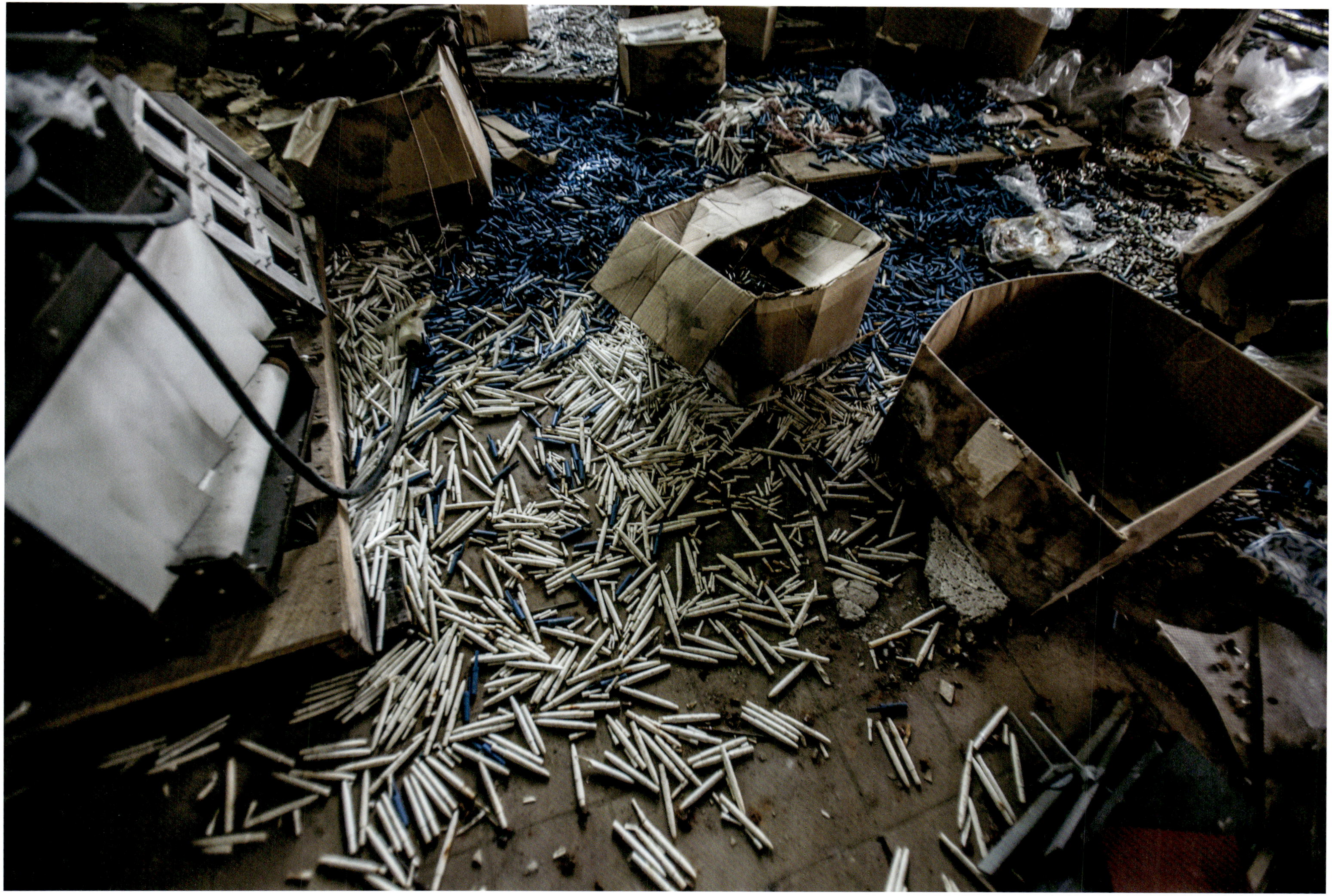

Hilton & Trump Hotels writing pen assembly in occupational therapy unit

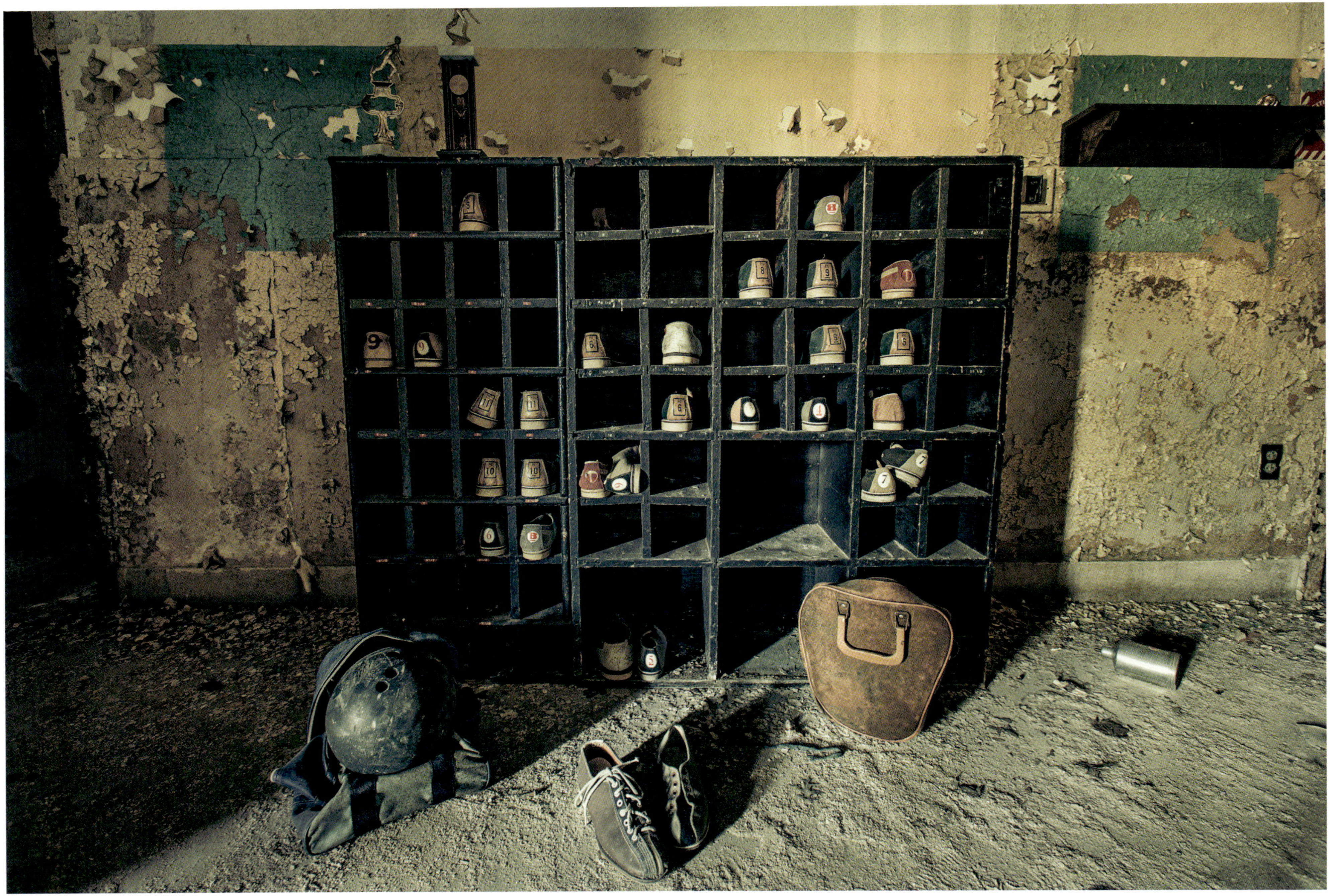

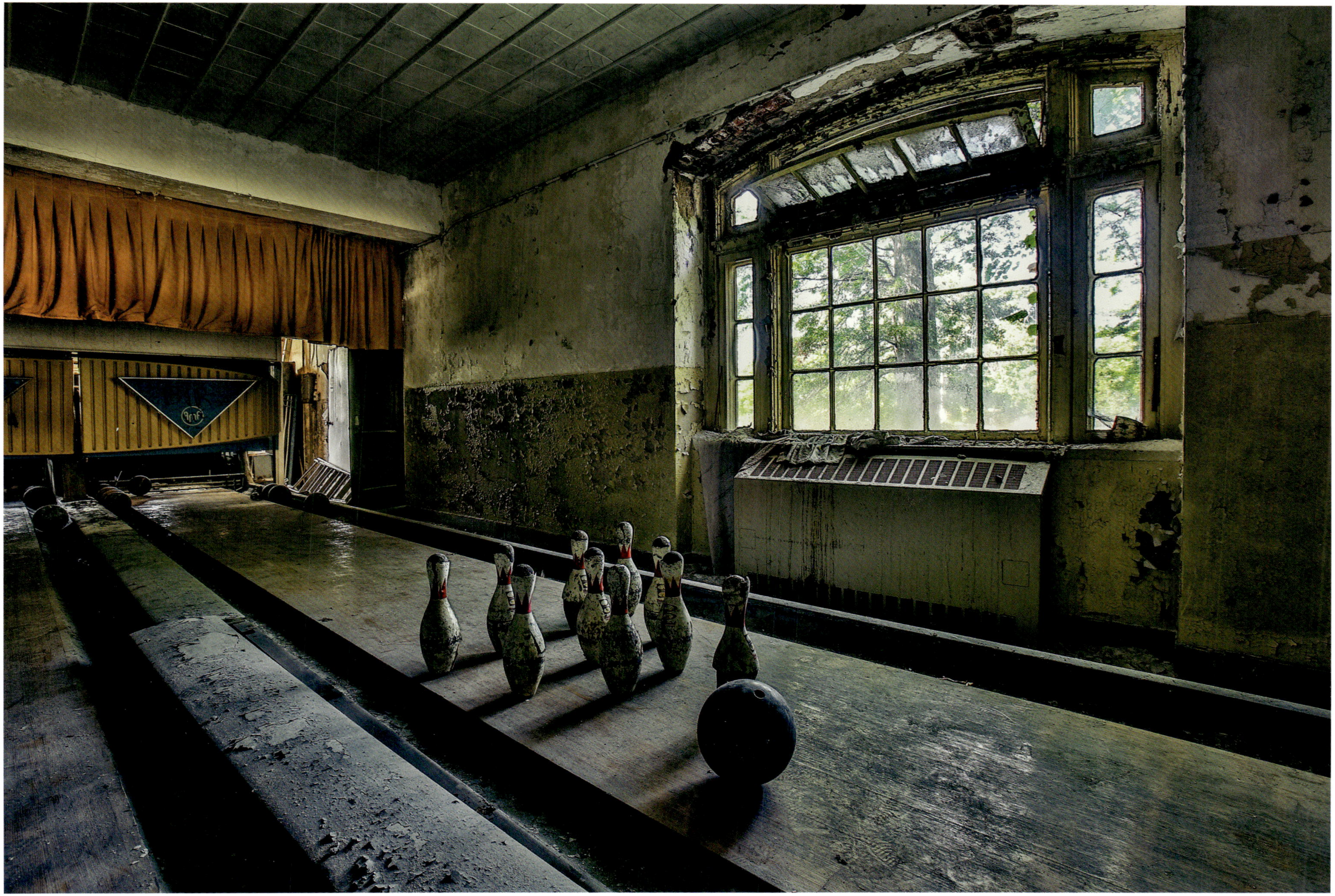

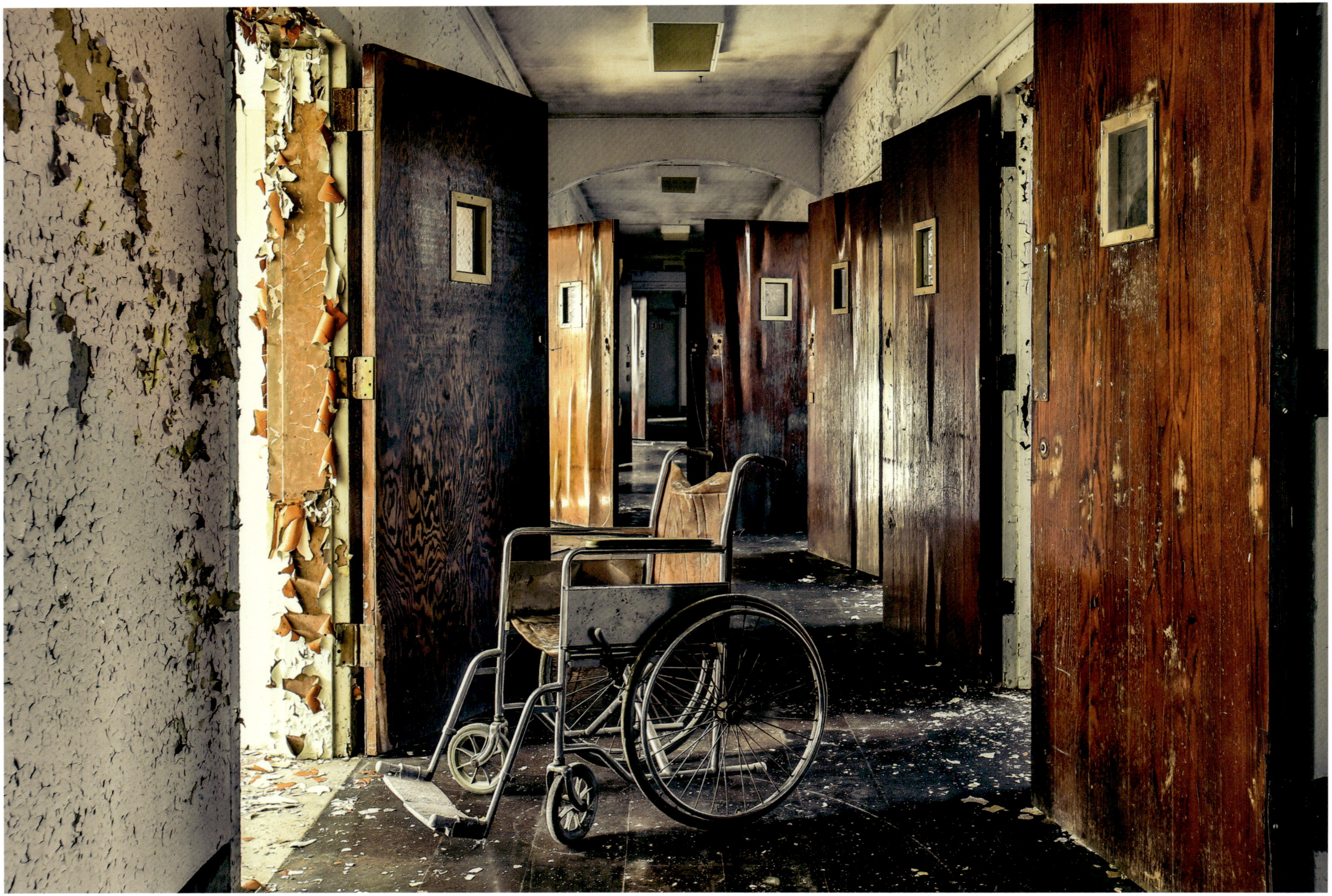

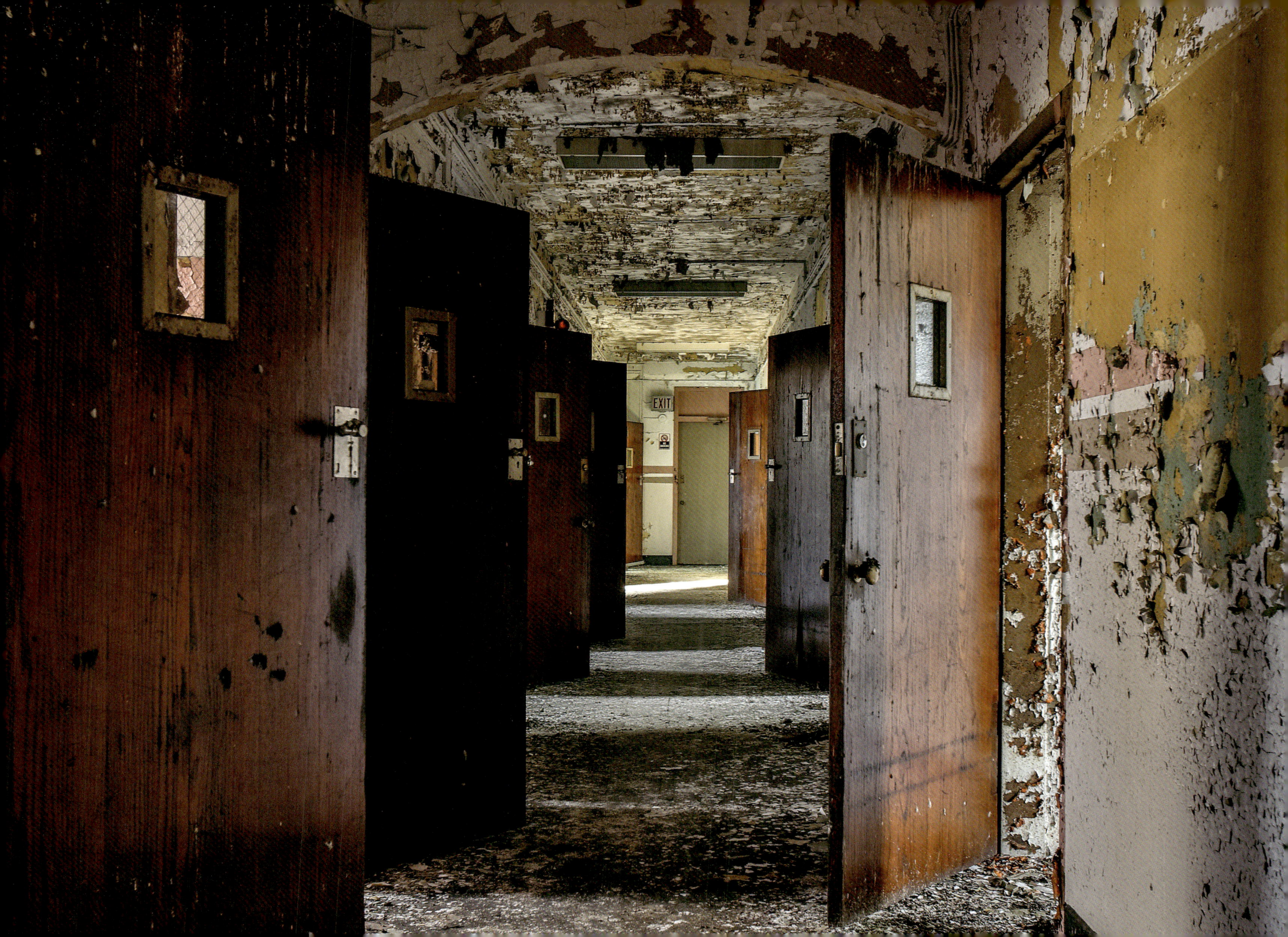
EXIT

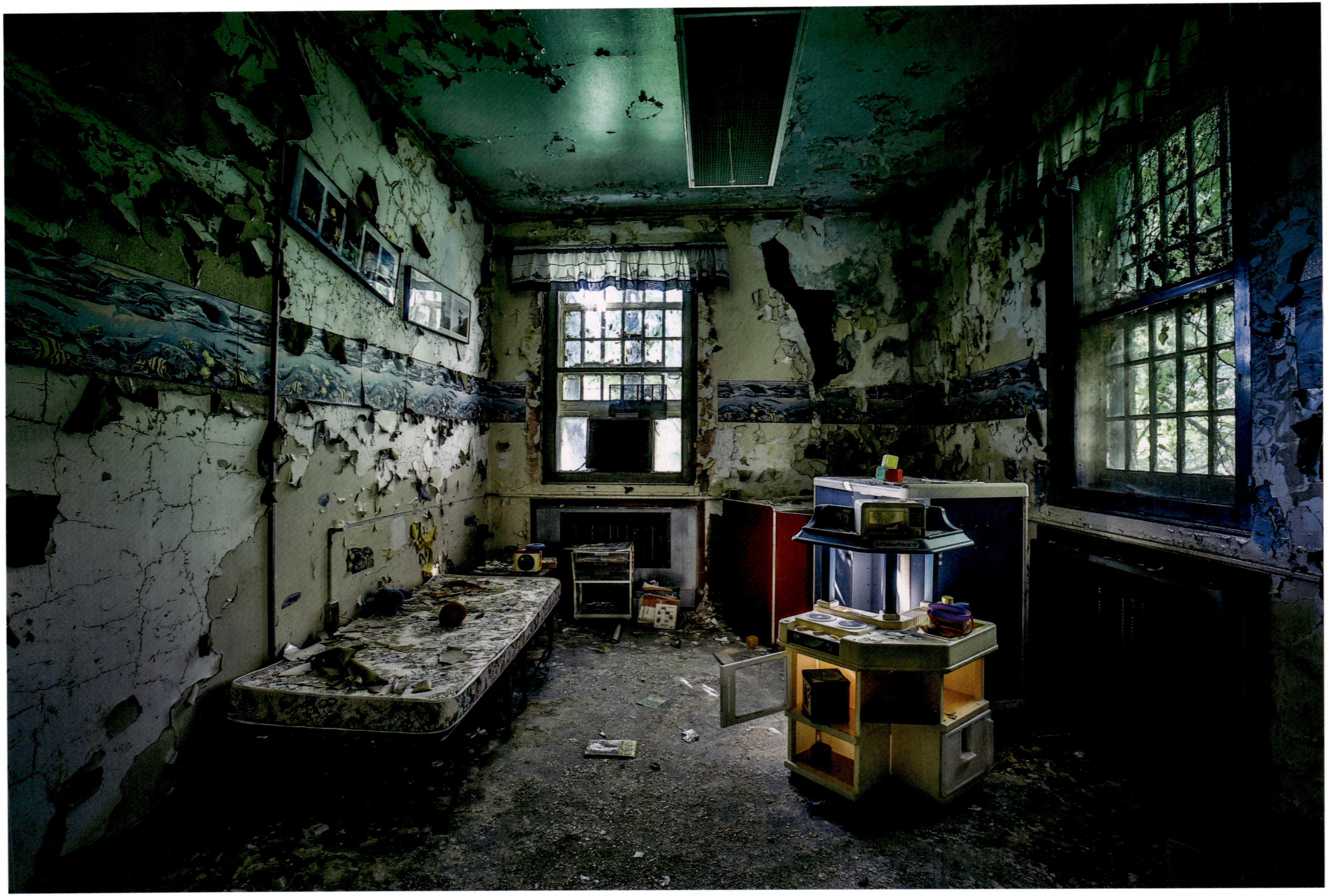

Children's Ward

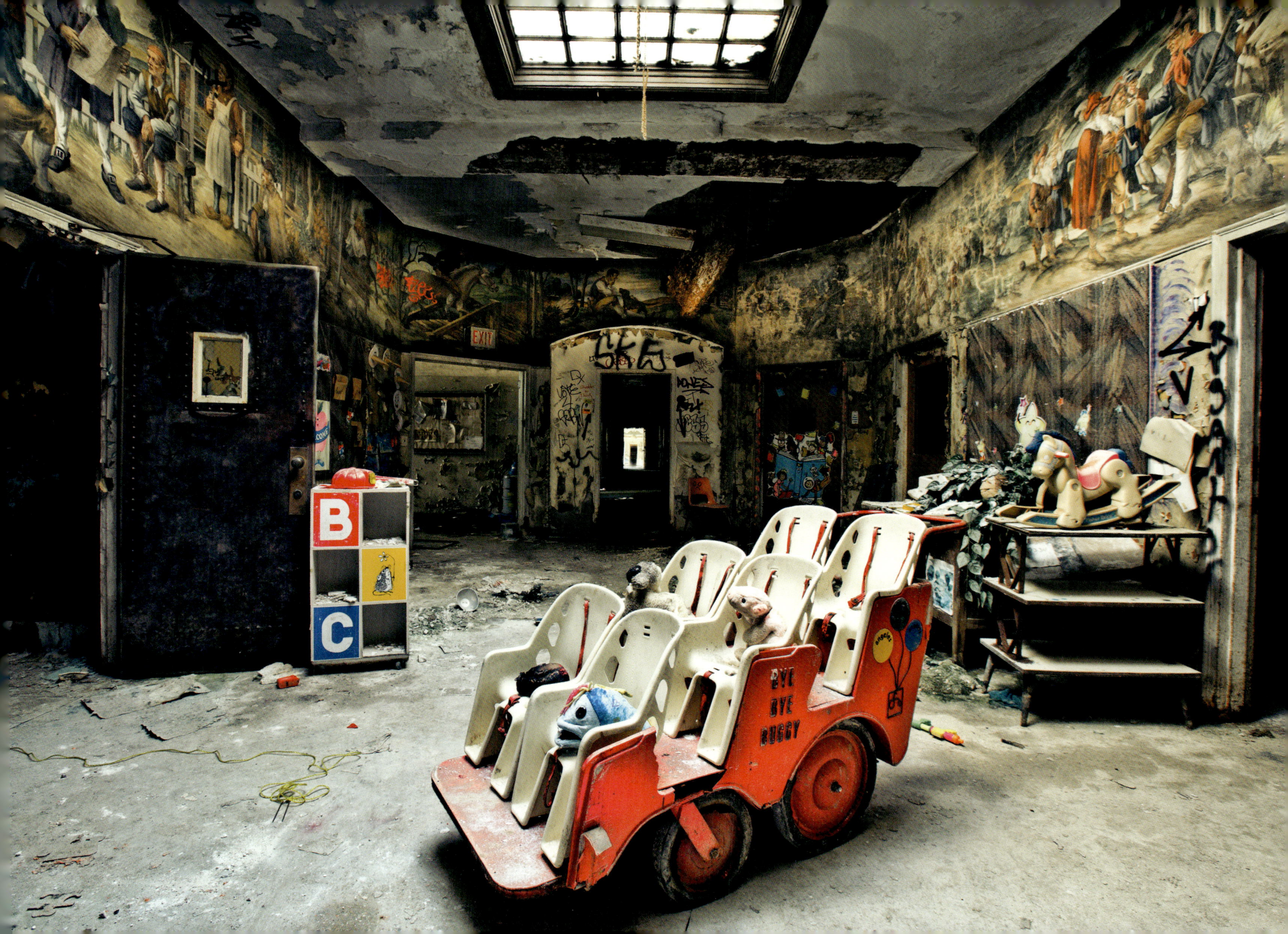
B
C
EXIT
BYE
BYE
BUGGY

Grafton State Hospital

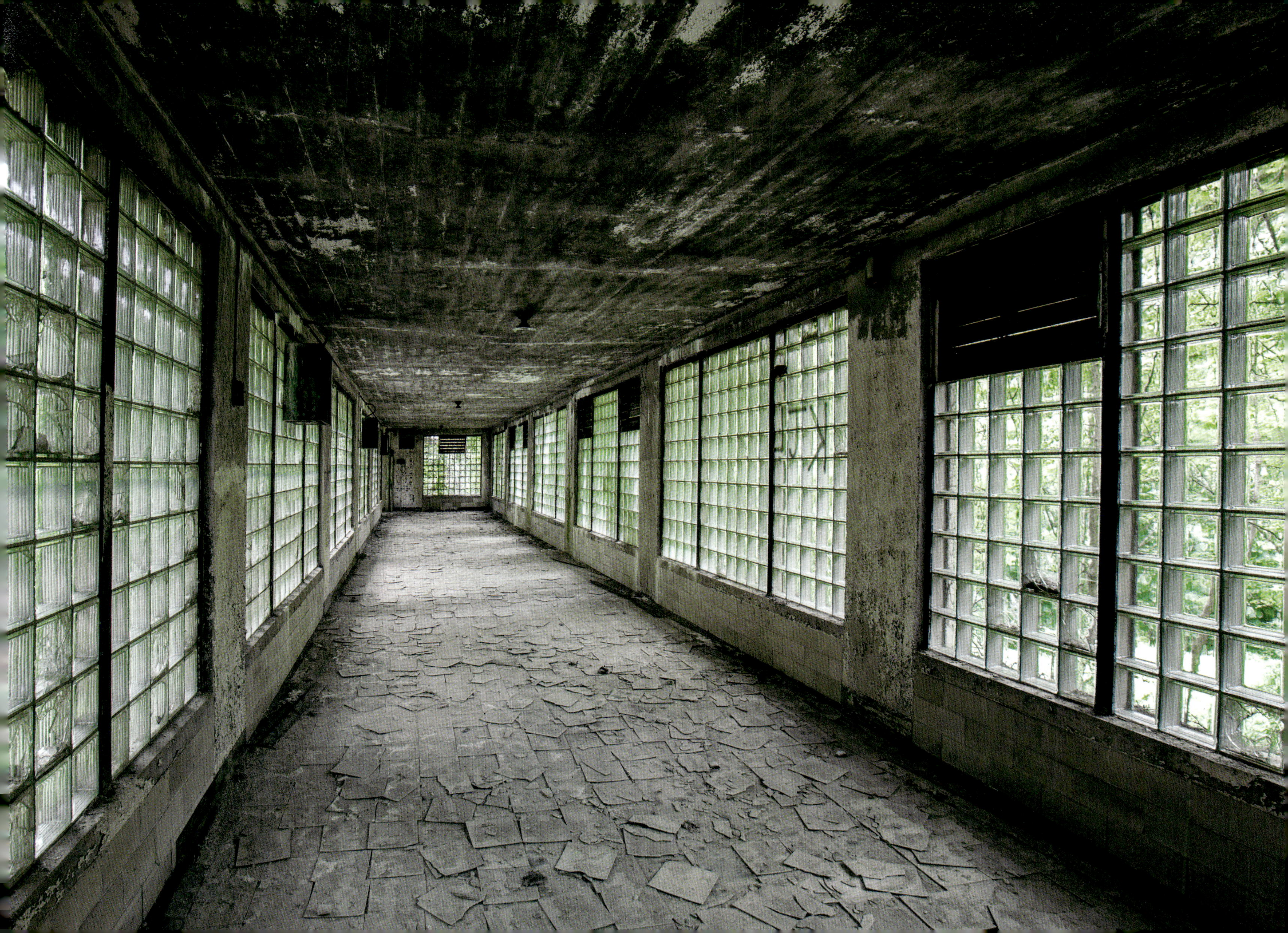

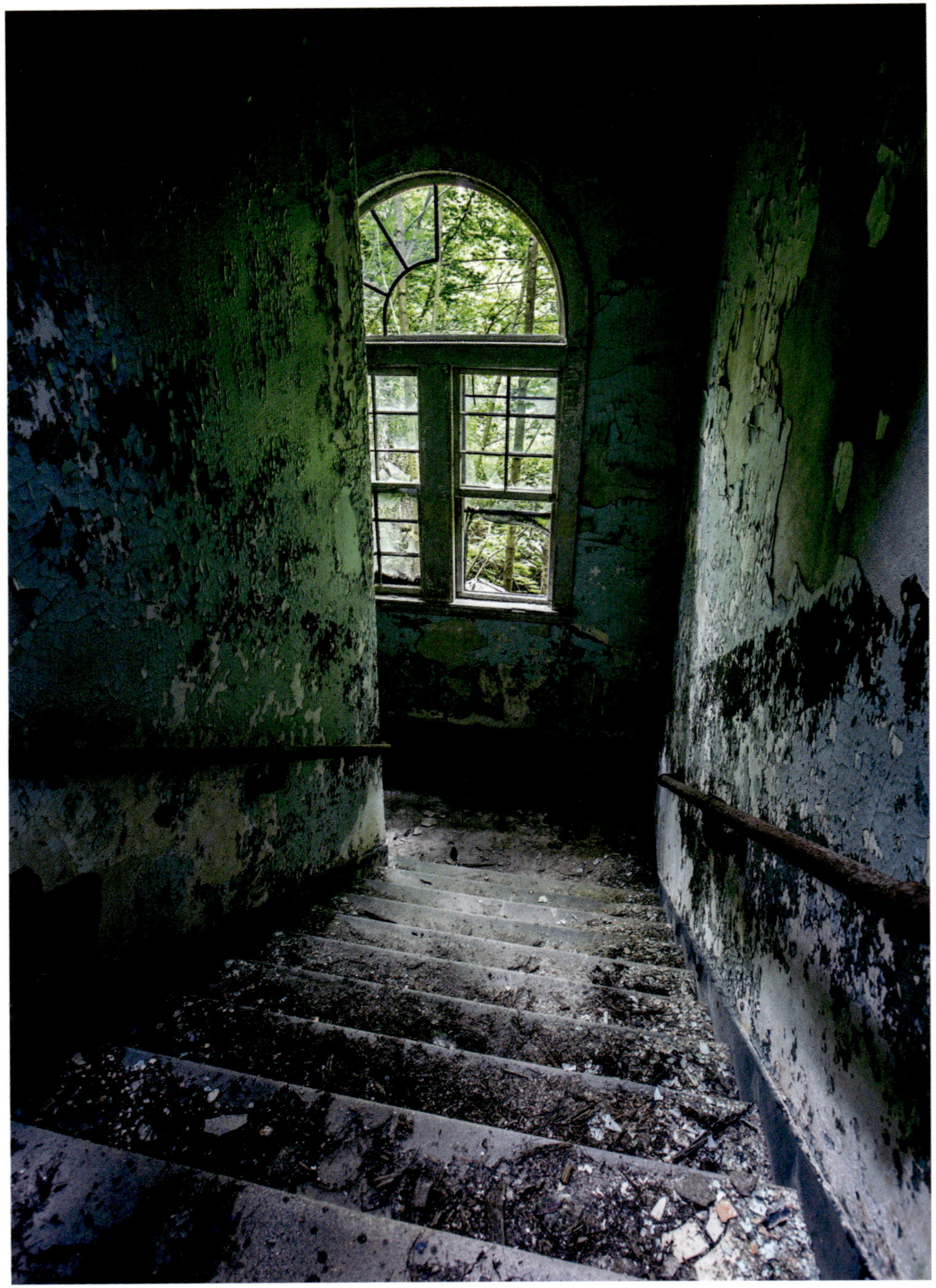

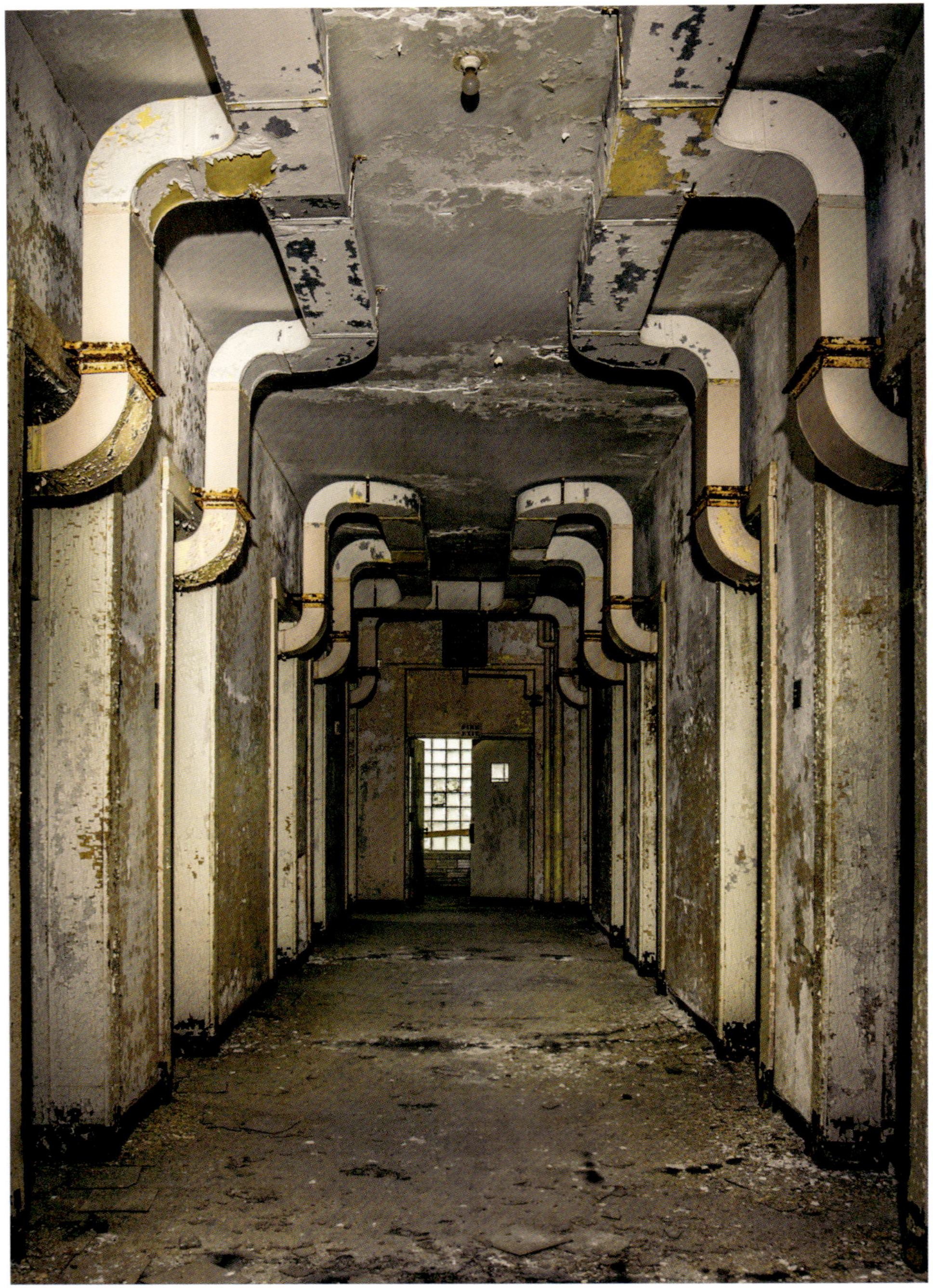

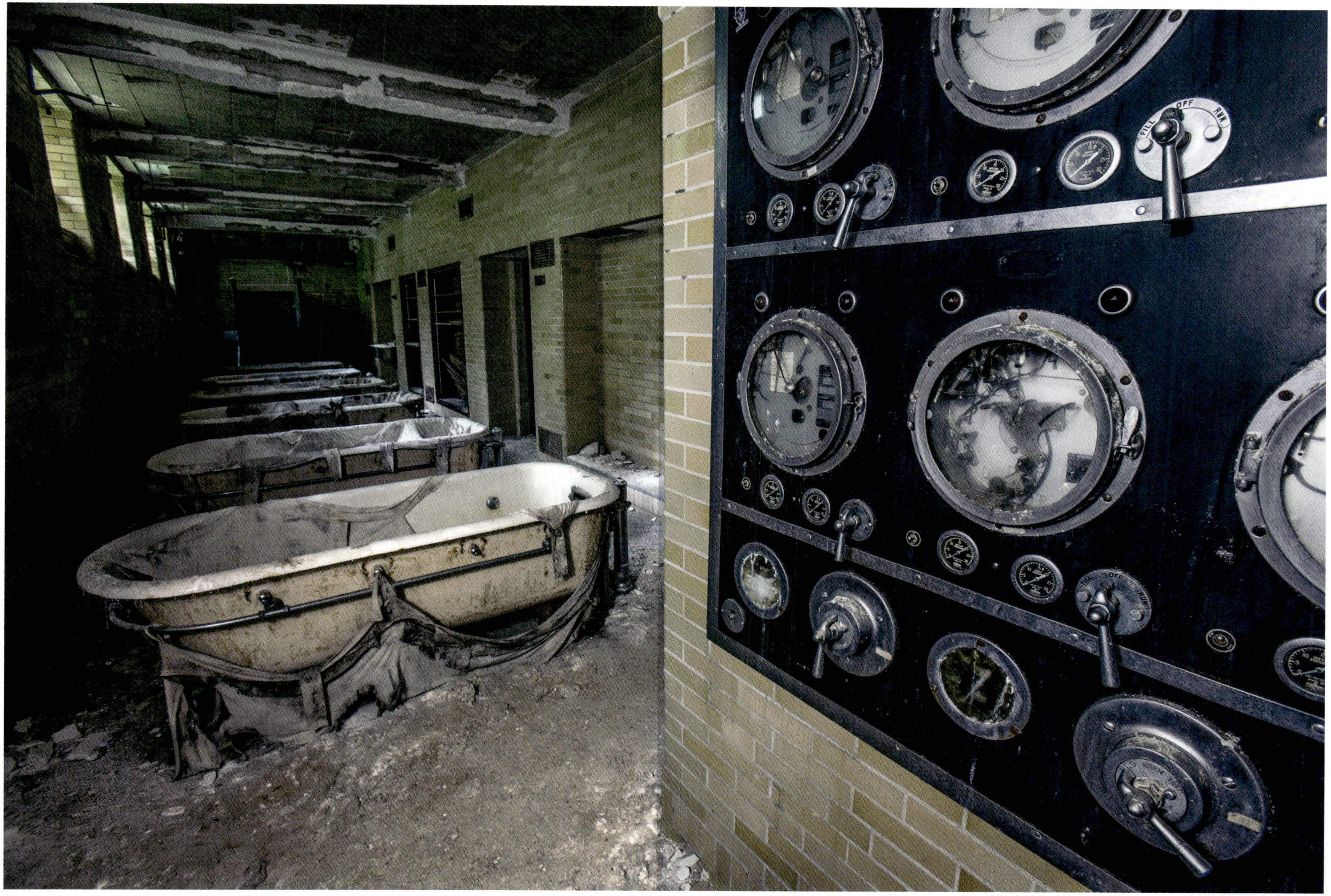
FILL OFF RUN

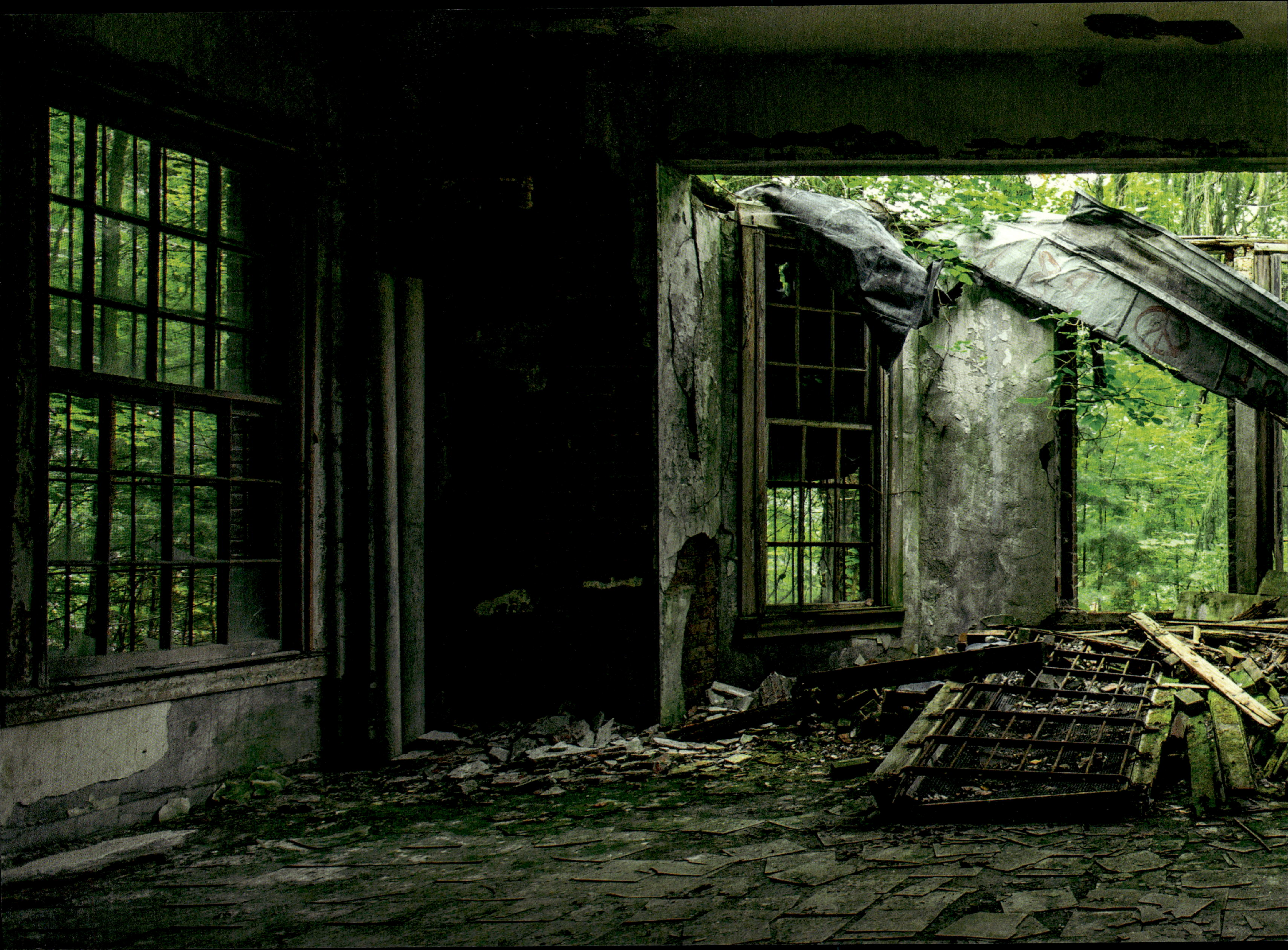

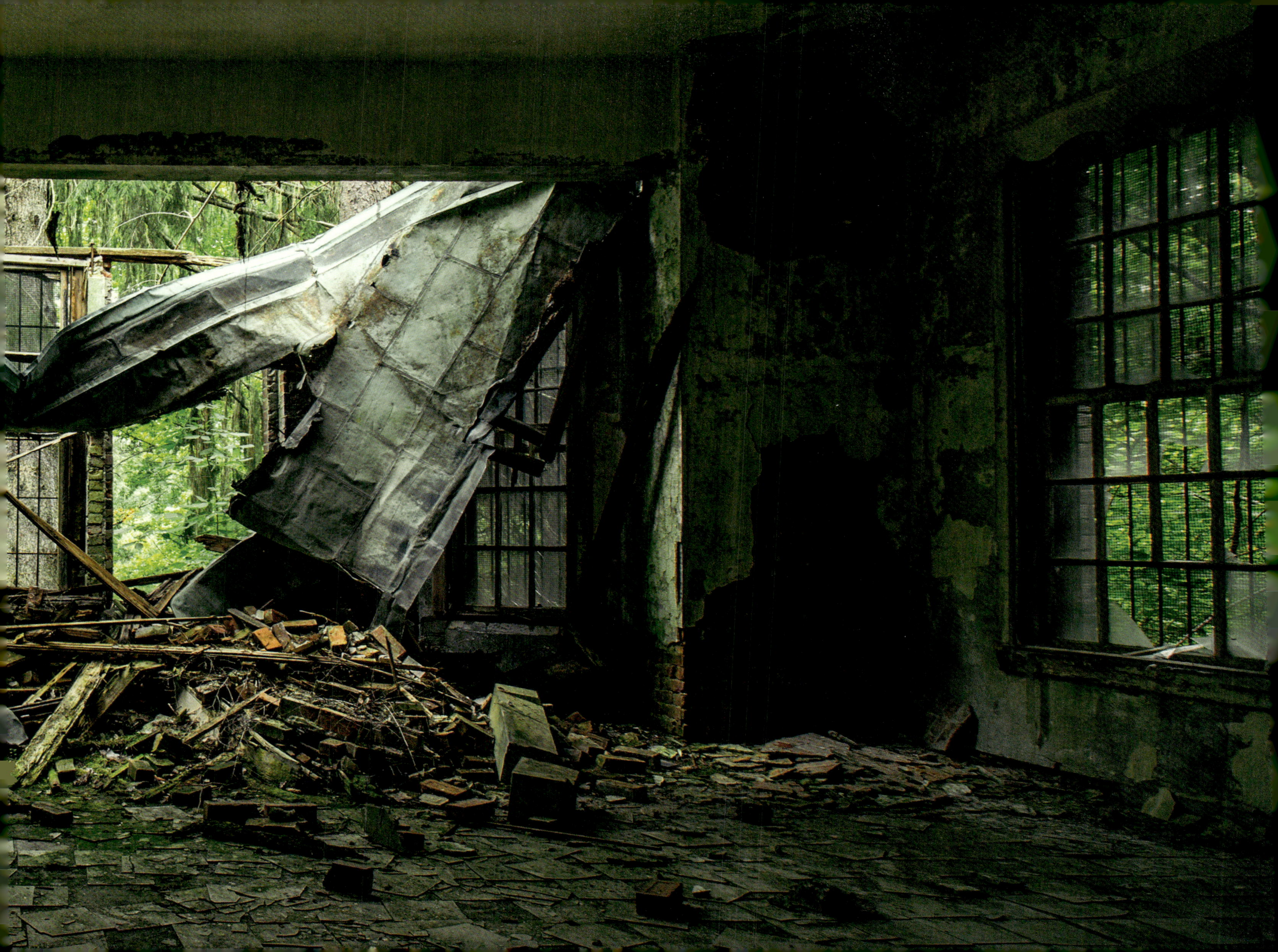

Forest Haven

Nestled discreetly in a heavily wooded area outside of Washington D.C., 22 vacant buildings stand on a 300-acre campus which, at its height, served over 1,300 children and adults with severe mental disabilities. It now lies abandoned as though its inhabitants had one day simply picked up and left – in reality, they did pretty much just that. When an institution closes, efforts are usually made to remove equipment and furniture, and empty the contents. Forest Haven, however, is an incredible time capsule, with all its contents frozen while the fabric of the buildings decays around them. Patients' suitcases with their personal belongings lie stacked ceiling-high; cribs, beds and furniture are strewn throughout its "cottage"-style wards; materials and dresses in various states of mid-manufacture still cling to the equipment in the occupational therapy building; and patient records (no doubt collected in a hurry and stuffed to the ceiling) spill into a hallway. The building's present state gives hardly any idea of its past horrors.

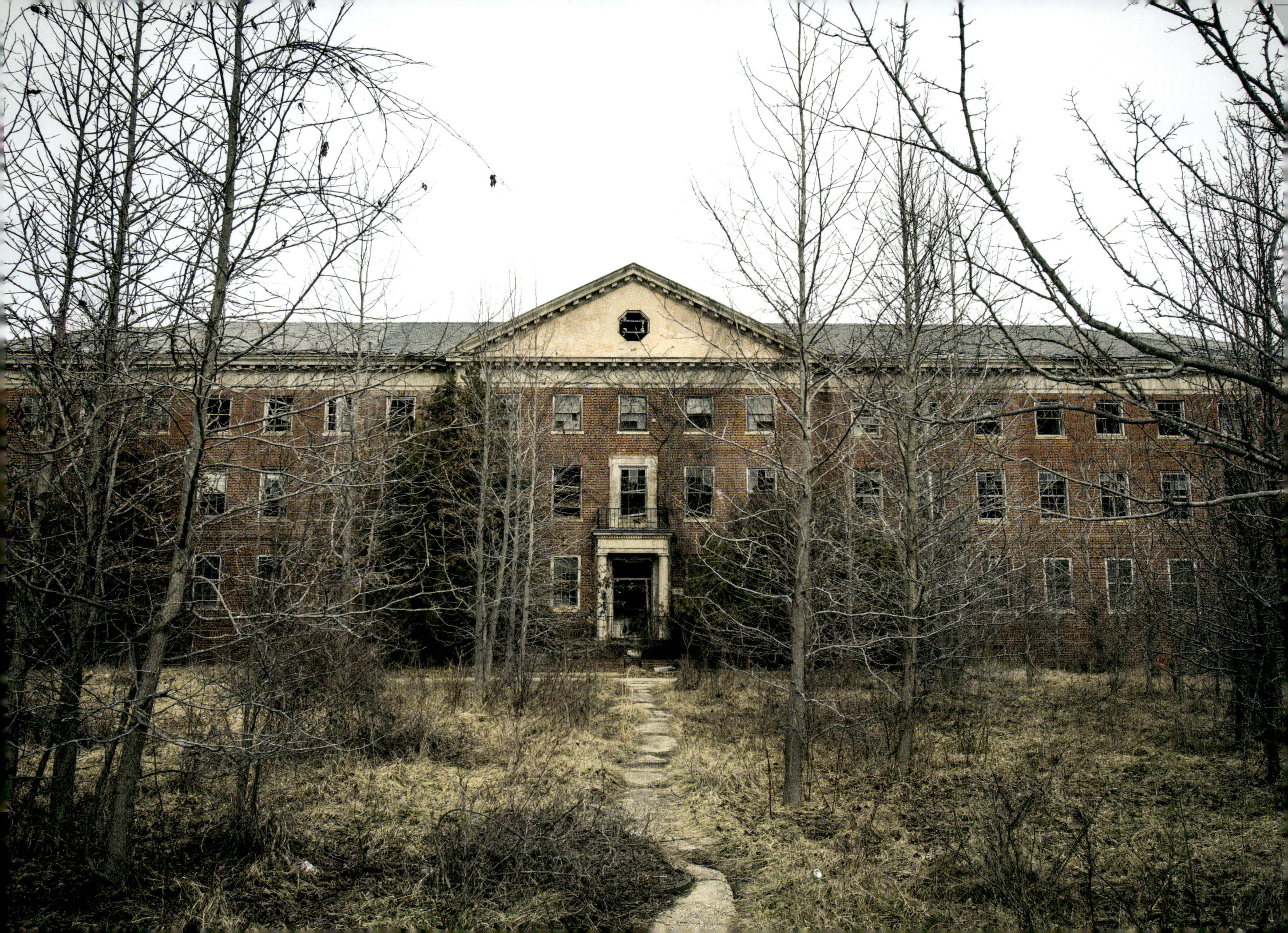

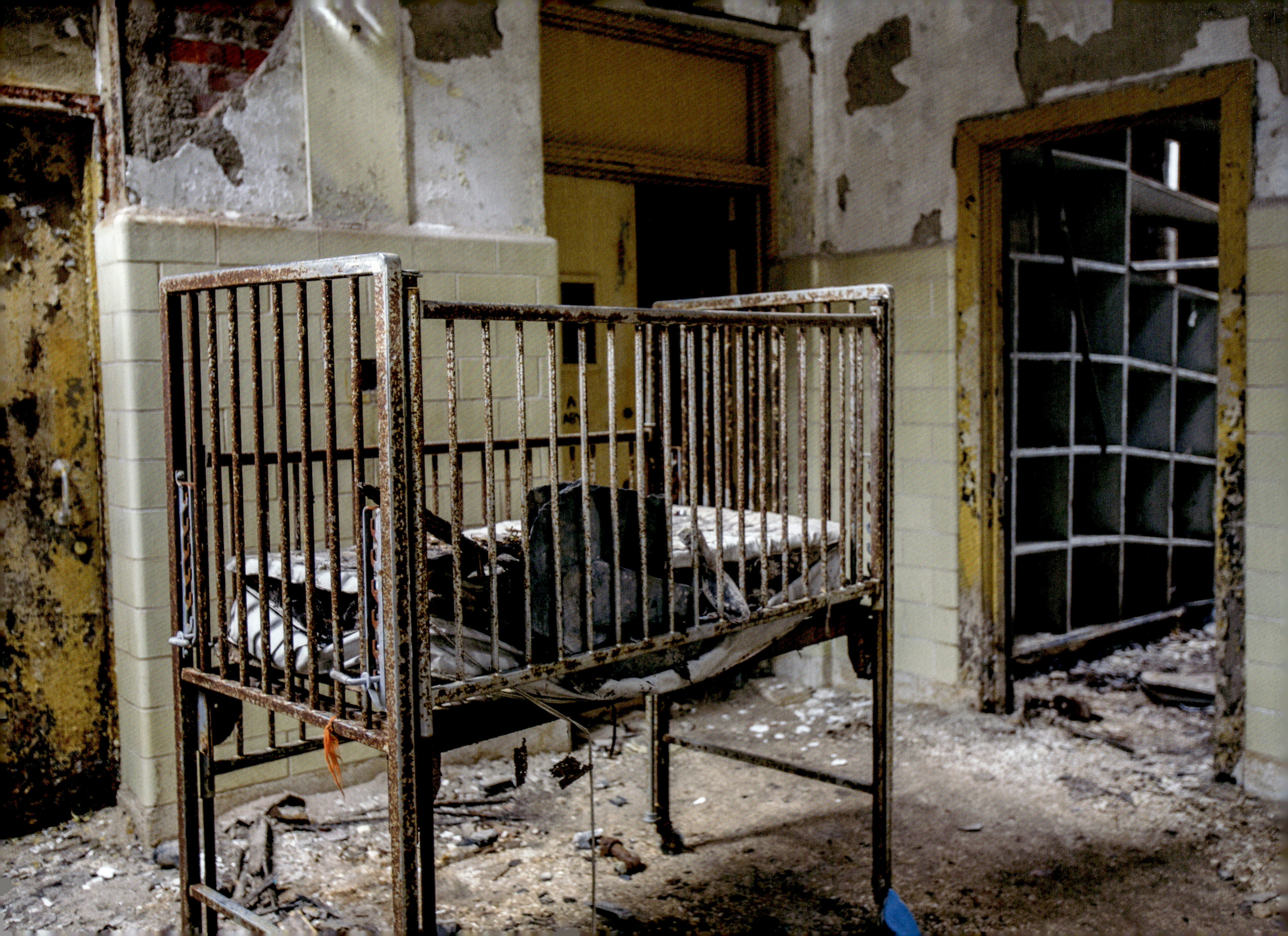

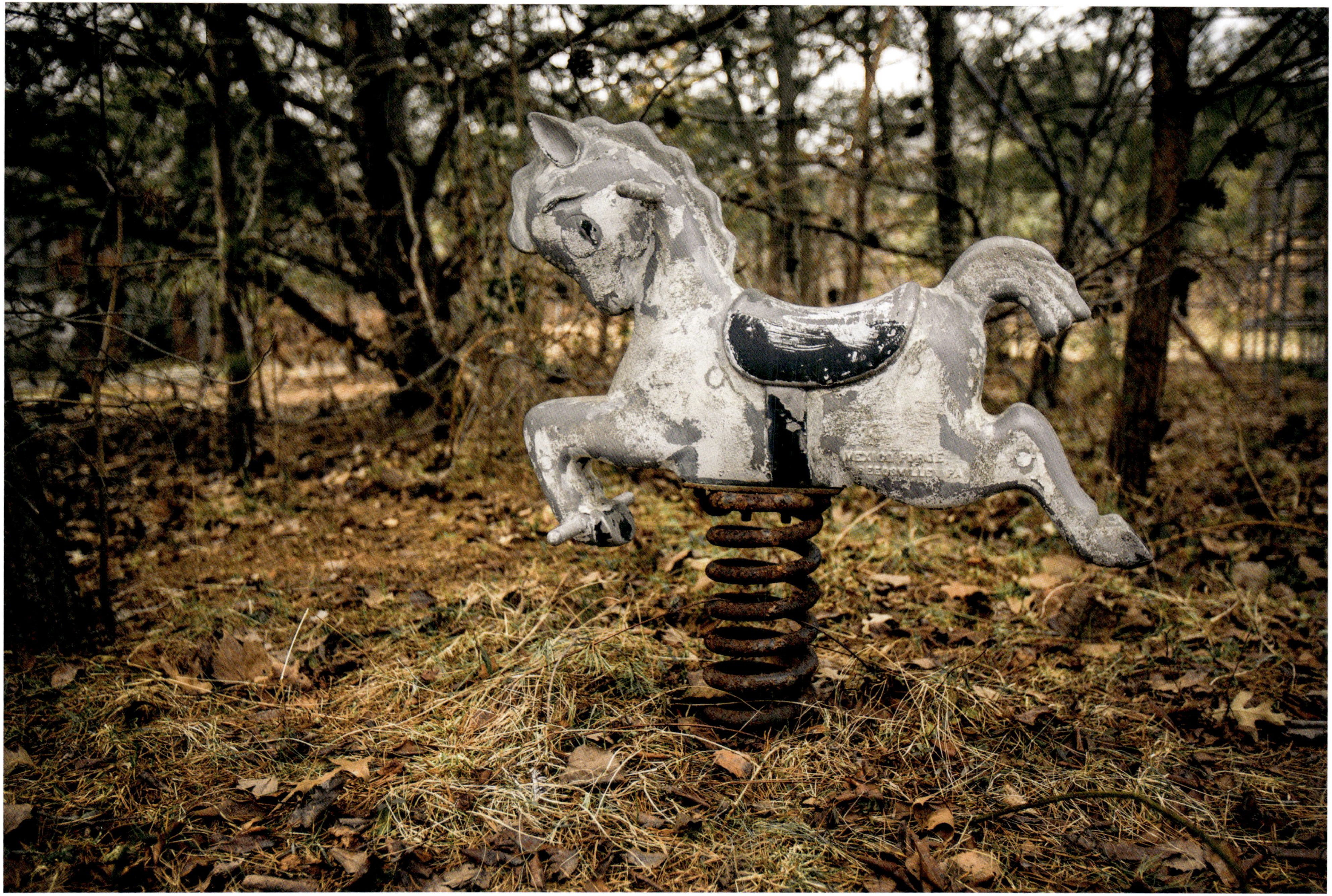

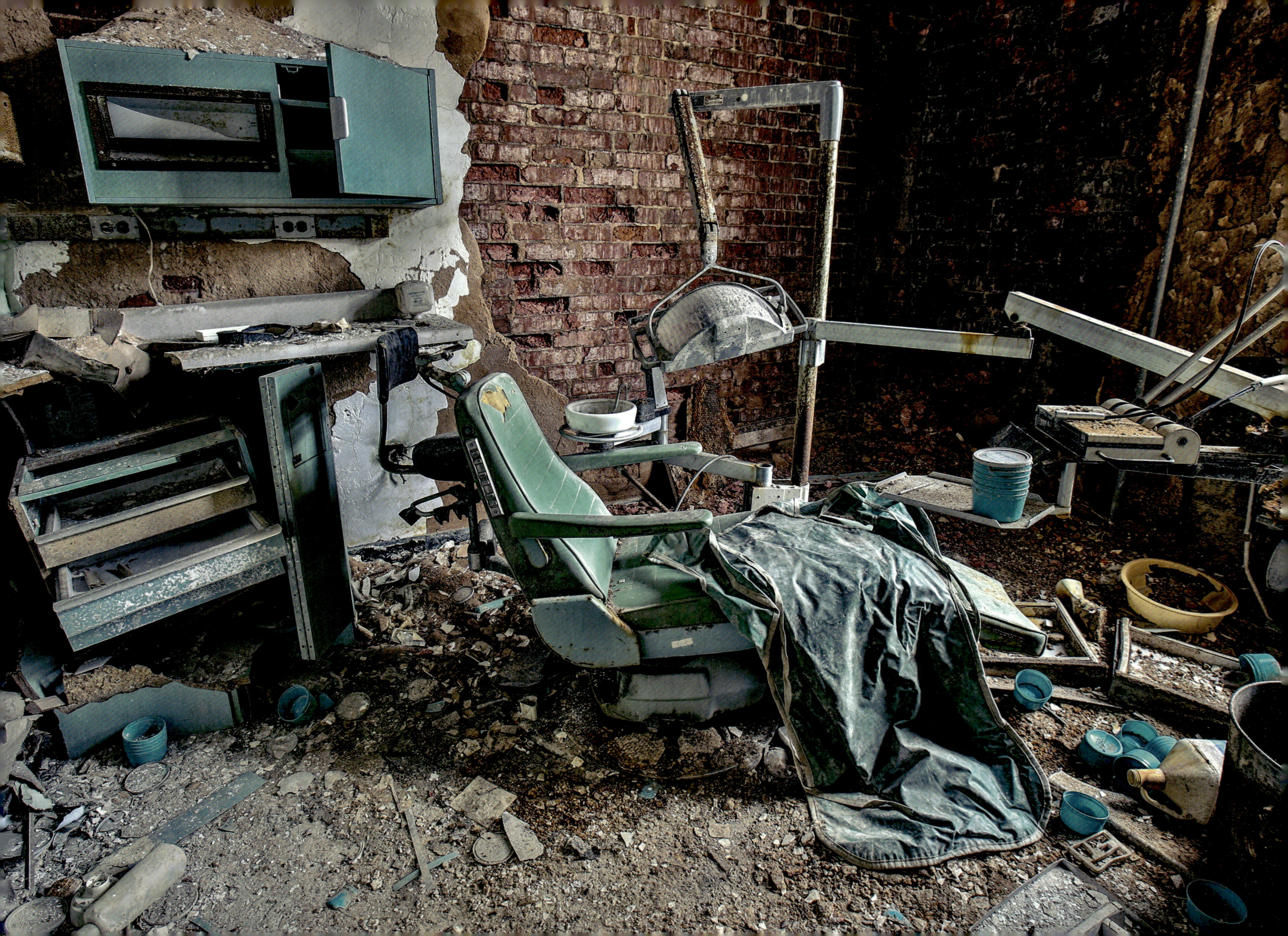

Opened in 1925, Forest Haven was closed on October 14, 1991 by order of a federal judge, citing years of alleged abuse, inhumane treatment and medical incompetence – some of which proved fatal to the patients. Staff incompetence and negligence probably account for several deaths from aspiration pneumonia: the end result of improper force-feeding, where food is regurgitated and forced into the lungs, suffocating the patient.

Murray Waas, an investigative reporter with the *Los Angeles Times*, summarized the abuses at Forest Haven like this: "Improper feeding and lack of movement can also cause potentially fatal gastrointestinal conditions, including 'volvulus', in which the intestines become so twisted that they may eventually, in the words of one physician, 'resemble an entangled telephone cord'. The inability of the intestines to function can, in turn, cause the crowding of other nearby body organs, internal hemorrhaging or asphyxiation." Marie Gil, who was only 21 years old, succumbed to volvulus at Forest Haven in 1989; at the time of her death, she weighed only 28 lbs.

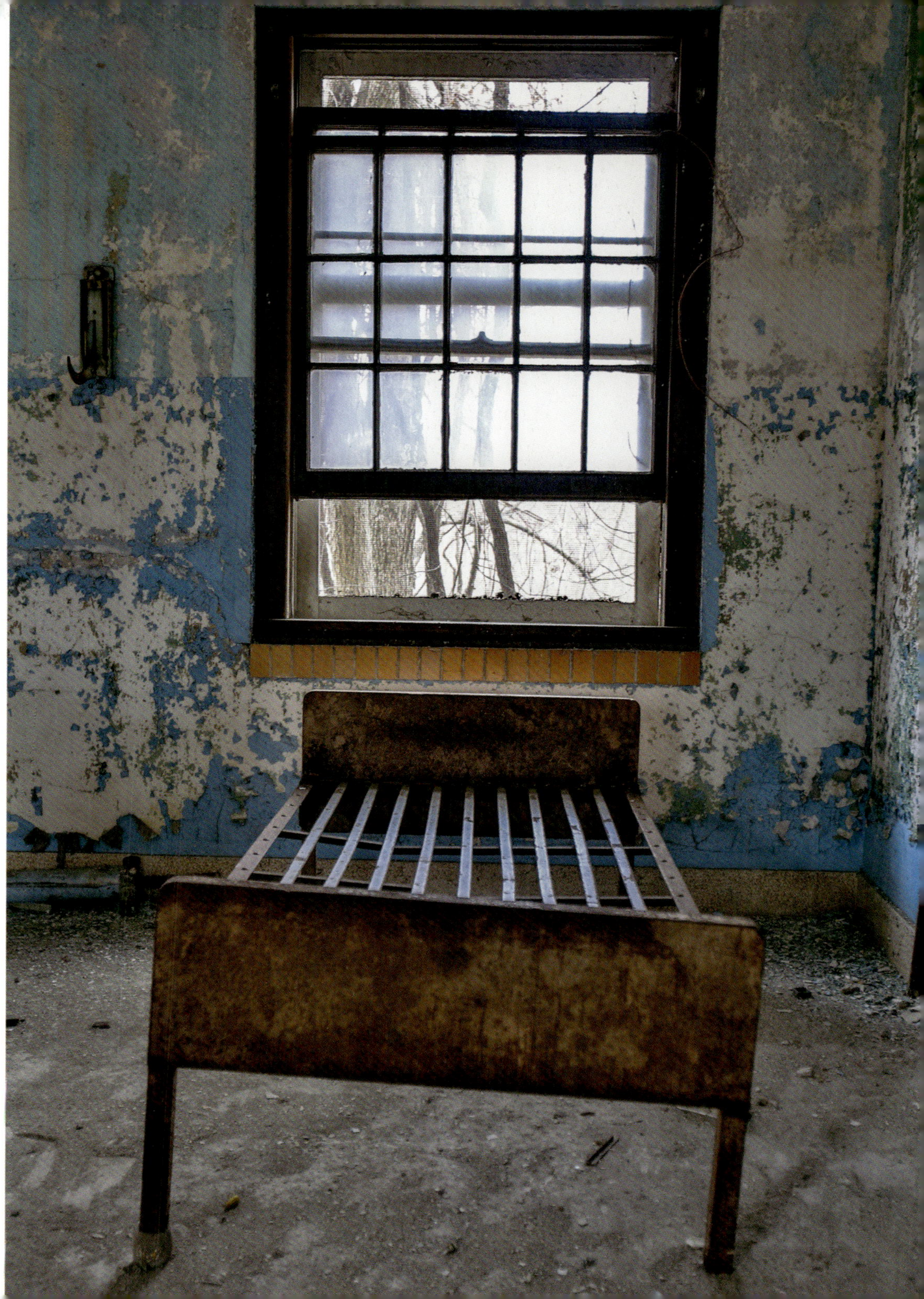

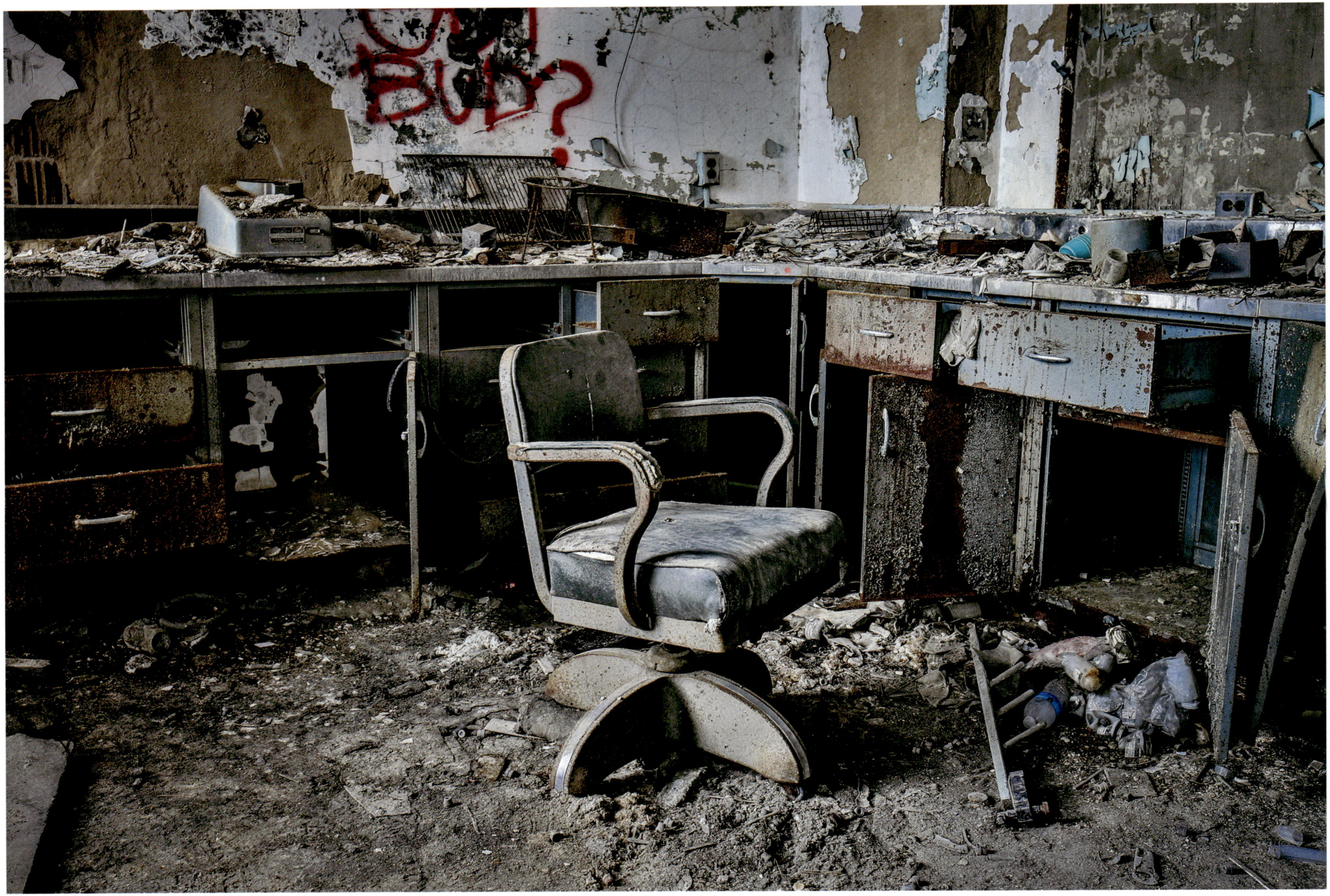

Laboratory

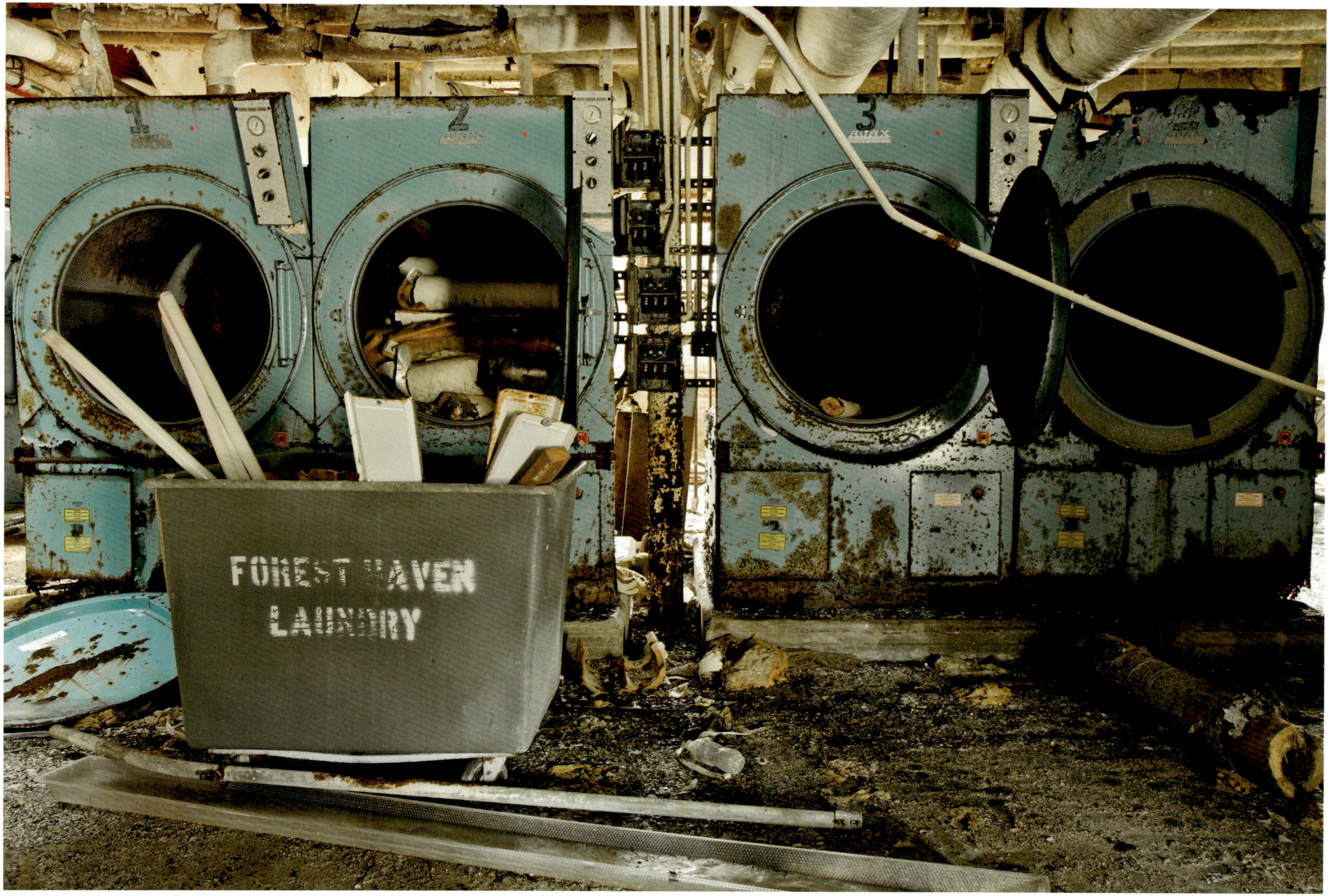
FOREST HAVEN
LAUNDRY

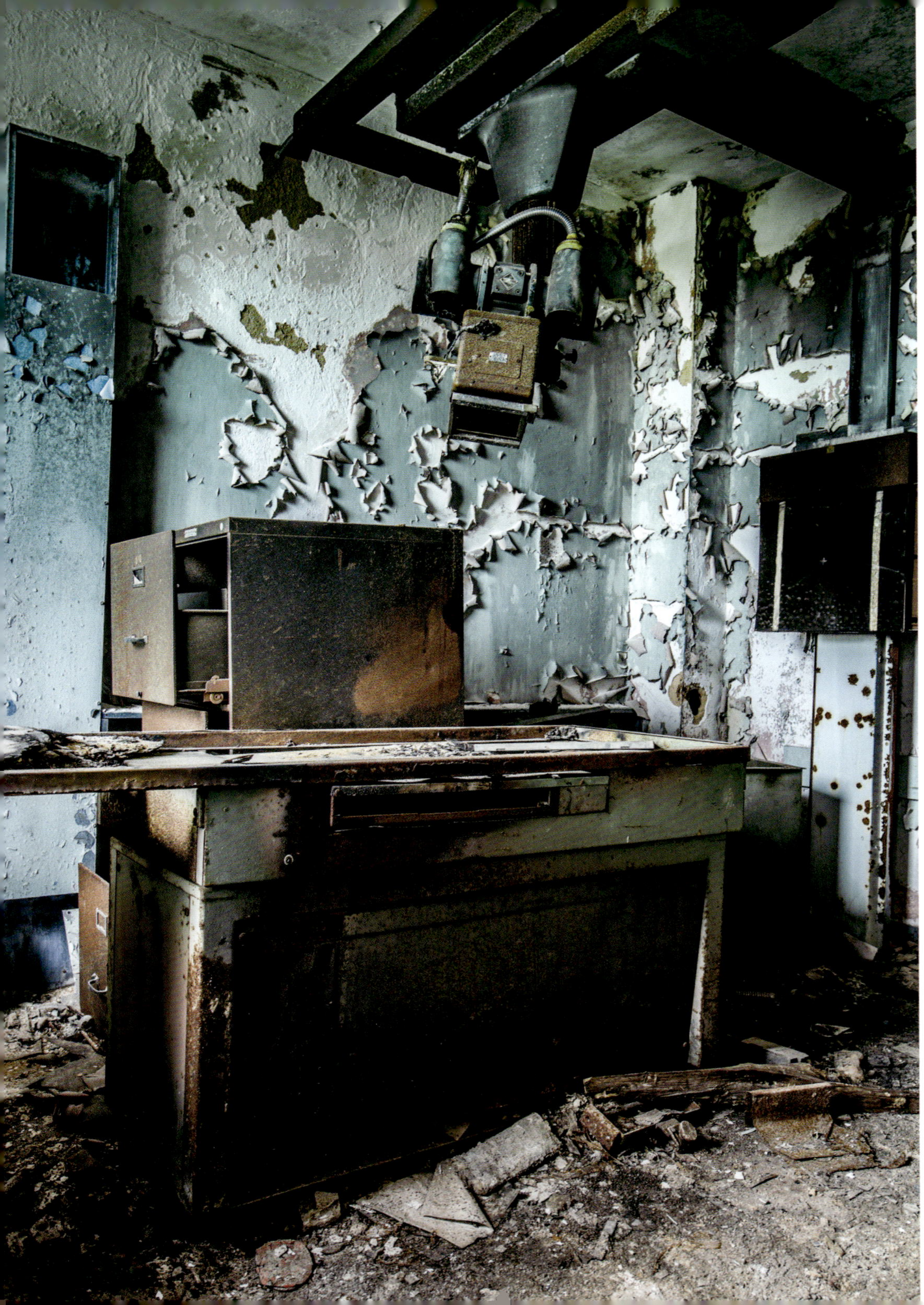

All these factors contributed to the worst known example of institutional abuse in recent American history and led to the long overdue closure of Forest Haven, which in reality was a "haven" for no one. John Dunne, the assistant Attorney General for Civil Rights during the Bush Sr administration, concluded: "Based on our various investigations around the country [...] there was no other institution of any kind in America where so many people died from abuse and neglect over such a short period of time." Between 1989 and 1990, ten poor souls at Forest Haven died from complications as a result of malpractice and neglect – nine of them over a nine-month period. At that time, the facility housed 252 individuals but could only afford 2 physicians. Although the city had received a huge number of warnings over a fifteen-year period – culminating in a 1978 lawsuit forced decree that Forest Haven should close – no action was taken until it was too late. In 1989 government-funded Medicaid was cut off. Although conditions were deplorable, Forest Haven continued to operate until 1991, when it was threatened with a $10,000 fine for every day it remained open.

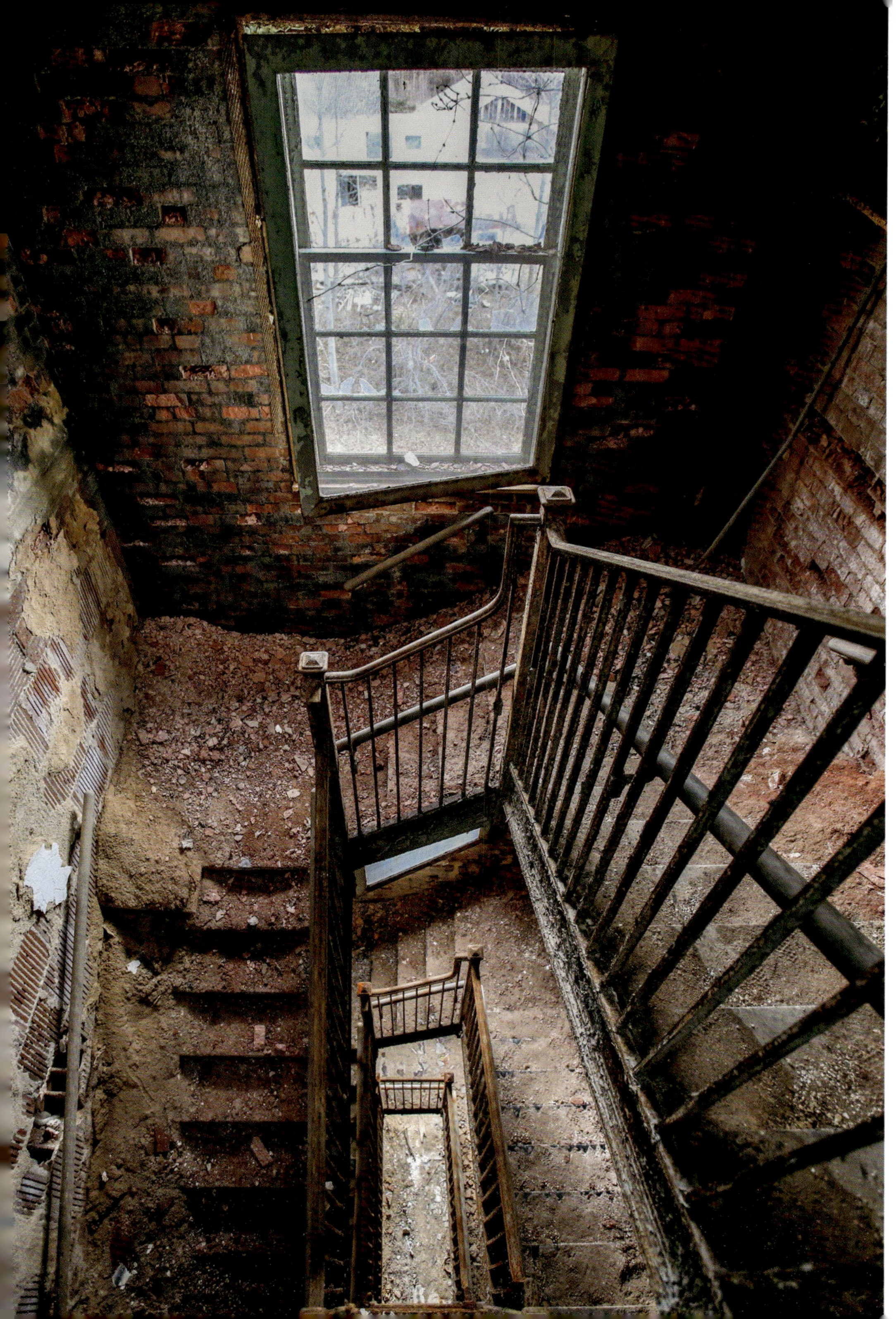

While society's impressions of these institutions have been unfairly influenced by the horrors portrayed in both books and films, very few facilities have a genuinely dark story or a truly infamous history. Institutions like Forest Haven, Letchworth Village, Pennhurst State School and Willowbrook State School were certainly the exceptions to the rule. All were subject to forced closure as a result of their abuses and the inhumane treatment of both children and adults.

Betty Evans (mother of Joy Evans, who died at Forest Haven aged 18) was the plaintiff in the 1978 court case *Evans vs. Washington*. She provided a sworn affidavit stating that, "Dogwood, the cottage where Joy lived, was a veritable snake pit. [...] I once witnessed a nurse open the cottage door only to find 80 half-clad screaming women come running to the door; the nurse quickly closed it shut." Further atrocities included adults being physically restrained in cribs; untreated bedsores that went so long without attention that they resulted in death; inadequate clothing, with residents wearing nothing more than an adult-sized diaper; and toothless mouths as a result of stomach acid rotting them away. These are just some of the inexcusable conditions endured by the residents of Forest Haven.

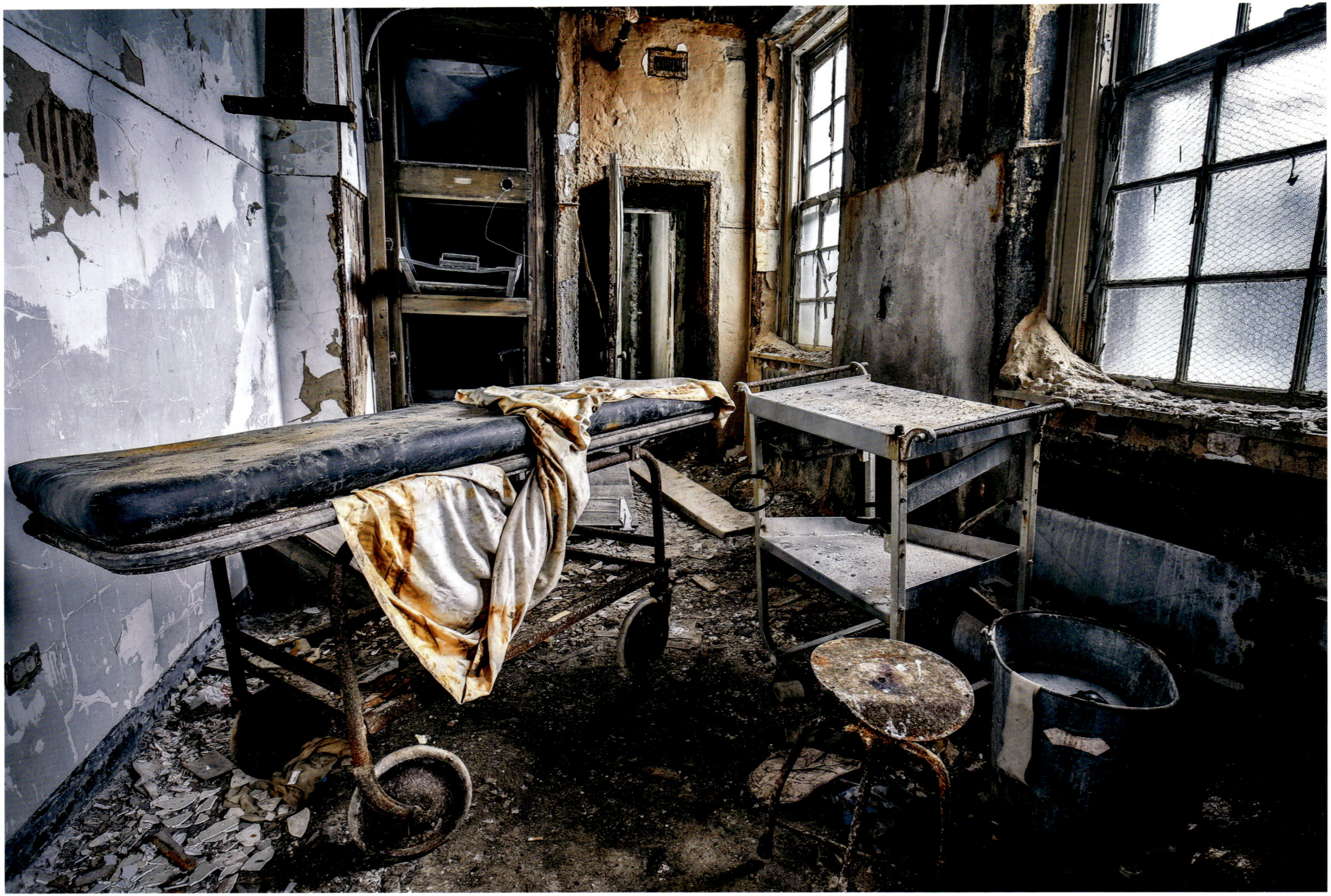

Occupational Therapy dress making shop

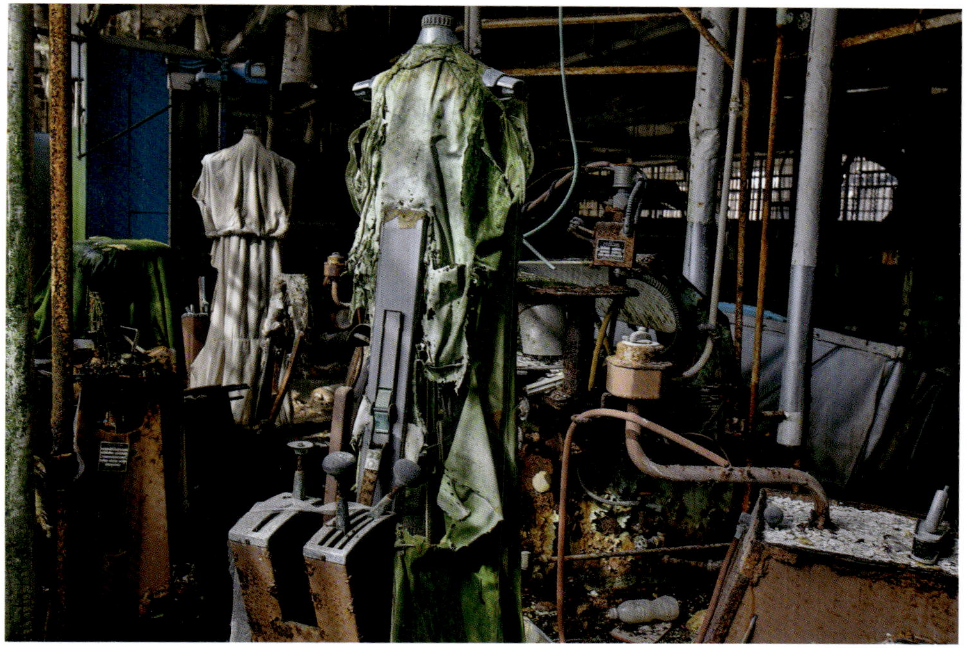

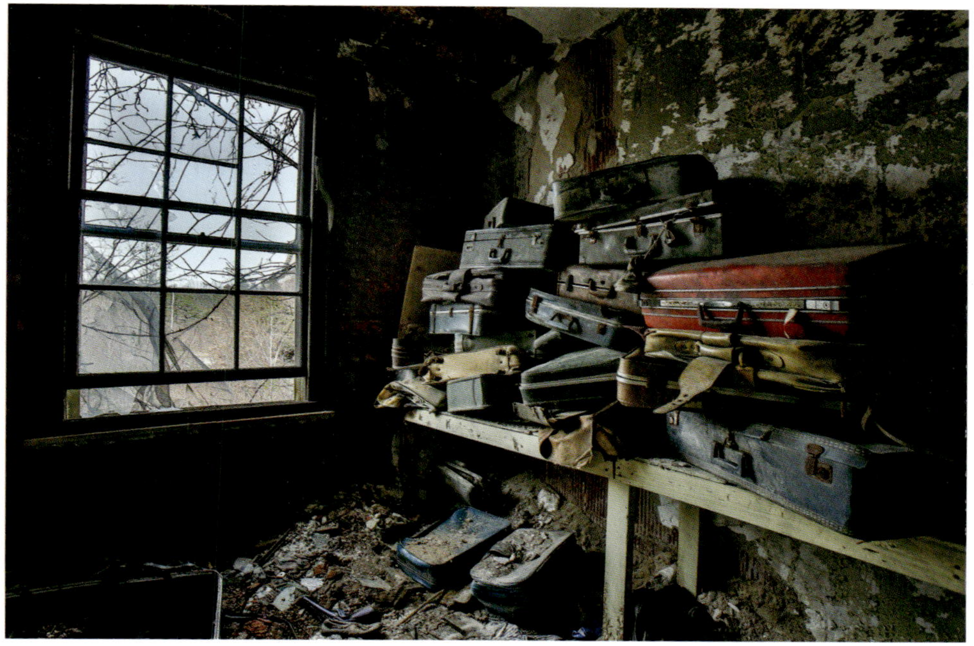

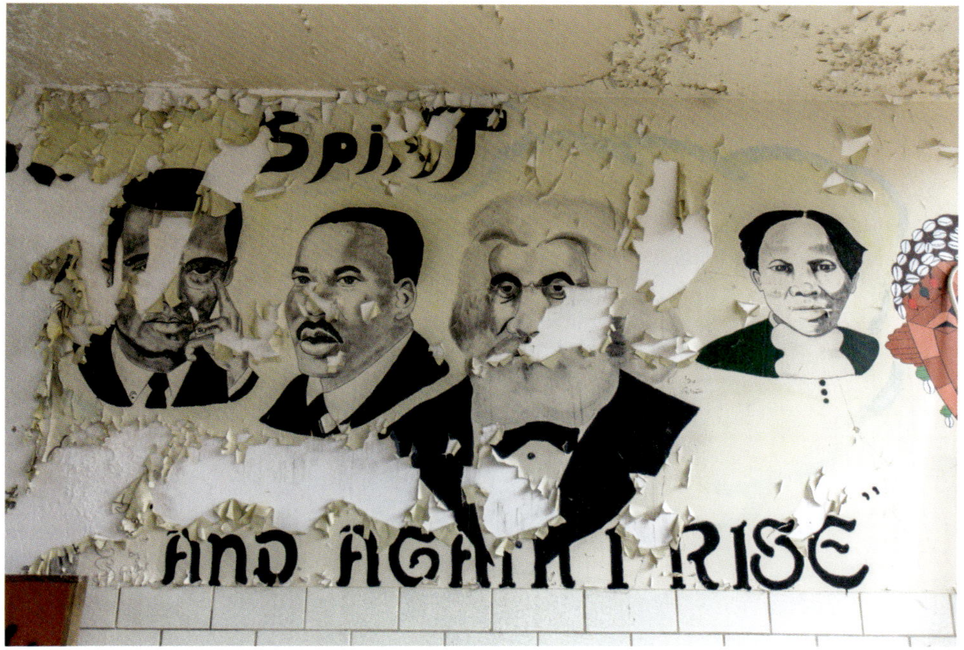

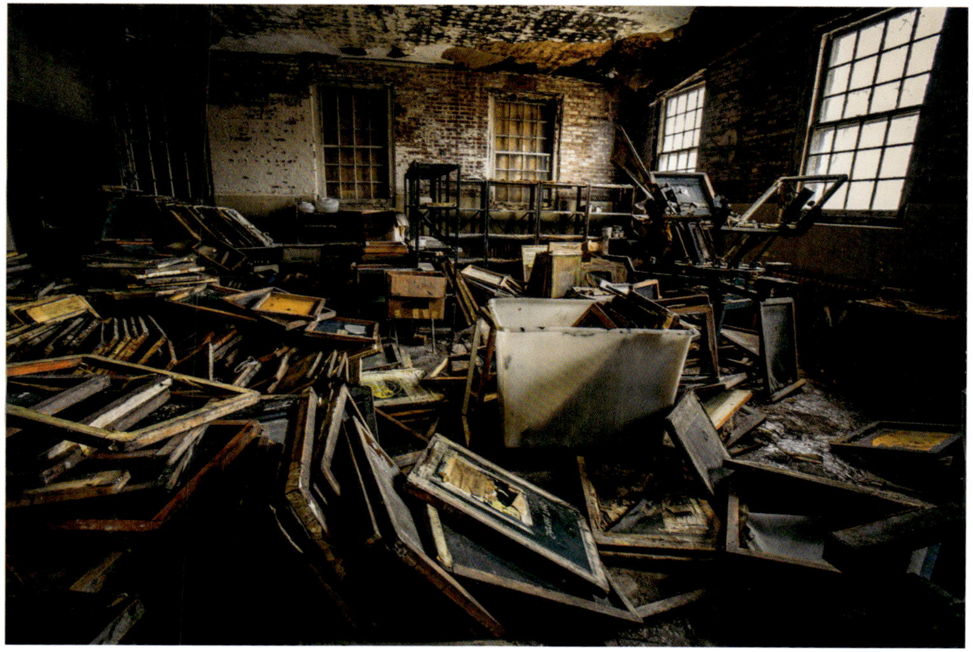

Occupational therapy silk screen print shop

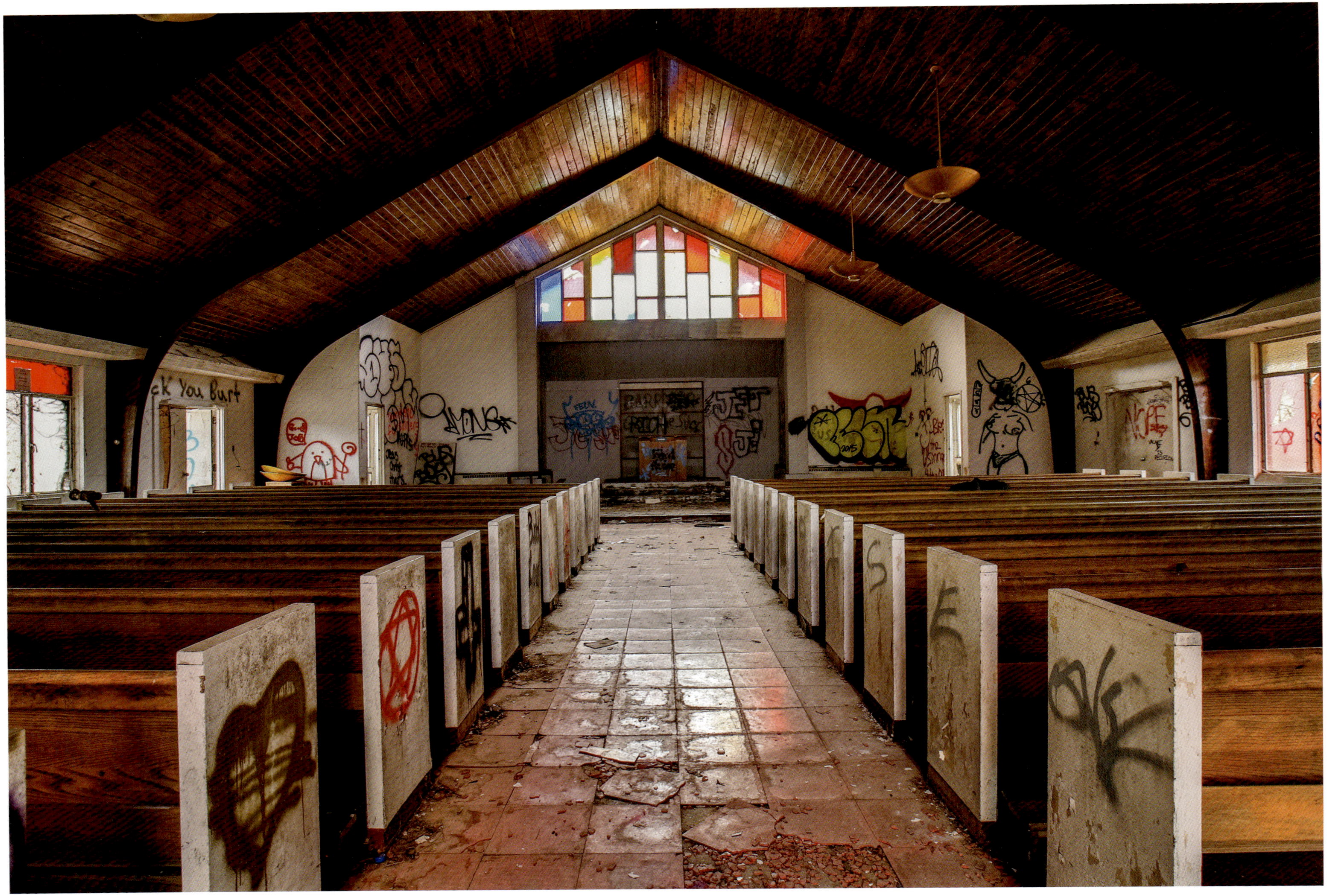
ck You Burt

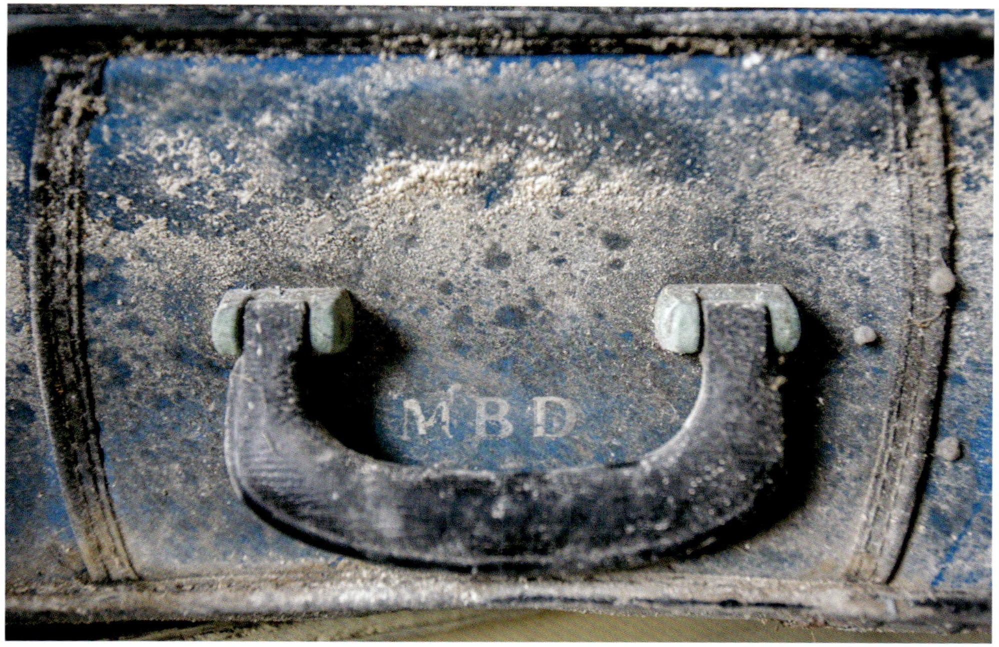

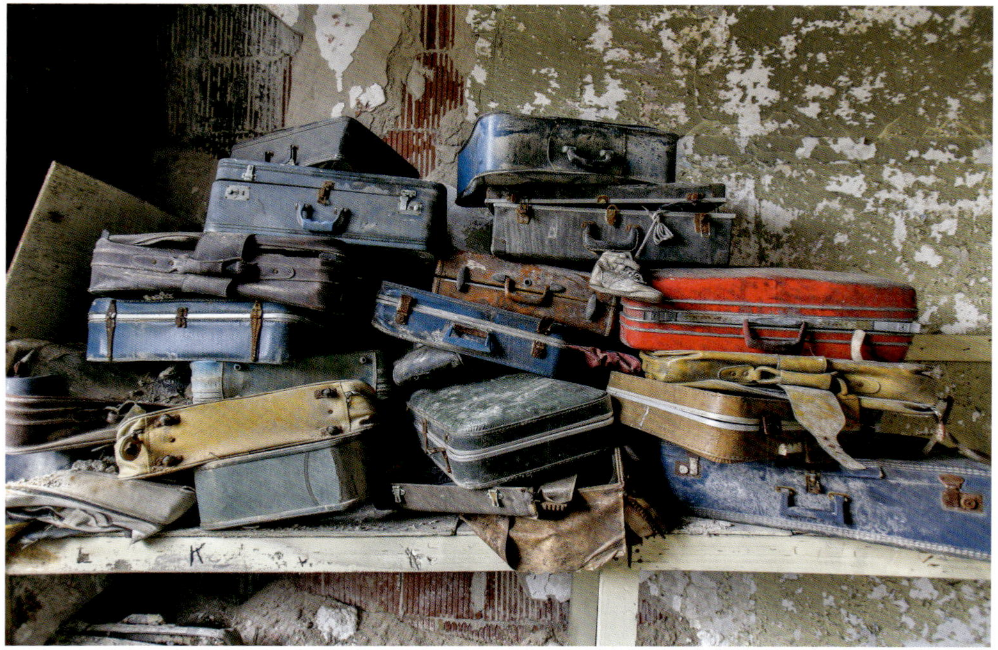

Patient Luggage

When the facility closed, the residents were placed in community homes throughout the area. The end of Forest Haven was not the solution to the wider problem, however: advocates warned that group homes and community living did not necessarily promise a better life. Reports of abuse were nearly as common in group homes as in large institutions. Moreover, the large influx of patients entering community care was not accompanied by the necessary increase in resources. However, this ushered in a new era in social policy: gradually, incarceration in centralized facilities was abandoned in favor of care in the community. The battle was won against Forest Haven, but in the darker corners of suburban America, abuse and exploitation of the mentally ill and developmentally challenged were still widespread.

Harlem Valley State Hospital

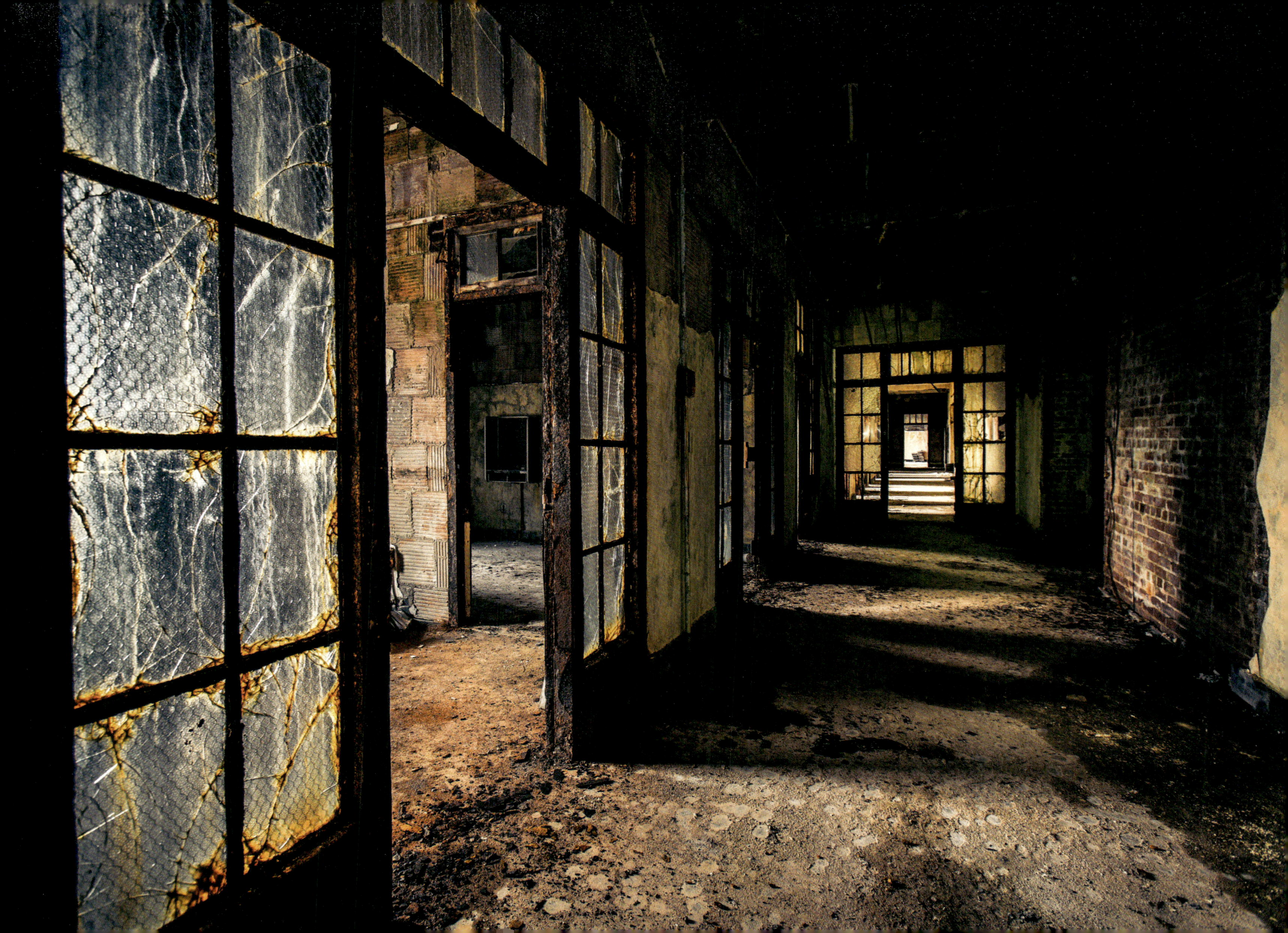

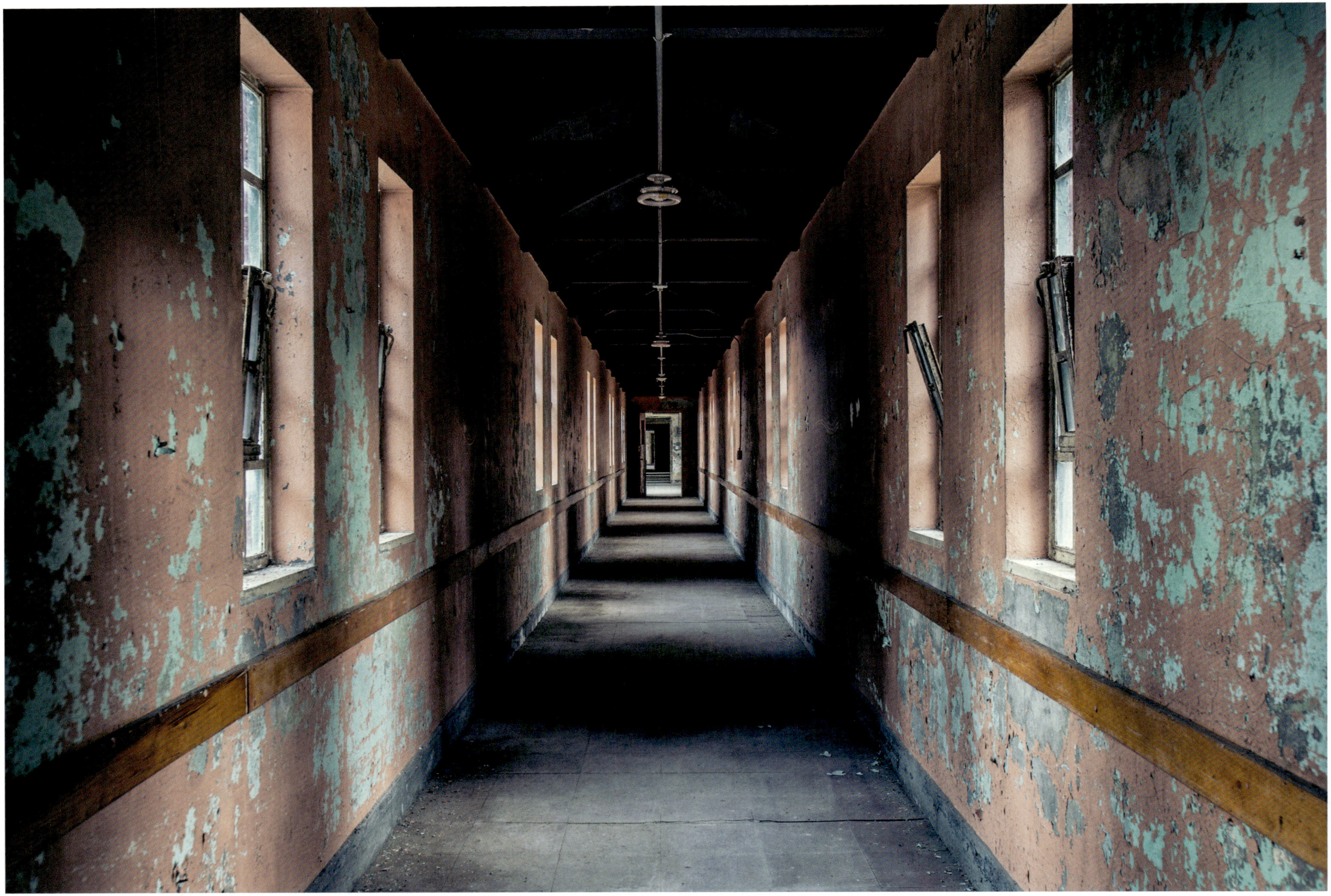

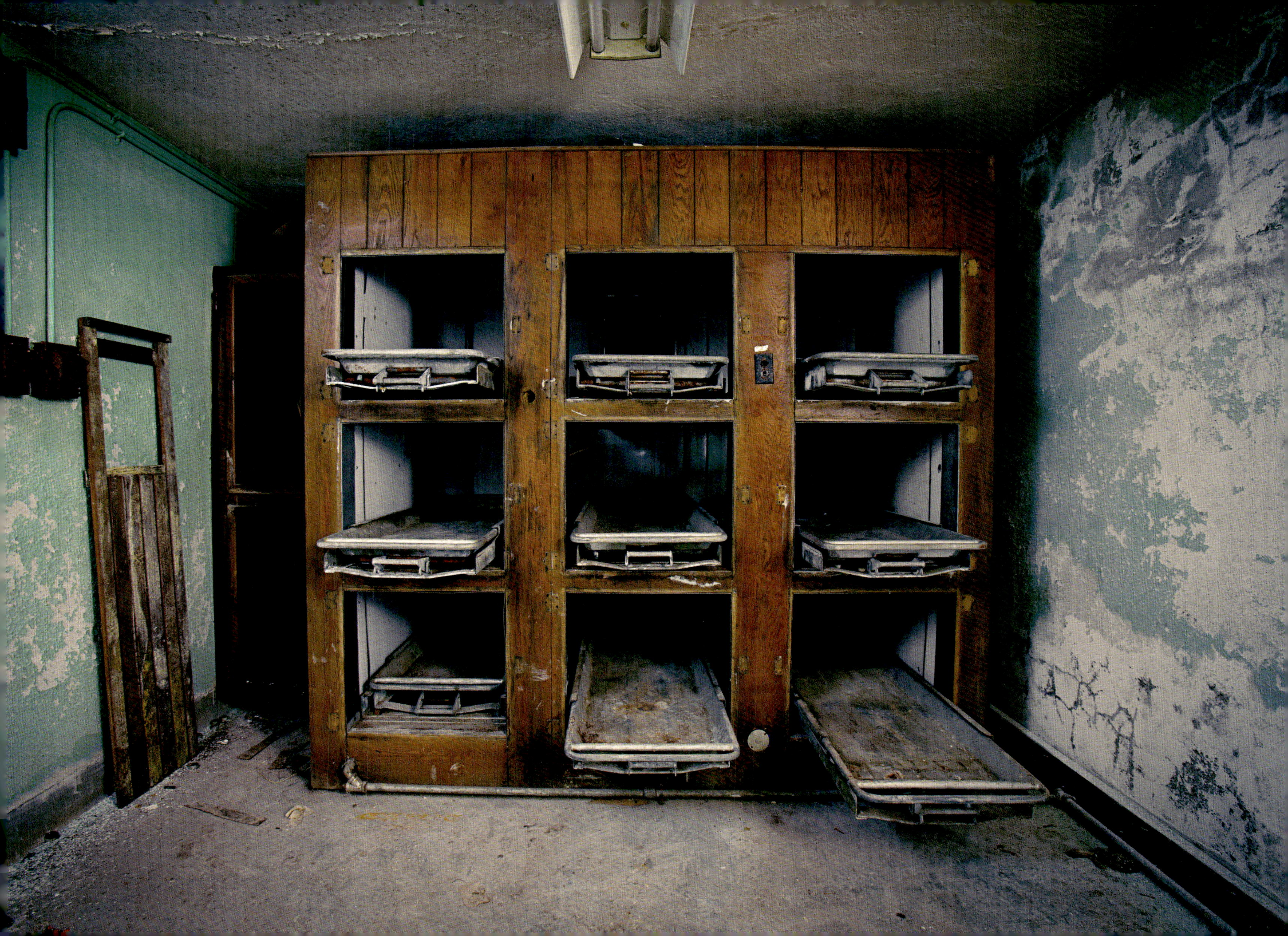

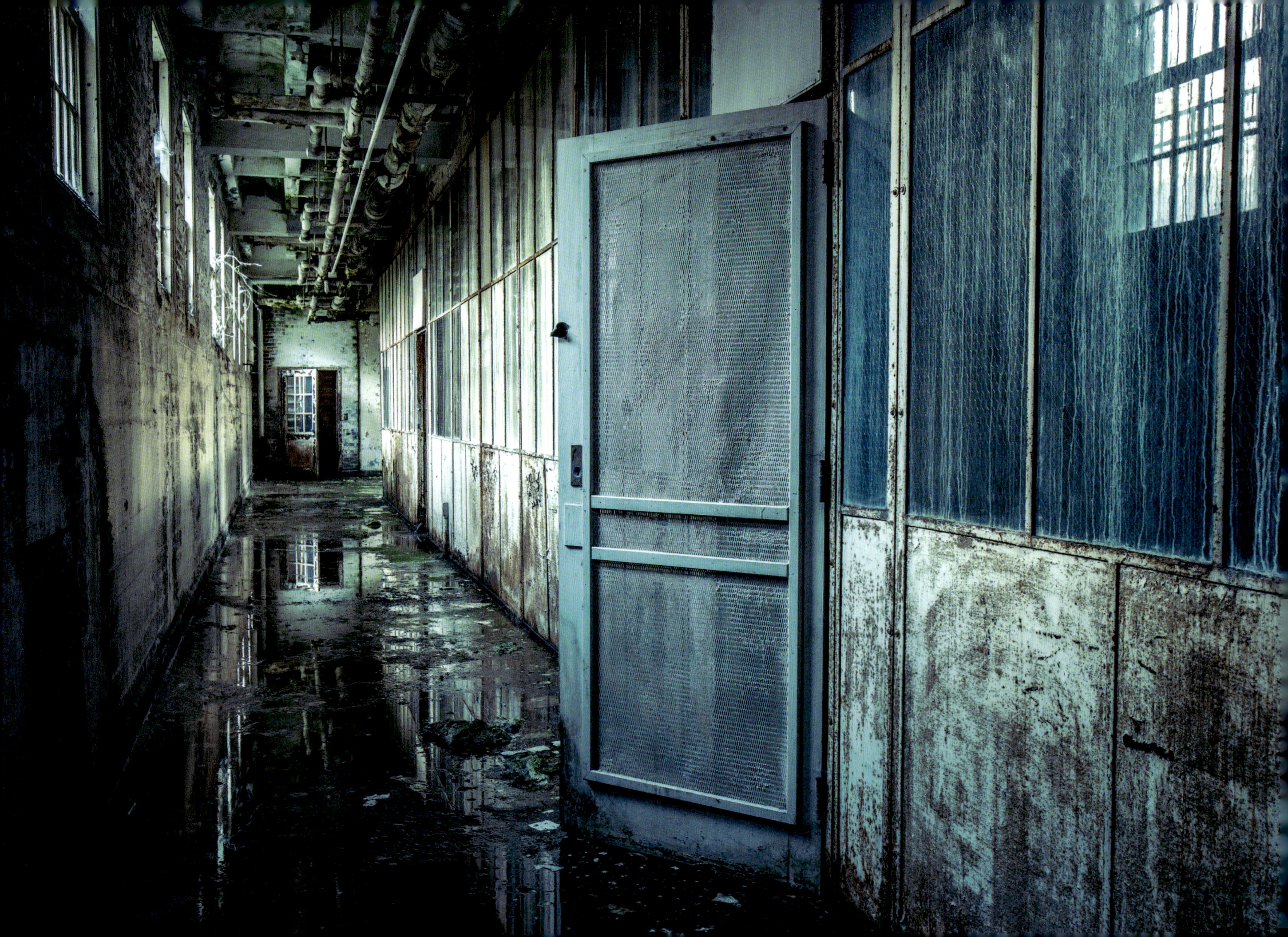

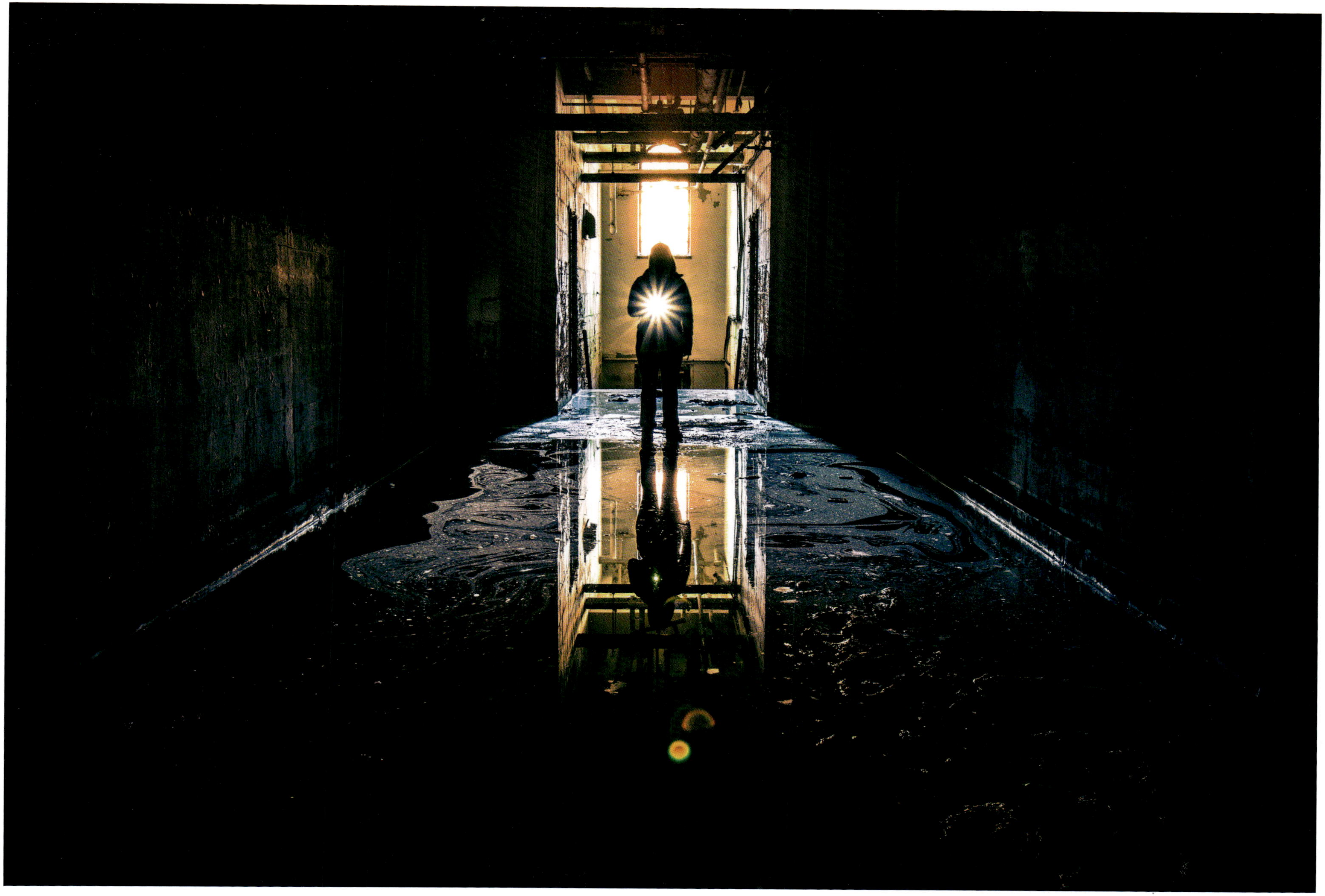

Underground tunnel system

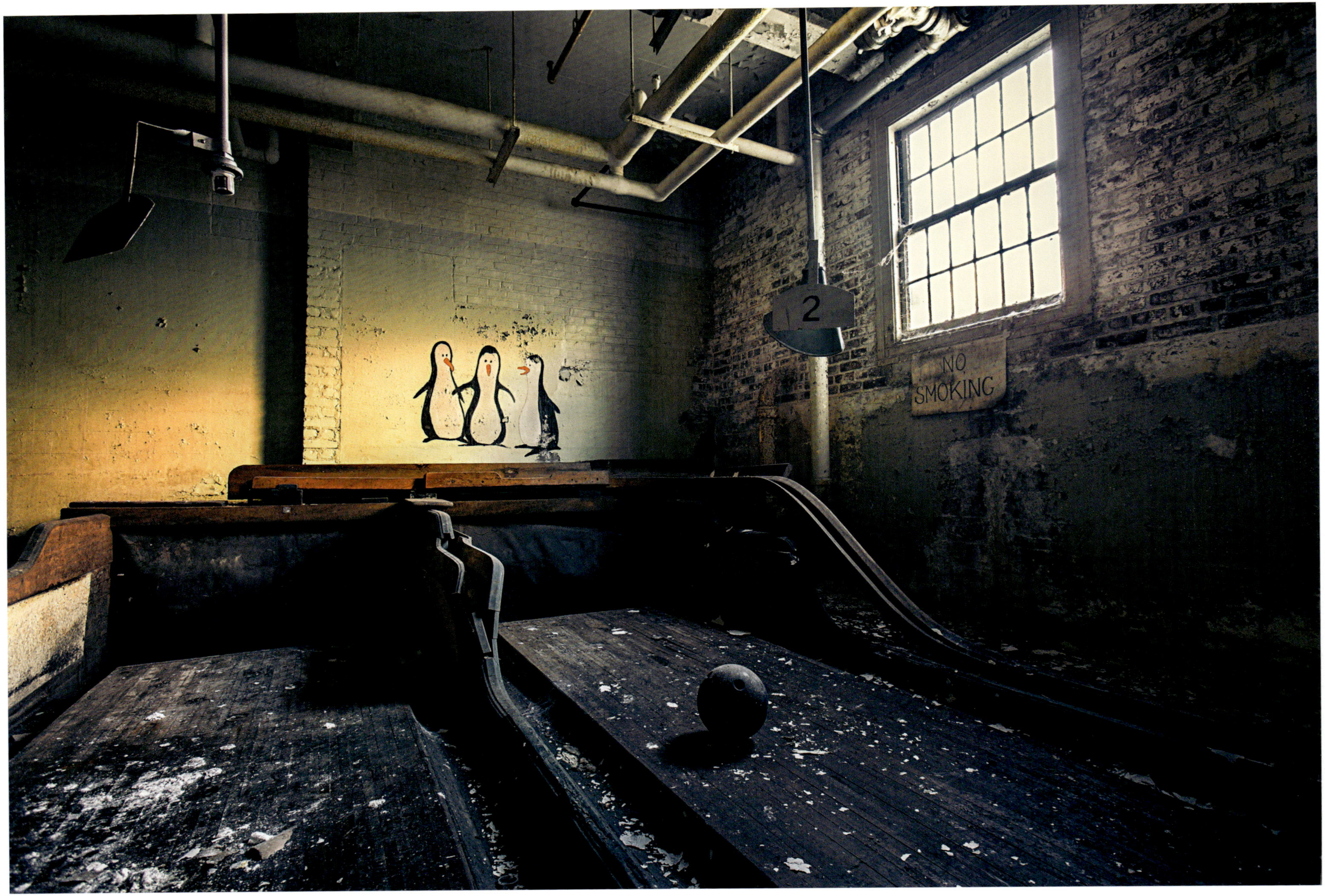
2
NO SMOKING

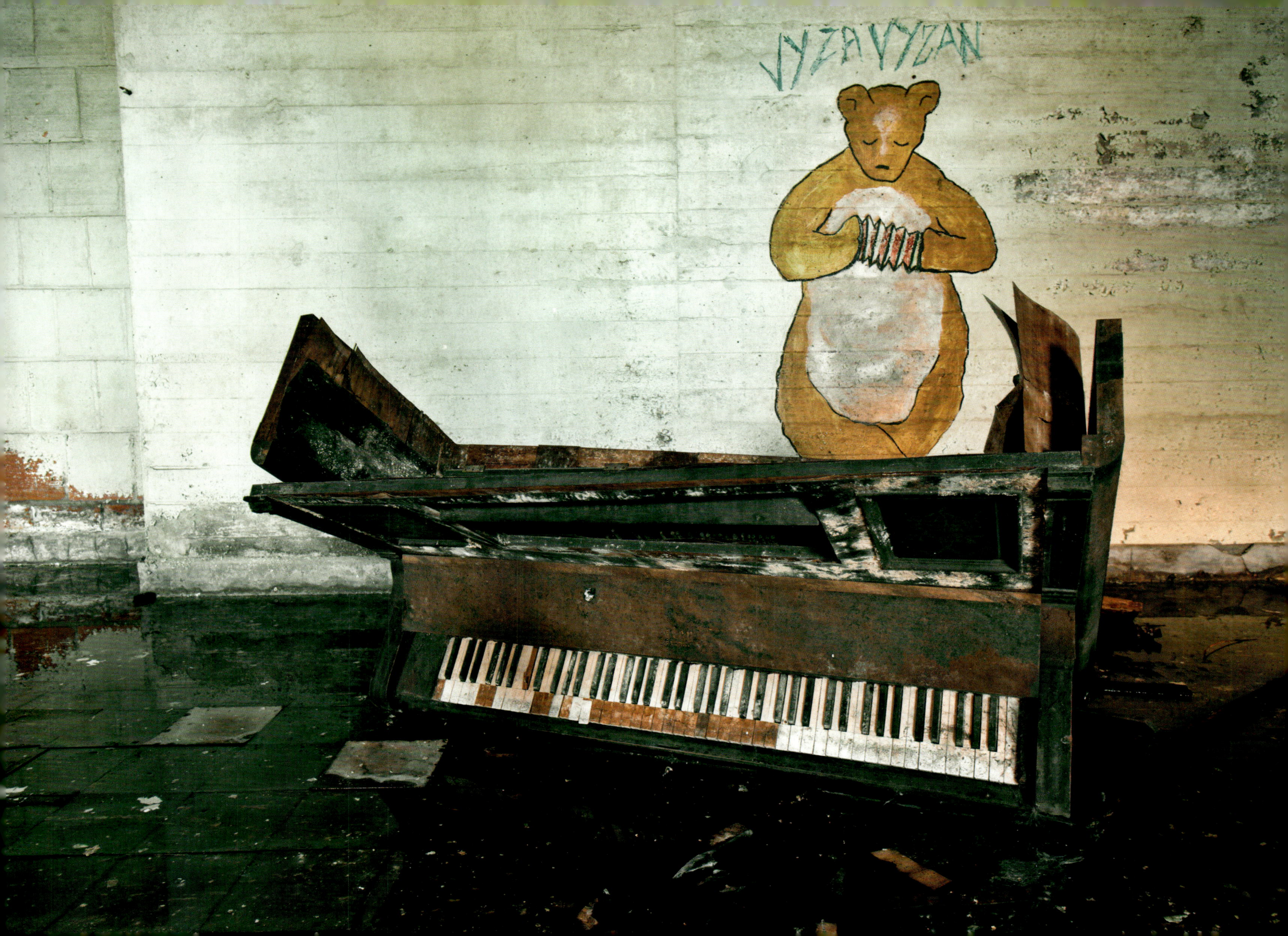
VYZAVYZAN

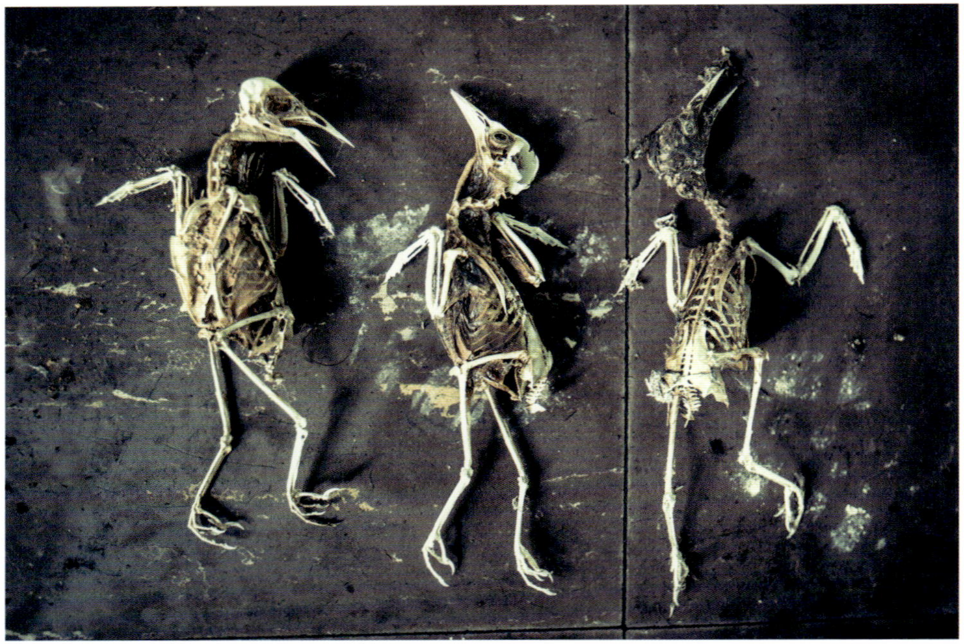

Padded room

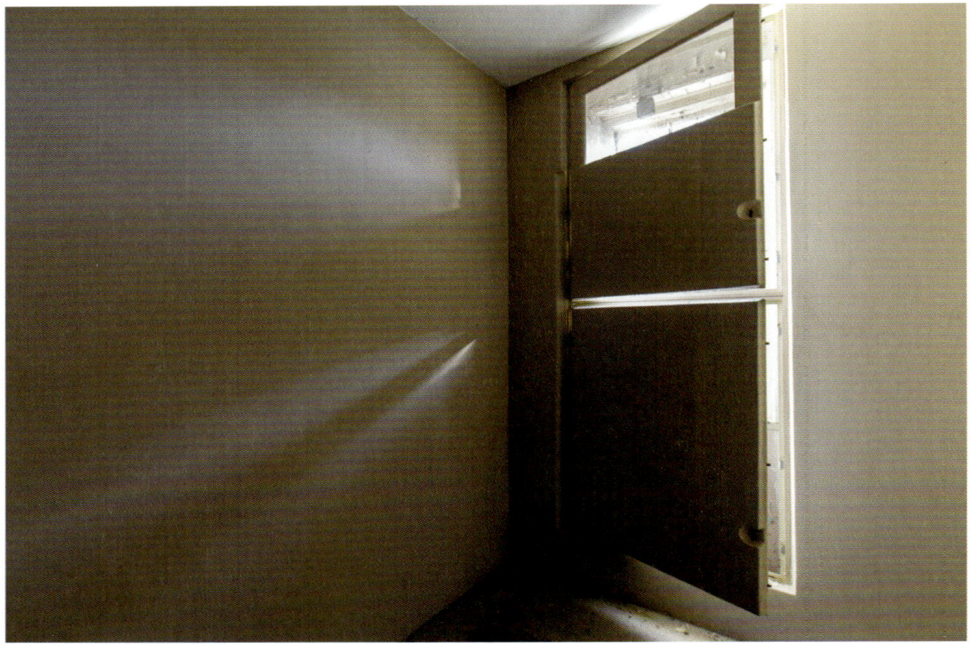

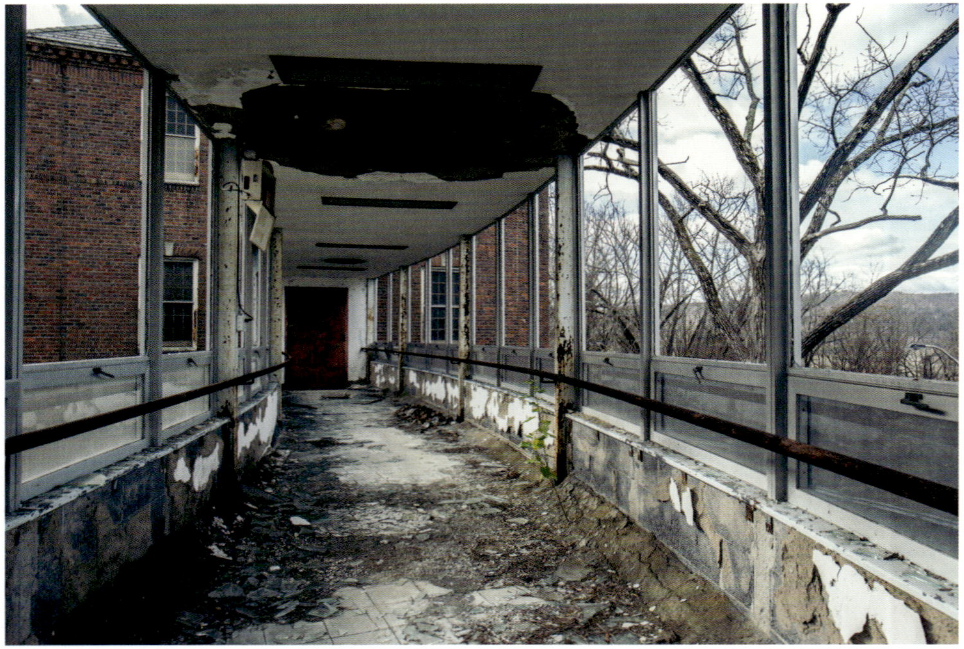

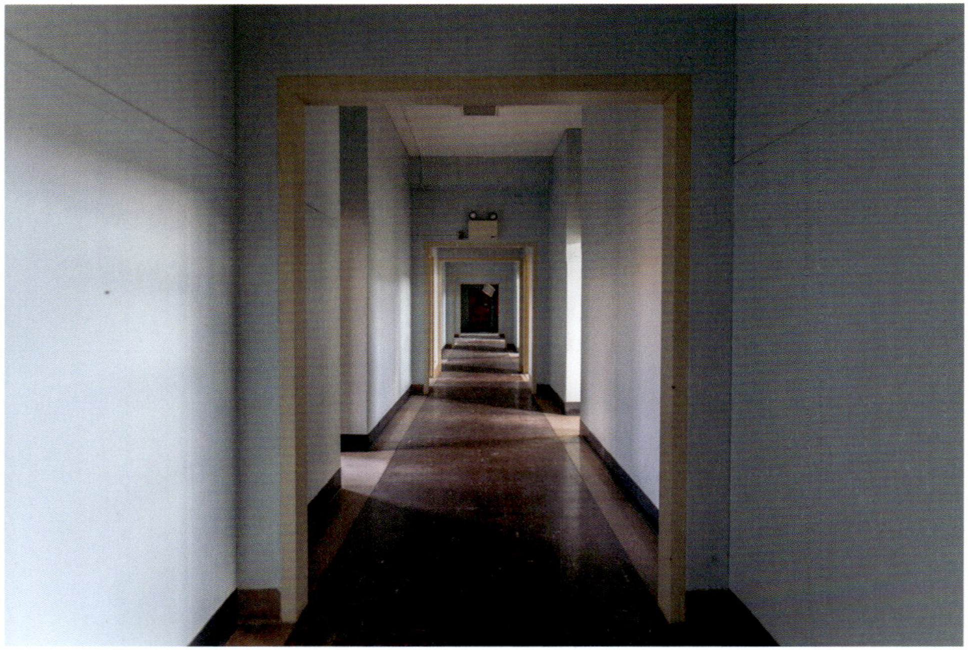

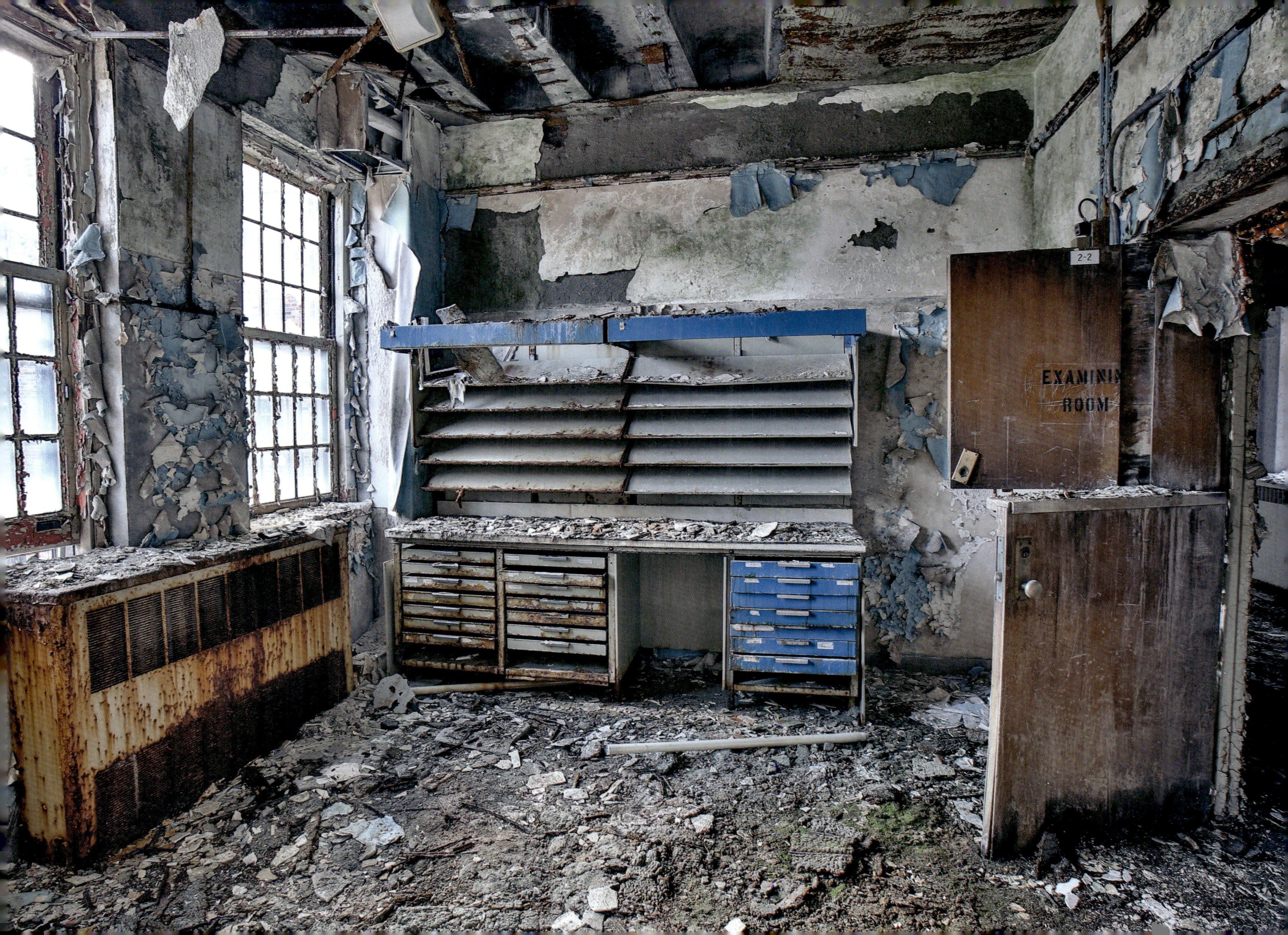
2-2
EXAMININ
ROOM

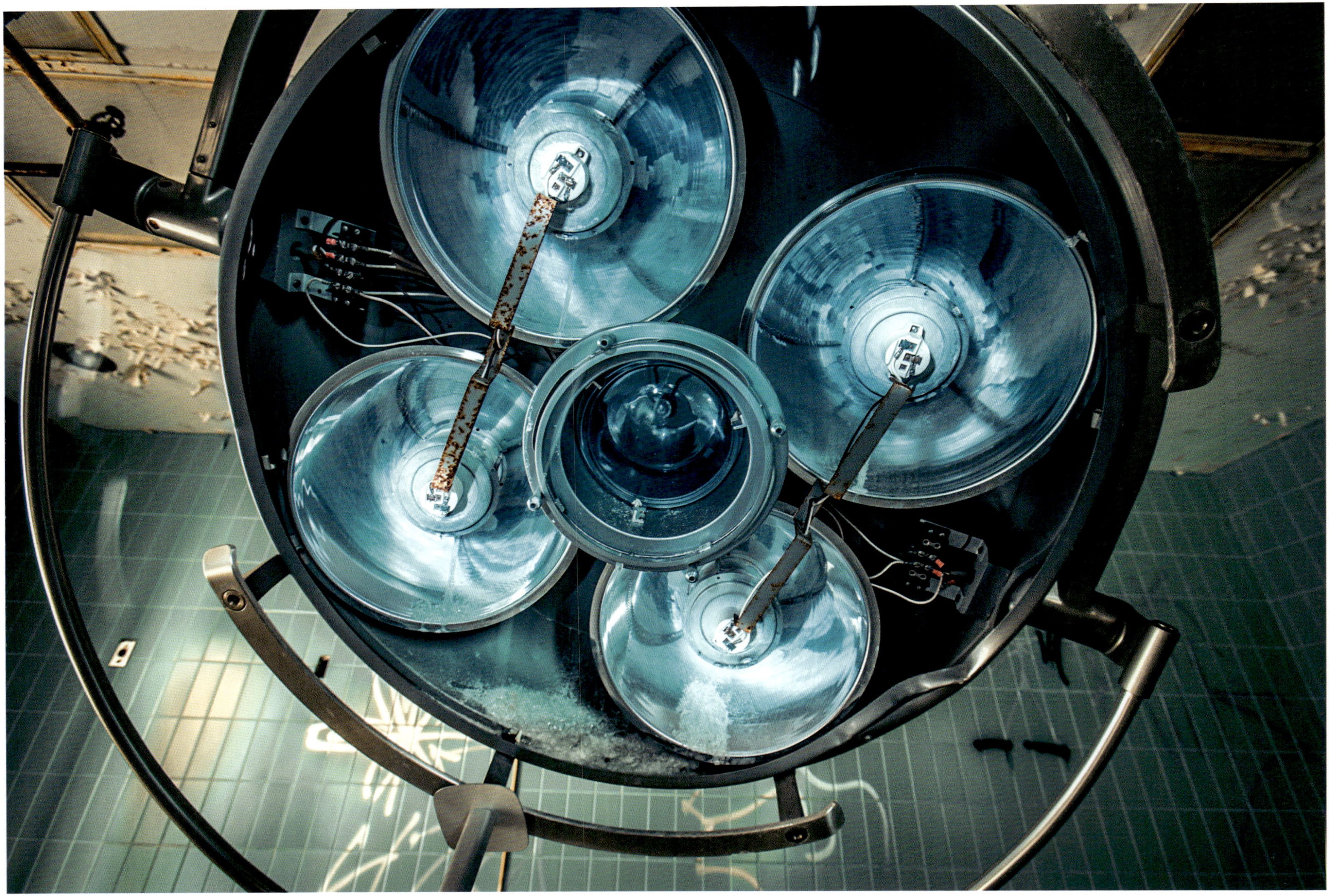

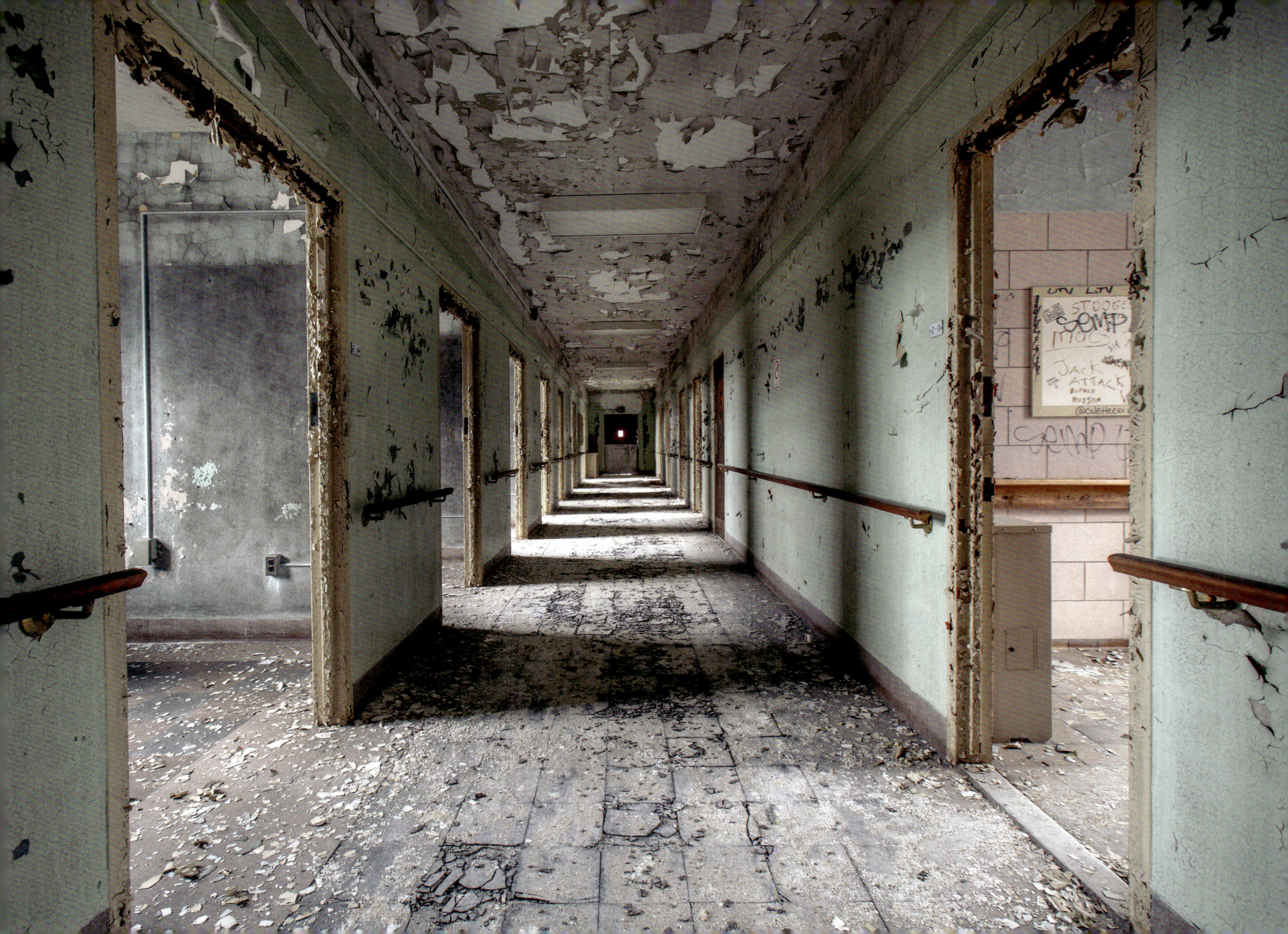
LTV LTV
JACK
ATTACK
HUDSON

Creedmoor State Hospital

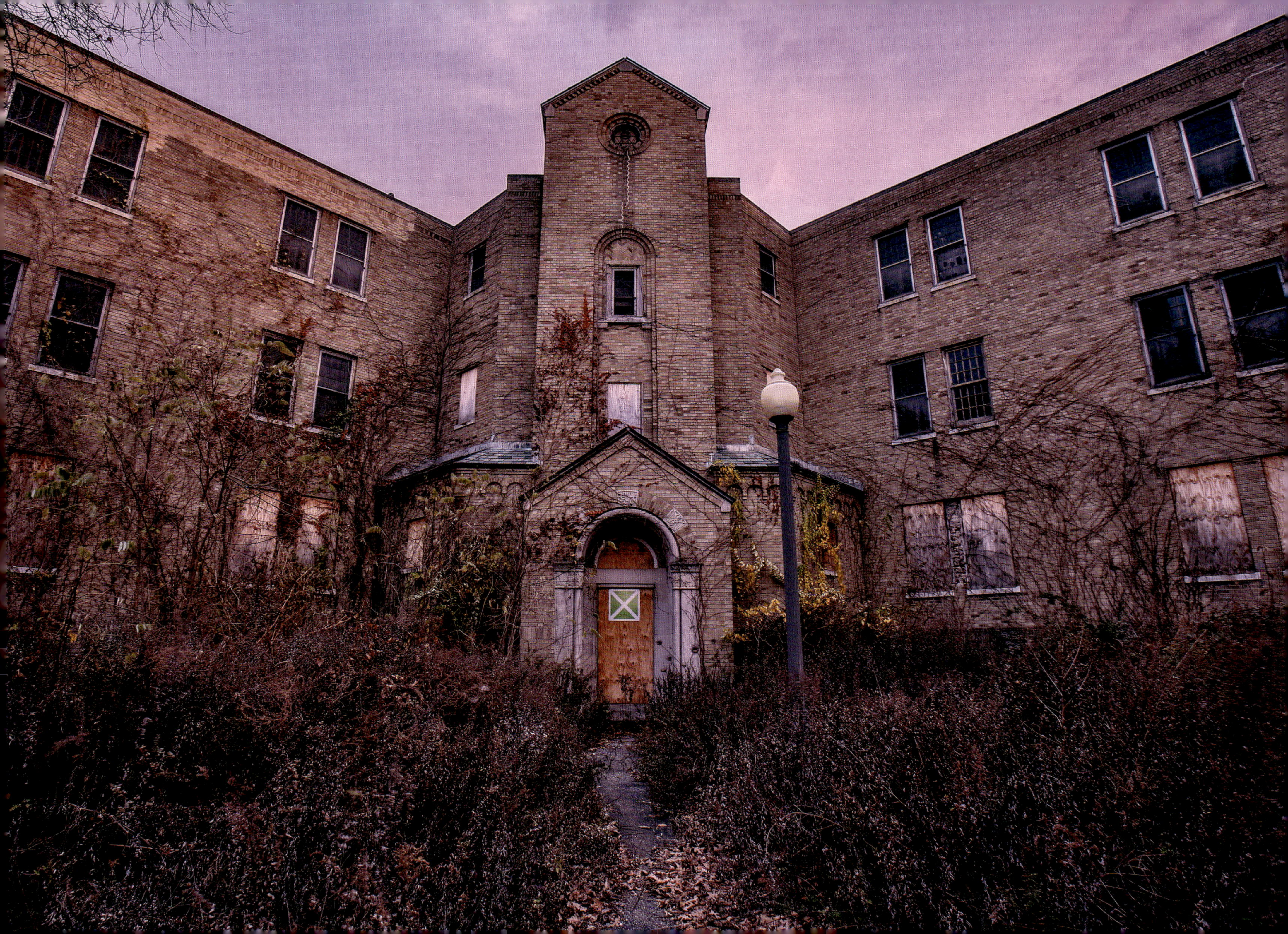

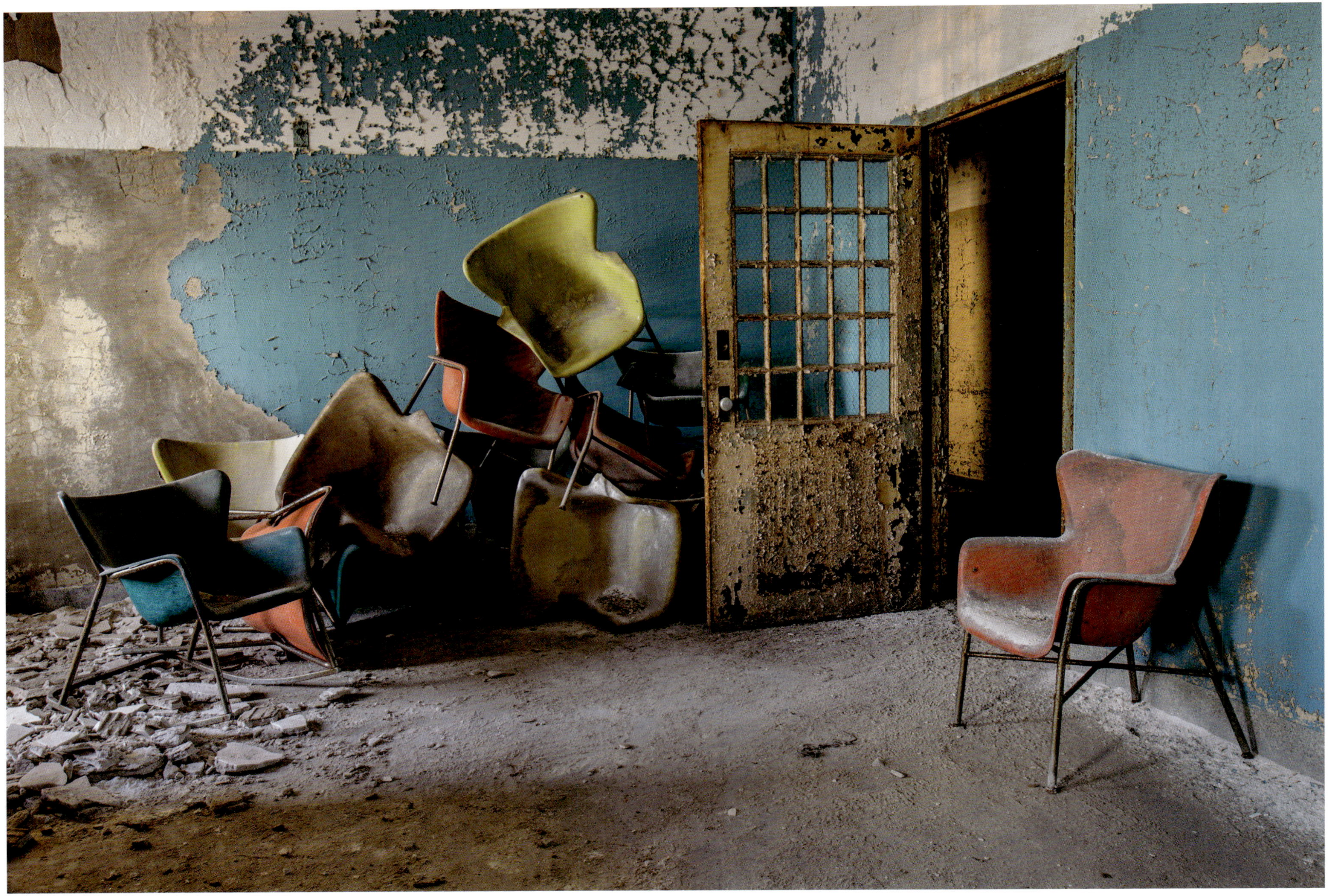

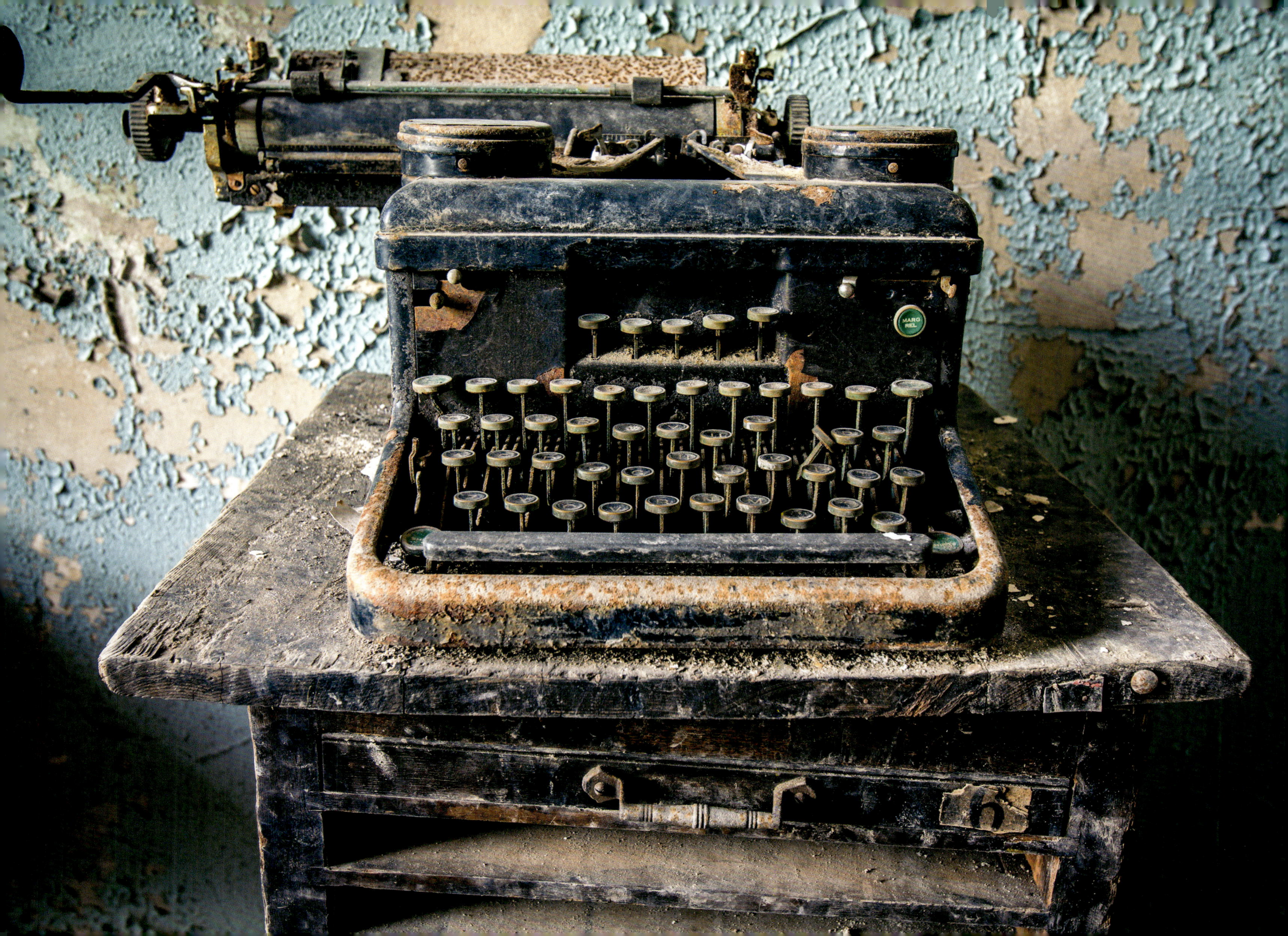
MARG
REL
6

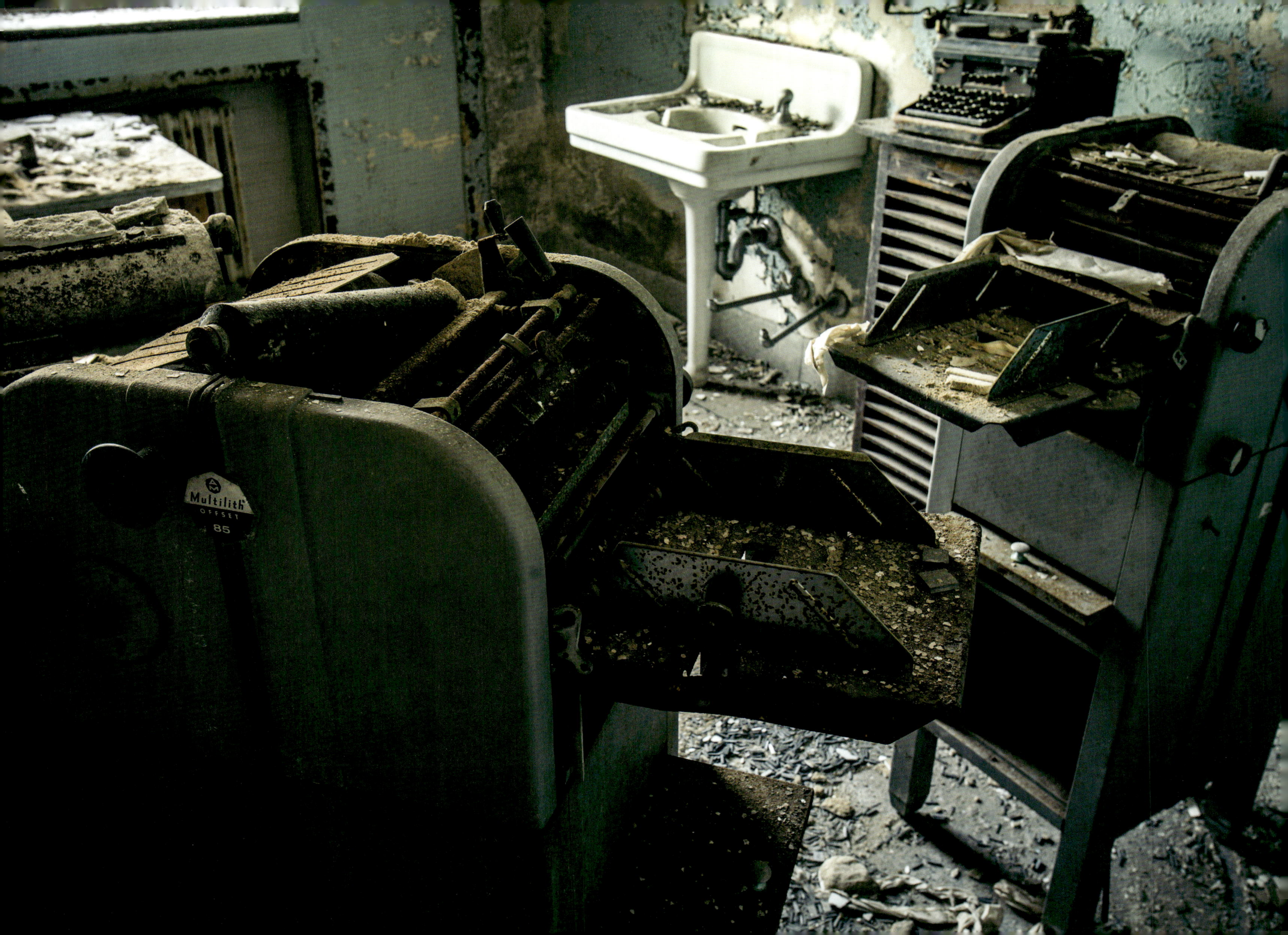
Multilith
OFFSET
85

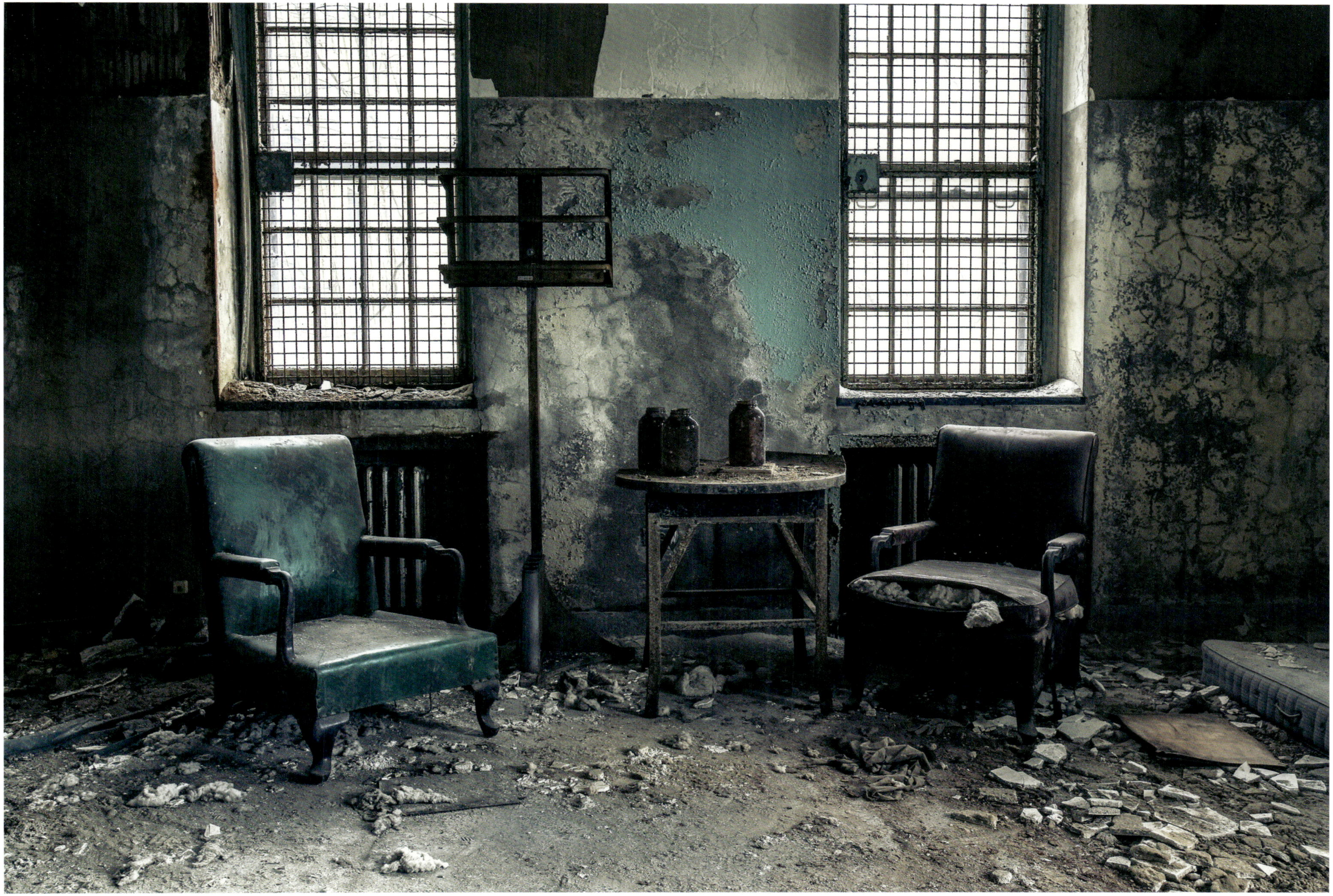

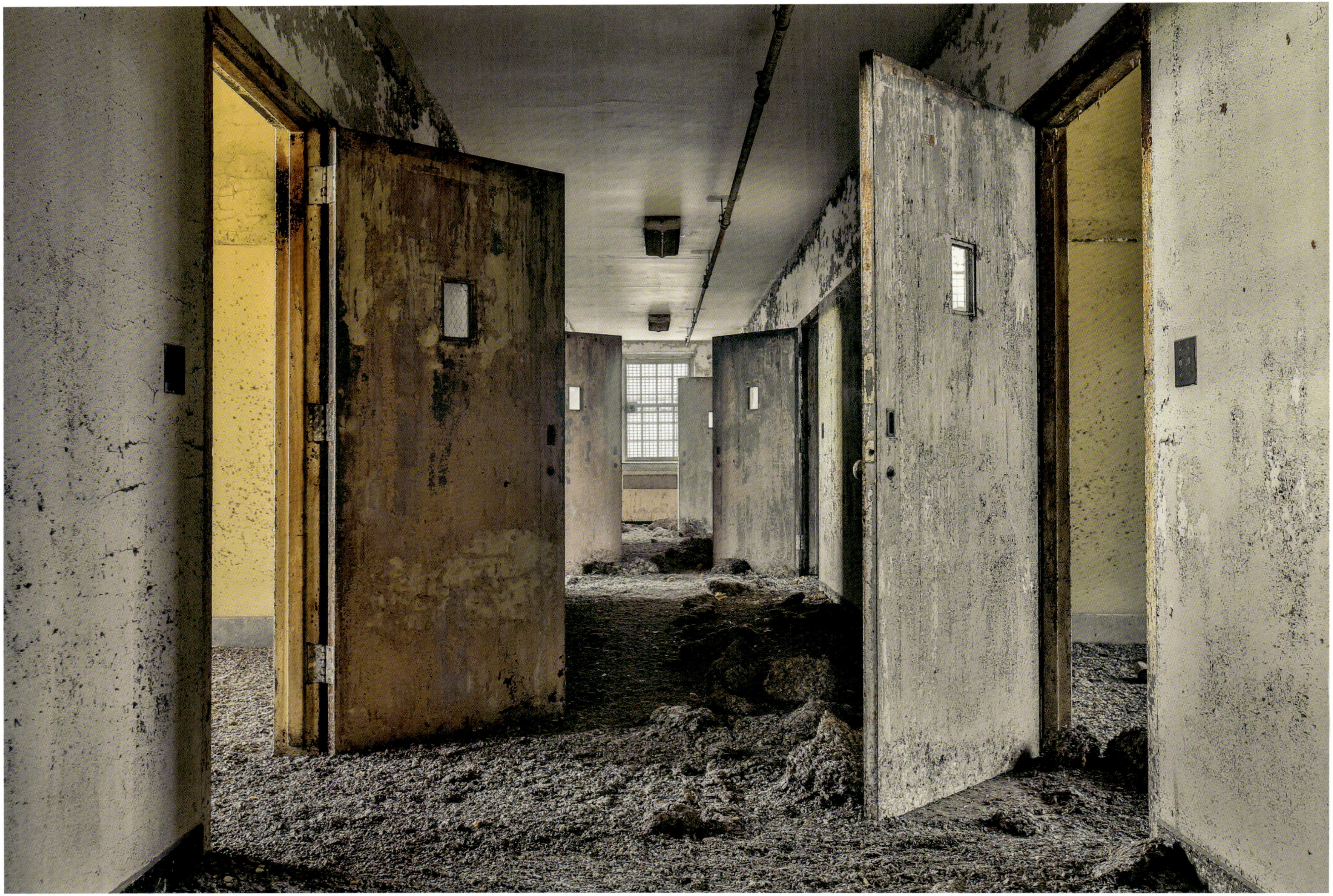

Decades of bird feces inches thick litter the ward floors

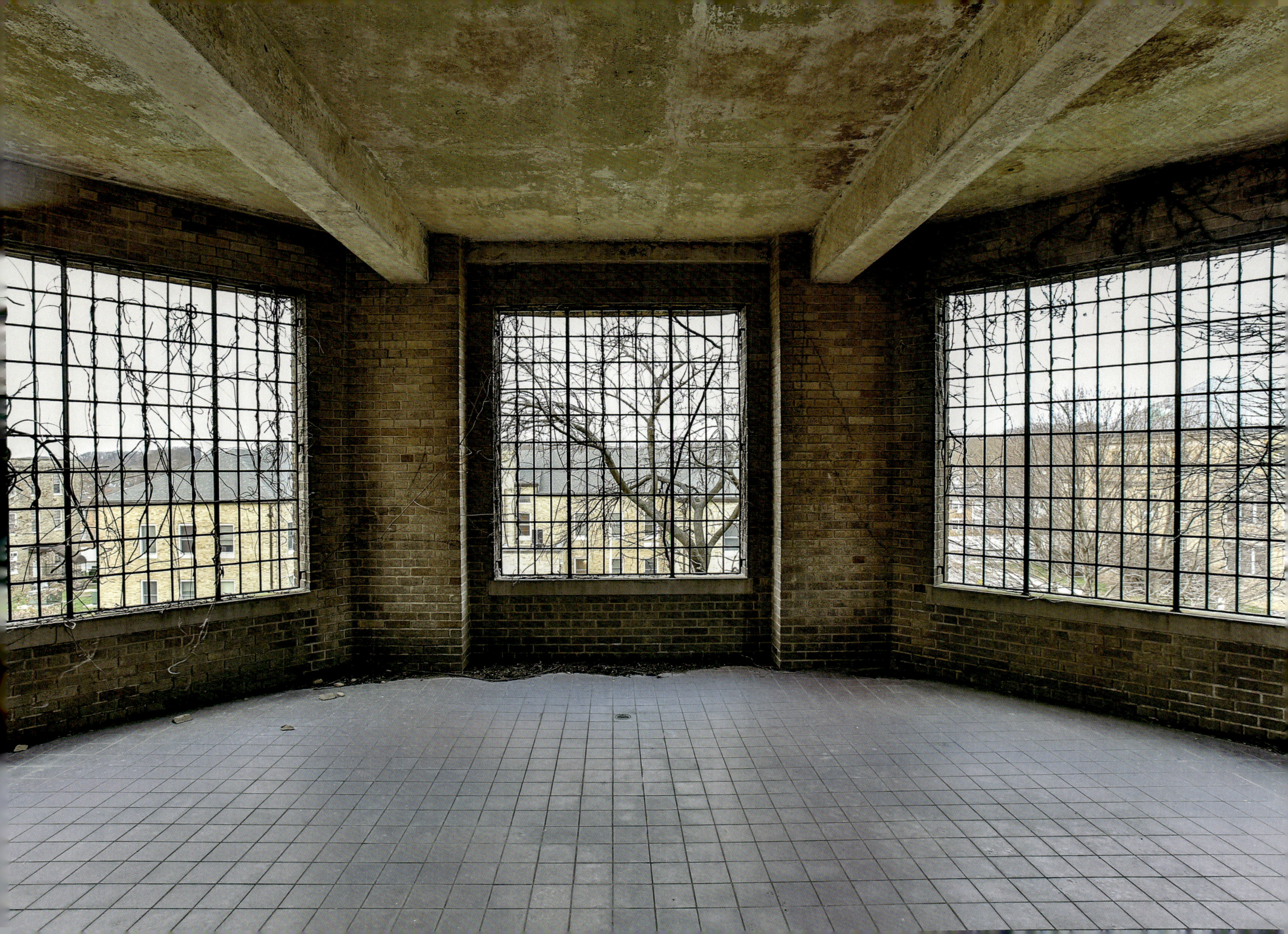

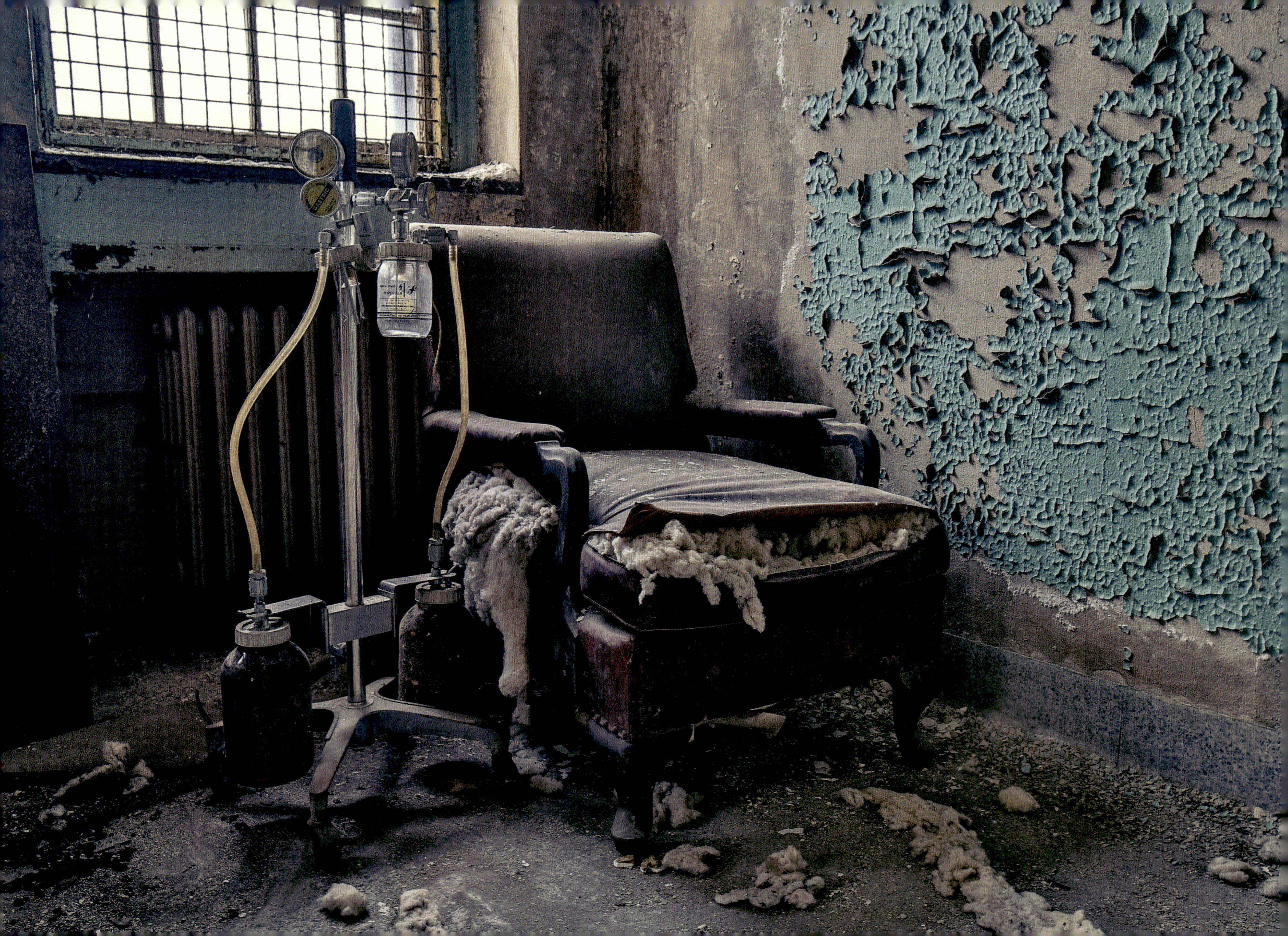

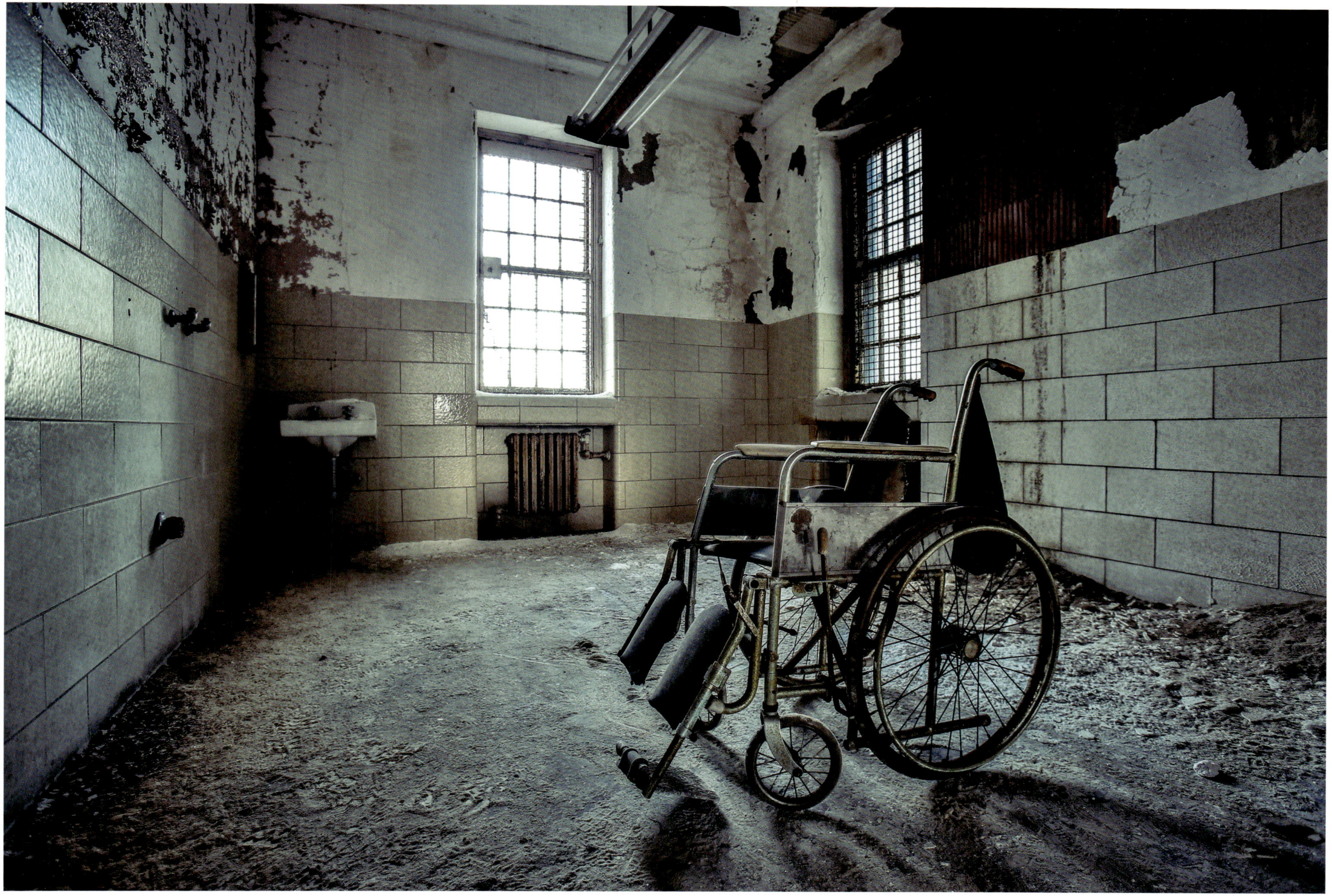

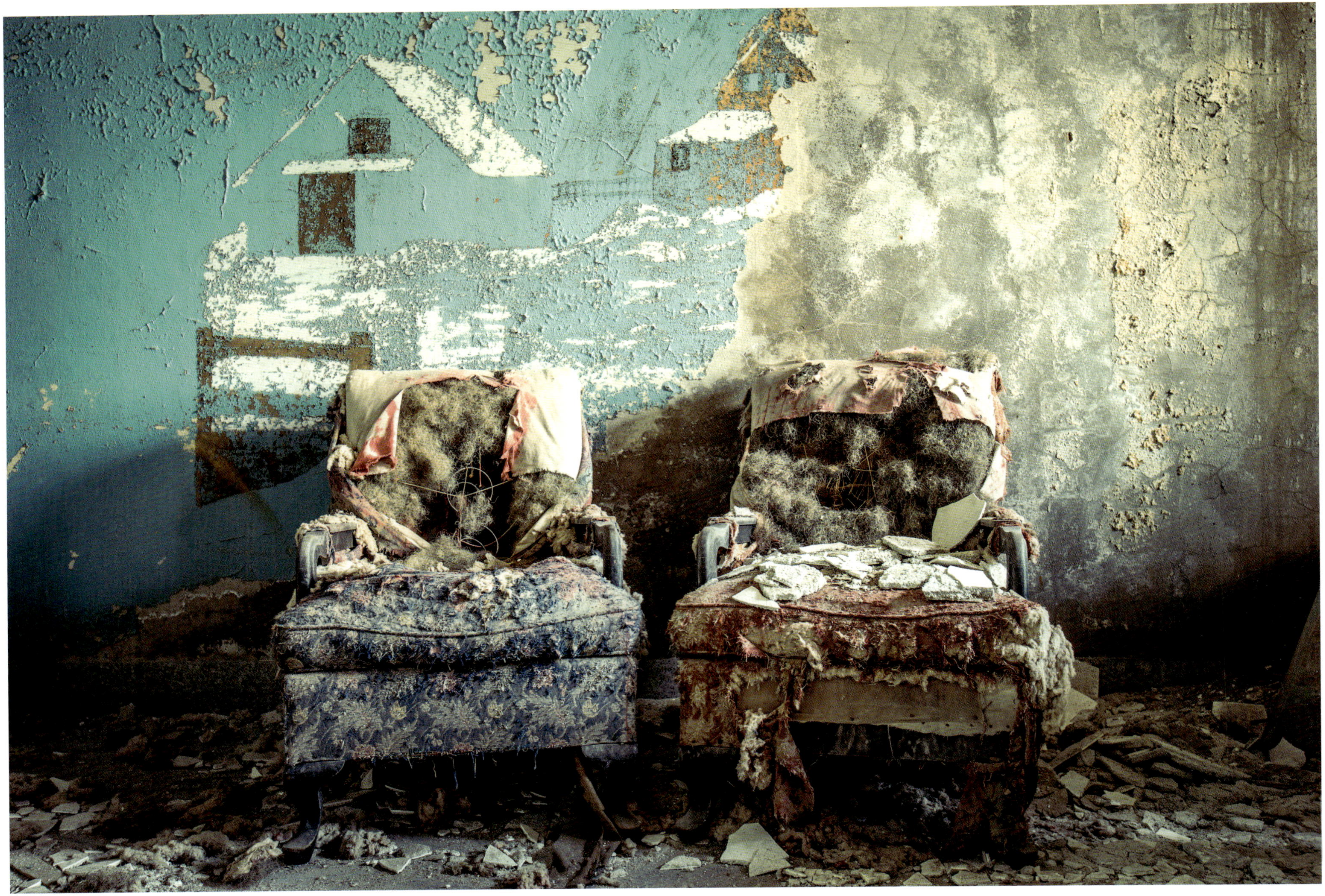

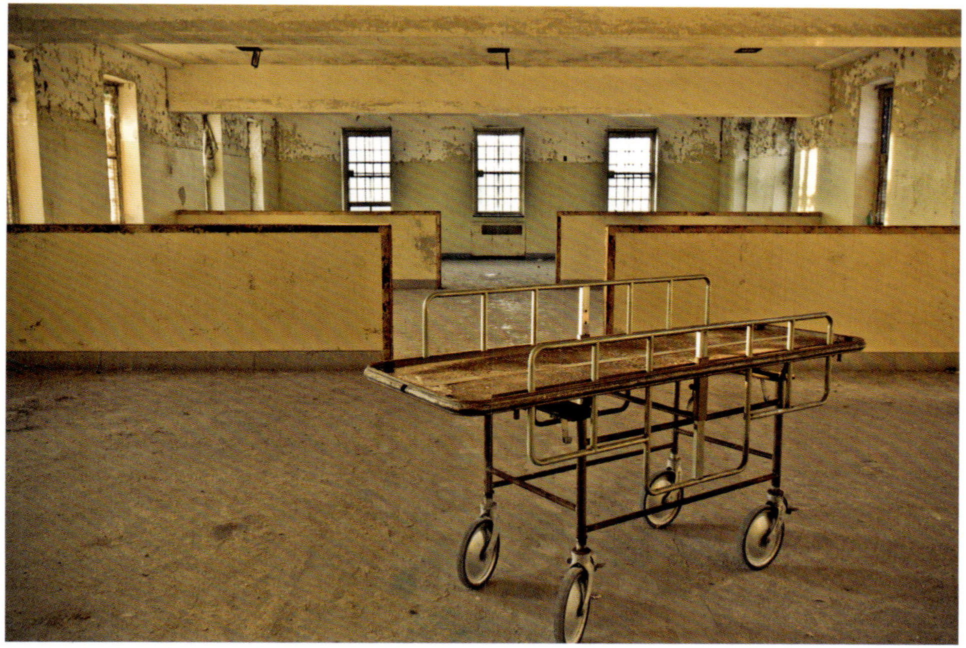
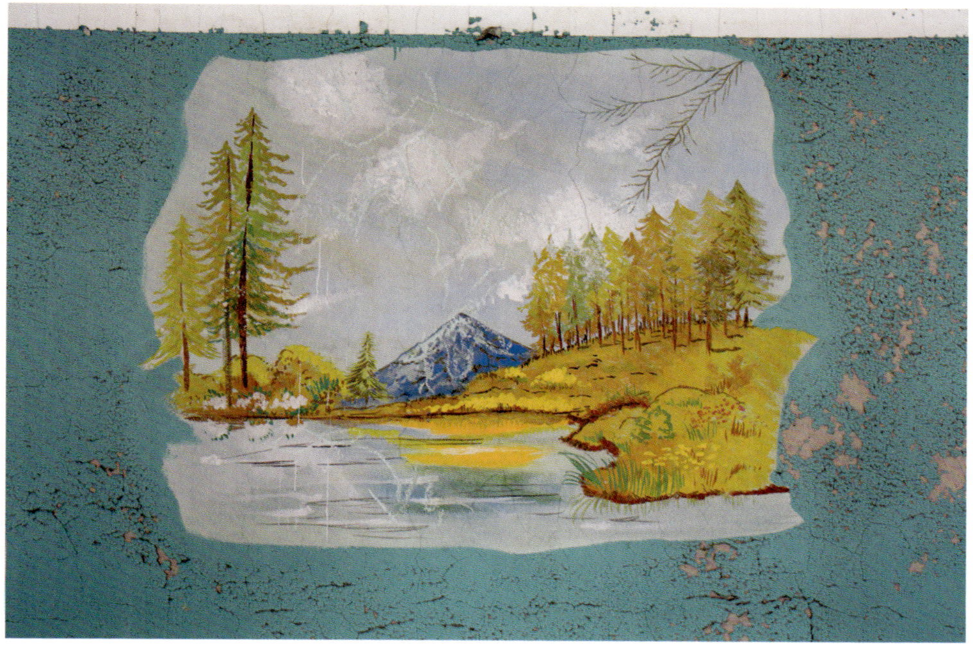
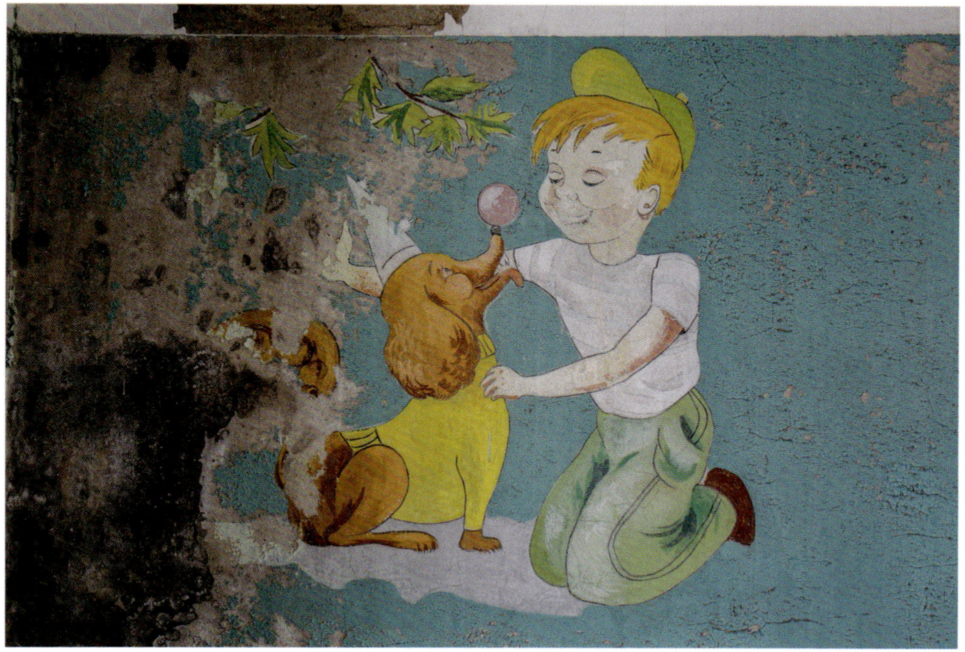
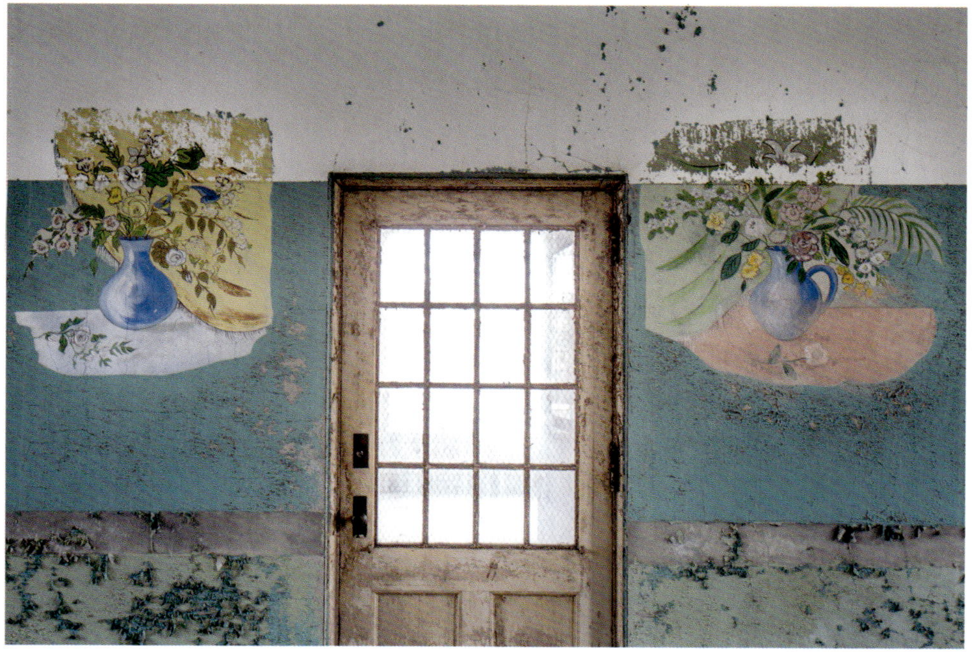

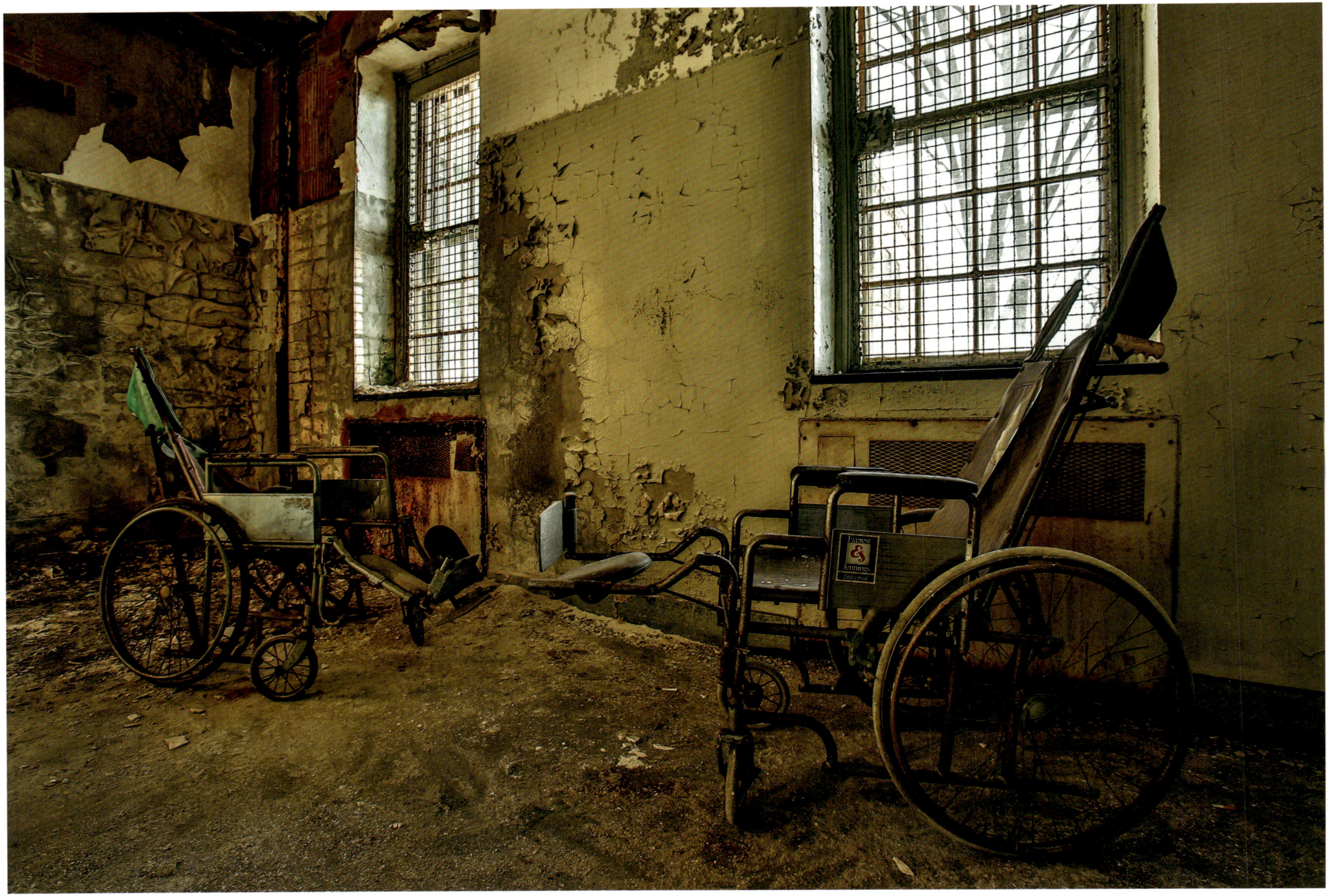
Everest
&
Jennings
Universal

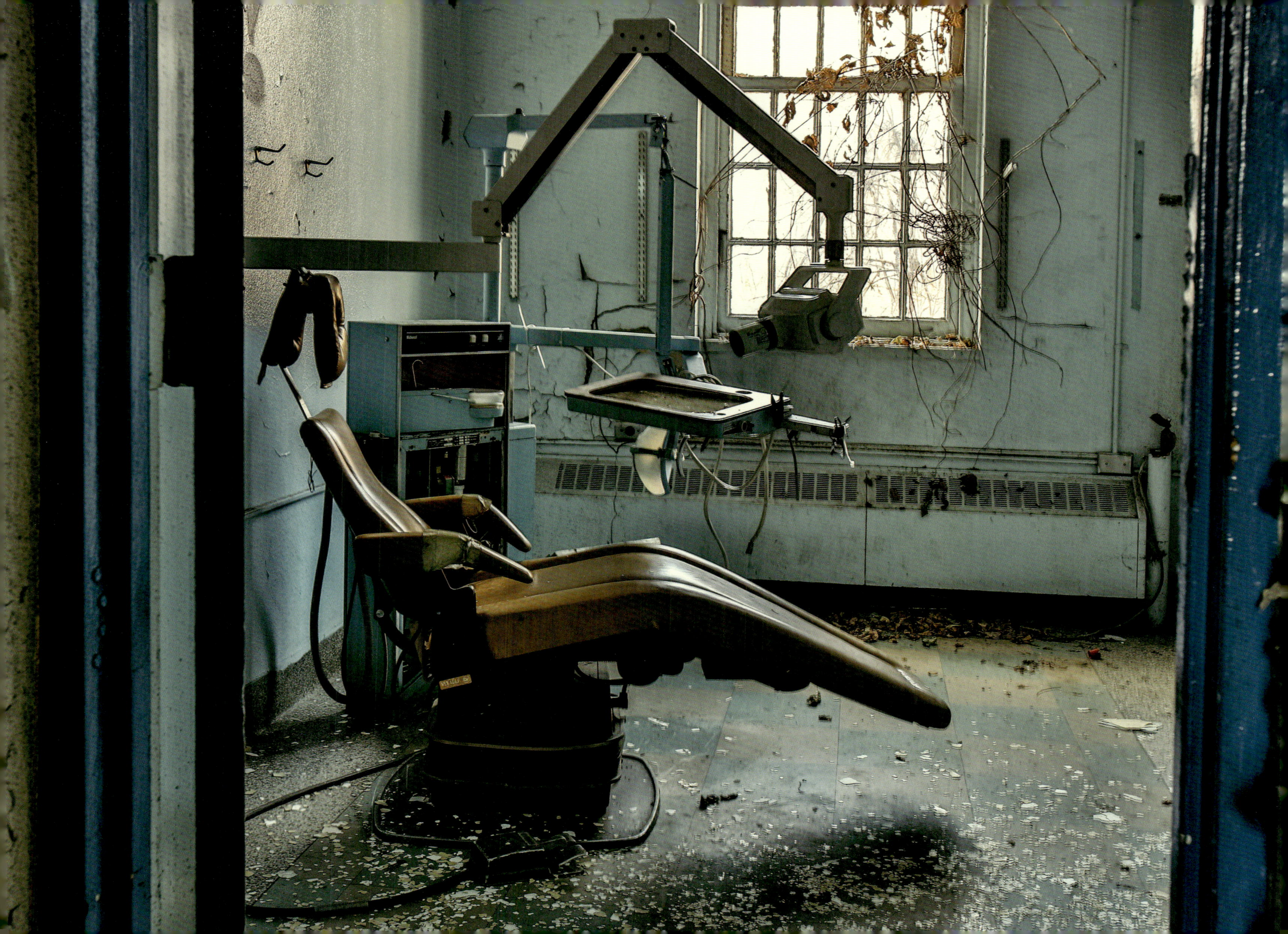

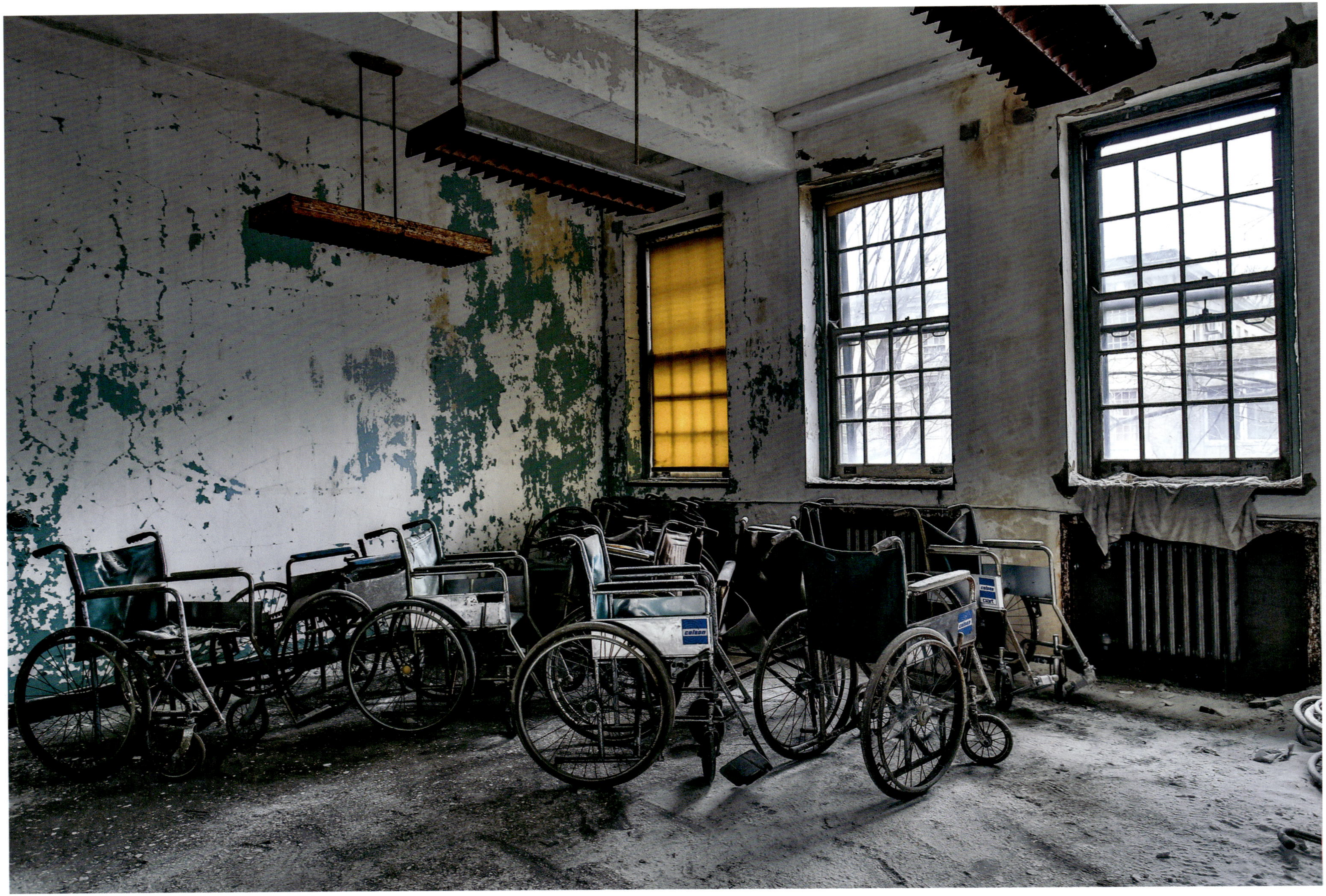

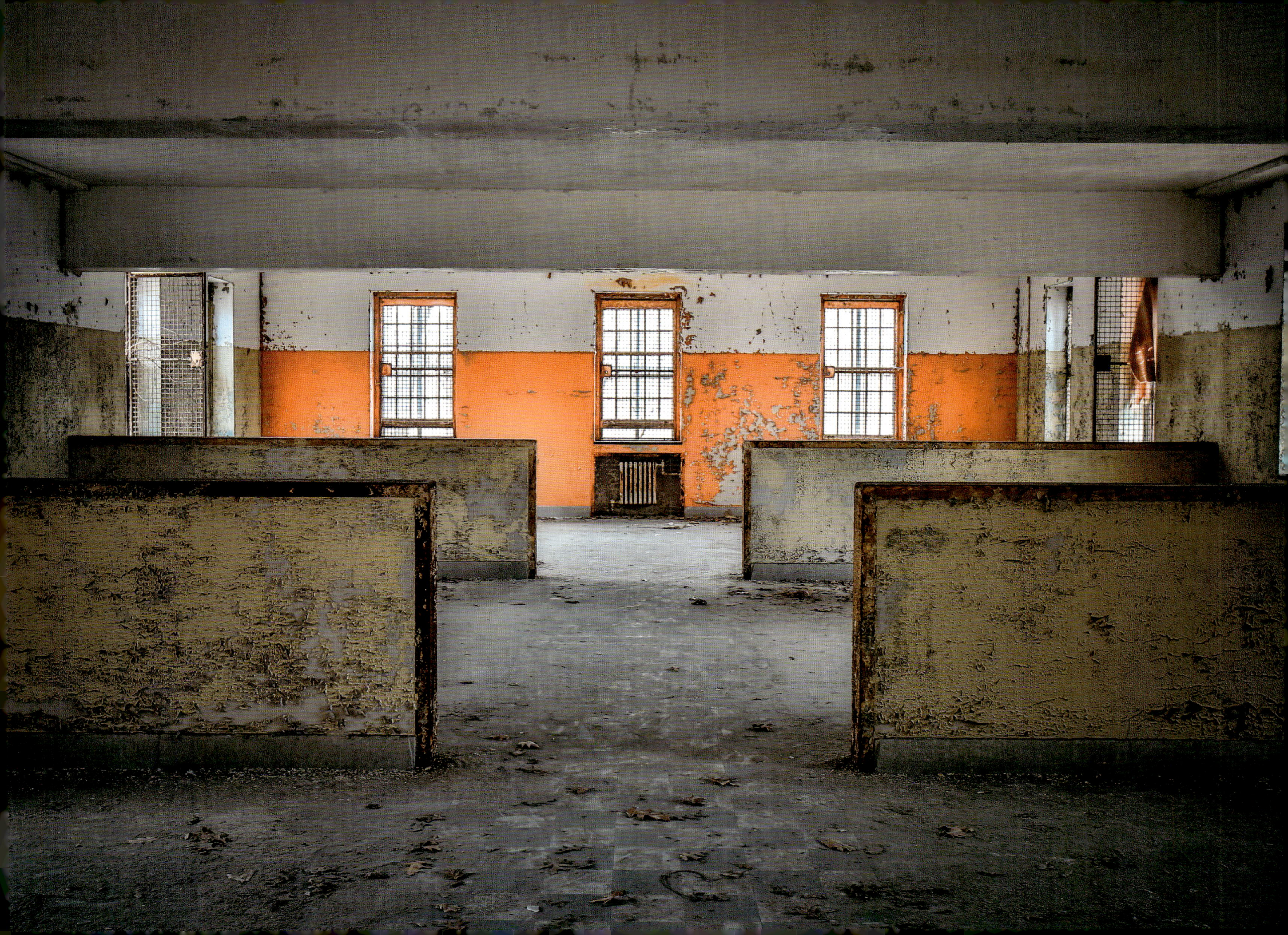

Forgotten in Life, Forgotten in Death

The most emotionally charged environments of the abandoned asylums lie neither in the vacant hallways, where motionless wheelchairs are randomly strewn about, nor the morgues, nor the untouched racks of patient clothing. If you look in the furthest corners of state hospital properties, you'll normally find the anonymous graves of thousands of tortured souls who once called the institutions 'home'. There are 55,000 patients, at 17 known sites, interred anonymously in New York State alone. As the asylums shuttered, the end of their operational maintenance efforts soon followed.

Grounds keeping ceased. You won't find these cemeteries with immaculately mowed grass, stone-worked gates or perimeter walls; there are no glistening marble grave markers displaying the names, dates of birth and death, or touching passages celebrating their lives. Rather, you'll see thousands of non-descript burial markers bearing only a number. In some tragic instances, such as Western State Hospital in Virginia, a century of exposure to the elements has worn away the numbers completely. All of this is assuming you can even locate the cemetery grounds to begin with - signage is rare and the grounds are usually tucked away in wooded areas, hidden from the view of patients and public alike.

Greystone Park Psychiatric Hospital burial ground

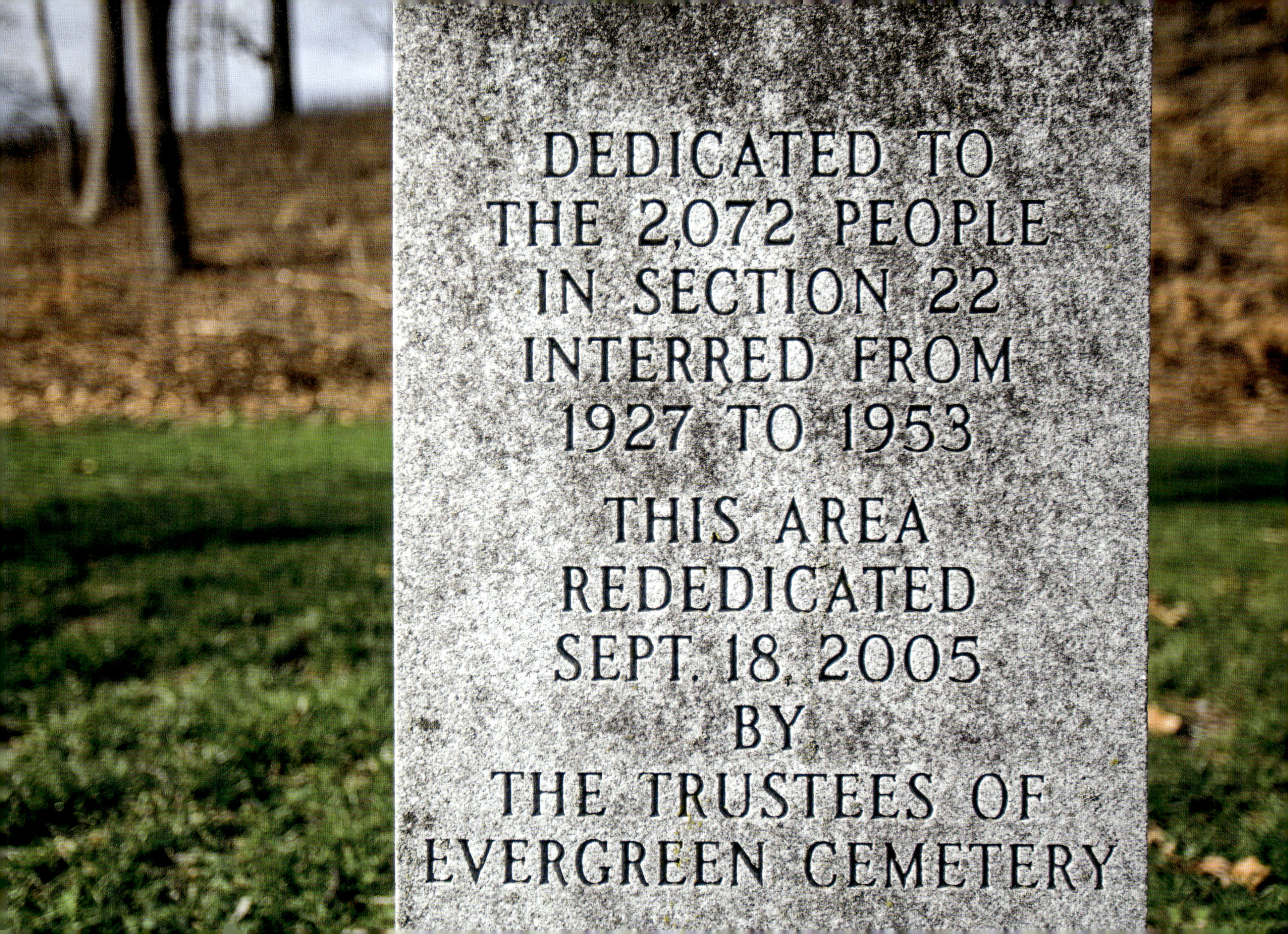
DEDICATED TO
THE 2,072 PEOPLE
IN SECTION 22
INTERRED FROM
1927 TO 1953
THIS AREA
REDEDICATED
SEPT. 18, 2005
BY
THE TRUSTEES OF
EVERGREEN CEMETERY

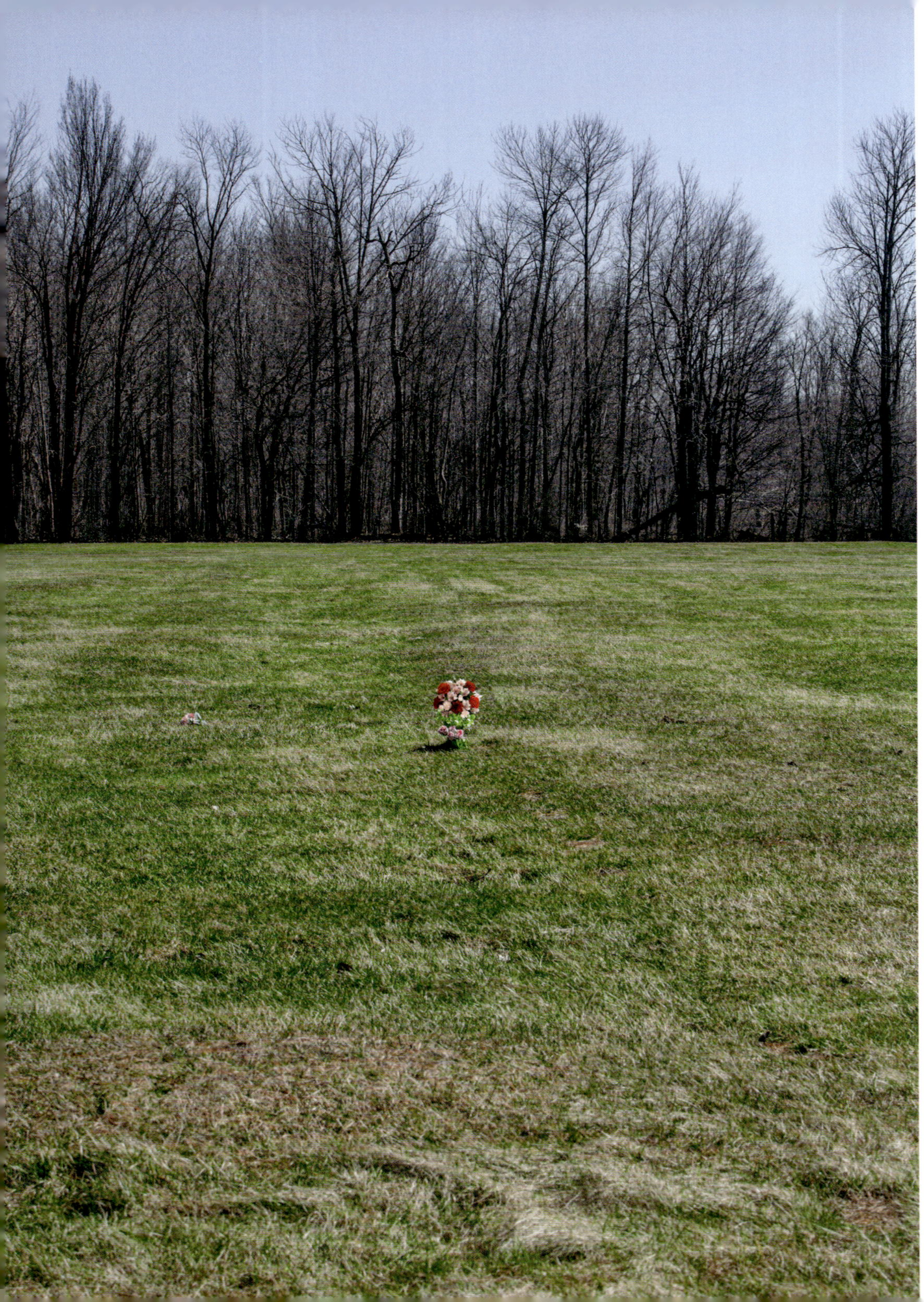

Saint Lawrence State Hospital cemetary

The size and style of grave marker differs from institution to institution. Some opted for a traditional cross, but the most commonly found are small circular metal/cement markers with just enough surface area to display the designated number. In the case of Willard State Hospital and Greystone Park State Hospital, for instance, these small circular markers have been forgotten to the extent that the earth surrounding them has buried every trace of their existence. The passage of time and neglect has allowed trees to spring up through the graves, in some cases toppling the markers over or moving them away from their original position, making tracing any record virtually impossible.

Patients have not only been stripped of their names, they have also been stripped of their dignity. Forgotten in life, forgotten in death. This is the result of state bureaucracy protecting privacy and a fear of stigma, which, unfortunately, is alive and well even today. The patient's final resting place now sits in a disgraceful state of neglect.

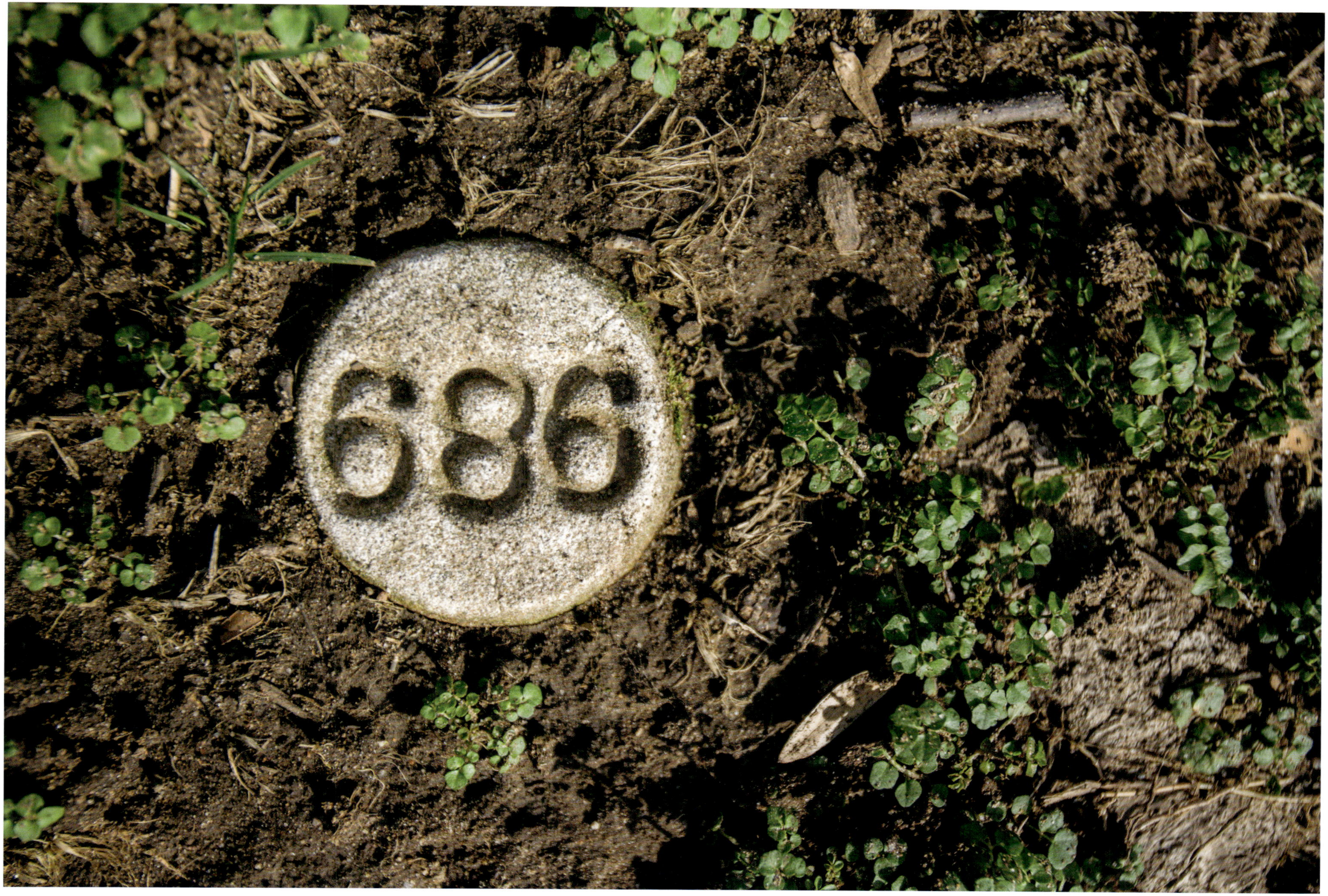

Greystone Park Psychiatric Hospital grave marker

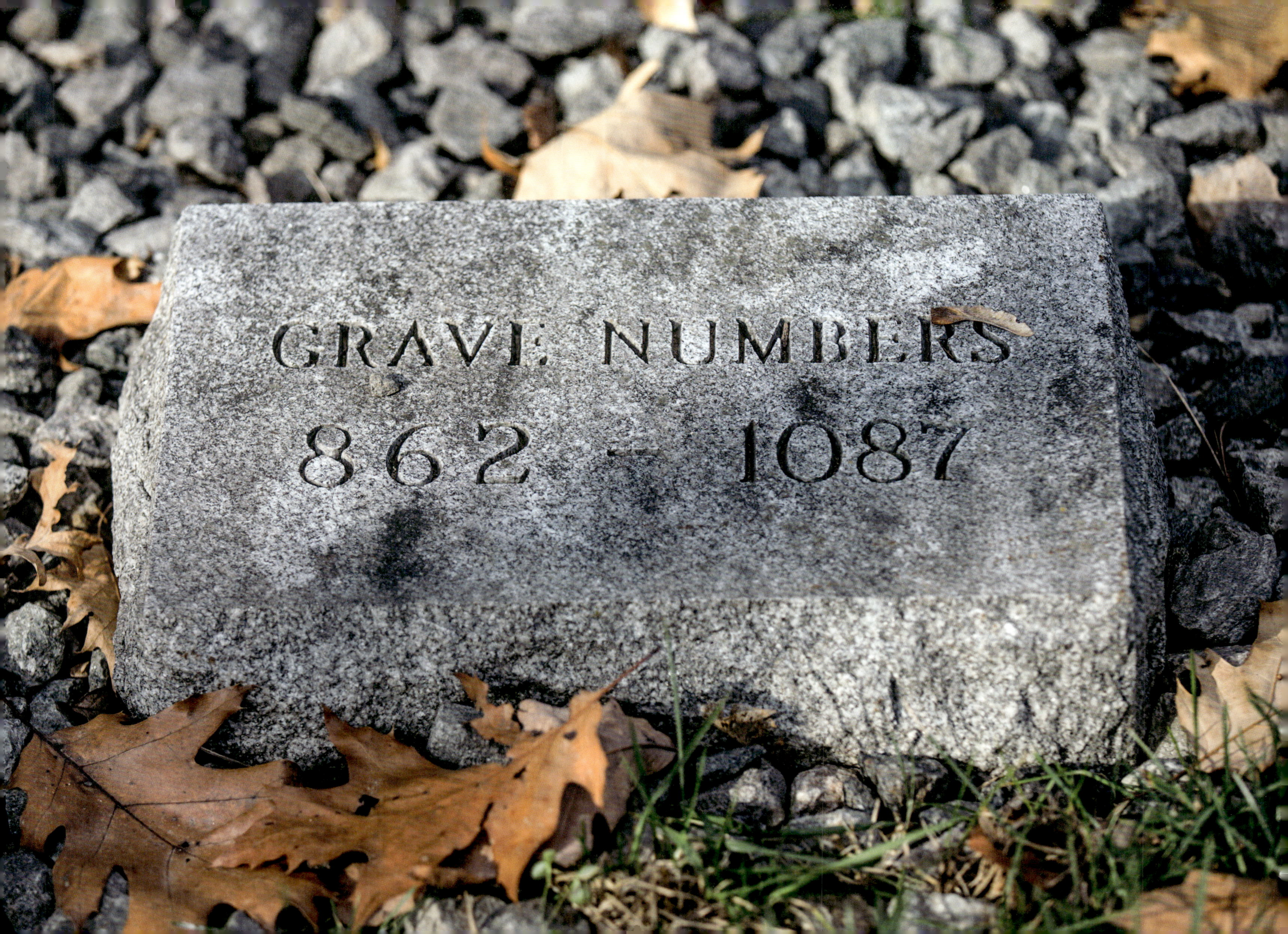
GRAVE NUMBERS
862 - 1087

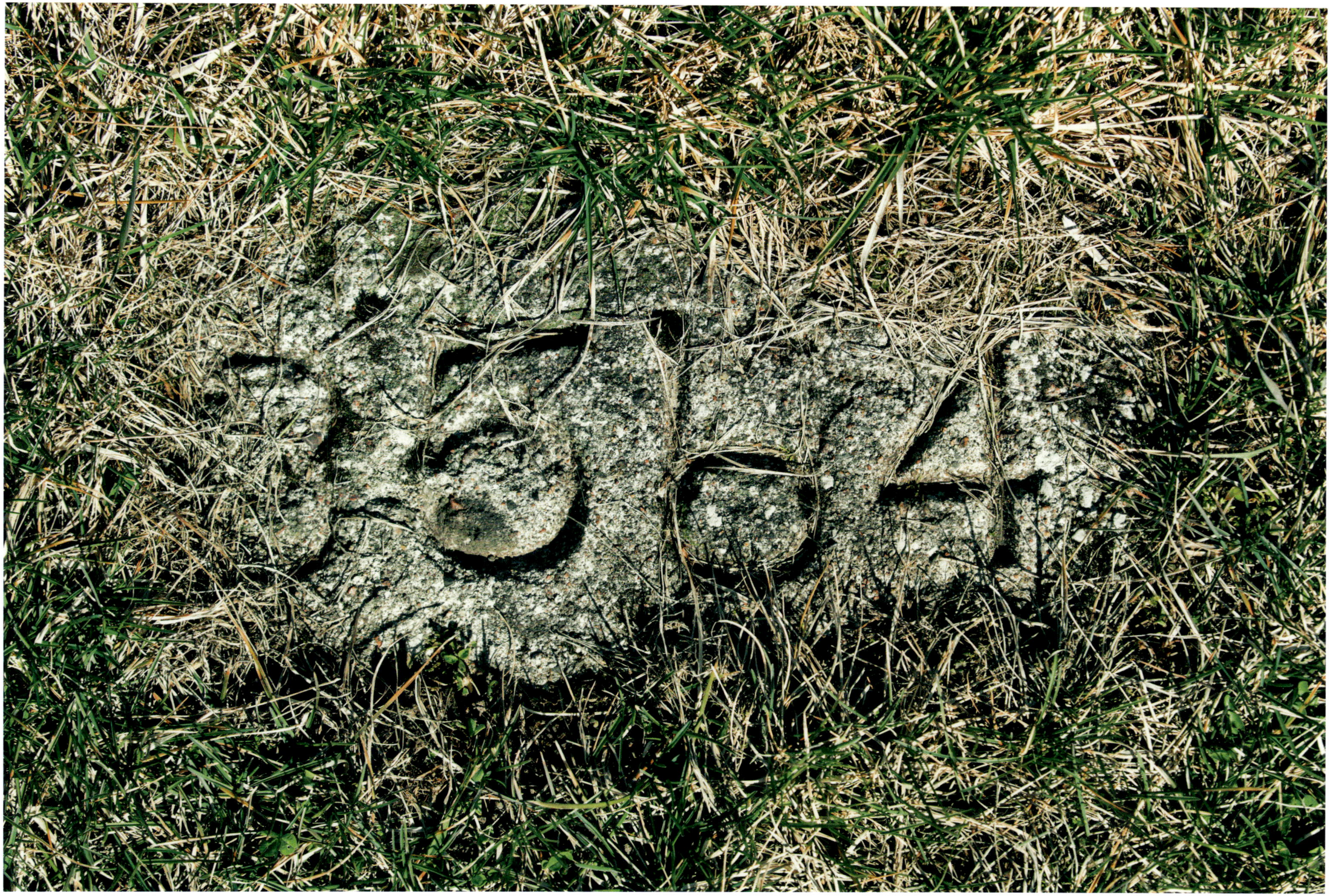

Saint Lawrence State Hospital grave marker

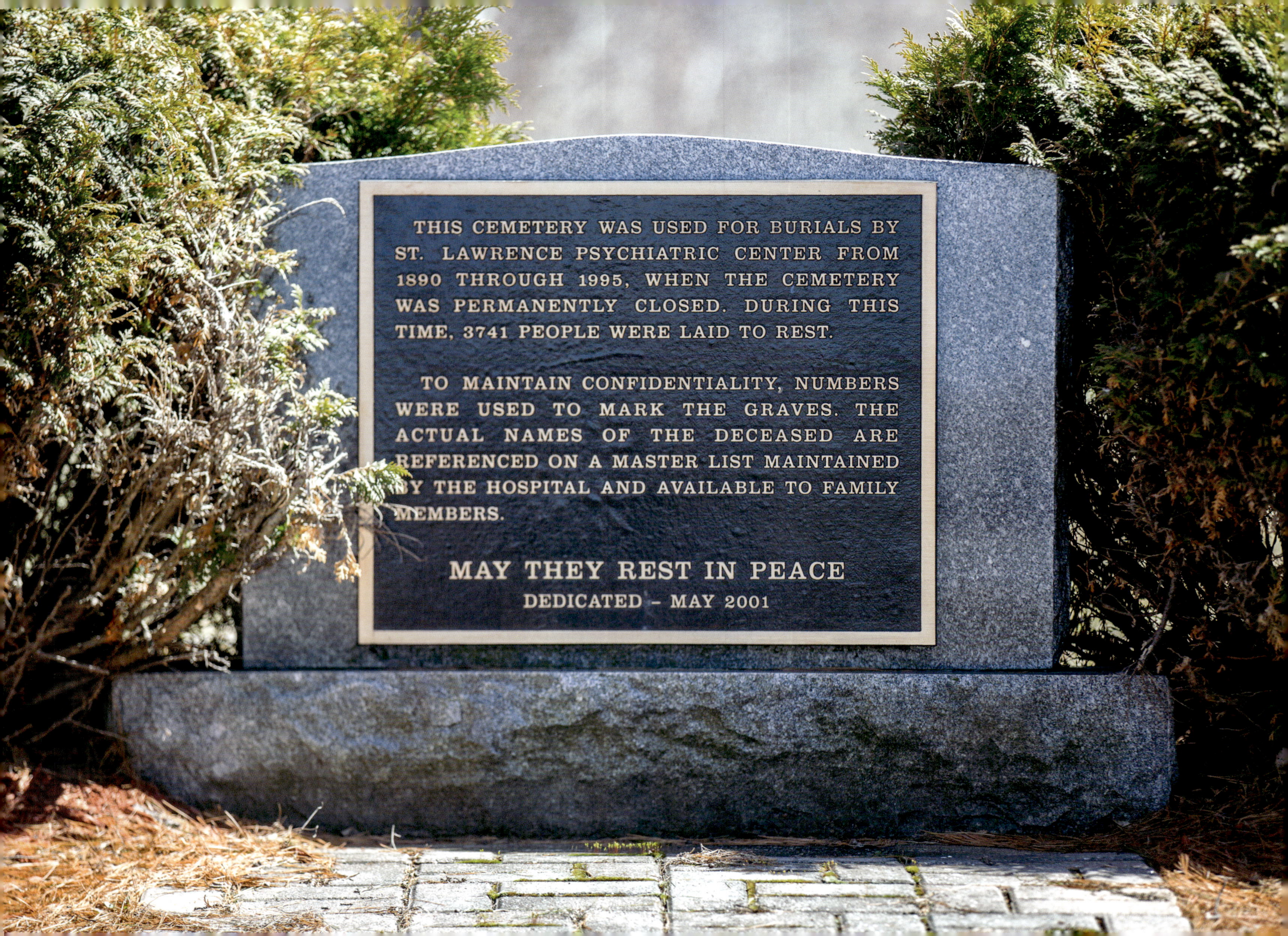
THIS CEMETERY WAS USED FOR BURIALS BY ST. LAWRENCE PSYCHIATRIC CENTER FROM 1890 THROUGH 1995, WHEN THE CEMETERY WAS PERMANENTLY CLOSED. DURING THIS TIME, 3741 PEOPLE WERE LAID TO REST.
TO MAINTAIN CONFIDENTIALITY, NUMBERS WERE USED TO MARK THE GRAVES. THE ACTUAL NAMES OF THE DECEASED ARE REFERENCED ON A MASTER LIST MAINTAINED BY THE HOSPITAL AND AVAILABLE TO FAMILY MEMBERS.
MAY THEY REST IN PEACE
DEDICATED – MAY 2001

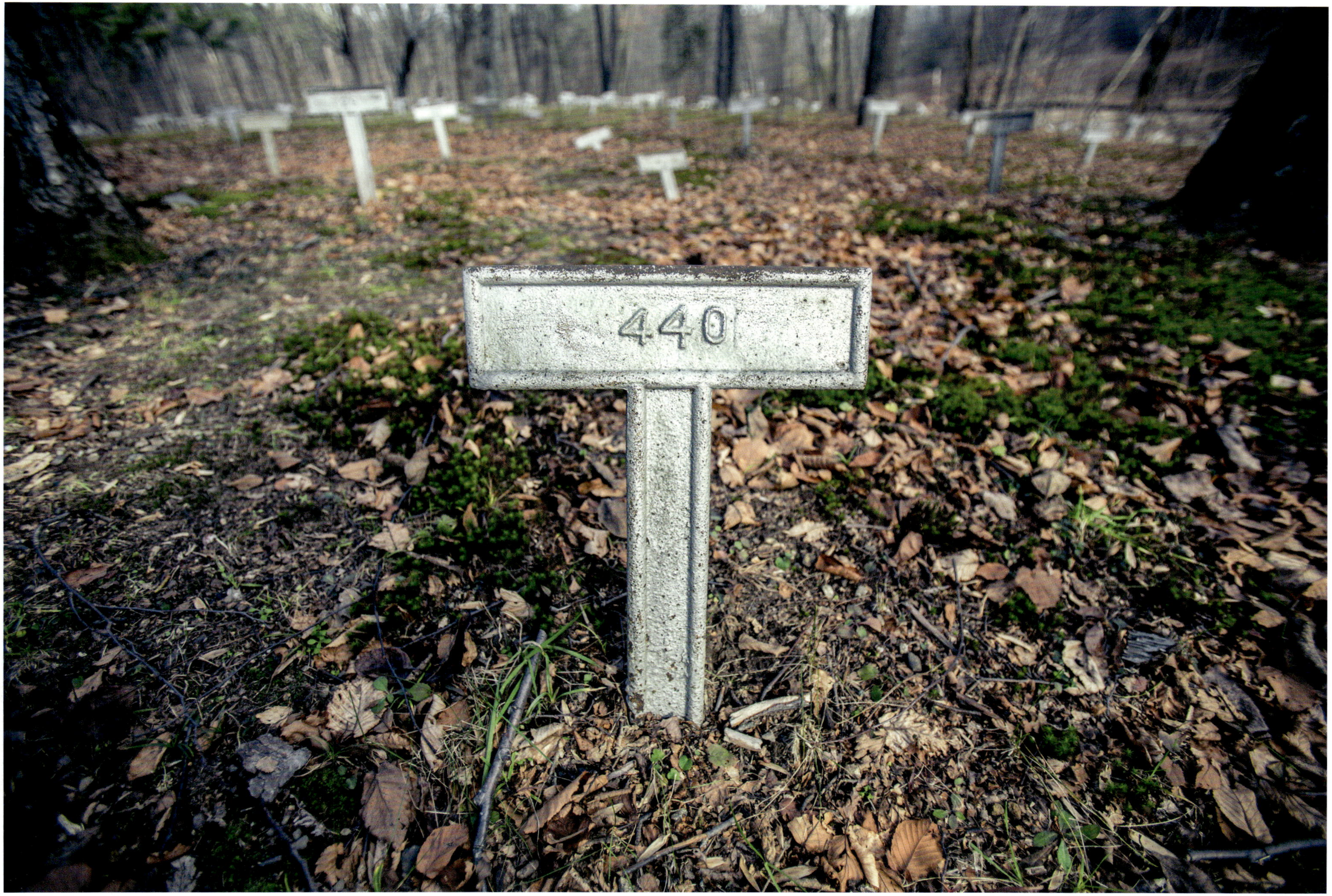

Letchworth Village grave marker

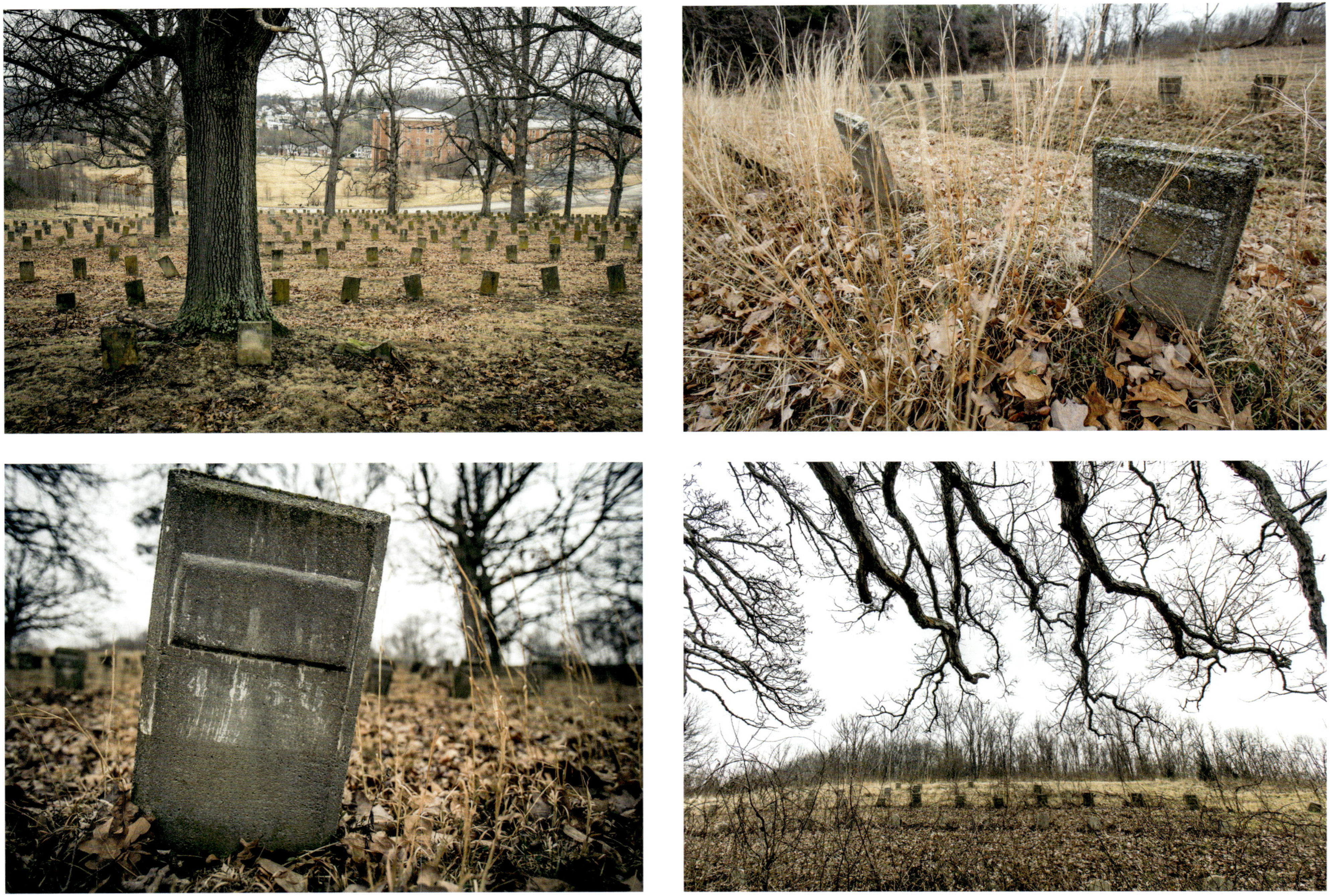

Western State Hospital cemetery

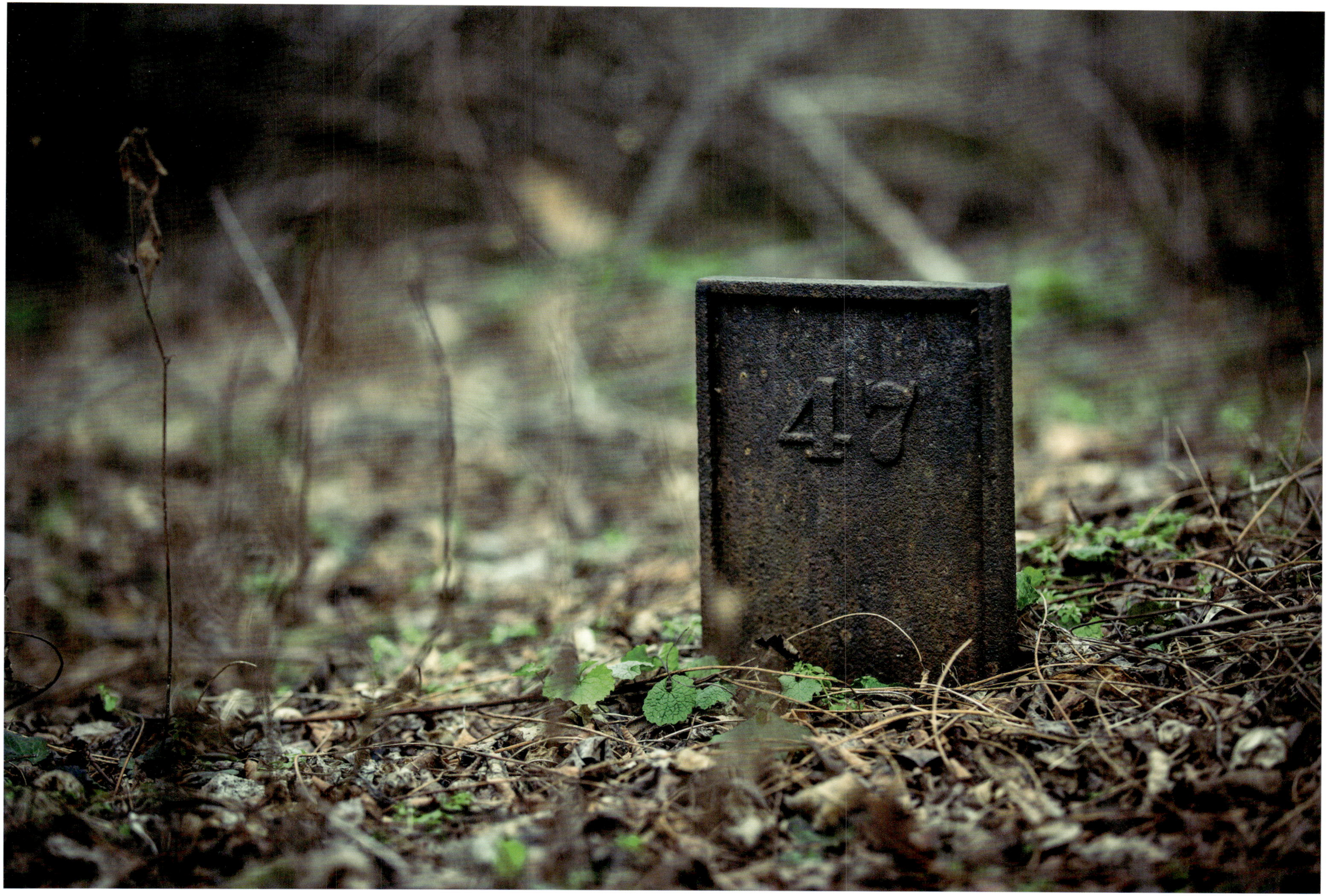
47

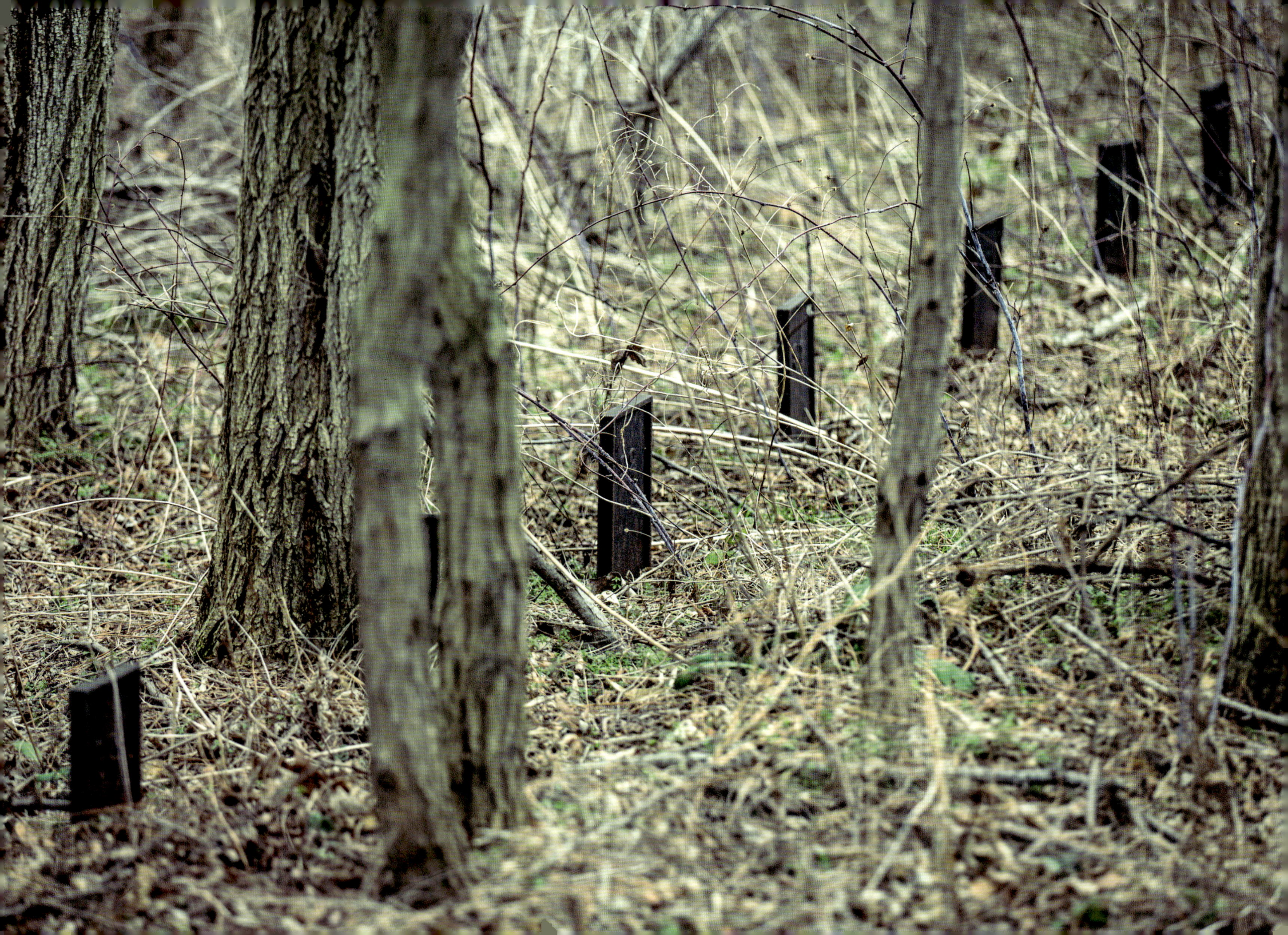

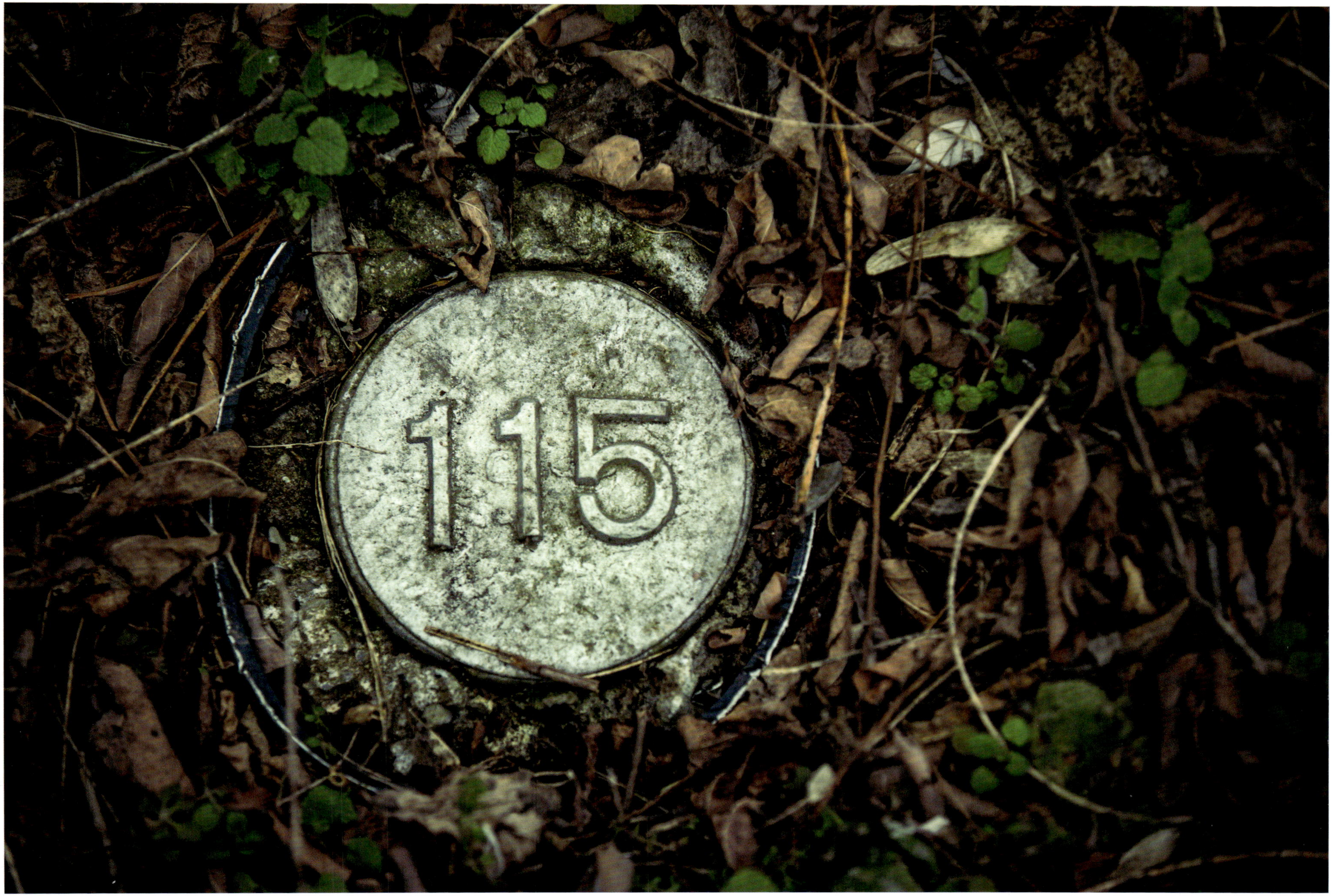

Willard Asylum for the Insane grave marker

Sources

Associated Press. 1968. "Doctor Quits At Pennhurst." *Gettysburg Times*, August 15.

Belofsky, N. 2013. *Strange Medicine: A Shocking History of Real Medical Practices Through the Ages.* London: Penguin Books.

Ben-Moshe, L., A. Carey, and C. Chapman. 2014. *Disability Incarcerated: Imprisonment and Disability in the United States and Canada.* Berlin: Springer Science & Business Media.

Braithwaite, W. 1853. *The Retrospect of Medicine, 4-6.*

Chandler, C. 2012. *Animal Assisted Therapy in Counselling.* New York: Routledge Publishing.

Doran, R.E. 1978. *History of Willard Asylum for the Insane and the Willard State Hospital.* Ovid, New York: Willard Psychiatric Center.

Dully, H., and C. Fleming. 2008. *My Lobotomy: A Memoir.* New York: Three Rivers Press.

El-Hai, J. 2005. *The Lobotomist: A Maverick Medical Genius and His Tragic Quest to Rid the World of Mental Illness.* Hoboken, New Jersey: JohnWiley & Sons, Inc.

Imbroglia, G., and N. Sheth. 1999. "Images in Psychiatry: Trenton Psychiatric Hospital." *The American Journal of Psychiatry* 156(2): 1982.

Koehler-Pentacoff, E. 2015. *The Missing Kennedy: Rosemary Kennedy and the Secret Bonds of Four Women.* Baltimore: Bancroft Press.

Kopelman, L.M., and J.C. Moskop. 2013. *Ethics and Mental Retardation.* Berlin: Springer Science & Business Media.

Lawrence, C. 1998. *Greater Than the Parts: Holism in Biomedicine.* Oxford: Oxford University Press.

Noll, R. 2009. *The Encyclopedia of Schizophrenia and Other Psychotic Disorders.* New York: Infobase Publishing.

Oshinsky, David M. 2005. *Polio: An American Story.* Oxford: Oxford University Press.

Payne, C., and O. Sacks. 2009. *Asylum: Inside the Closed World of State Mental Hospitals.* Cambridge, Massachusetts: MIT Press.

Penney, D., L. Rinzler, and P. Stastny. 2009. *The Lives They Left Behind: Suitcases from a State Hospital Attic.* New York: Bellevue Literary Press.

Raz, M. 2013. *The Lobotomy Letters: The Making of American Psychosurgery.* Rochester, New York: University of Rochester Press.

Scull, A. 2005. "Desperate Remedies: Embrace of a Deadly Cure." *Princeton Alumni Weekly* 6(13).

Scull, A. 2006. *The Insanity of Place / The Place of Insanity: Essays on the History of Psychiatry.* New York: Routledge Publishing.

Scull, A. 2007. *Madhouse: A Tragic Tale of Megalomania and Modern Medicine.* New Haven: Yale University Press.

Shutts, D. 1982. *Lobotomy: Resort to the Knife.* New York: Van Nostrand Reinhold.

Stuhler, L. 2015. *The Inmates of Willard 1870 to 1900: A Genealogy Resource.* Accessed on October 23 from http://www.inmatesofwillard.com.

Trent, J.W. 1994. *Inventing the Feeble Mind: A History of Mental Retardation in the United States.* Oakland: University of California Press.

Tucker, R. 2016. "NYC's First Supermodel Died Alone in an Insane Asylum." *New York Post*, March 5.

Yanni, C. 2007. *The Architecture of Madness: Insane Asylums in the United States.* Minneapolis: University of Minnesota Press.

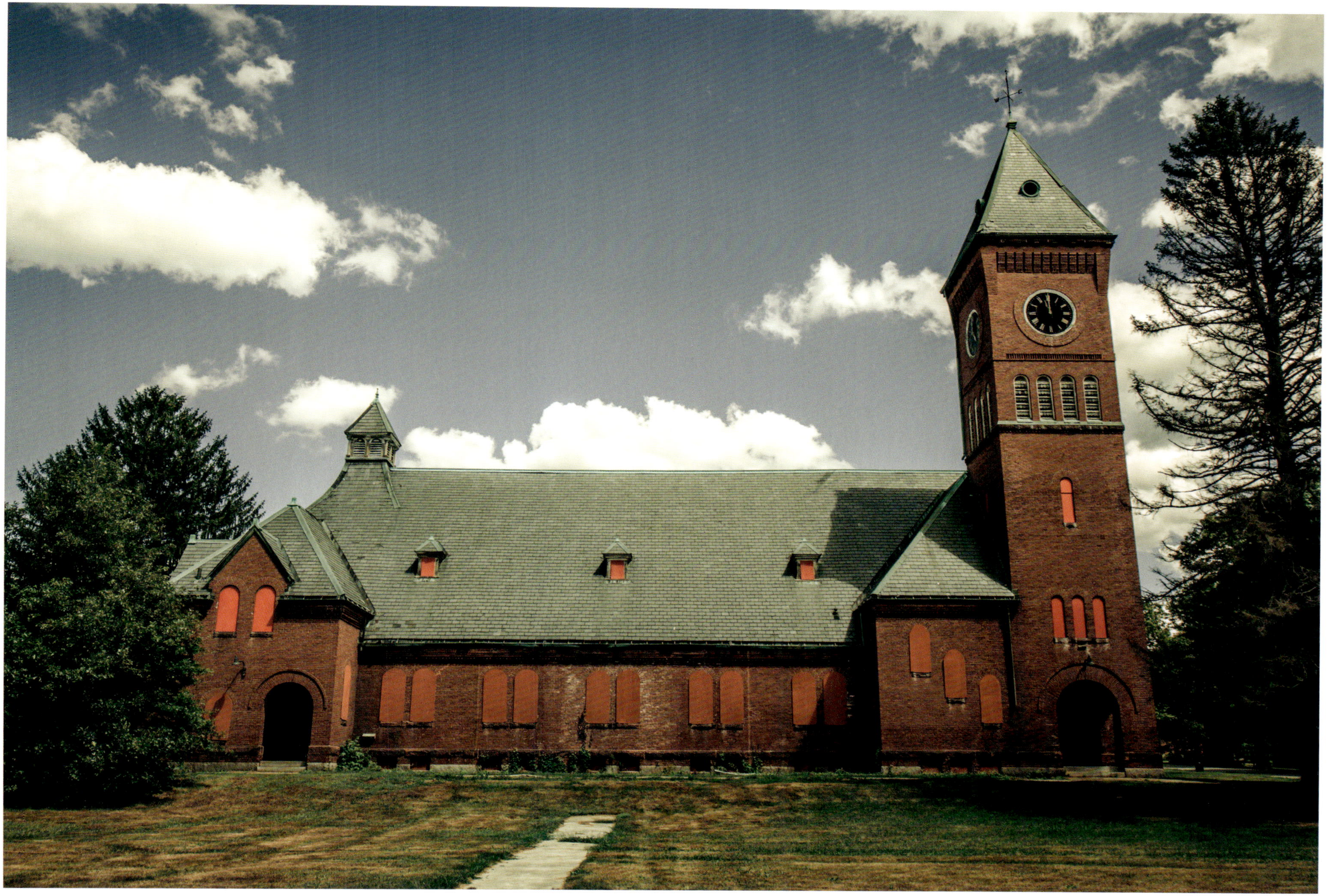

Medfield Insane Asylum Chapel as seen in 2010 film 'Shutter Island' starring Leonardo DiCaprio

Acknowledgements

This book would not have been possible withcut the help, assistance and guidance of many individuals whose contributions I hold dear. Producing the images in this book was no easy task. Endless travel, research and planning. Long days, early mornings and late nights. Acquiring permissions and jumping through bureaucratic hoops. There are countless individuals to whom I'm indebted. These are but a few:

Firstly, I need to extend a thank you to JonGlez Publishing for taking the leap and showing such impassioned interest in my work. From our very first conversations, Thomas expressed his desire to collaborate on a historical reference guide, highlighting the importance of documenting these incredible places before they are gone forever. You have given me a voice and platform to share with the world the images I have created. And although these places may not last forever in the physical reclm, their photographic documentation will live on.

Thank you to the incredible Carla Yanni, who graciously penned the foreword – the largest body of text in this book. Without you, this book would not be the gateway by which the non-academics meet the scholarly world. You have provided historical reference and legitimacy to my photographs in a world where "ruin-porn" has stripped the institutions of context, dignity and respect. Our collaboration, shared views and enduring appreciation for the architecture and history form a symbiotic relationship that I value extremely. Without your knowledge and expertise I wield only a set of photographs. With your contribution, the scholar meets the artist and thus completes the circle.

Thank you to my mother, Pam, my father, Reynolds, and my stepfather, Mark. Each of your contributions has helped me make this dream a reality; for that, I am forever indebted. You are the voices of reason and encouragement; the protectors and saviours in times of need; the sources of unconditional love; and the greatest parents a man could ask for. This book is dedicated to my late grandparents, Harry and Lillian, whose endless support still echoes throughout my life.

Thank you to Daniel Carleton, who I'm privileged to not only call my best friend, but also my confidant. Daniel has a special way with words and generously donated his time providing the peer editing for this book. Without Dan, I can't imagine the unintelligible scribblings I would have presented on these pages. Dan you are an incredible soul, an invaluable ally in life and an endless source of kindness to the world, which will forever be bettered by your charitable efforts and selflessness.

Thank you to Ben Rosen of the New York State Office of Mental Health and to countless other state officials who have supported my vision and provided assistance in securing the necessary permissions and access for me to document such sensitive sites where privacy and respect are of utmost concern. Without you this book would not have been possible.

Thank you, Martin Johnson, for mentoring me in my early days of holding a camera, and for instilling in me a curiosity about the closed off, inaccessible corners of society that few eyes get to see. Thank you to Colleen Shannon for being my inspiration and motivation for success; Colleen was the first person to suggest I should produce a book and share my images with the world. Thank you to Anthony Perretta for endless guidance, direction and friendship; Melissa Gagnon; John Diak and the crew at Pennhurst State School; Shawn Cooper; Ed Piccola, who graciously donated the display of his antique artifacts; Rebecca Jordan Gleason and everyone at Trans-Allegheny Lunatic Asylum.

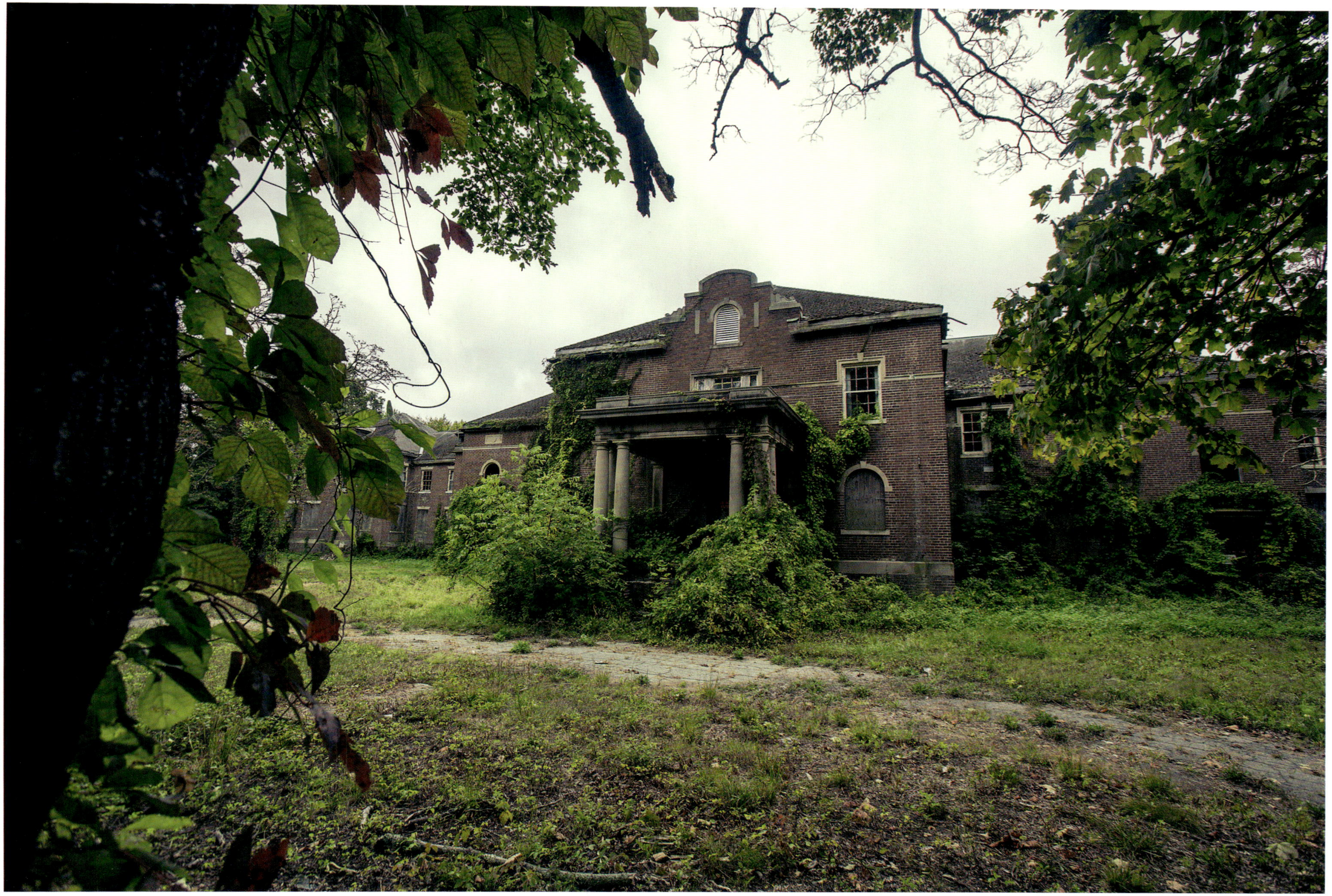

Norwich State Hospital for the Insane

All photographs by Matt Van der Velde

Photo copyrights: Matt Van der Velde
Design: Stéphanie Benoit
Editing: Matt Gay
Proof-reading: Kimberly Bess

Registration of copyright: April 2023 – Edition: 01
ISBN: 978-2-36195-163-4
Printed in Slovakia by Polygraf